LOC S

Sayaka Kanamori would like to thank you for your purchase of *Keep Your Hands off Eizouken!* and reminds all customers that this manga reads in the traditional Japanese style, right-to-left. To get your money's worth, please flip the book around and begin reading.

1
HMM...
2
YES, THAT'S IT!
3
HOW 'BOUT THAT, YOU!
4
A PEG PUNCHER! WITH THREE HOLES FOR ANIME PAPER. IF WE CAN GET ONE FOR UNDER 30,000...
5
...WE'LL SOON RECOVER THE COST!
6
HMPH!
7
NOT TOO BAD!
8
YOURS IS NOT TOO BAD? CHECK THIS OUT... IT'S PERFECT!
9
...WHAT CAN WE MAKE FROM THIS? IT COULD BE...

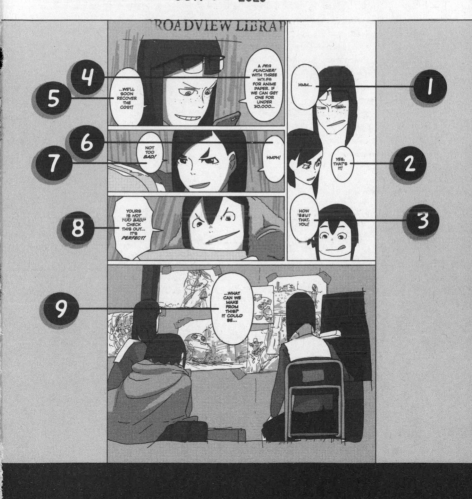

EMANON

FROM KENJI TSURUTA, THE ARTIST OF THE
EISNER-NOMINATED *WANDERING ISLAND*,
AND THE AWARD-WINNING JAPANESE
SCIENCE FICTION AUTHOR SHINJI KAJIO!

Emanon is the eternal stranger who belongs here
more than any of us— a woman possessing a
mind that evolved over the entire history of life
on earth, and who carries within her over three
billion years of memories. Set in 1960s and 70s
Japan, *Emanon* tells of her encounters with the
lives of people who can no more forget her, than
she can forget any person. Drawn in both
Tsuruta's elegant black-and-white linework and
his signature painted color, *Emanon* is a literary
SF manga at the intersection of life, memory,
family, and existence.

$14.99 EACH!

FOR MORE INFORMATION OR TO ORDER DIRECT, VISIT DARKHORSE.COM.
*PRICES AND AVAILABILITY SUBJECT TO CHANGE WITHOUT NOTICE.

KEEP YOUR HANDS OFF EIZOUKEN!

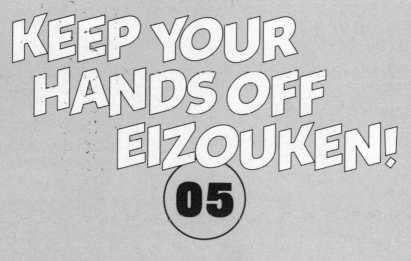

05

STORY AND ART BY

大童澄瞳

SUMITO OOWARA

CONTENTS

KEEP YOUR HANDS OFF EIZOUKEN! VOL. 5
TRANSLATED BY KUMAR SIVASUBRAMANIAN
SPECIAL THANKS FOR TRANSLATION ASSISTANCE: CHITOKU TESHIMA
LETTERING AND RETOUCH BY SUSIE LEE AND STUDIO CUTIE
EDITED BY CARL GUSTAV HORN

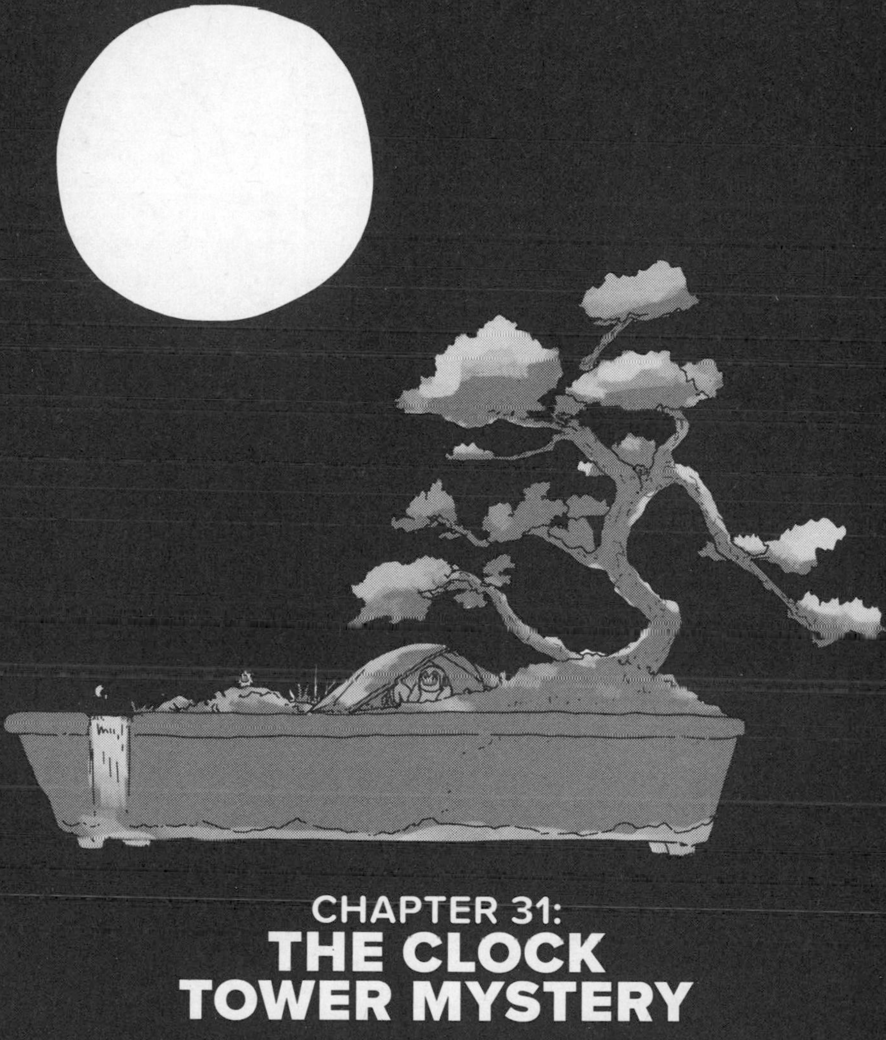

CHAPTER 31:
THE CLOCK TOWER MYSTERY

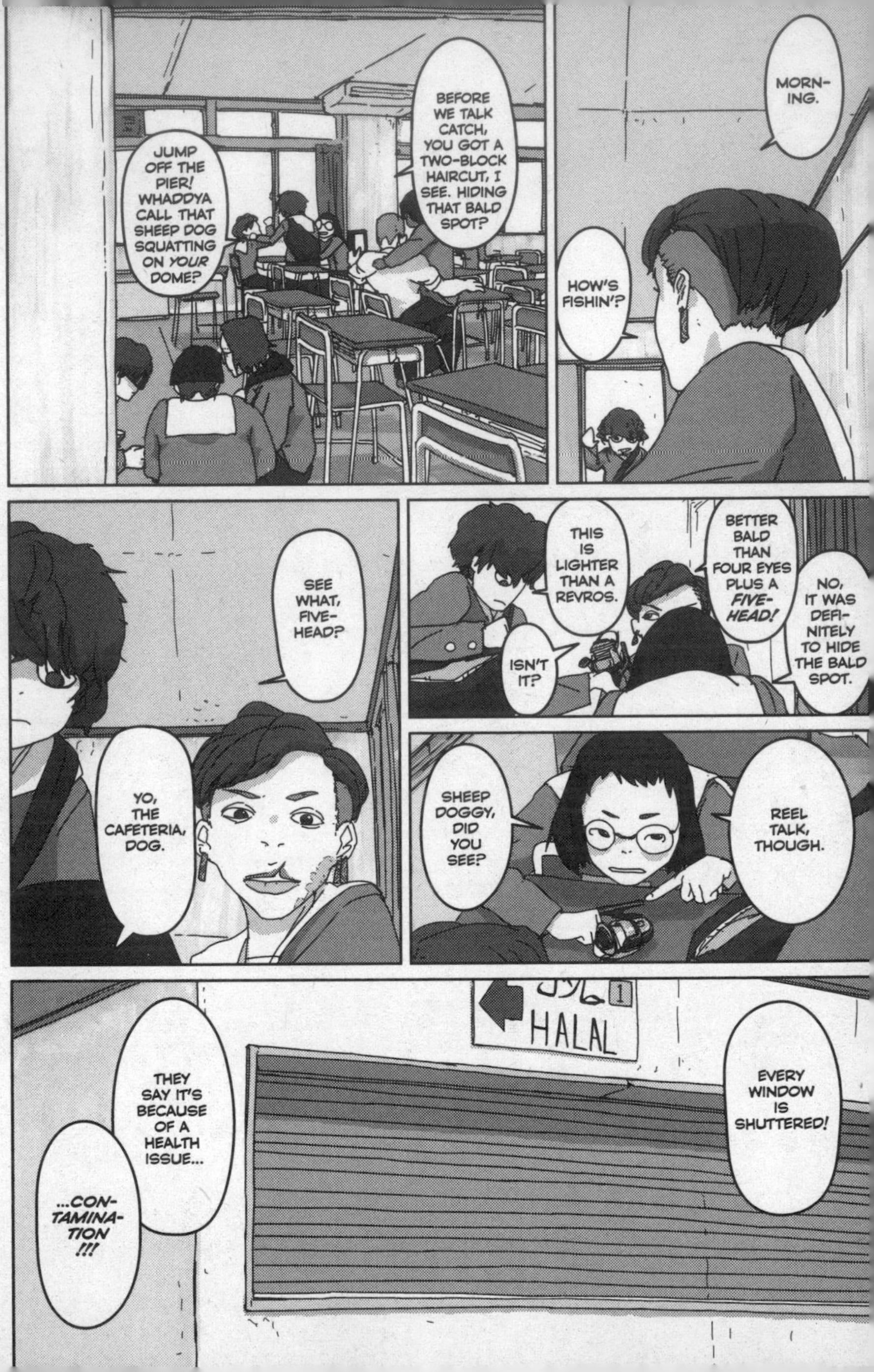
MORNING.
HOW'S FISHIN'?
BEFORE WE TALK CATCH, YOU GOT A TWO-BLOCK HAIRCUT, I SEE. HIDING THAT BALD SPOT?
JUMP OFF THE PIER! WHADDYA CALL THAT SHEEP DOG SQUATTING ON *YOUR* DOME?
BETTER BALD THAN FOUR EYES PLUS A *FIVE-HEAD!*
NO, IT WAS DEFINITELY TO HIDE THE BALD SPOT.
THIS IS LIGHTER THAN A REVROS.
ISN'T IT?
REEL TALK, THOUGH.
SHEEP DOGGY, DID YOU SEE?
SEE WHAT, FIVE-HEAD?
YO, THE CAFETERIA, DOG.
HALAL
EVERY WINDOW IS SHUTTERED!
THEY SAY IT'S BECAUSE OF A HEALTH ISSUE...
...CONTAMINATION!!!

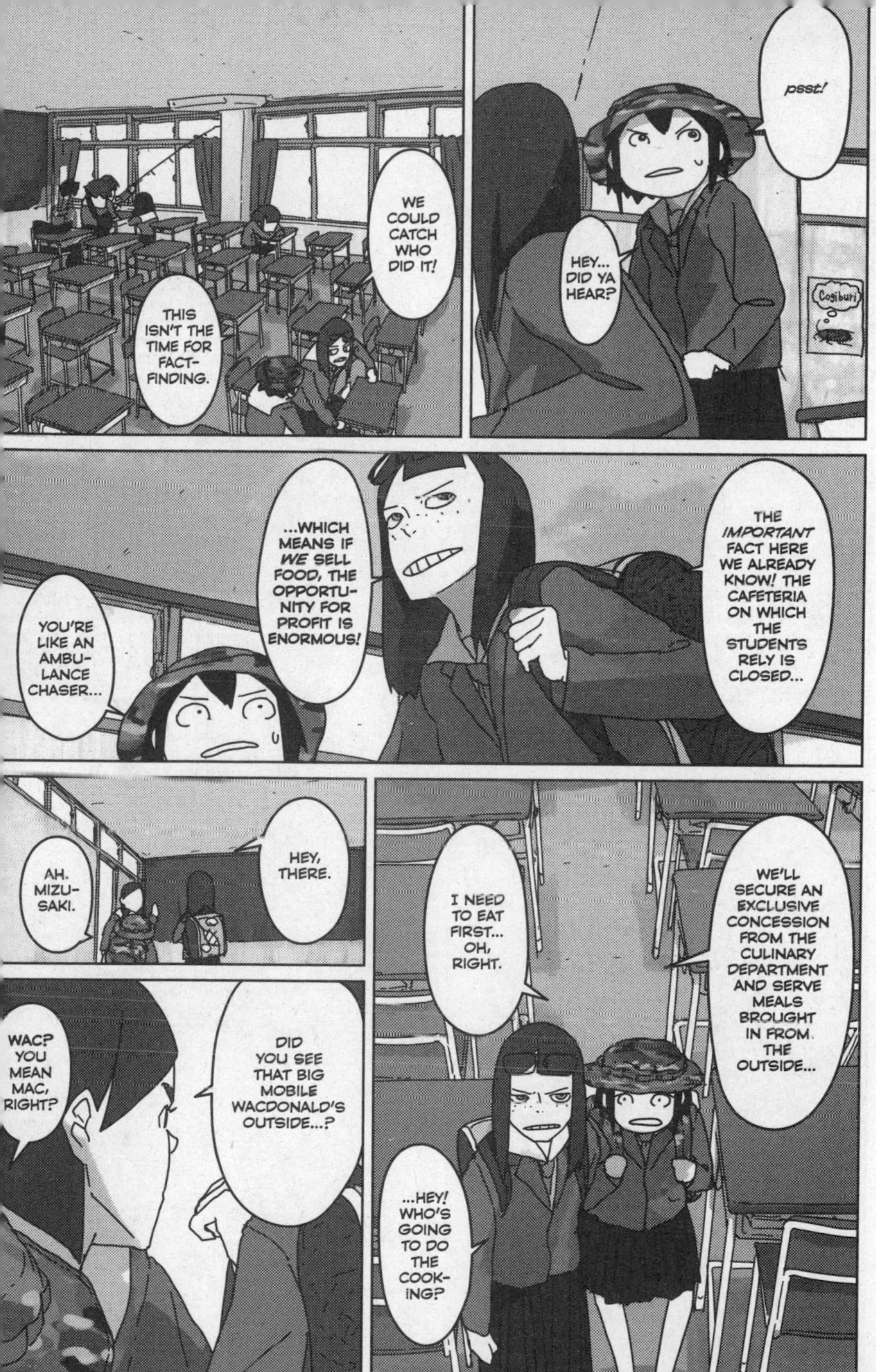
psst!
HEY... DID YA HEAR?
Cogiburi
WE COULD CATCH WHO DID IT!
THIS ISN'T THE TIME FOR FACT-FINDING.
THE *IMPORTANT* FACT HERE WE ALREADY KNOW! THE CAFETERIA ON WHICH THE STUDENTS RELY IS CLOSED...
...WHICH MEANS IF *WE* SELL FOOD, THE OPPORTUNITY FOR PROFIT IS ENORMOUS!
YOU'RE LIKE AN AMBULANCE CHASER...
WE'LL SECURE AN EXCLUSIVE CONCESSION FROM THE CULINARY DEPARTMENT AND SERVE MEALS BROUGHT IN FROM THE OUTSIDE...
I NEED TO EAT FIRST... OH, RIGHT.
...HEY! WHO'S GOING TO DO THE COOKING?
HEY, THERE.
AH. MIZUSAKI.
DID YOU SEE THAT BIG MOBILE WACDONALD'S OUTSIDE...?
WAC? YOU MEAN MAC, RIGHT?

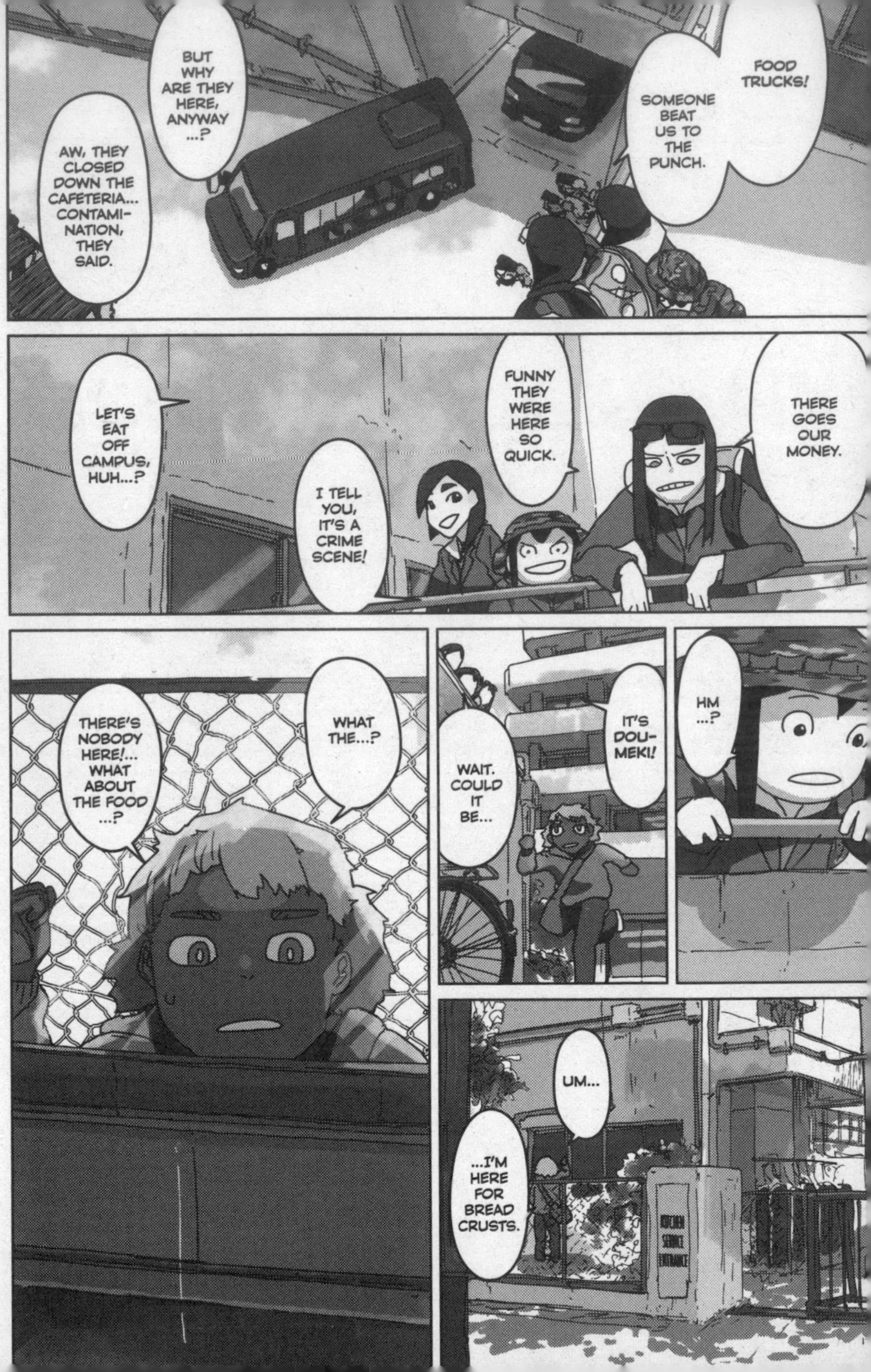
FOOD TRUCKS!
SOMEONE BEAT US TO THE PUNCH.
BUT WHY ARE THEY HERE, ANYWAY ...?
AW, THEY CLOSED DOWN THE CAFETERIA... CONTAMINATION, THEY SAID.
THERE GOES OUR MONEY.
FUNNY THEY WERE HERE SO QUICK.
I TELL YOU, IT'S A CRIME SCENE!
LET'S EAT OFF CAMPUS, HUH...?
HM ...?
IT'S DOU-MEKI!
WAIT. COULD IT BE...
UM...
...I'M HERE FOR BREAD CRUSTS.
WHAT THE...?
THERE'S NOBODY HERE!... WHAT ABOUT THE FOOD ...?

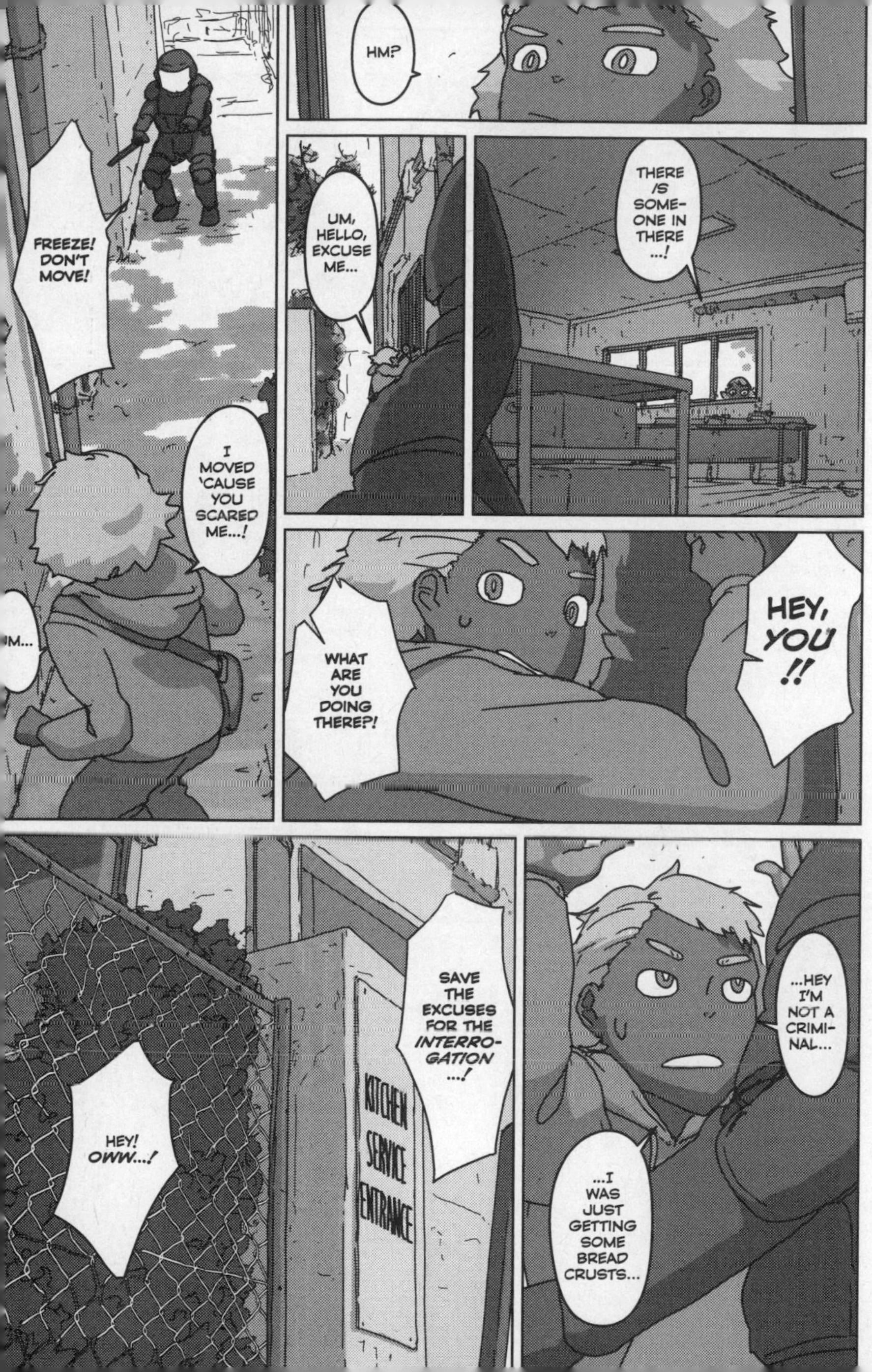
HM?
THERE IS SOMEONE IN THERE ...!
UM, HELLO, EXCUSE ME...
HEY, YOU!!
WHAT ARE YOU DOING THERE?!
FREEZE! DON'T MOVE!
I MOVED 'CAUSE YOU SCARED ME...!
...HEY I'M NOT A CRIMINAL...
...I WAS JUST GETTING SOME BREAD CRUSTS...
SAVE THE EXCUSES FOR THE INTERROGATION ...!
KITCHEN SERVICE ENTRANCE
HEY! OWW...!

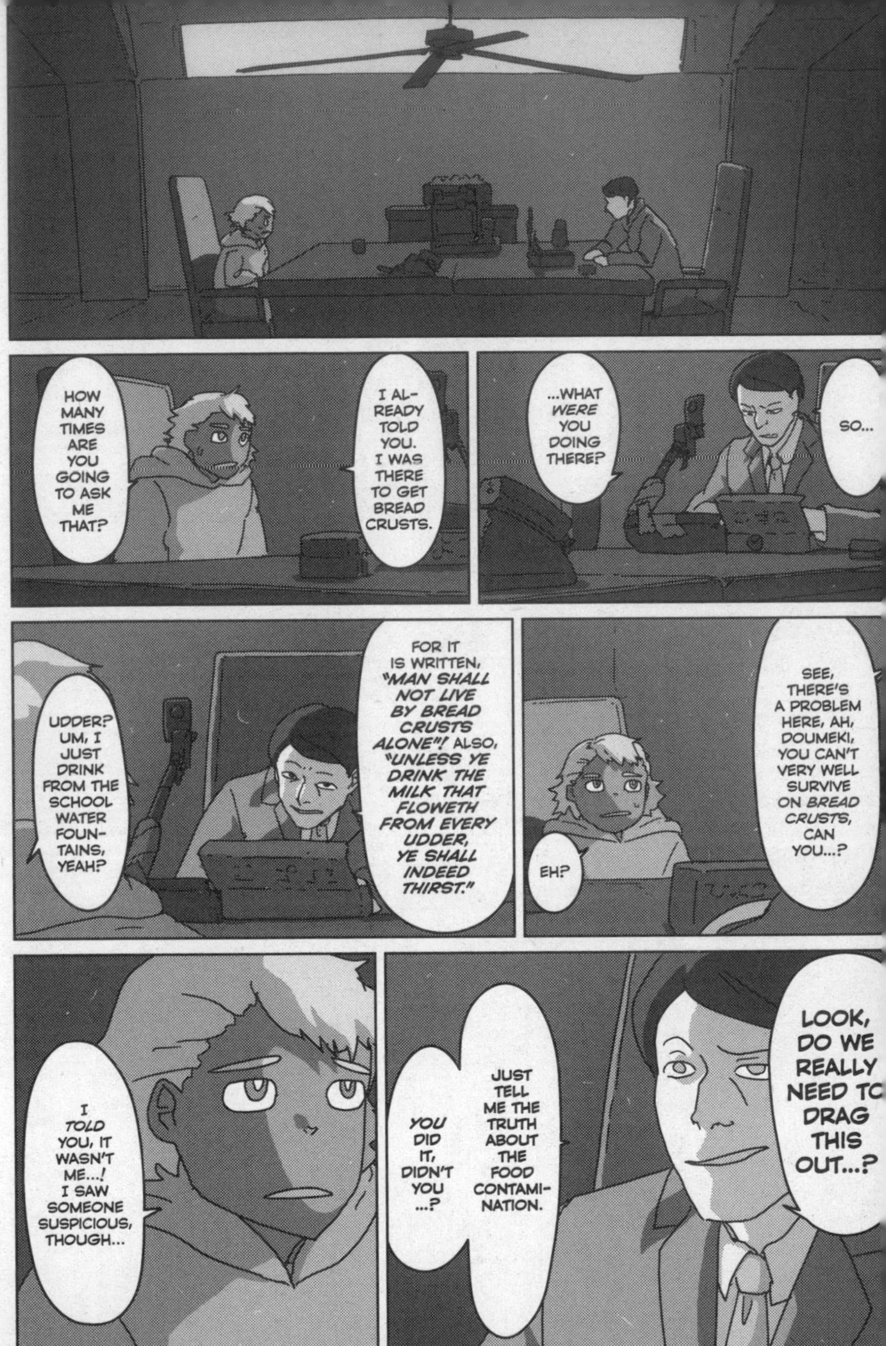
SO...
...WHAT WERE YOU DOING THERE?
I ALREADY TOLD YOU. I WAS THERE TO GET BREAD CRUSTS.
HOW MANY TIMES ARE YOU GOING TO ASK ME THAT?
SEE, THERE'S A PROBLEM HERE, AH, DOUMEKI, YOU CAN'T VERY WELL SURVIVE ON *BREAD CRUSTS*, CAN YOU...?
EH?
FOR IT IS WRITTEN, *"MAN SHALL NOT LIVE BY BREAD CRUSTS ALONE"!* ALSO, *"UNLESS YE DRINK THE MILK THAT FLOWETH FROM EVERY UDDER, YE SHALL INDEED THIRST."*
UDDER? UM, I JUST DRINK FROM THE SCHOOL WATER FOUNTAINS, YEAH?
LOOK, DO WE REALLY NEED TO DRAG THIS OUT...?
JUST TELL ME THE TRUTH ABOUT THE FOOD CONTAMINATION.
YOU DID IT, DIDN'T YOU ...?
I *TOLD* YOU, IT WASN'T ME...! I SAW SOMEONE SUSPICIOUS, THOUGH...

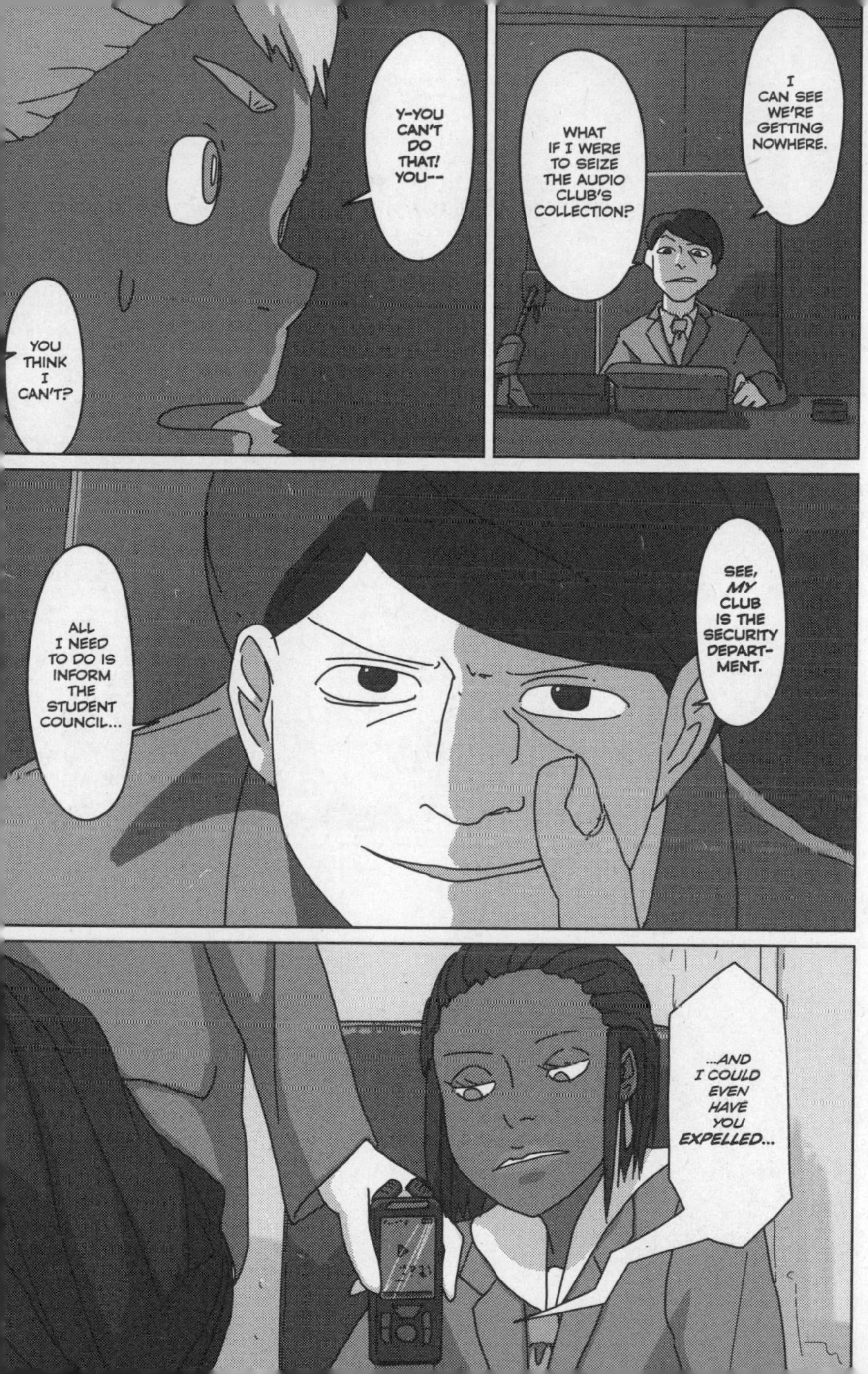
I CAN SEE WE'RE GETTING NOWHERE.
WHAT IF I WERE TO SEIZE THE AUDIO CLUB'S COLLECTION?
Y-YOU CAN'T DO THAT! YOU--
YOU THINK I CAN'T?
SEE, *MY* CLUB IS THE SECURITY DEPART-MENT.
ALL I NEED TO DO IS INFORM THE STUDENT COUNCIL...
...AND I COULD EVEN HAVE YOU EXPELLED...

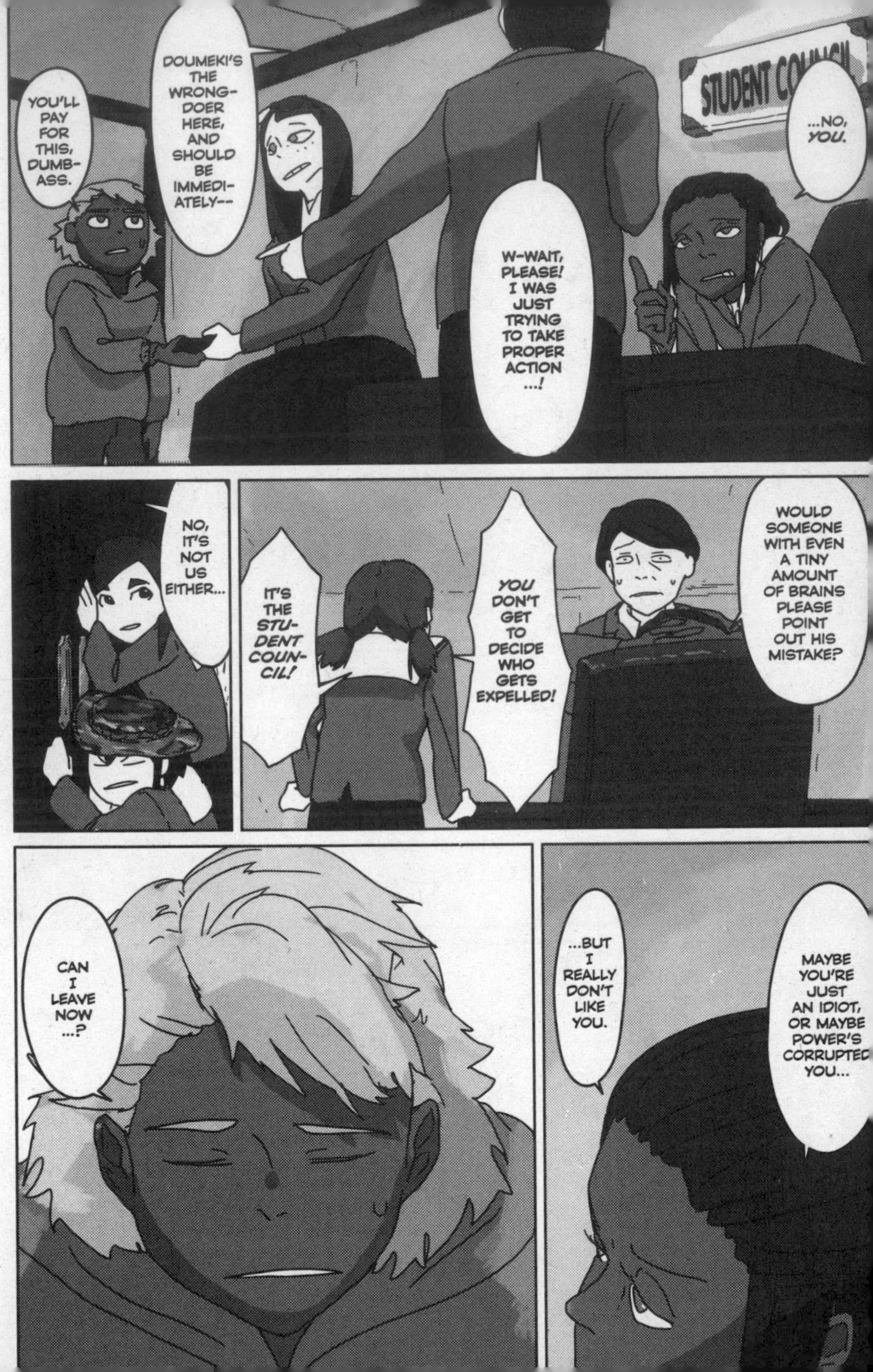
DOUMEKI'S THE WRONGDOER HERE, AND SHOULD BE IMMEDIATELY--
...NO, *YOU.*
W-WAIT, PLEASE! I WAS JUST TRYING TO TAKE PROPER ACTION ...!
YOU'LL PAY FOR THIS, DUMBASS.
WOULD SOMEONE WITH EVEN A TINY AMOUNT OF BRAINS PLEASE POINT OUT HIS MISTAKE?
YOU DON'T GET TO DECIDE WHO GETS EXPELLED!
IT'S THE *STUDENT COUNCIL!*
NO, IT'S NOT US EITHER...
MAYBE YOU'RE JUST AN IDIOT, OR MAYBE POWER'S CORRUPTED YOU...
...BUT I REALLY DON'T LIKE YOU.
CAN I LEAVE NOW ...?

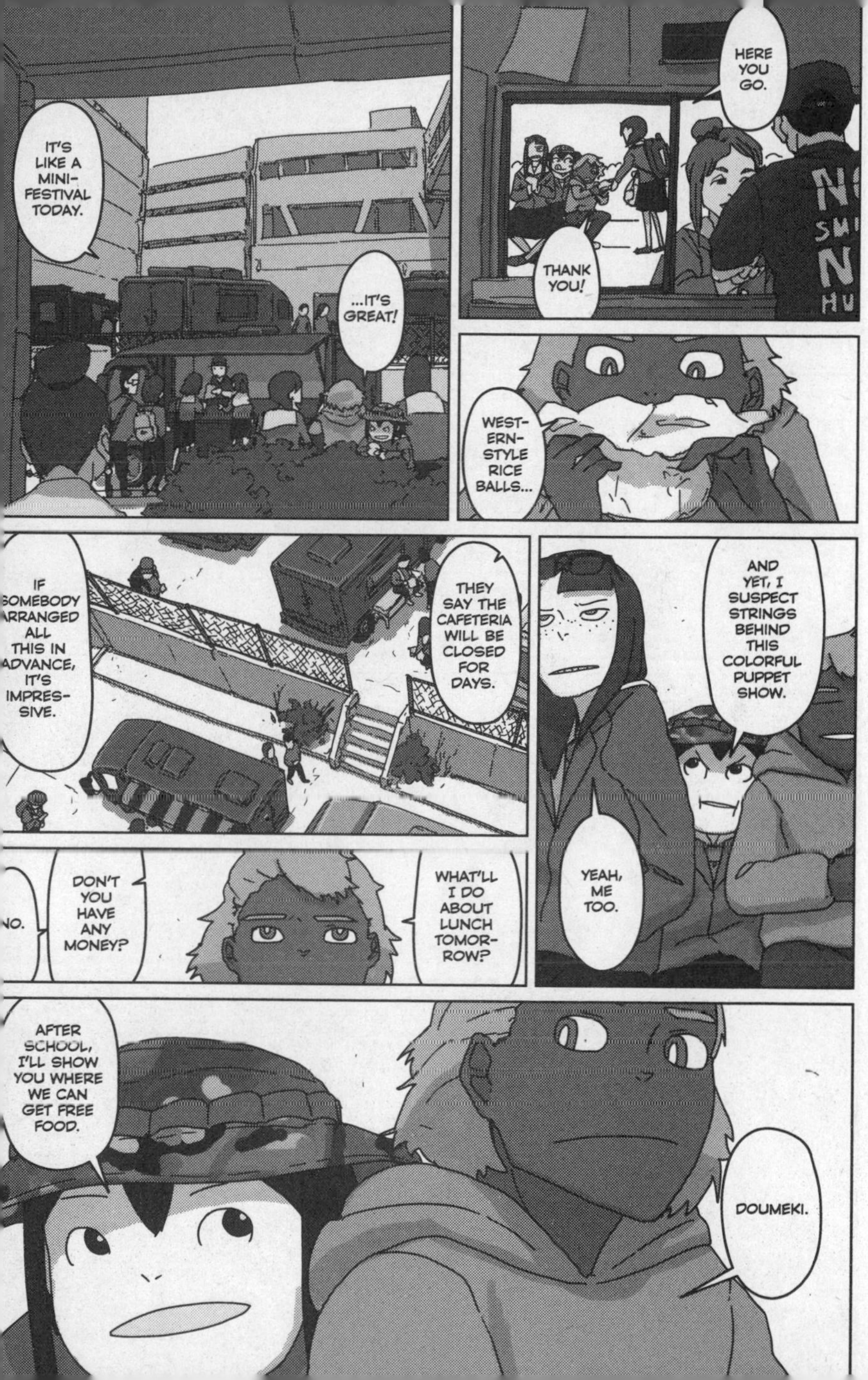
HERE YOU GO.
THANK YOU!
WESTERN-STYLE RICE BALLS...
IT'S LIKE A MINI-FESTIVAL TODAY.
...IT'S GREAT!
AND YET, I SUSPECT STRINGS BEHIND THIS COLORFUL PUPPET SHOW.
YEAH, ME TOO.
THEY SAY THE CAFETERIA WILL BE CLOSED FOR DAYS.
IF SOMEBODY ARRANGED ALL THIS IN ADVANCE, IT'S IMPRESSIVE.
WHAT'LL I DO ABOUT LUNCH TOMORROW?
DON'T YOU HAVE ANY MONEY?
NO.
DOUMEKI.
AFTER SCHOOL, I'LL SHOW YOU WHERE WE CAN GET FREE FOOD.

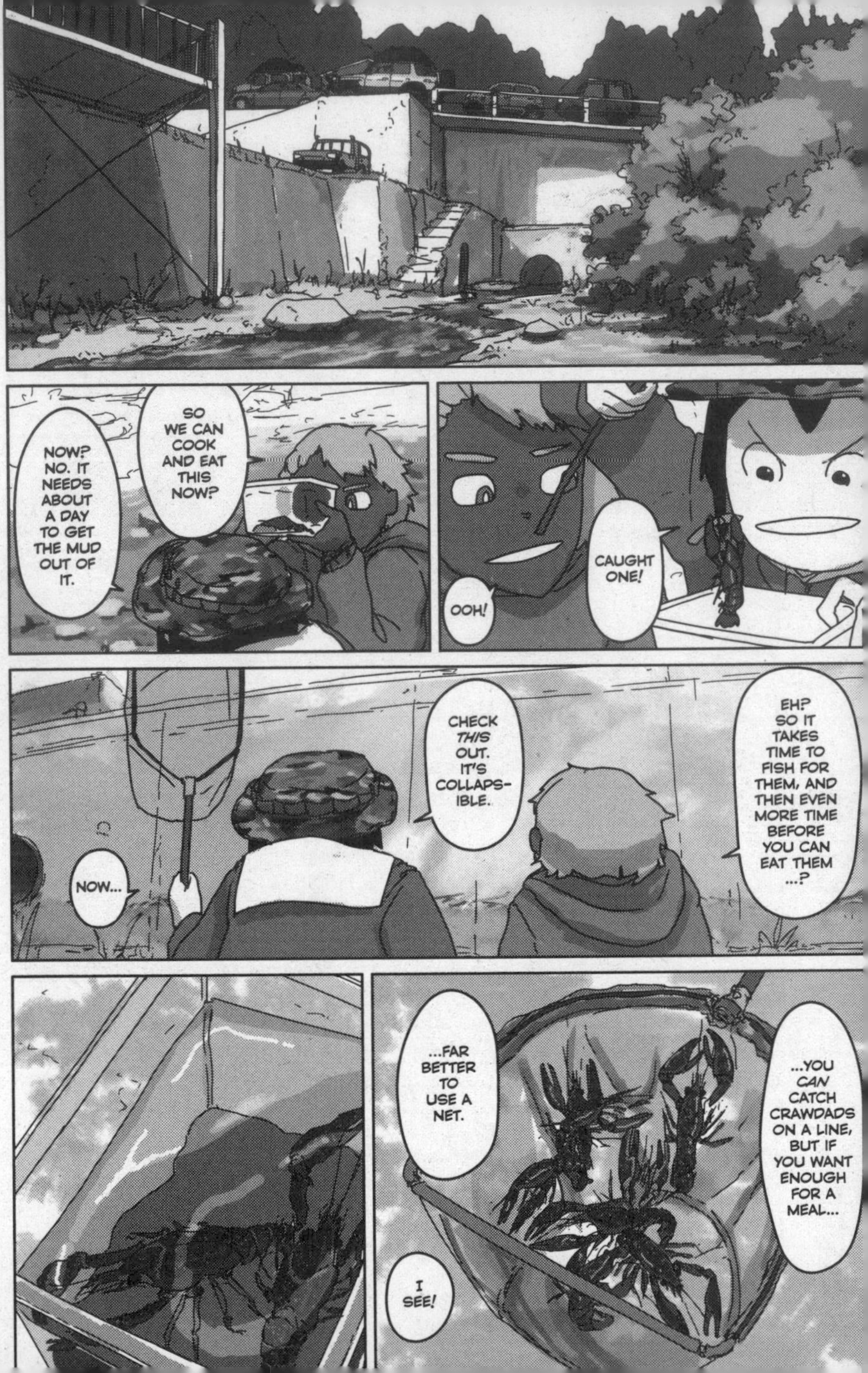
CAUGHT ONE!
OOH!
SO WE CAN COOK AND EAT THIS NOW?
NOW? NO. IT NEEDS ABOUT A DAY TO GET THE MUD OUT OF IT.
EH? SO IT TAKES TIME TO FISH FOR THEM, AND THEN EVEN MORE TIME BEFORE YOU CAN EAT THEM ...?
CHECK *THIS* OUT. IT'S COLLAPS-IBLE.
NOW...
...YOU *CAN* CATCH CRAWDADS ON A LINE, BUT IF YOU WANT ENOUGH FOR A MEAL...
...FAR BETTER TO USE A NET.
I SEE!

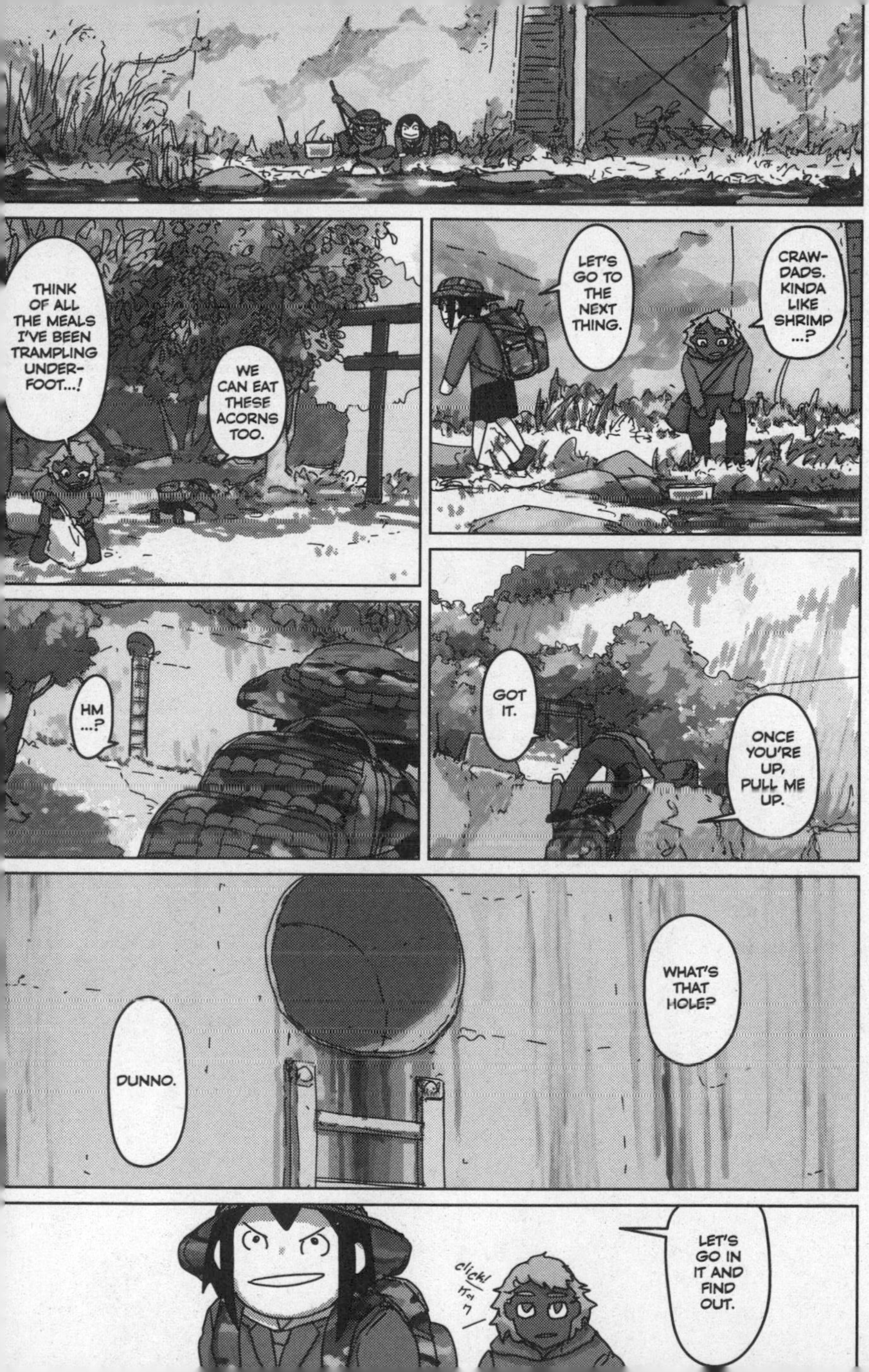
CRAW-DADS. KINDA LIKE SHRIMP ...?
LET'S GO TO THE NEXT THING.
WE CAN EAT THESE ACORNS TOO.
THINK OF ALL THE MEALS I'VE BEEN TRAMPLING UNDER-FOOT...!
ONCE YOU'RE UP, PULL ME UP.
GOT IT.
HM ...?
WHAT'S THAT HOLE?
DUNNO.
LET'S GO IN IT AND FIND OUT.
click!

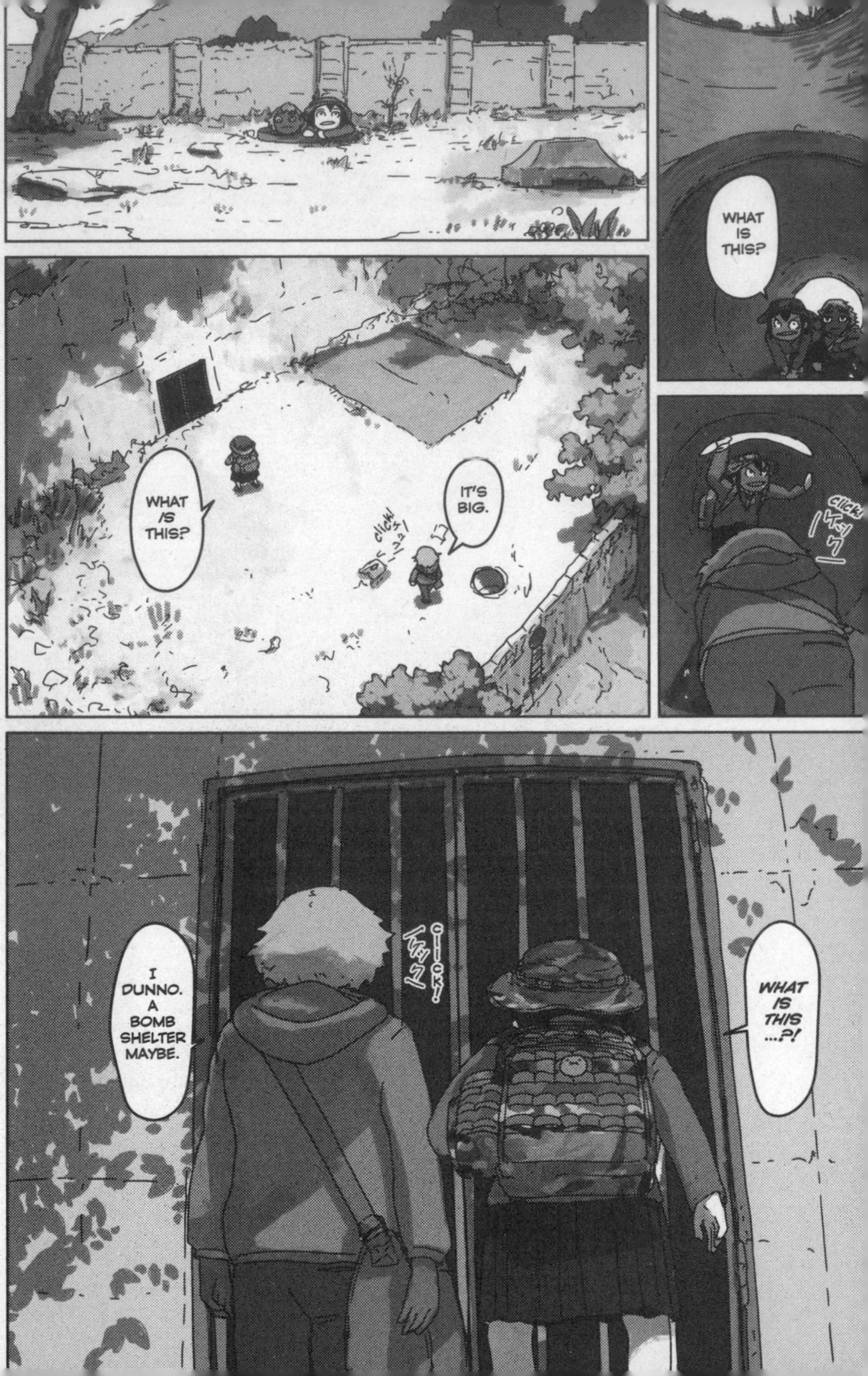
WHAT IS THIS?
CLICK
IT'S BIG.
WHAT IS THIS?
CLICK
WHAT IS THIS ...?!
CLICK!
I DUNNO. A BOMB SHELTER MAYBE.

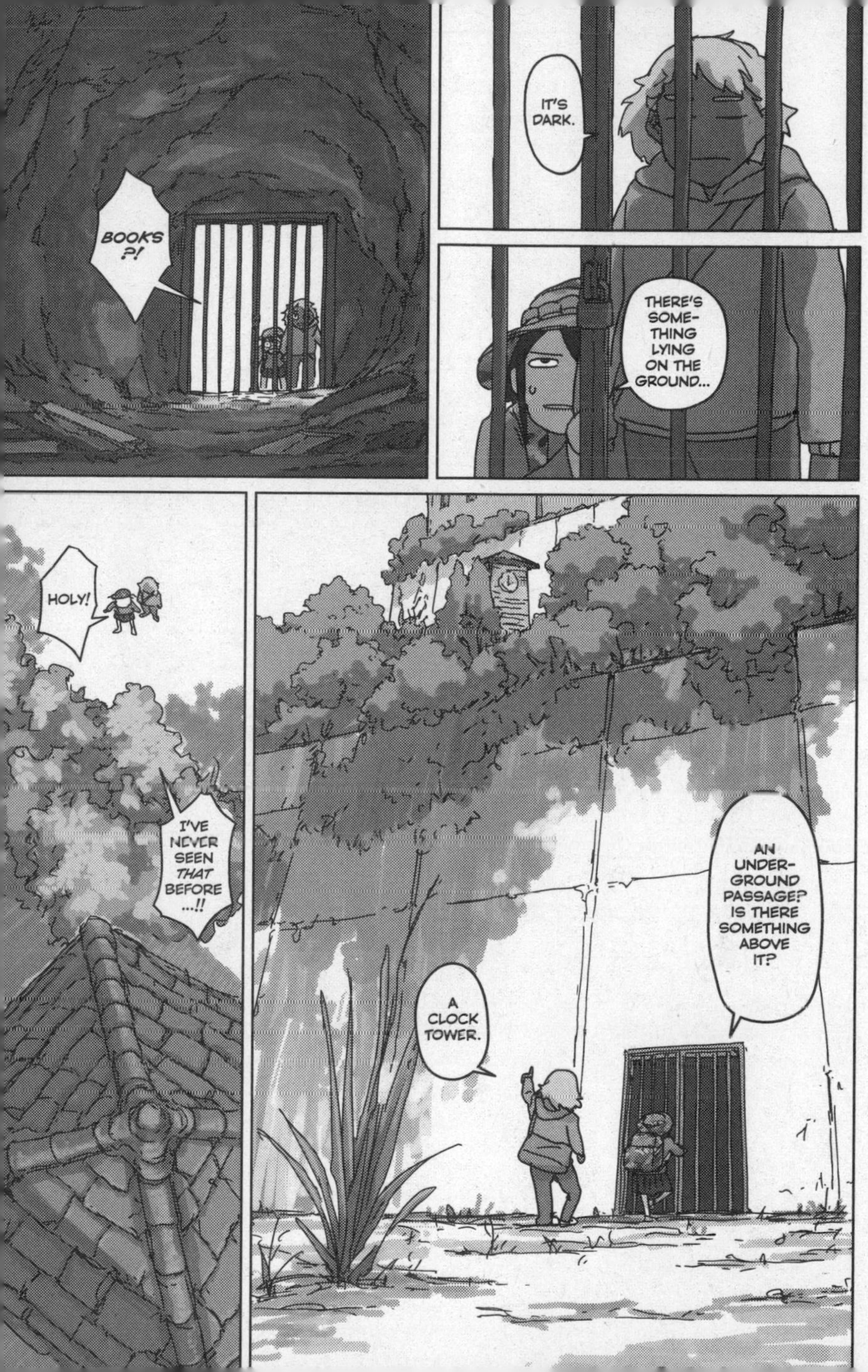
IT'S DARK.
THERE'S SOME-THING LYING ON THE GROUND...
BOOKS ?!
AN UNDER-GROUND PASSAGE? IS THERE SOMETHING ABOVE IT?
A CLOCK TOWER.
HOLY!
I'VE NEVER SEEN *THAT* BEFORE ...!!

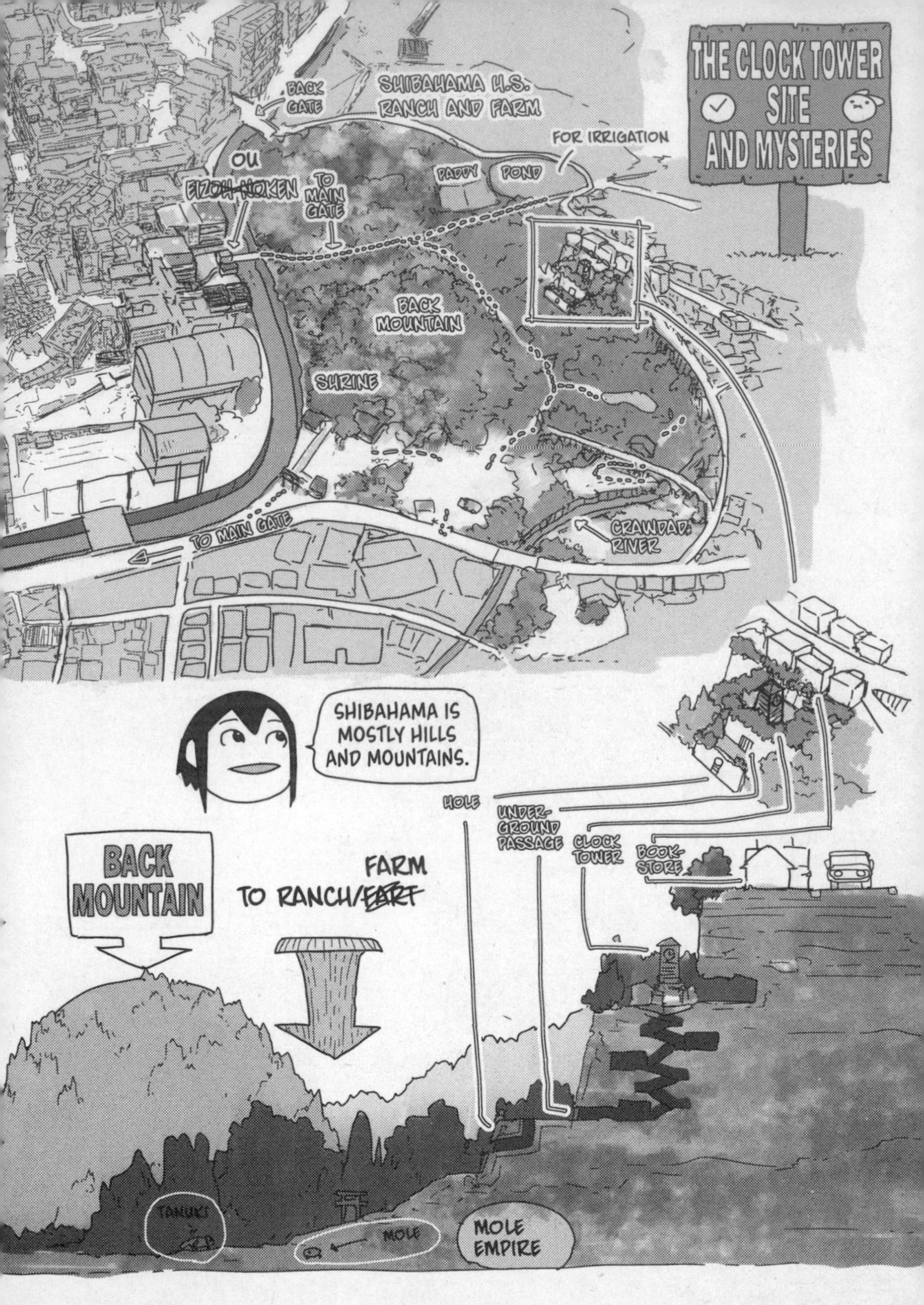
THE CLOCK TOWER SITE AND MYSTERIES
BACK GATE
SHIBAHAMA H.S. RANCH AND FARM
FOR IRRIGATION
PADDY
POND
OU
~~EIZOH HOKEN~~
TO MAIN GATE
BACK MOUNTAIN
SHRINE
TO MAIN GATE
CRAWDAD RIVER
SHIBAHAMA IS MOSTLY HILLS AND MOUNTAINS.
HOLE
UNDERGROUND PASSAGE
CLOCK TOWER
BOOKSTORE
BACK MOUNTAIN
FARM
TO RANCH/~~FART~~
TANUKI
MOLE
MOLE EMPIRE

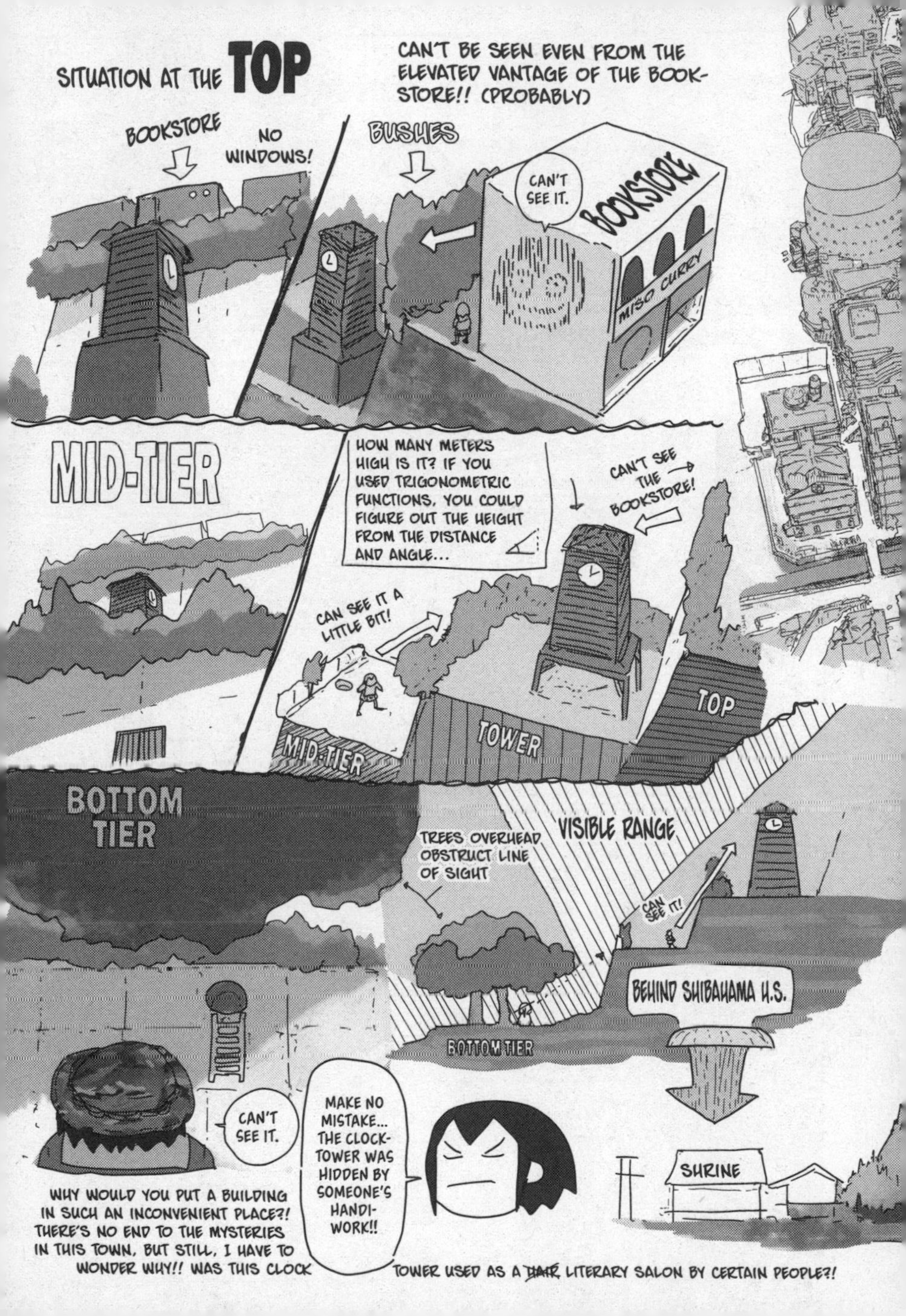
SITUATION AT THE TOP
CAN'T BE SEEN EVEN FROM THE ELEVATED VANTAGE OF THE BOOKSTORE!! (PROBABLY)
BUSHES
CAN'T SEE IT.
BOOKSTORE
MISO CURRY
BOOKSTORE
NO WINDOWS!
CAN'T SEE THE BOOKSTORE!
HOW MANY METERS HIGH IS IT? IF YOU USED TRIGONOMETRIC FUNCTIONS, YOU COULD FIGURE OUT THE HEIGHT FROM THE DISTANCE AND ANGLE...
CAN SEE IT A LITTLE BIT!
TOP
TOWER
MID-TIER
MID-TIER
VISIBLE RANGE
CAN SEE IT!
TREES OVERHEAD OBSTRUCT LINE OF SIGHT
BEHIND SHIBAHAMA H.S.
BOTTOM TIER
BOTTOM TIER
SHRINE
MAKE NO MISTAKE... THE CLOCKTOWER WAS HIDDEN BY SOMEONE'S HANDIWORK!!
CAN'T SEE IT.
WHY WOULD YOU PUT A BUILDING IN SUCH AN INCONVENIENT PLACE?! THERE'S NO END TO THE MYSTERIES IN THIS TOWN, BUT STILL, I HAVE TO WONDER WHY!! WAS THIS CLOCK
TOWER USED AS A LITERARY SALON BY CERTAIN PEOPLE?!

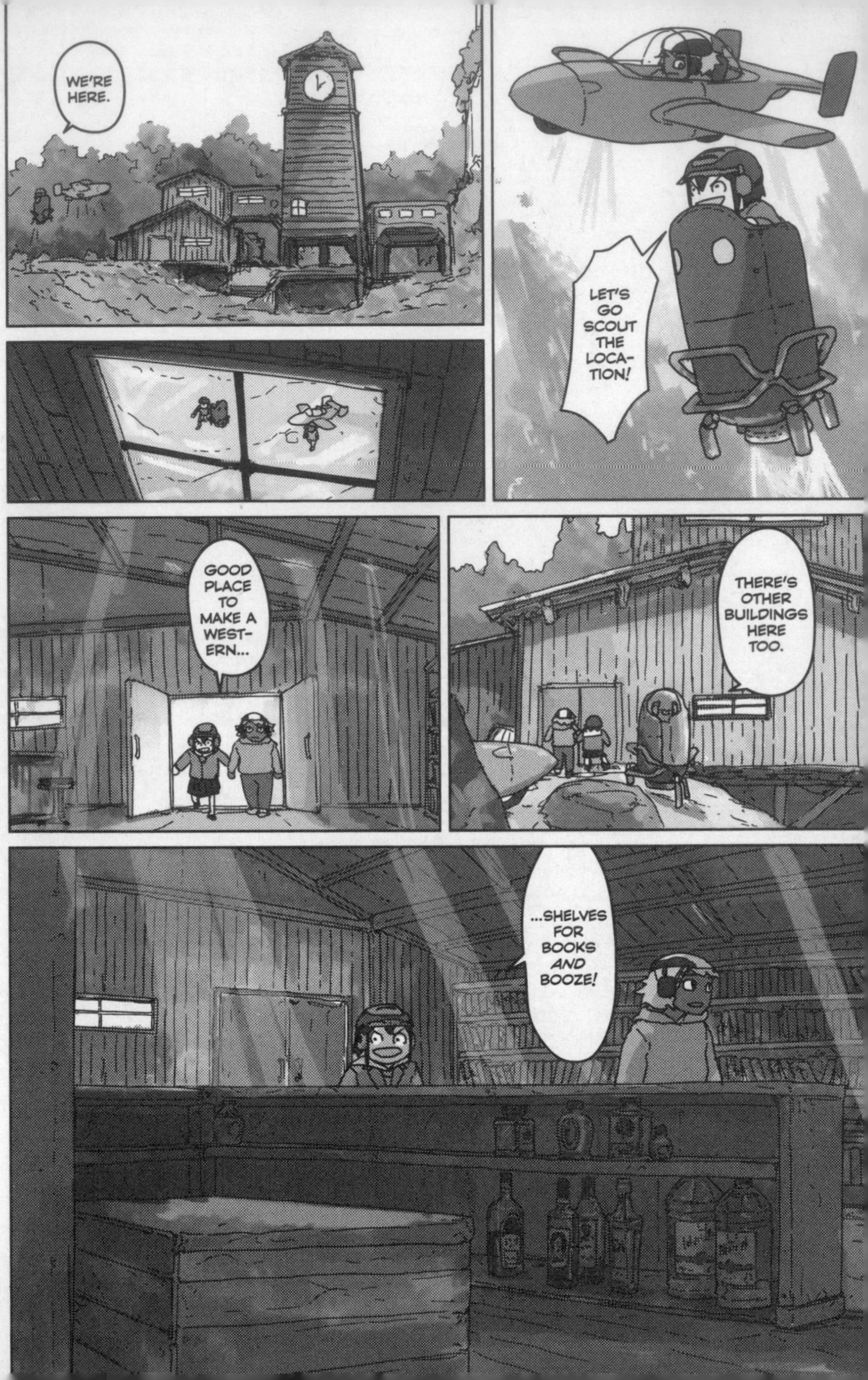
LET'S GO SCOUT THE LOCATION!
WE'RE HERE.
THERE'S OTHER BUILDINGS HERE TOO.
GOOD PLACE TO MAKE A WESTERN...
...SHELVES FOR BOOKS AND BOOZE!

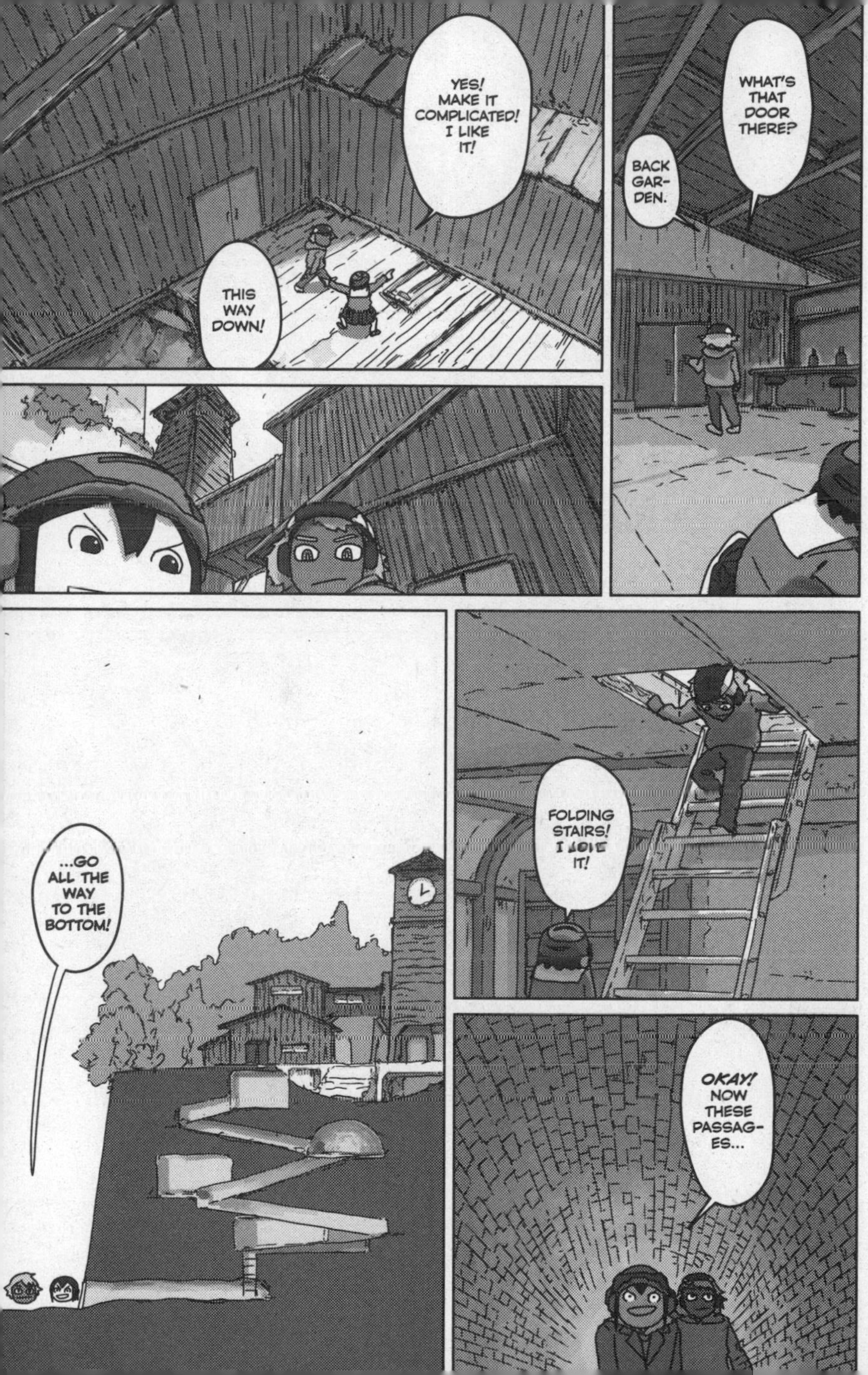
WHAT'S THAT DOOR THERE?
BACK GAR-DEN.
YES! MAKE IT COMPLICATED! I LIKE IT!
THIS WAY DOWN!
FOLDING STAIRS!
OKAY! NOW THESE PASSAG-ES...
...GO ALL THE WAY TO THE BOTTOM!

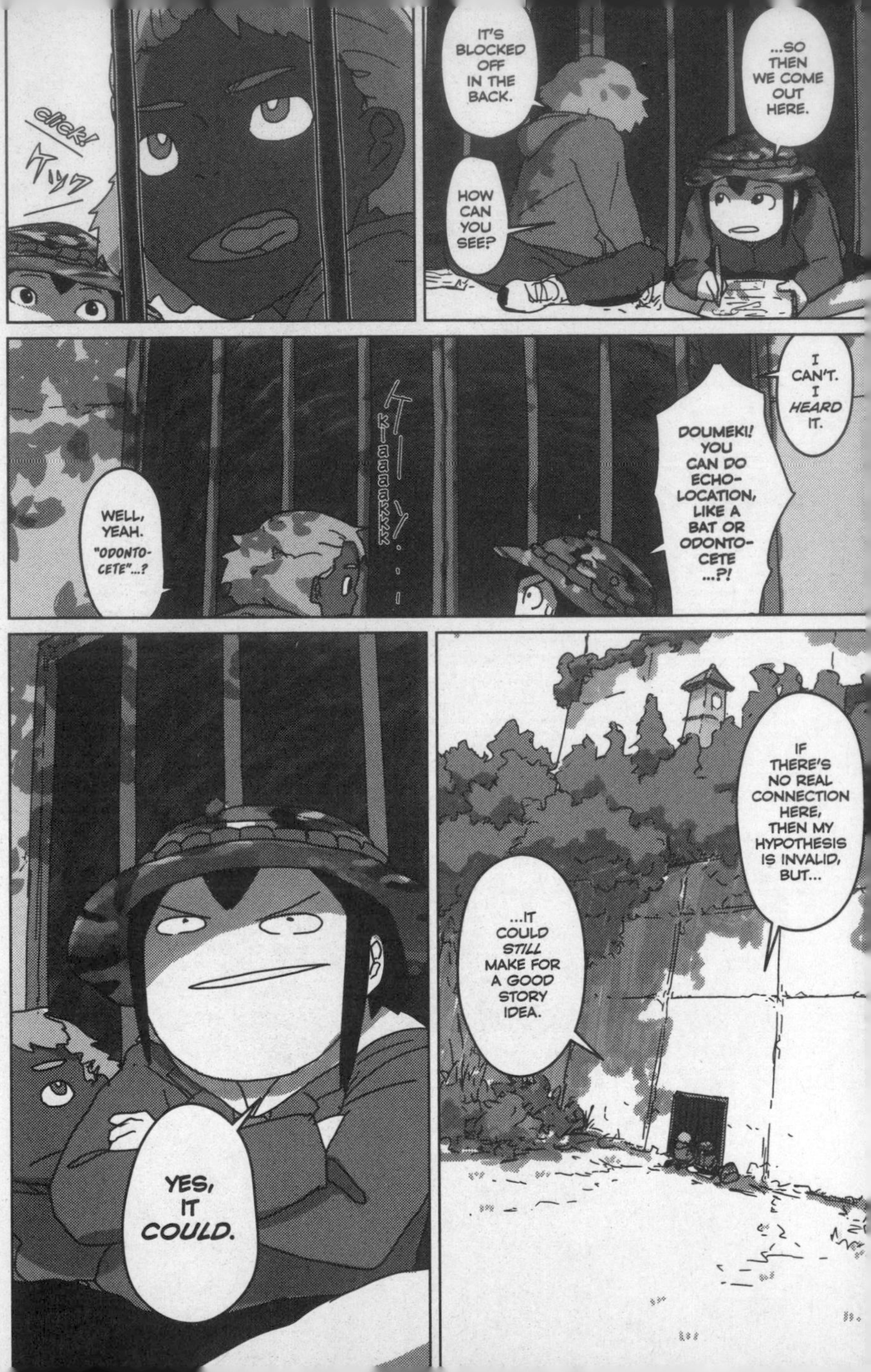
...SO THEN WE COME OUT HERE.
IT'S BLOCKED OFF IN THE BACK.
HOW CAN YOU SEE?
click!
I CAN'T. I *HEARD* IT.
DOUMEKI! YOU CAN DO ECHO-LOCATION, LIKE A BAT OR ODONTO-CETE ...?!
ケーン!...
k-aaaakkk
WELL, YEAH. "ODONTO-CETE"...?
IF THERE'S NO REAL CONNECTION HERE, THEN MY HYPOTHESIS IS INVALID, BUT...
...IT COULD *STILL* MAKE FOR A GOOD STORY IDEA.
YES, IT *COULD.*

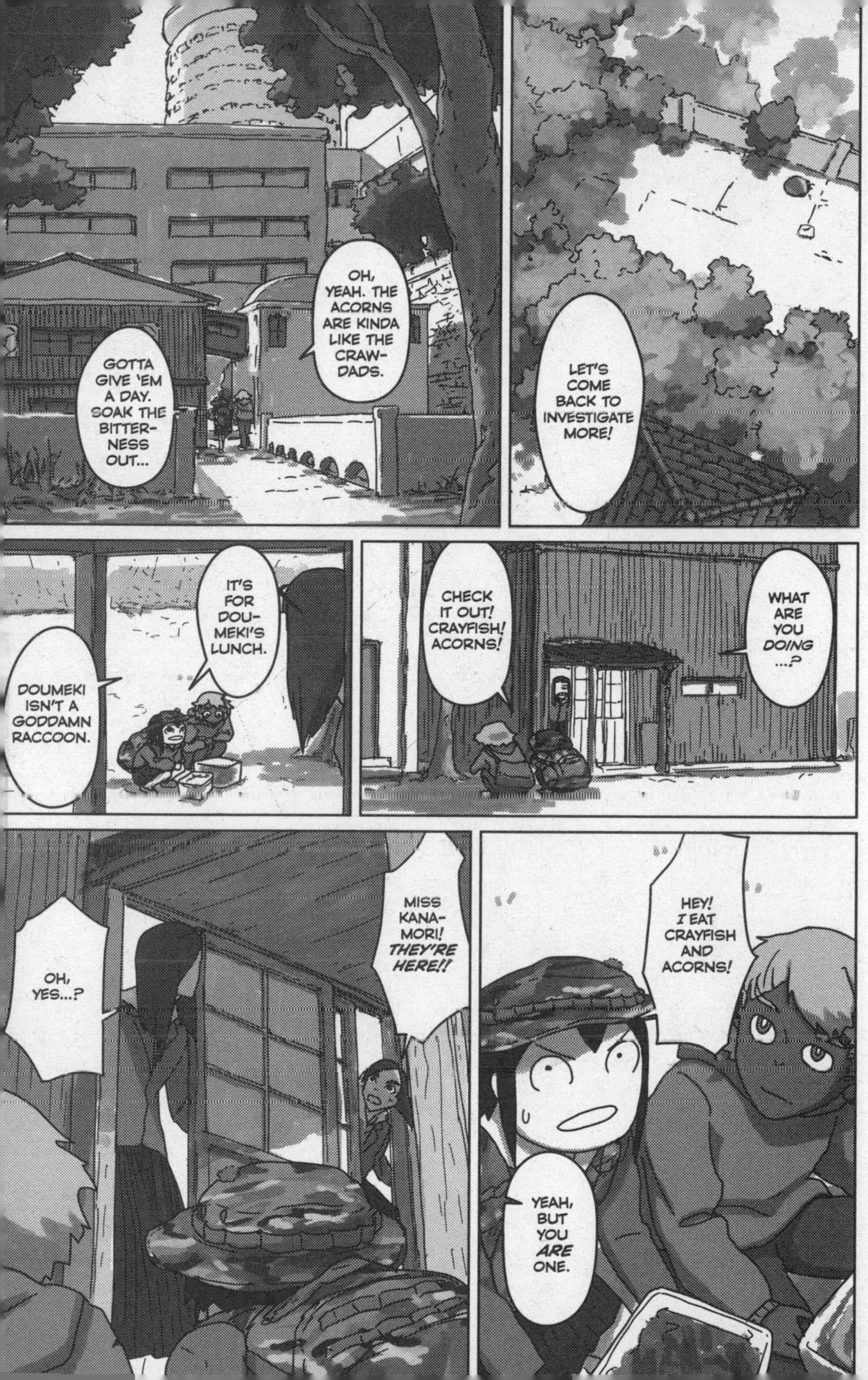
LET'S COME BACK TO INVESTIGATE MORE!
OH, YEAH. THE ACORNS ARE KINDA LIKE THE CRAW-DADS.
GOTTA GIVE 'EM A DAY. SOAK THE BITTER-NESS OUT...
WHAT ARE YOU *DOING* ...?
CHECK IT OUT! CRAYFISH! ACORNS!
IT'S FOR DOU-MEKI'S LUNCH.
DOUMEKI ISN'T A GODDAMN RACCOON.
HEY! *I* EAT CRAYFISH AND ACORNS!
YEAH, BUT YOU *ARE* ONE.
MISS KANA-MORI! ***THEY'RE HERE!!***
OH, YES...?

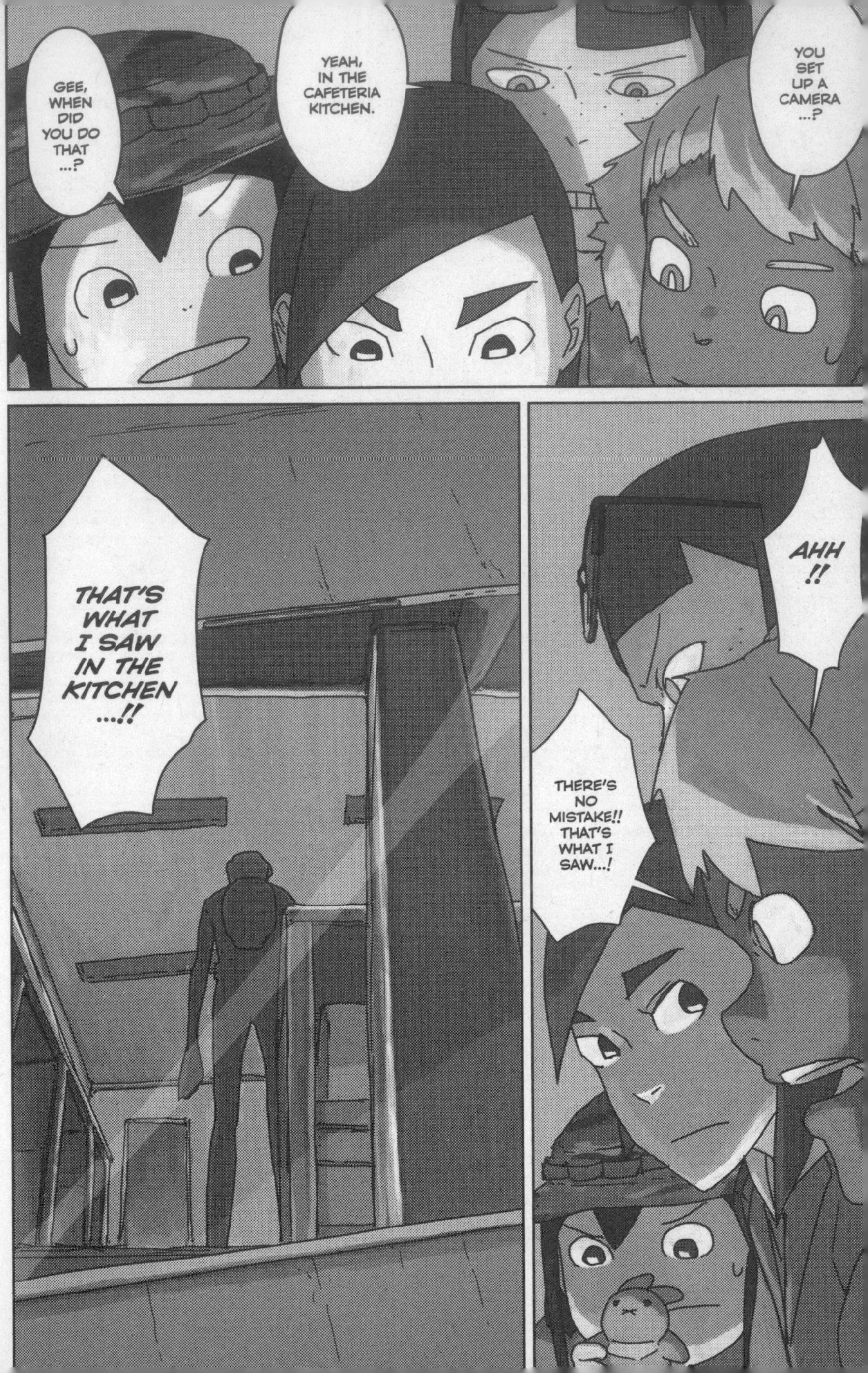
YOU SET UP A CAMERA ...?
YEAH, IN THE CAFETERIA KITCHEN.
GEE, WHEN DID YOU DO THAT ...?
AHH !!
THERE'S NO MISTAKE!! THAT'S WHAT I SAW...!
THAT'S WHAT I SAW IN THE KITCHEN ....!!

KEEP YOUR HANDS OFF EIZOUKEN!

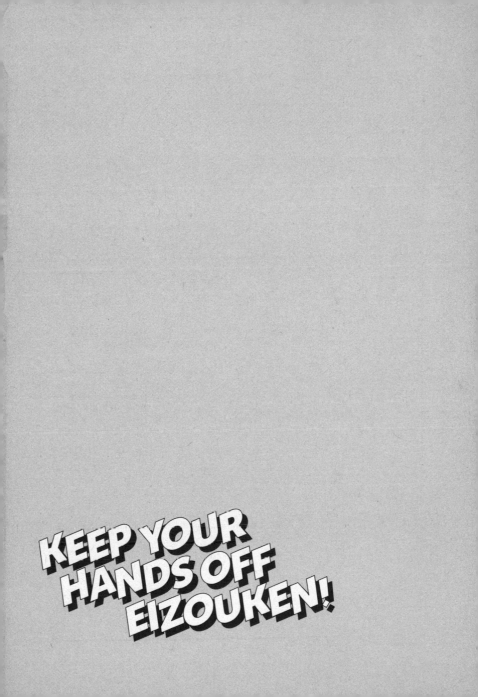

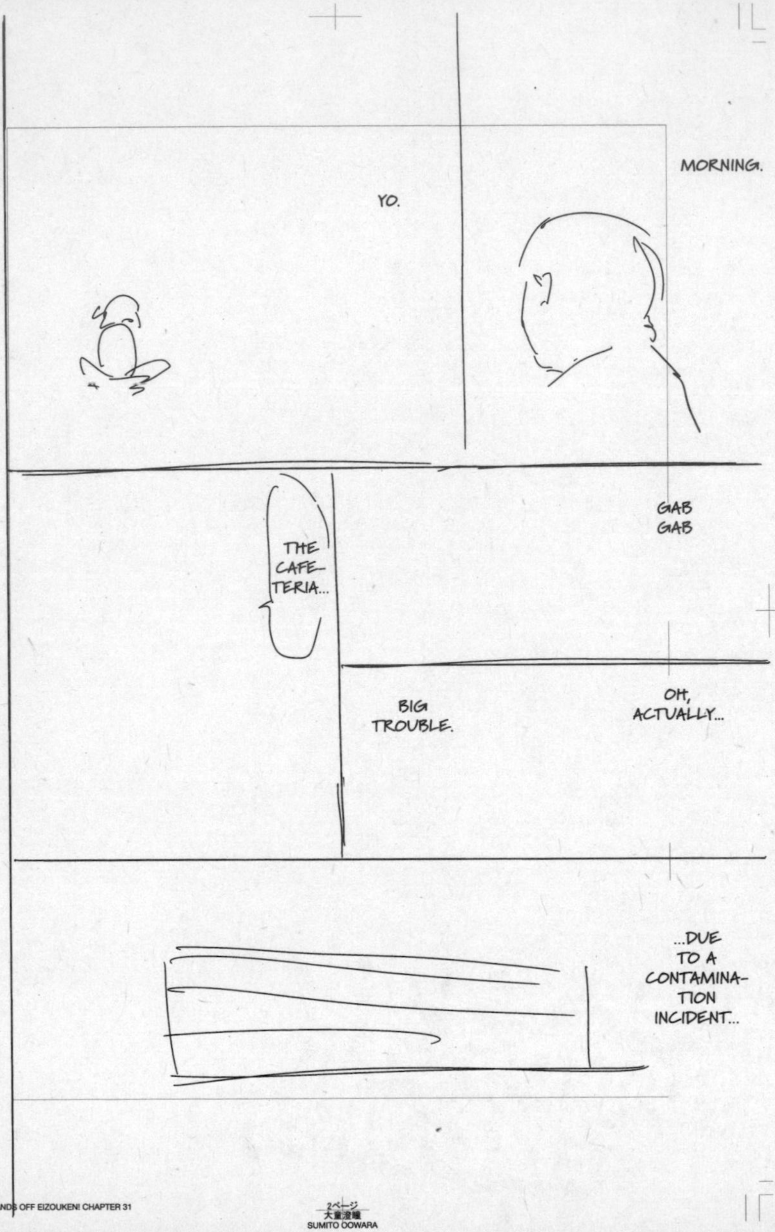
MORNING.
YO.
GAB GAB
OH, ACTUALLY...
BIG TROUBLE.
THE CAFETERIA...
...DUE TO A CONTAMINATION INCIDENT...

CHAPTER 32: THE KAPPA WERE REAL! (KAPPA VS. WEIRD FISH)

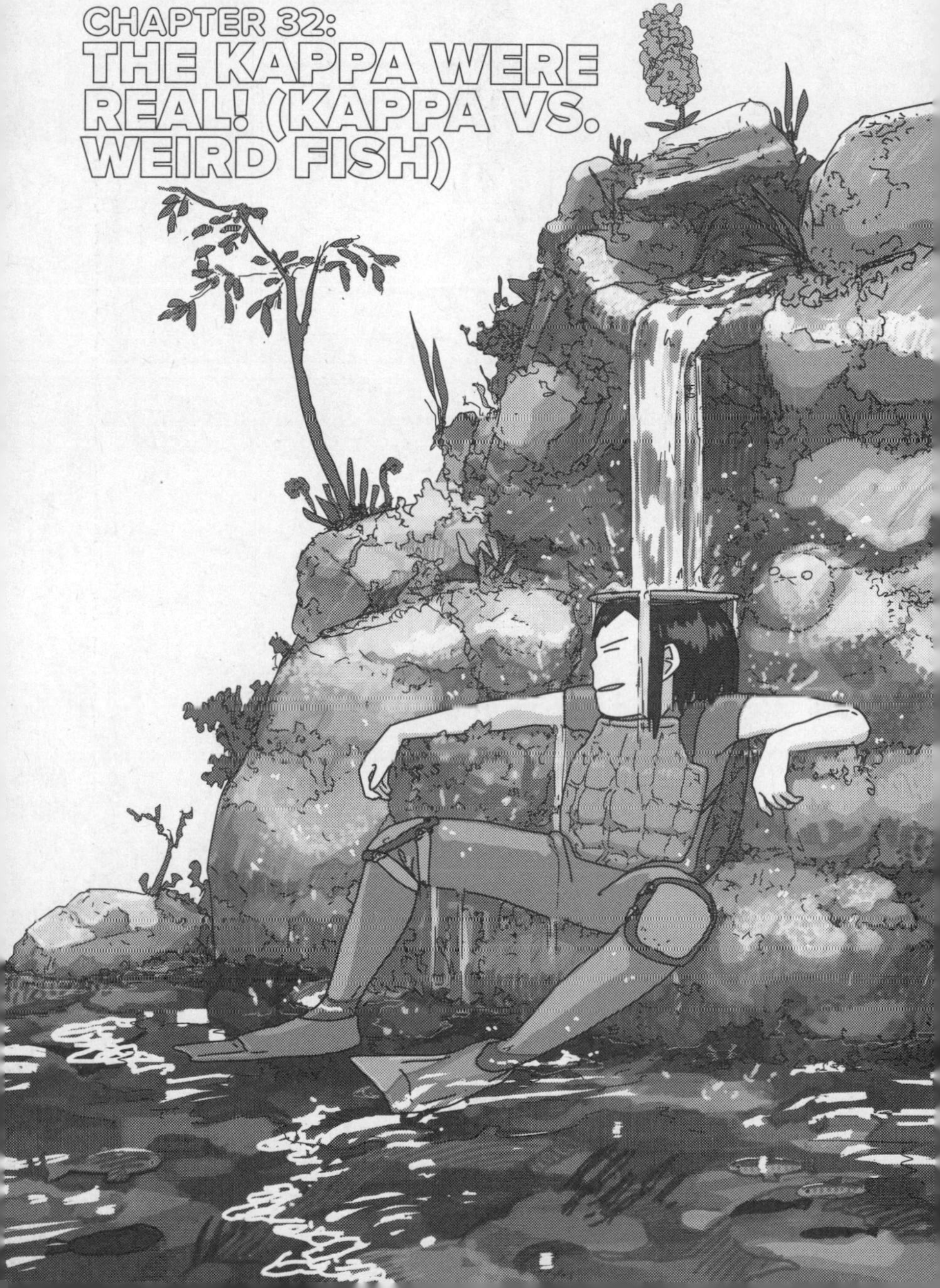

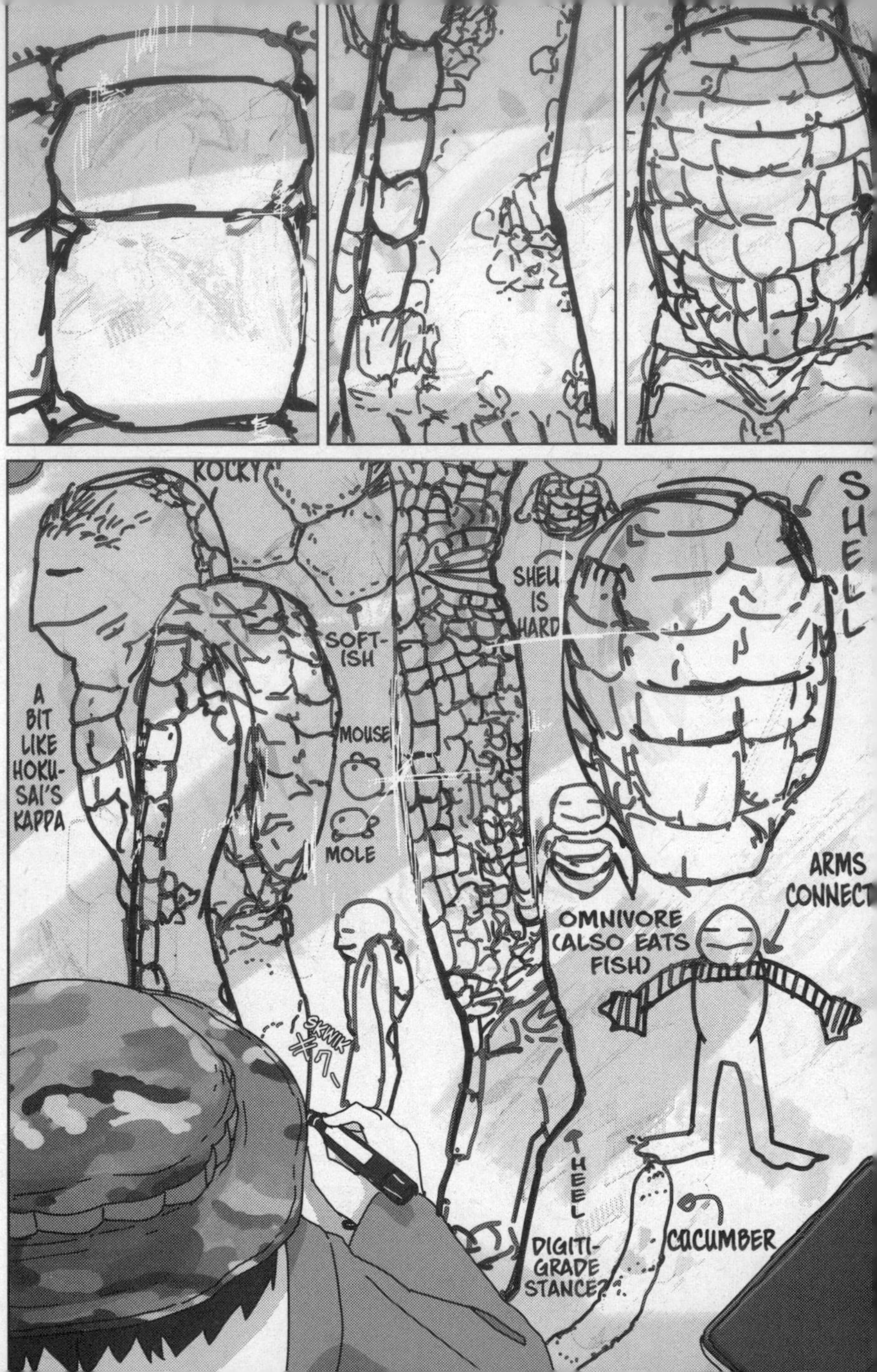
SHELL
SHELL IS HARD
ROCKY
SOFT-ISH
ARMS CONNECT
OMNIVORE (ALSO EATS FISH)
MOUSE
MOLE
A BIT LIKE HOKUSAI'S KAPPA
SKWIK
HEEL
CUCUMBER
DIGITI-GRADE STANCE?

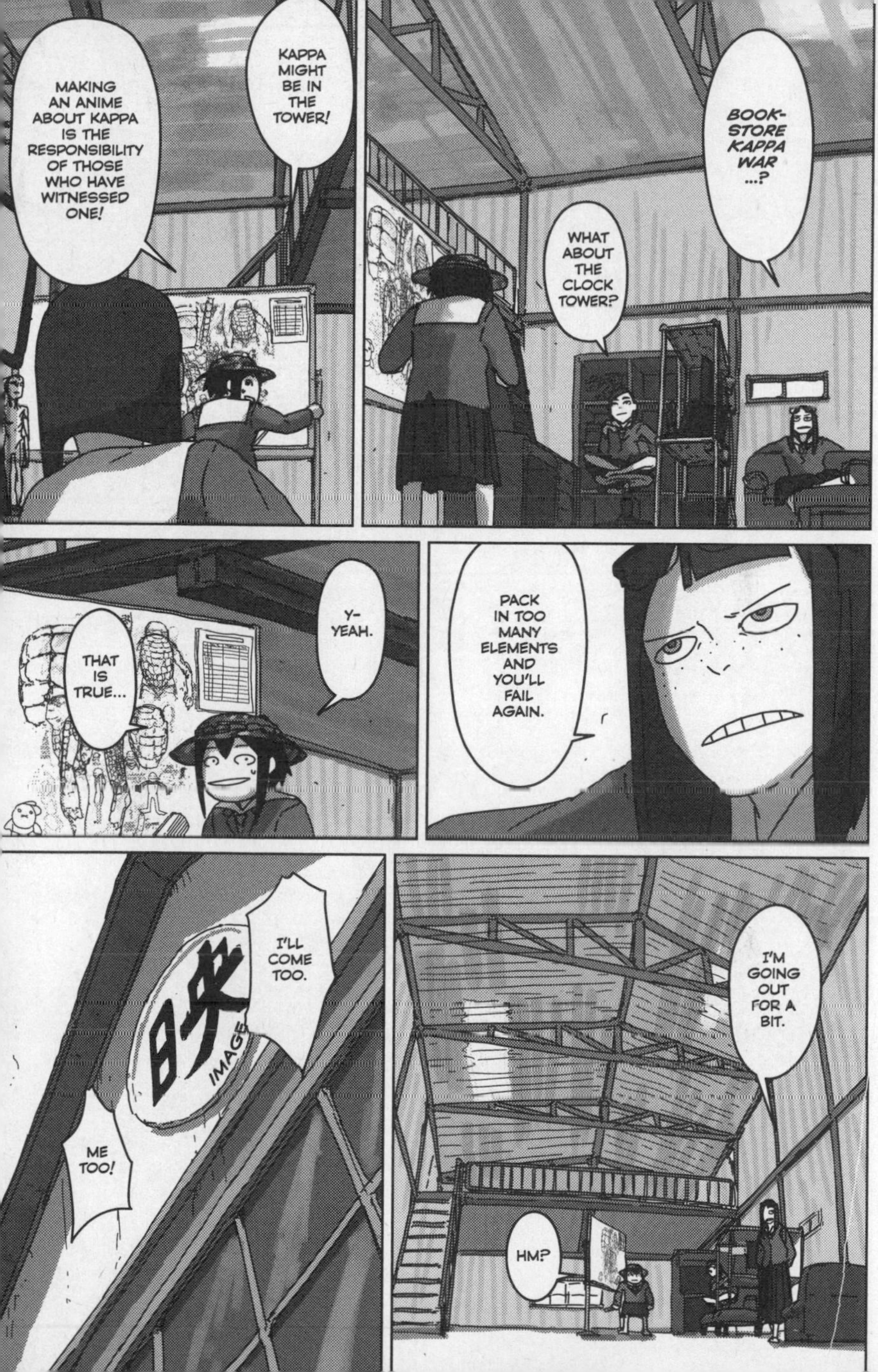
BOOK-STORE KAPPA WAR ...?
WHAT ABOUT THE CLOCK TOWER?
KAPPA MIGHT BE IN THE TOWER!
MAKING AN ANIME ABOUT KAPPA IS THE RESPONSIBILITY OF THOSE WHO HAVE WITNESSED ONE!
PACK IN TOO MANY ELEMENTS AND YOU'LL FAIL AGAIN.
Y-YEAH.
THAT IS TRUE...
I'M GOING OUT FOR A BIT.
HM?
I'LL COME TOO.
IMAGE
ME TOO!

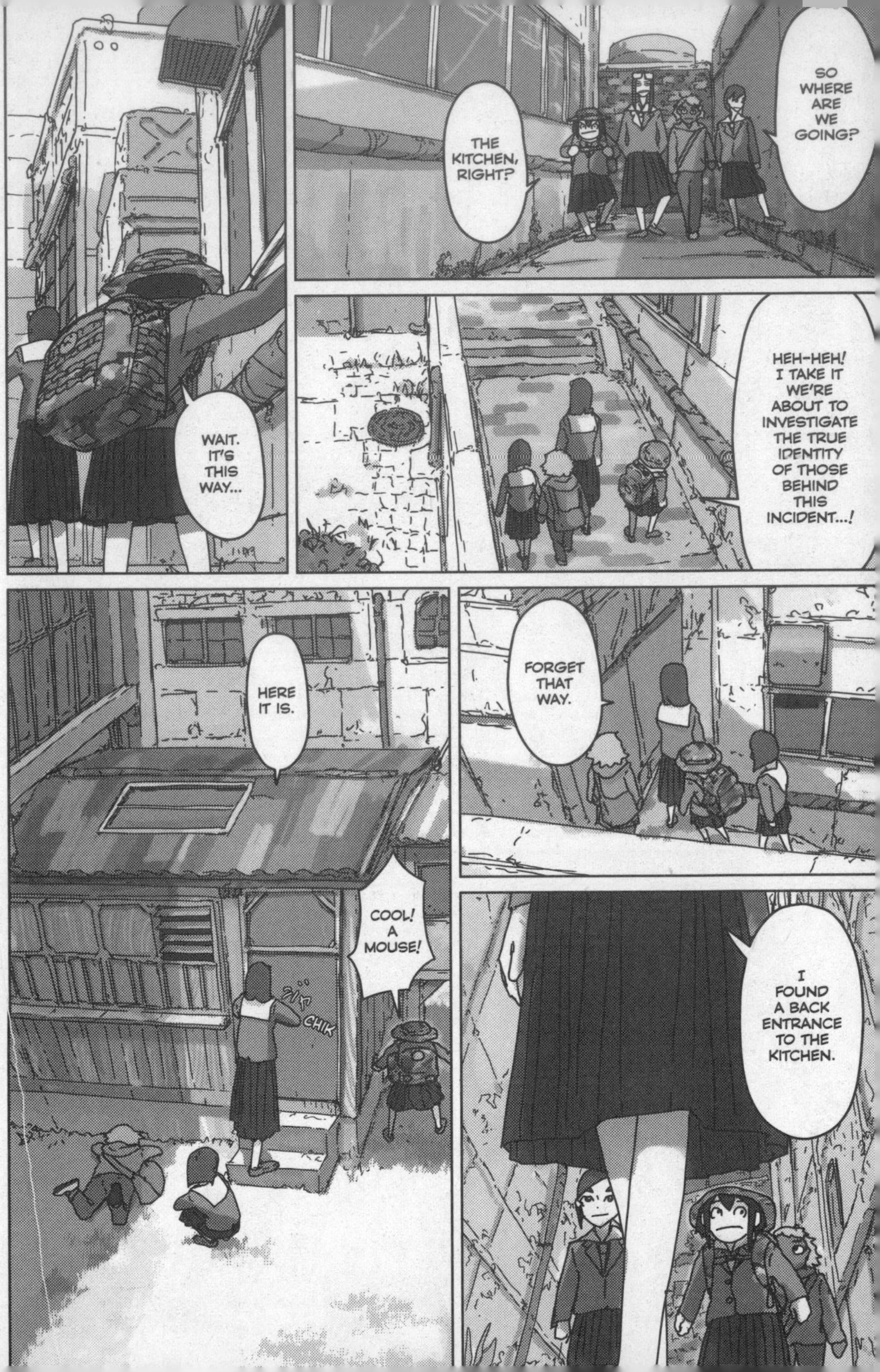
SO WHERE ARE WE GOING?
THE KITCHEN, RIGHT?
HEH-HEH! I TAKE IT WE'RE ABOUT TO INVESTIGATE THE TRUE IDENTITY OF THOSE BEHIND THIS INCIDENT...!
WAIT. IT'S THIS WAY...
FORGET THAT WAY.
I FOUND A BACK ENTRANCE TO THE KITCHEN.
HERE IT IS.
COOL! A MOUSE!
CHIK

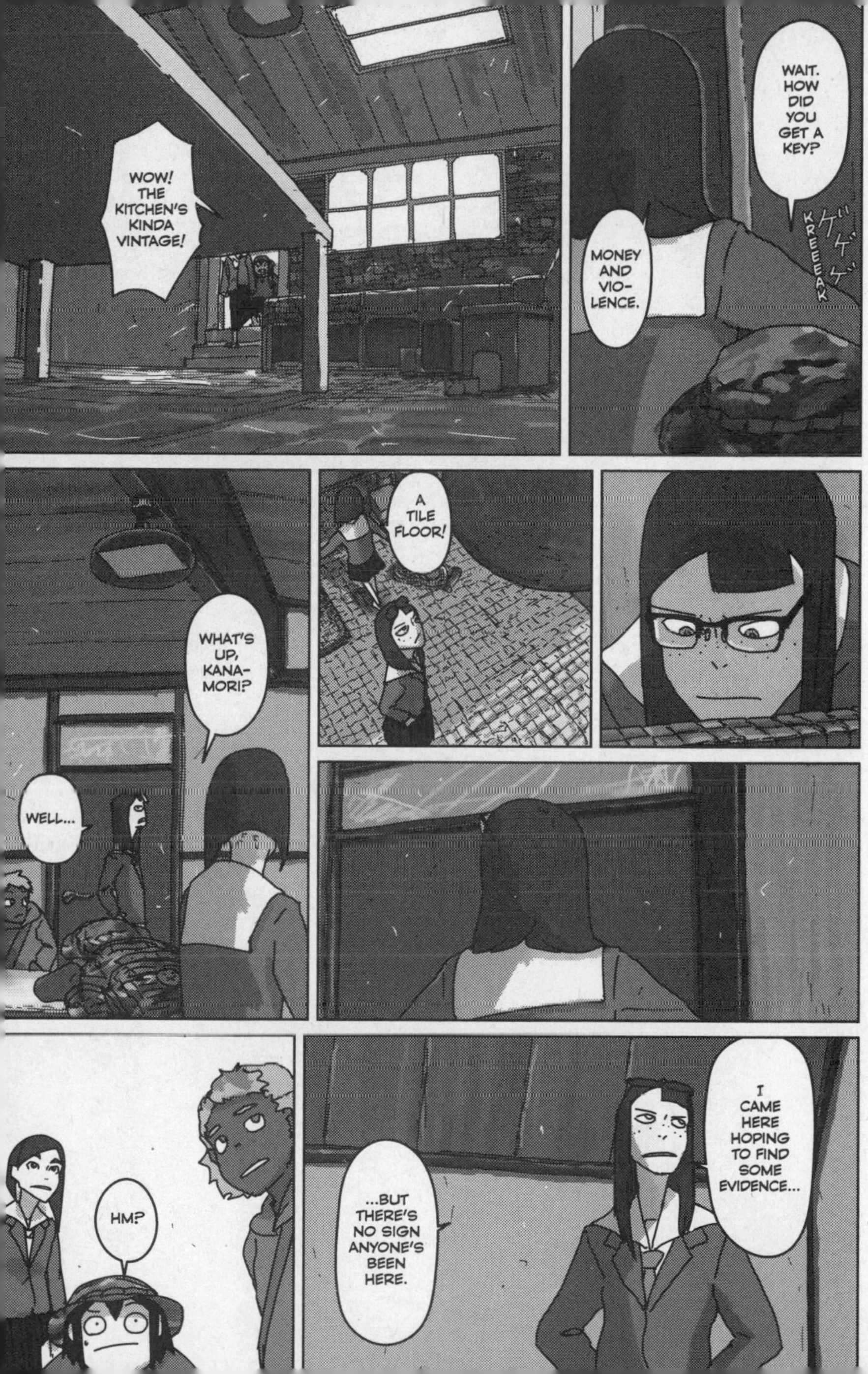
WAIT. HOW DID YOU GET A KEY?
KREEEAK
MONEY AND VIO-LENCE.
WOW! THE KITCHEN'S KINDA VINTAGE!
A TILE FLOOR!
WHAT'S UP, KANA-MORI?
WELL...
I CAME HERE HOPING TO FIND SOME EVIDENCE...
...BUT THERE'S NO SIGN ANYONE'S BEEN HERE.
HM?

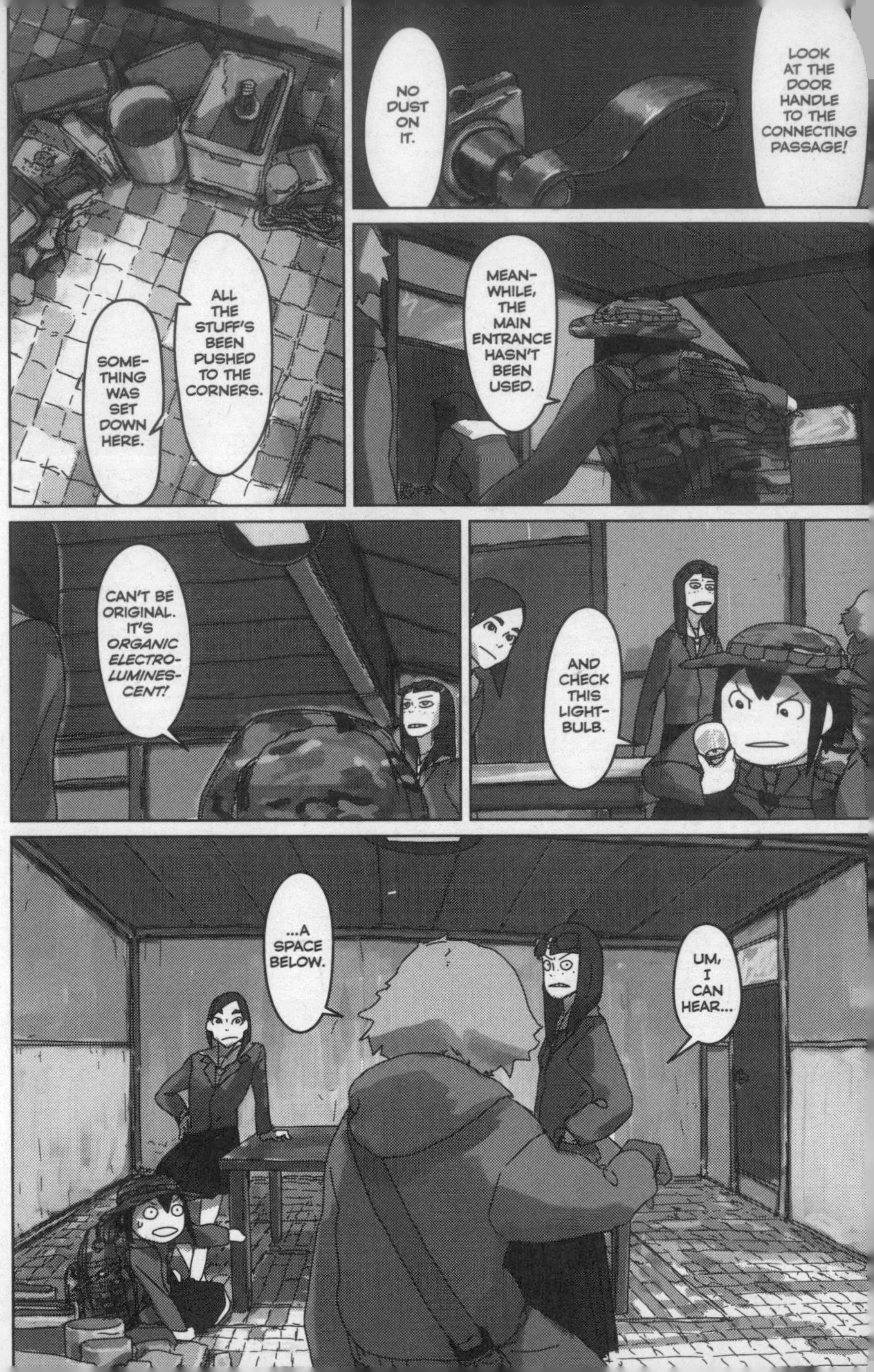
LOOK AT THE DOOR HANDLE TO THE CONNECTING PASSAGE!
NO DUST ON IT.
MEAN-WHILE, THE MAIN ENTRANCE HASN'T BEEN USED.
ALL THE STUFF'S BEEN PUSHED TO THE CORNERS.
SOME-THING WAS SET DOWN HERE.
AND CHECK THIS LIGHT-BULB.
CAN'T BE ORIGINAL. IT'S *ORGANIC ELECTRO-LUMINES-CENT!*
UM, I CAN HEAR...
...A SPACE BELOW.

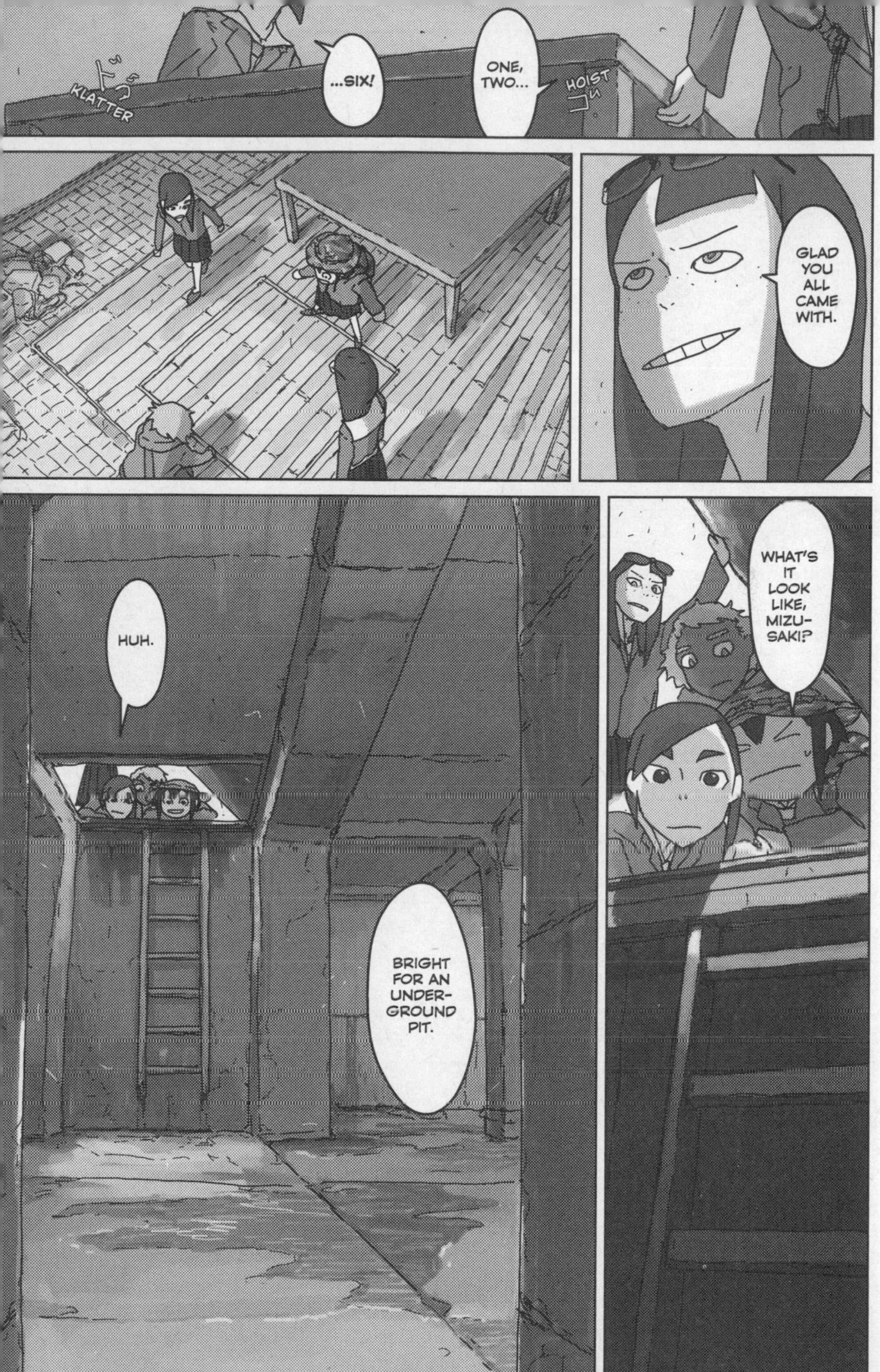
HOIST
ONE, TWO...
...SIX!
KLATTER
GLAD YOU ALL CAME WITH.
WHAT'S IT LOOK LIKE, MIZUSAKI?
HUH.
BRIGHT FOR AN UNDER-GROUND PIT.

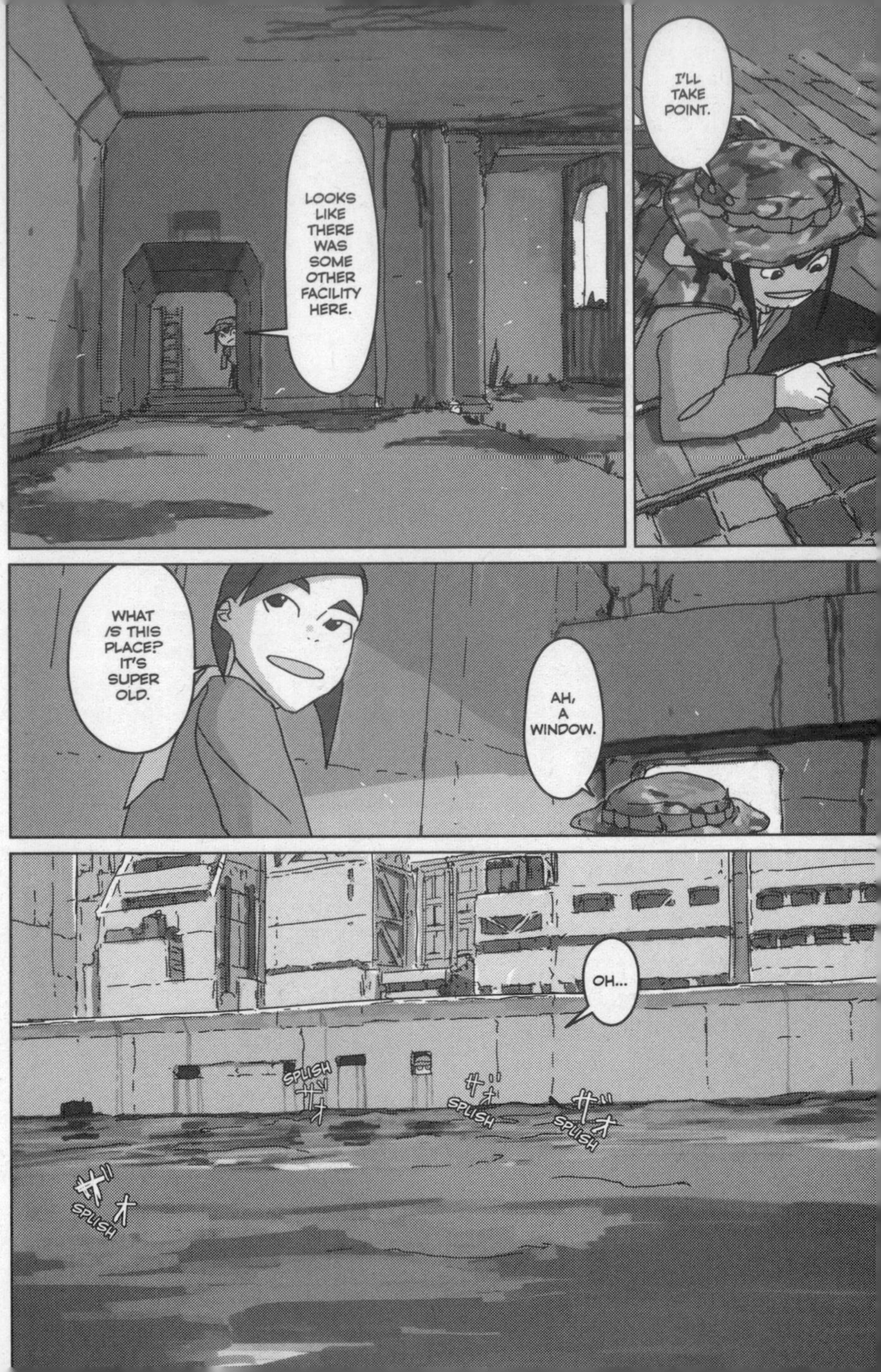
I'LL TAKE POINT.
LOOKS LIKE THERE WAS SOME OTHER FACILITY HERE.
AH, A WINDOW.
WHAT IS THIS PLACE? IT'S SUPER OLD.
OH...
SPLISH
SPLISH
SPLISH
SPLISH

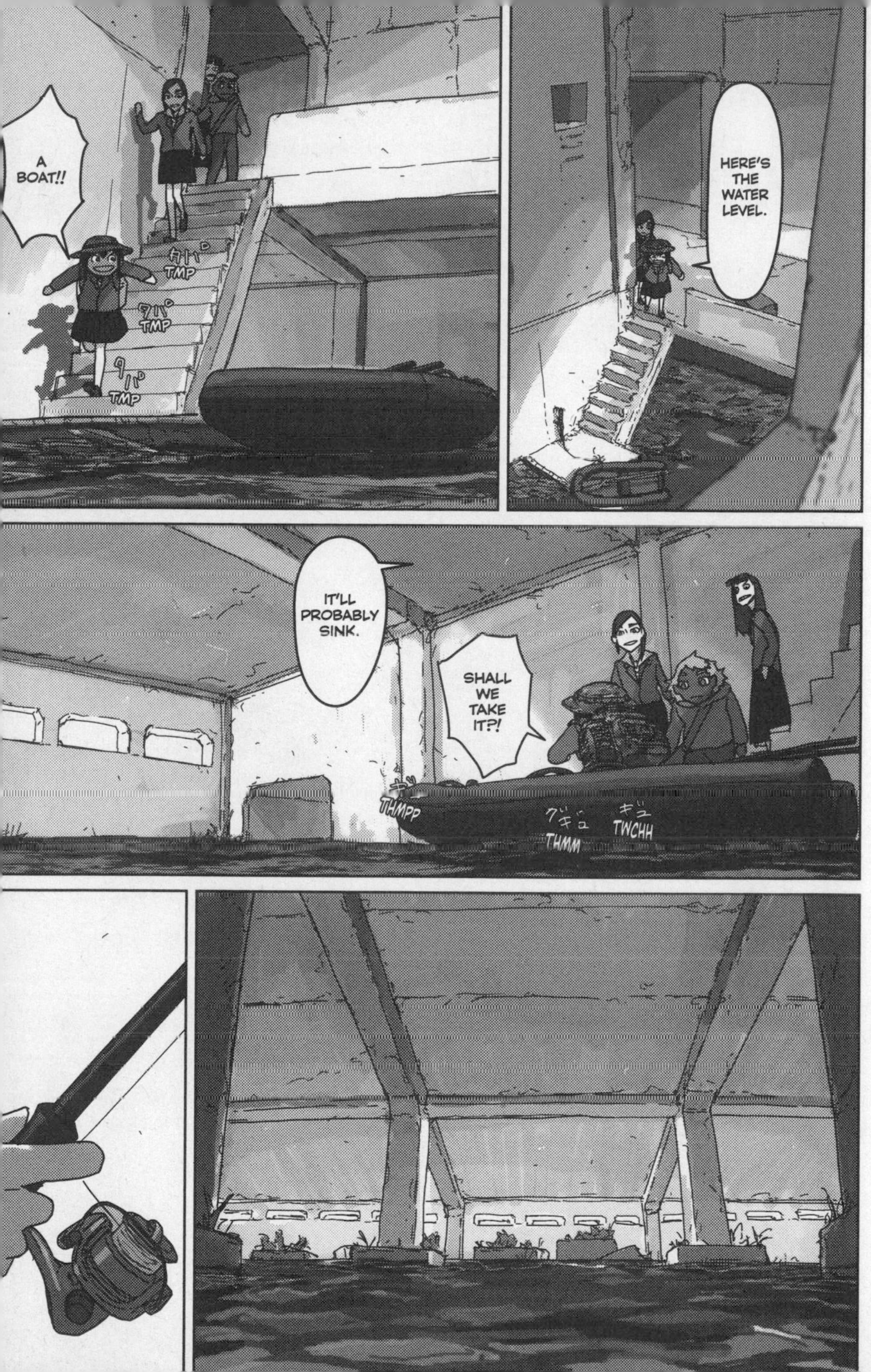
HERE'S THE WATER LEVEL.
A BOAT!!
TMP
TMP
TMP
SHALL WE TAKE IT?!
IT'LL PROBABLY SINK.
THMPP
TWCHH
THMM

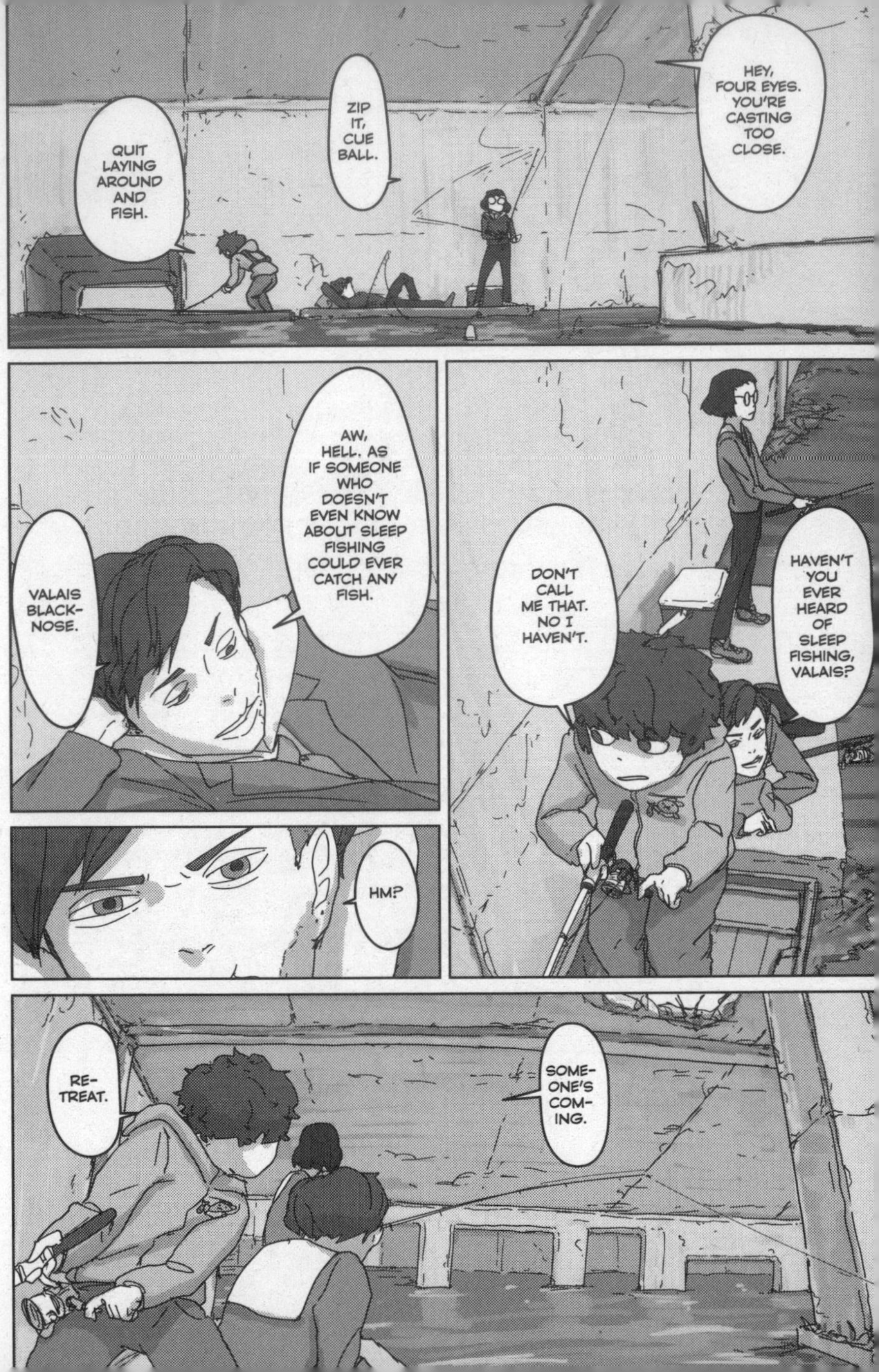
HEY, FOUR EYES. YOU'RE CASTING TOO CLOSE.
ZIP IT, CUE BALL.
QUIT LAYING AROUND AND FISH.
HAVEN'T YOU EVER HEARD OF SLEEP FISHING, VALAIS?
DON'T CALL ME THAT. NO I HAVEN'T.
AW, HELL. AS IF SOMEONE WHO DOESN'T EVEN KNOW ABOUT SLEEP FISHING COULD EVER CATCH ANY FISH.
VALAIS BLACK-NOSE.
HM?
SOME-ONE'S COM-ING.
RE-TREAT.

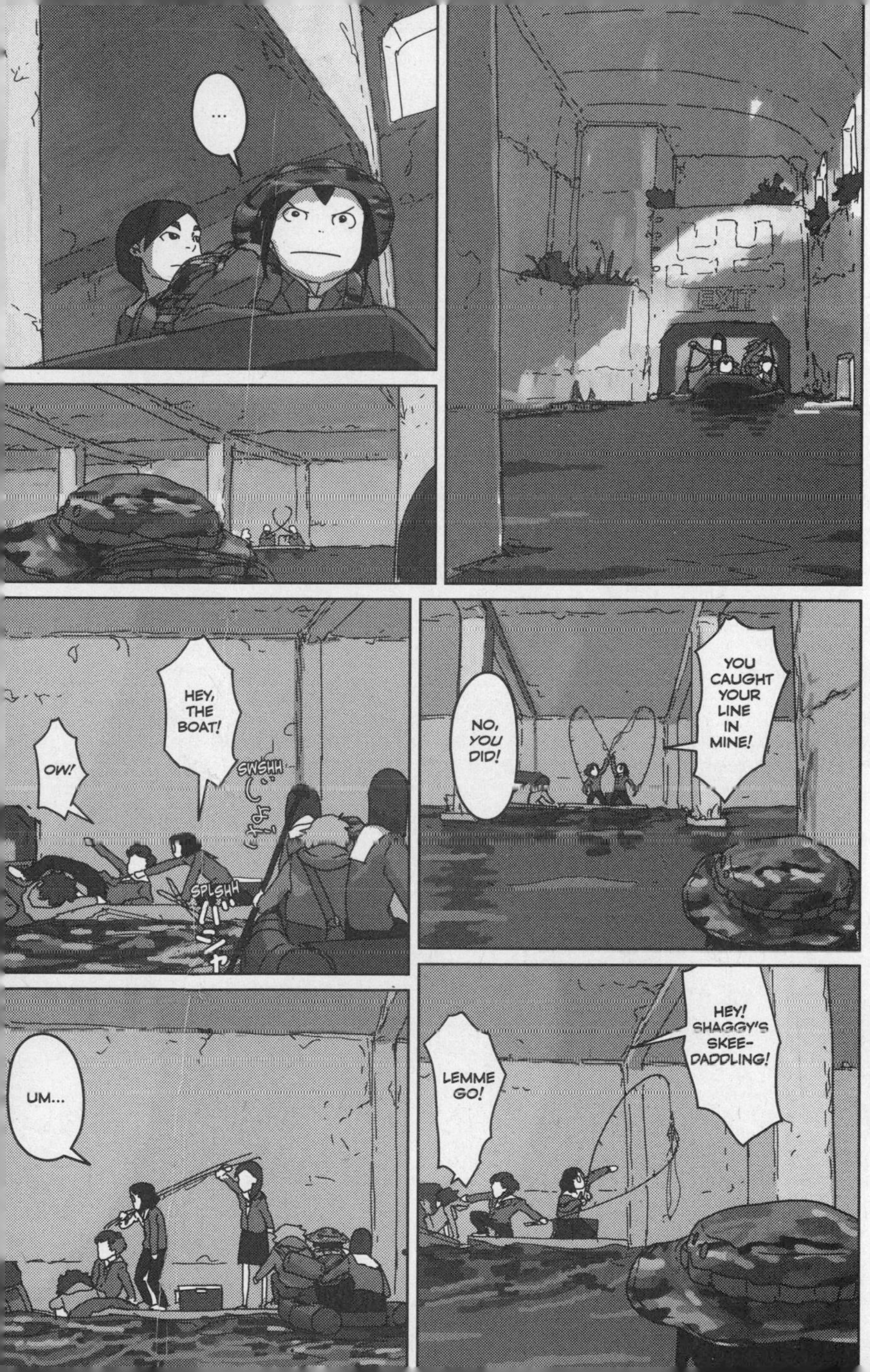
EXIT
...
YOU CAUGHT YOUR LINE IN MINE!
NO, YOU DID!
HEY, THE BOAT!
SWSHH
OW!
SPLSHH
HEY! SHAGGY'S SKEE-DADDLING!
LEMME GO!
UM...

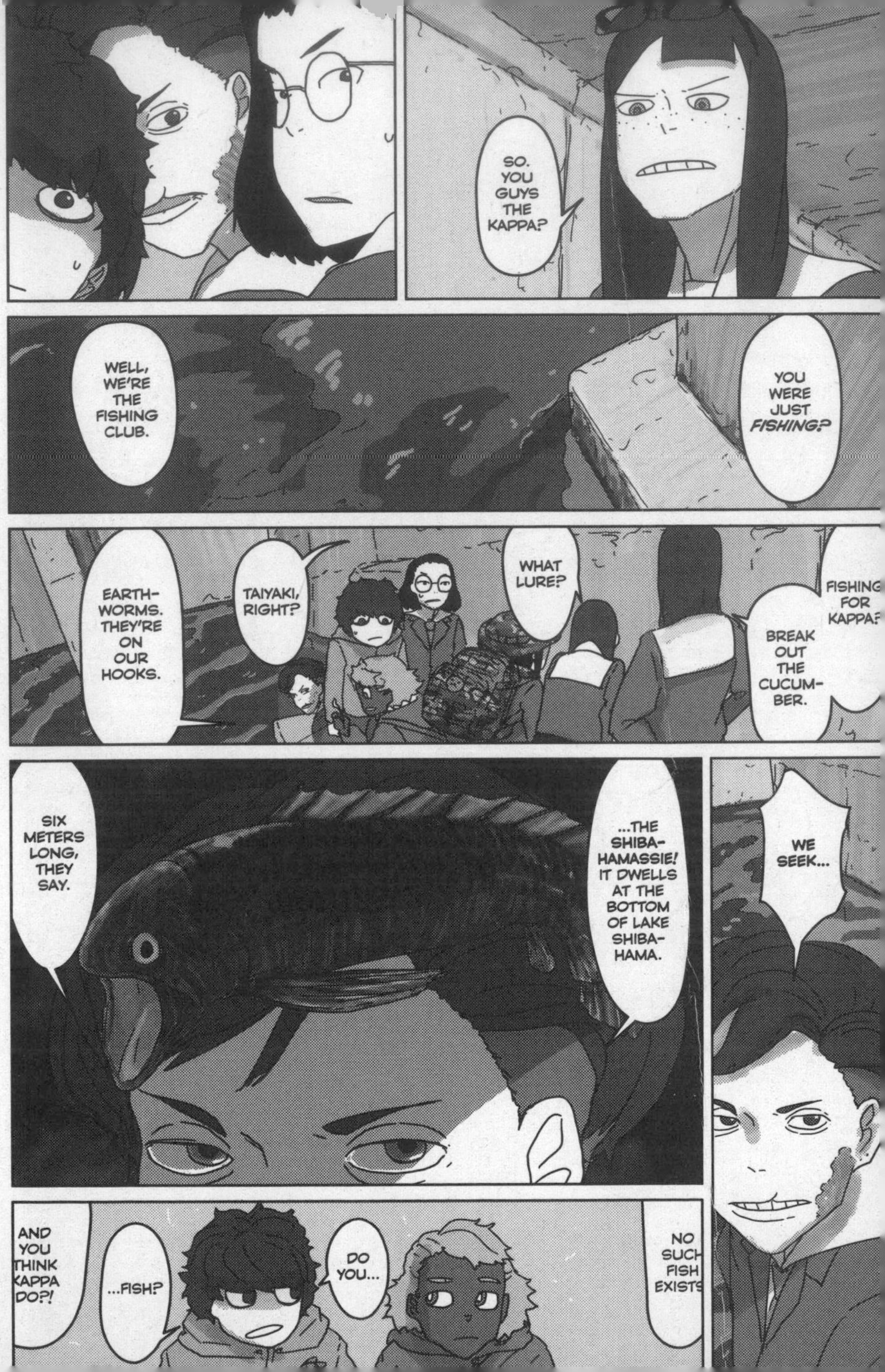
SO. YOU GUYS THE KAPPA?
YOU WERE JUST *FISHING?*
WELL, WE'RE THE FISHING CLUB.
FISHING FOR KAPPA?
BREAK OUT THE CUCUMBER.
WHAT LURE?
TAIYAKI, RIGHT?
EARTHWORMS. THEY'RE ON OUR HOOKS.
WE SEEK...
...THE SHIBAHAMASSIE! IT DWELLS AT THE BOTTOM OF LAKE SHIBAHAMA.
SIX METERS LONG, THEY SAY.
NO SUCH FISH EXISTS
DO YOU...
...FISH?
AND YOU THINK KAPPA DO?!

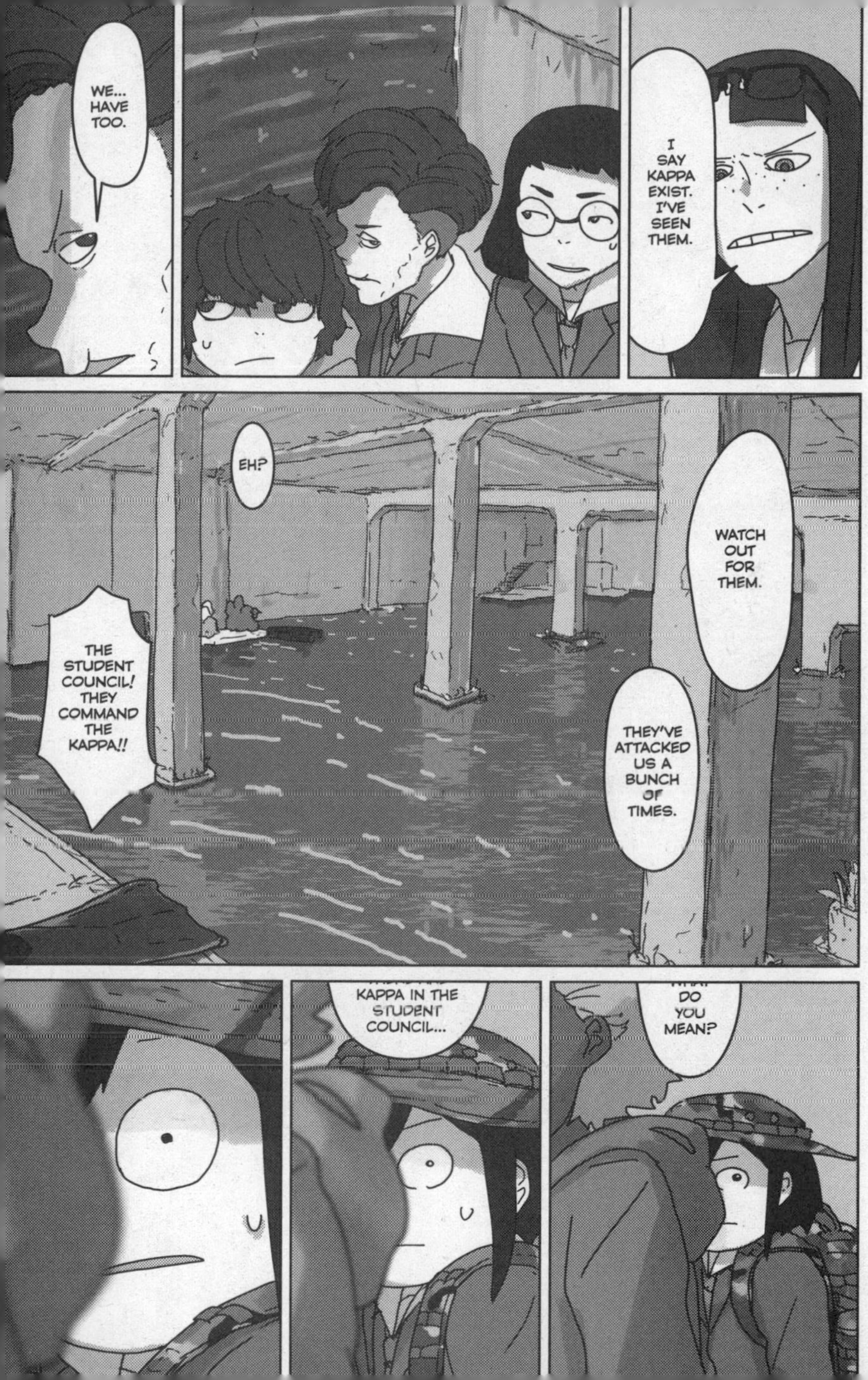
I SAY KAPPA EXIST. I'VE SEEN THEM.
WE... HAVE TOO.
WATCH OUT FOR THEM.
THEY'VE ATTACKED US A BUNCH OF TIMES.
EH?
THE STUDENT COUNCIL! THEY COMMAND THE KAPPA!!
DO YOU MEAN?
KAPPA IN THE STUDENT COUNCIL...

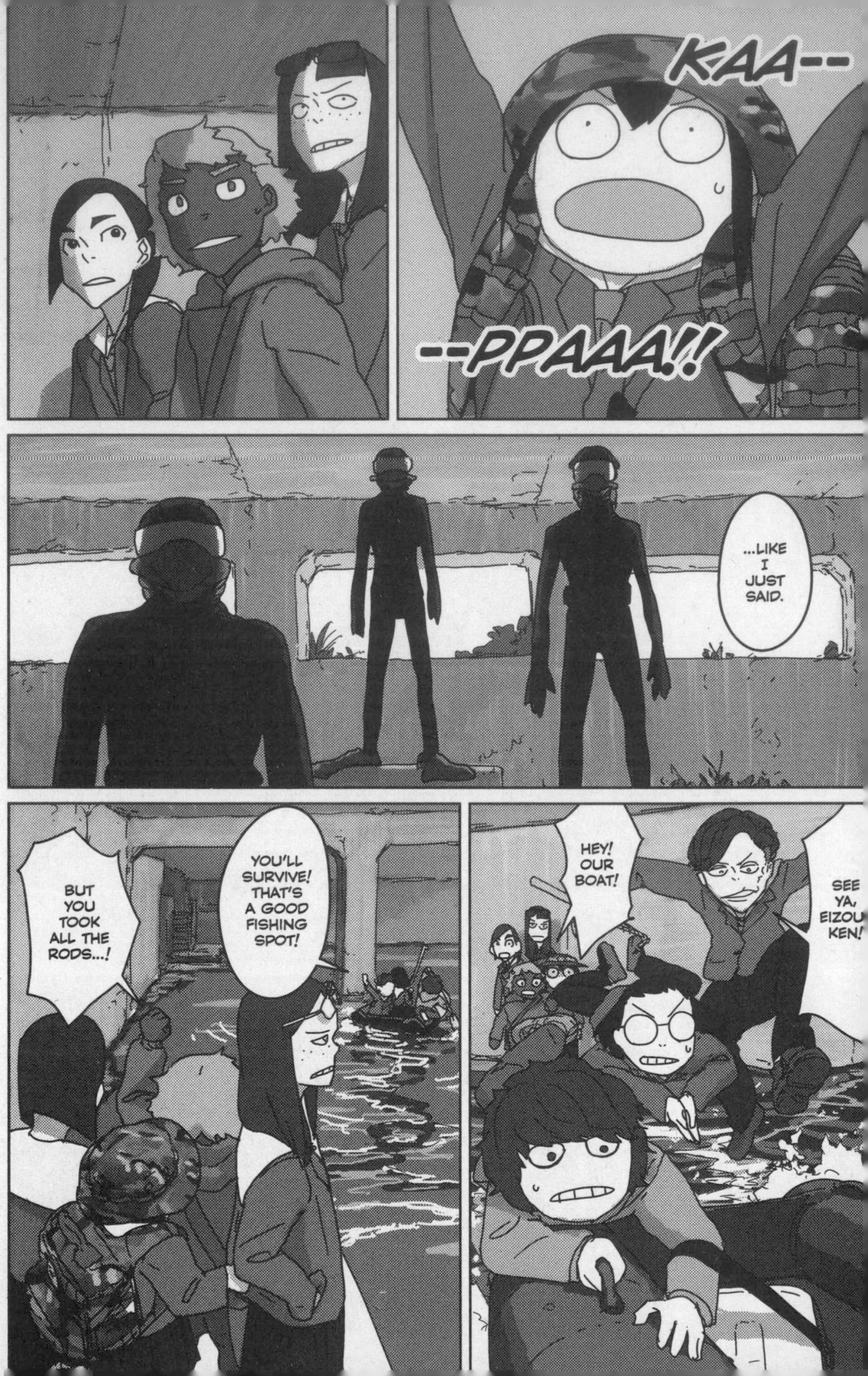
KAA--
--PPAAA!!
...LIKE I JUST SAID.
SEE YA, EIZOUKEN!
HEY! OUR BOAT!
YOU'LL SURVIVE! THAT'S A GOOD FISHING SPOT!
BUT YOU TOOK ALL THE RODS...!

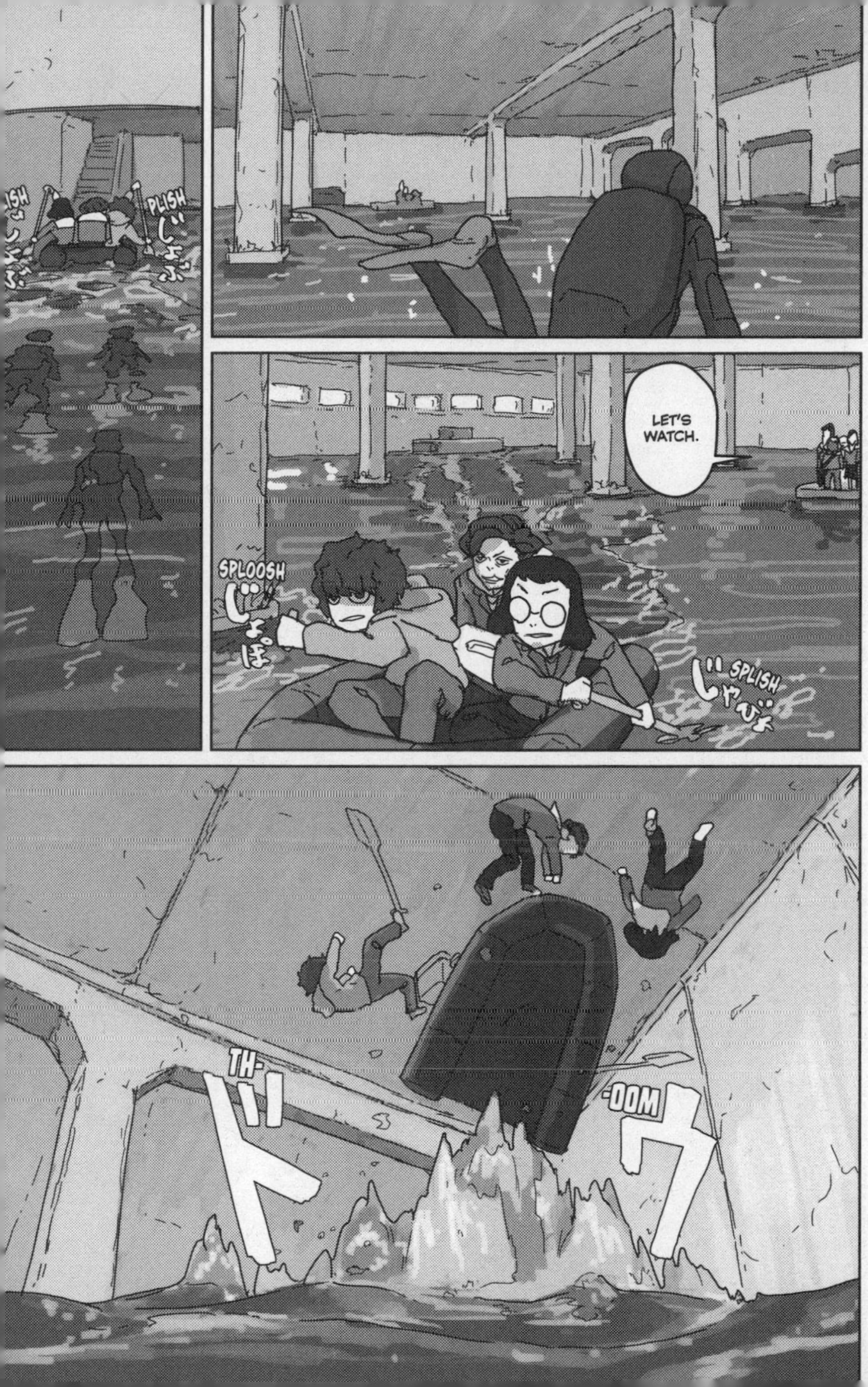
LET'S WATCH.
SPLASH
SPLOOSH
PLISH
TH-
-OOM

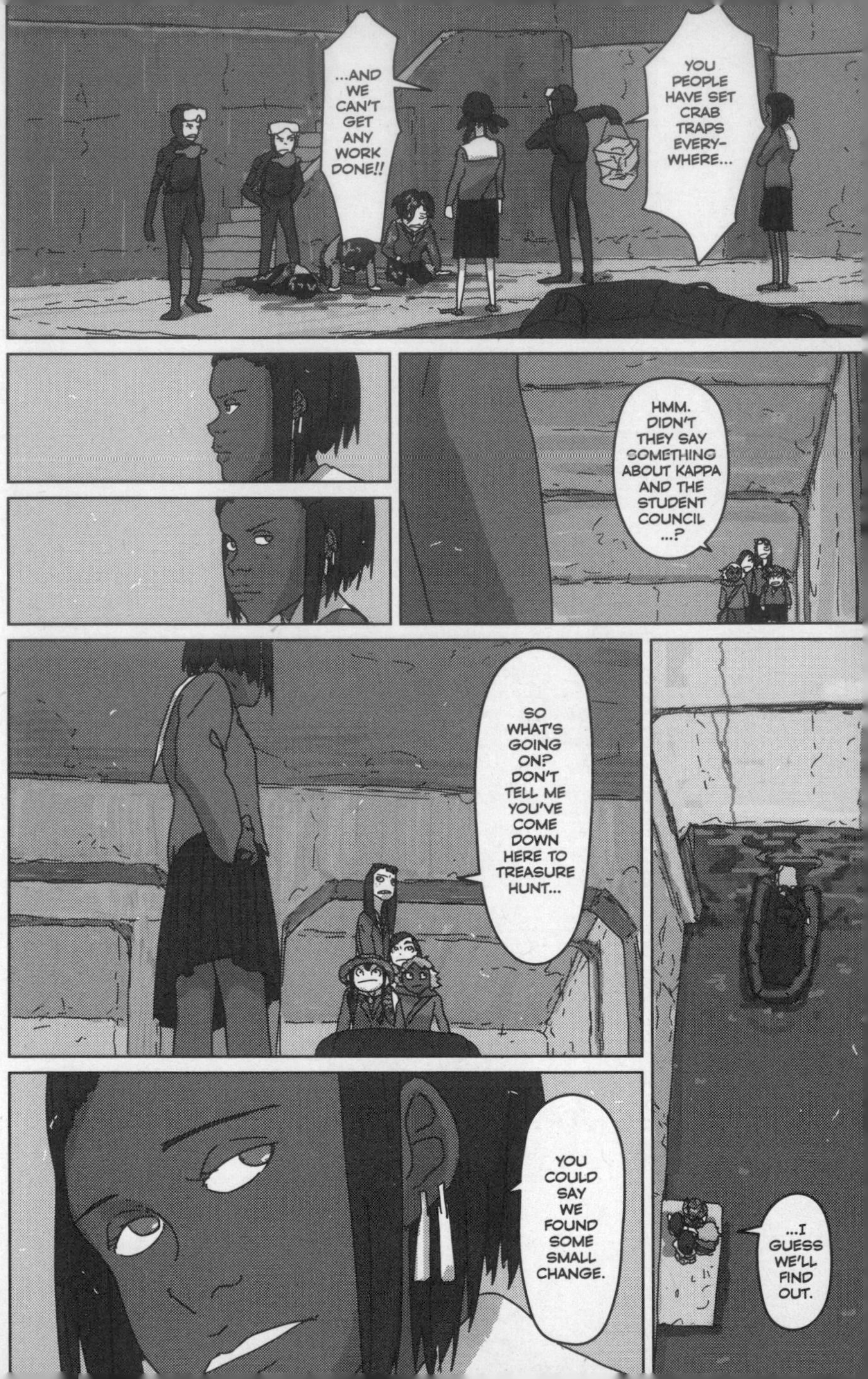
YOU PEOPLE HAVE SET CRAB TRAPS EVERY-WHERE...
...AND WE CAN'T GET ANY WORK DONE!!
HMM. DIDN'T THEY SAY SOMETHING ABOUT KAPPA AND THE STUDENT COUNCIL ...?
...I GUESS WE'LL FIND OUT.
SO WHAT'S GOING ON? DON'T TELL ME YOU'VE COME DOWN HERE TO TREASURE HUNT...
YOU COULD SAY WE FOUND SOME SMALL CHANGE.

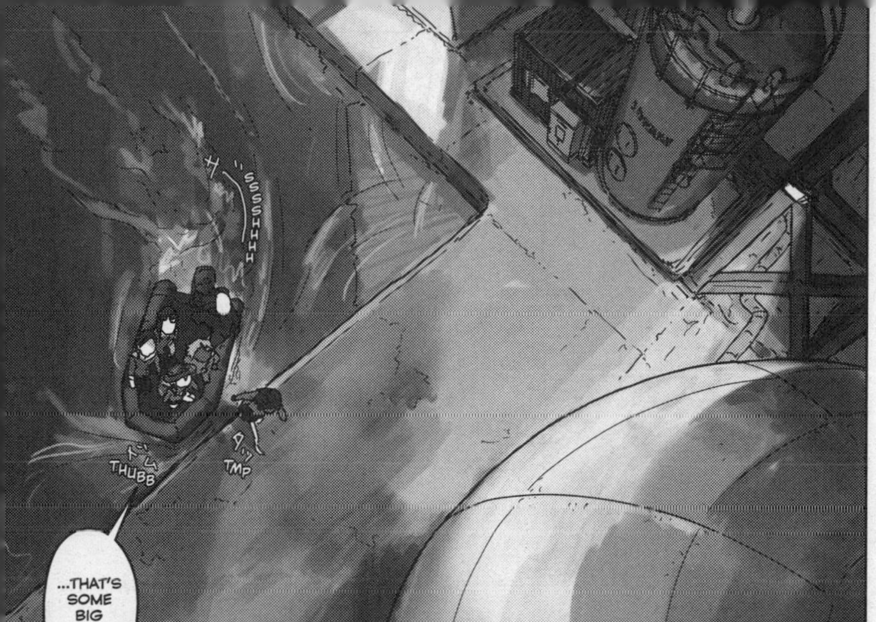
SSSSHHHH
TMP
THUBB
...THAT'S SOME BIG SMALL CHANGE.

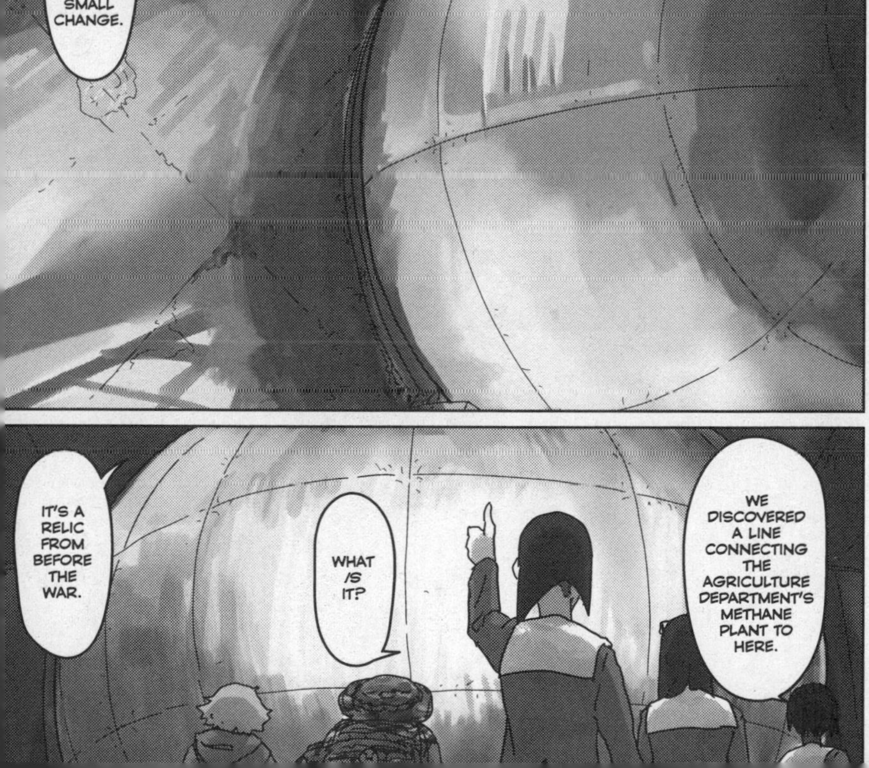
WE DISCOVERED A LINE CONNECTING THE AGRICULTURE DEPARTMENT'S METHANE PLANT TO HERE.
WHAT IS IT?
IT'S A RELIC FROM BEFORE THE WAR.

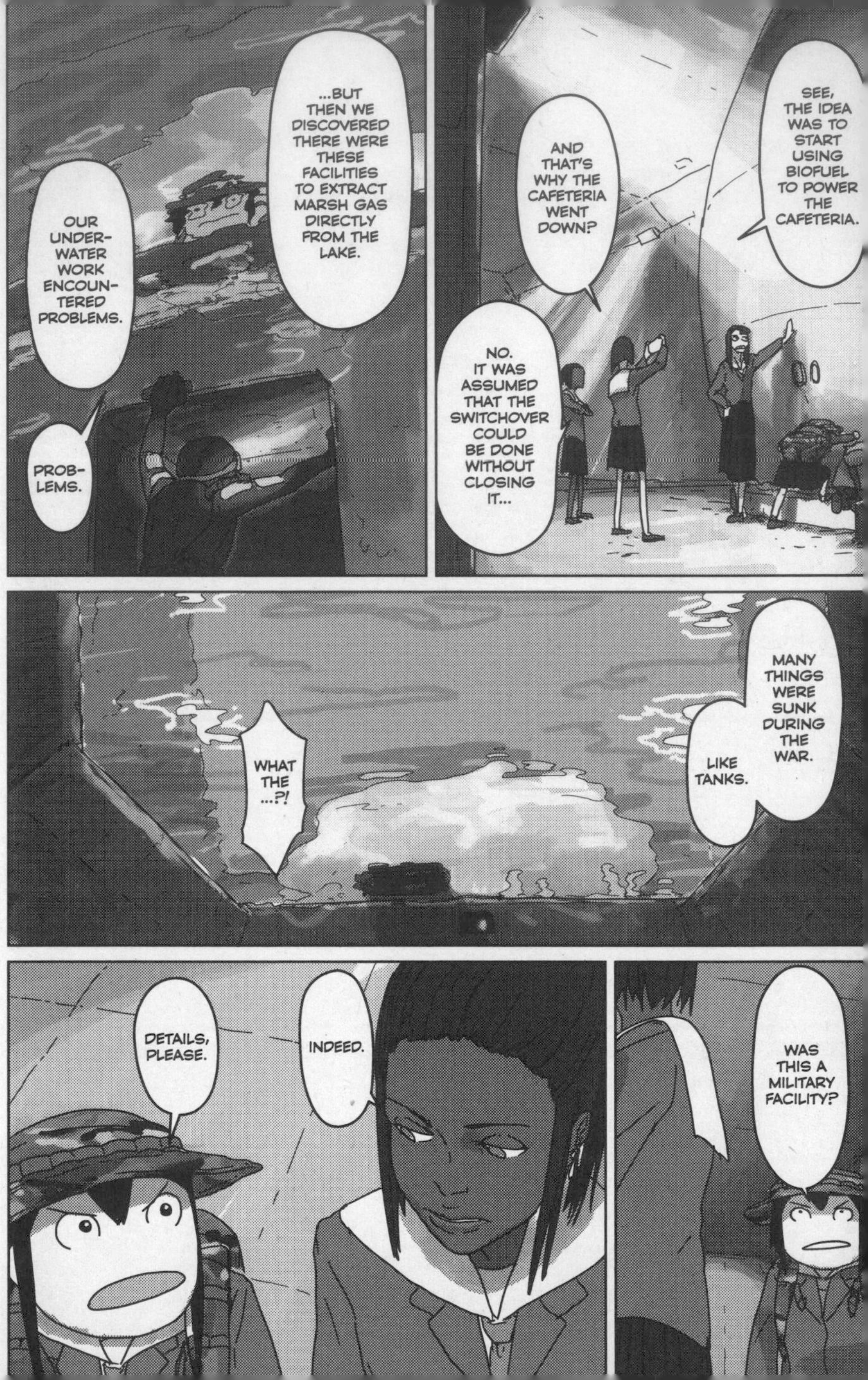
SEE, THE IDEA WAS TO START USING BIOFUEL TO POWER THE CAFETERIA.
AND THAT'S WHY THE CAFETERIA WENT DOWN?
NO. IT WAS ASSUMED THAT THE SWITCHOVER COULD BE DONE WITHOUT CLOSING IT...
...BUT THEN WE DISCOVERED THERE WERE THESE FACILITIES TO EXTRACT MARSH GAS DIRECTLY FROM THE LAKE.
OUR UNDERWATER WORK ENCOUNTERED PROBLEMS.
PROBLEMS.
MANY THINGS WERE SUNK DURING THE WAR.
LIKE TANKS.
WHAT THE ...?!
WAS THIS A MILITARY FACILITY?
INDEED.
DETAILS, PLEASE.

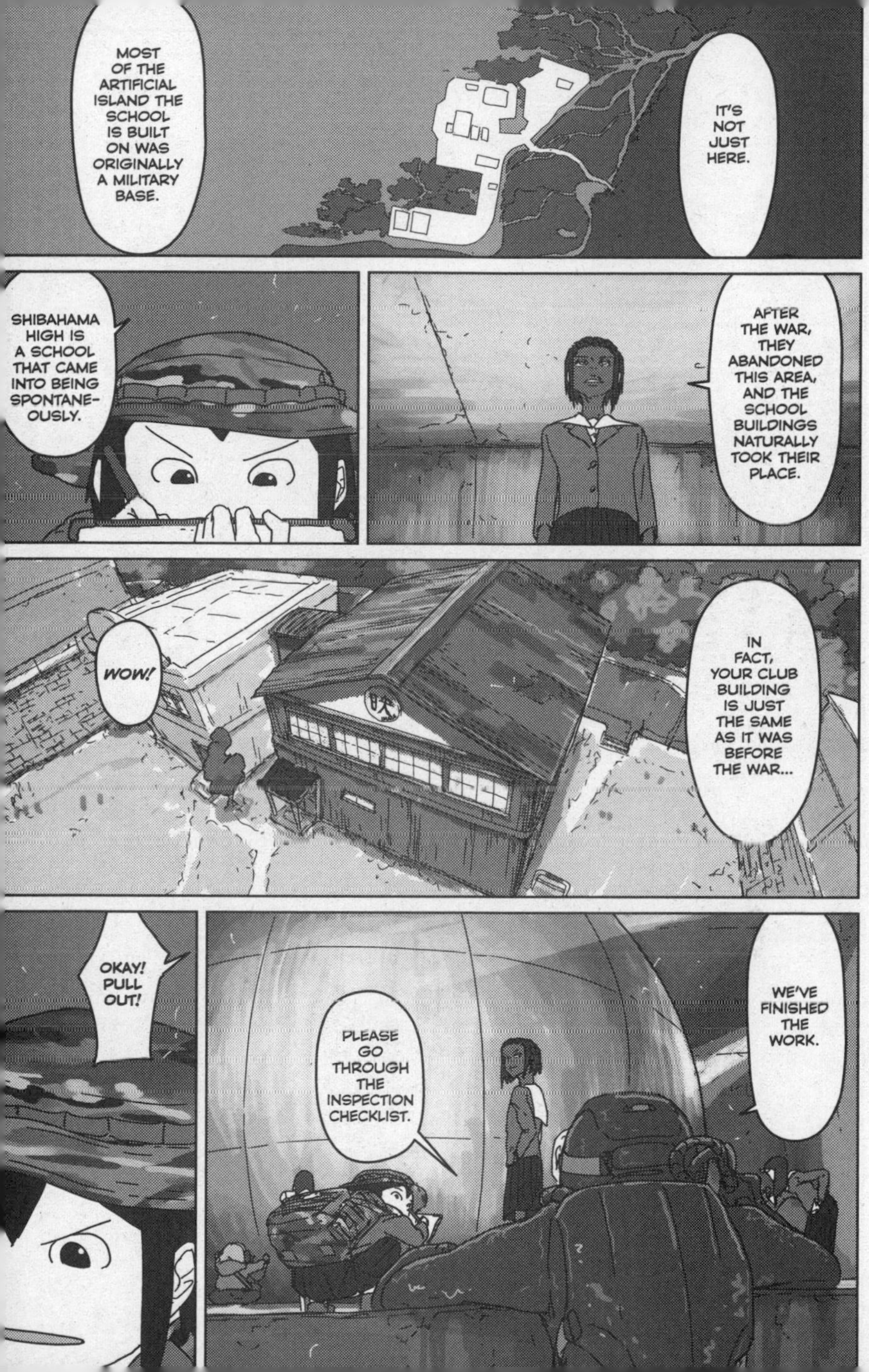
IT'S NOT JUST HERE.
MOST OF THE ARTIFICIAL ISLAND THE SCHOOL IS BUILT ON WAS ORIGINALLY A MILITARY BASE.
AFTER THE WAR, THEY ABANDONED THIS AREA, AND THE SCHOOL BUILDINGS NATURALLY TOOK THEIR PLACE.
SHIBAHAMA HIGH IS A SCHOOL THAT CAME INTO BEING SPONTANE-OUSLY.
IN FACT, YOUR CLUB BUILDING IS JUST THE SAME AS IT WAS BEFORE THE WAR...
WOW!
WE'VE FINISHED THE WORK.
PLEASE GO THROUGH THE INSPECTION CHECKLIST.
OKAY! PULL OUT!

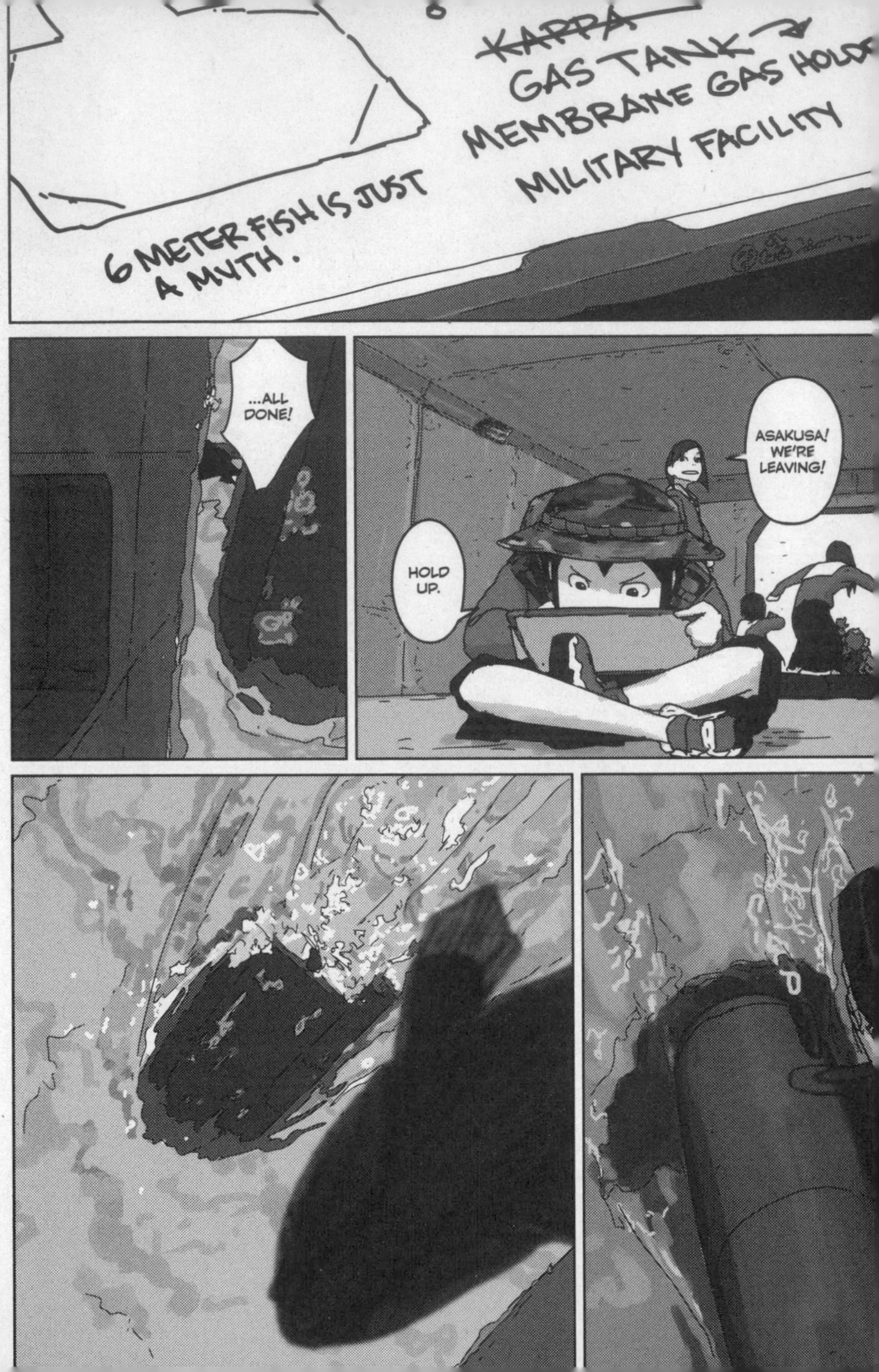
KAPPA
GAS TANK
MEMBRANE GAS HOLD
MILITARY FACILITY
6 METER FISH IS JUST A MYTH.
ASAKUSA! WE'RE LEAVING!
HOLD UP.
...ALL DONE!

KEEP YOUR HANDS OFF EIZOUKEN!

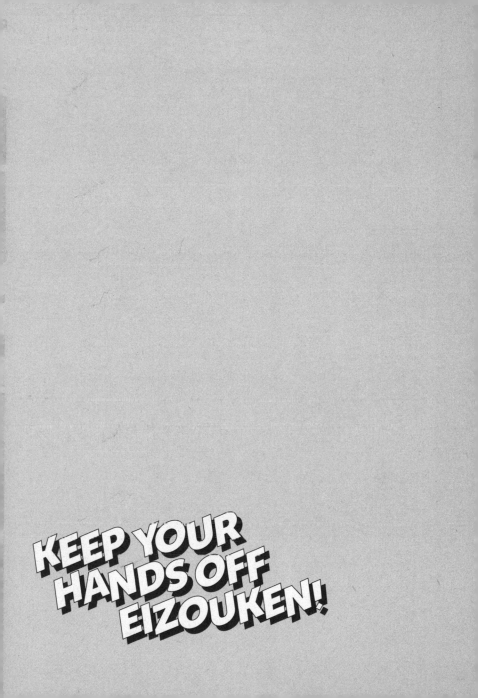

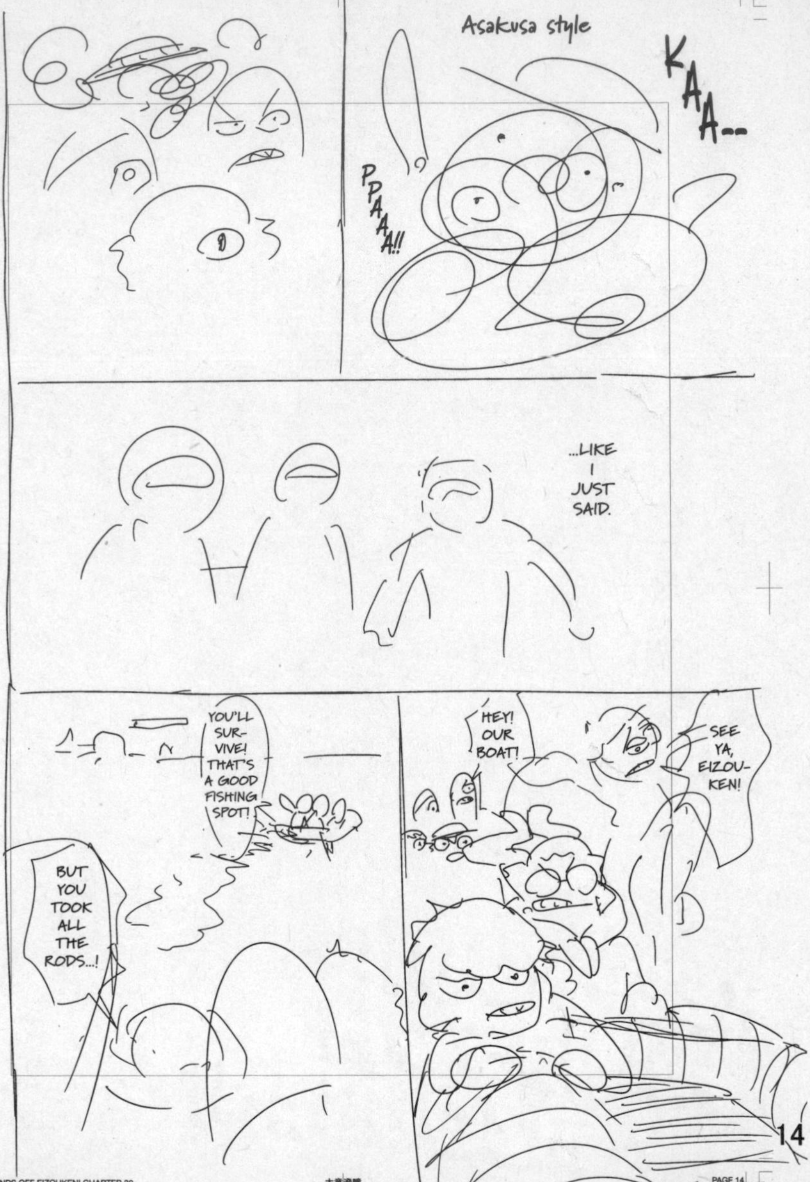
Asakusa style
KAA...
PPAAAA!!
...LIKE I JUST SAID.
SEE YA, EIZOU-KEN!
HEY! OUR BOAT!
YOU'LL SUR-VIVE! THAT'S A GOOD FISHING SPOT!
BUT YOU TOOK ALL THE RODS...!

CHAPTER 33:
SECRET OF THE CLOCK TOWER

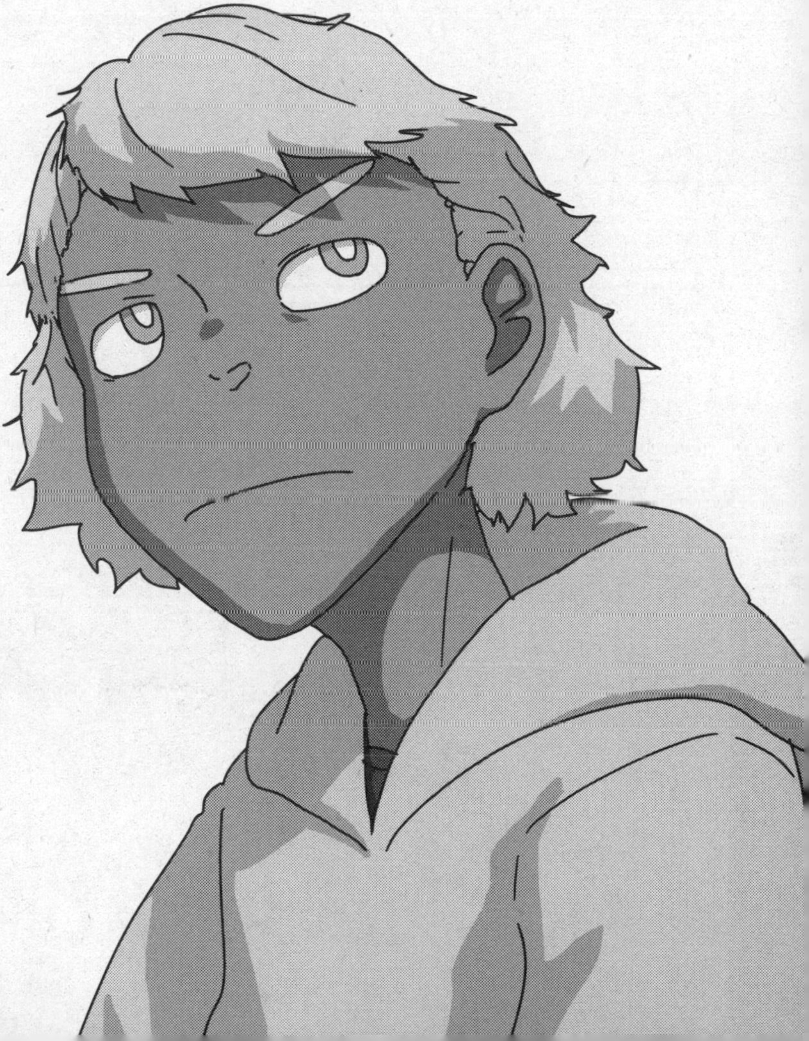

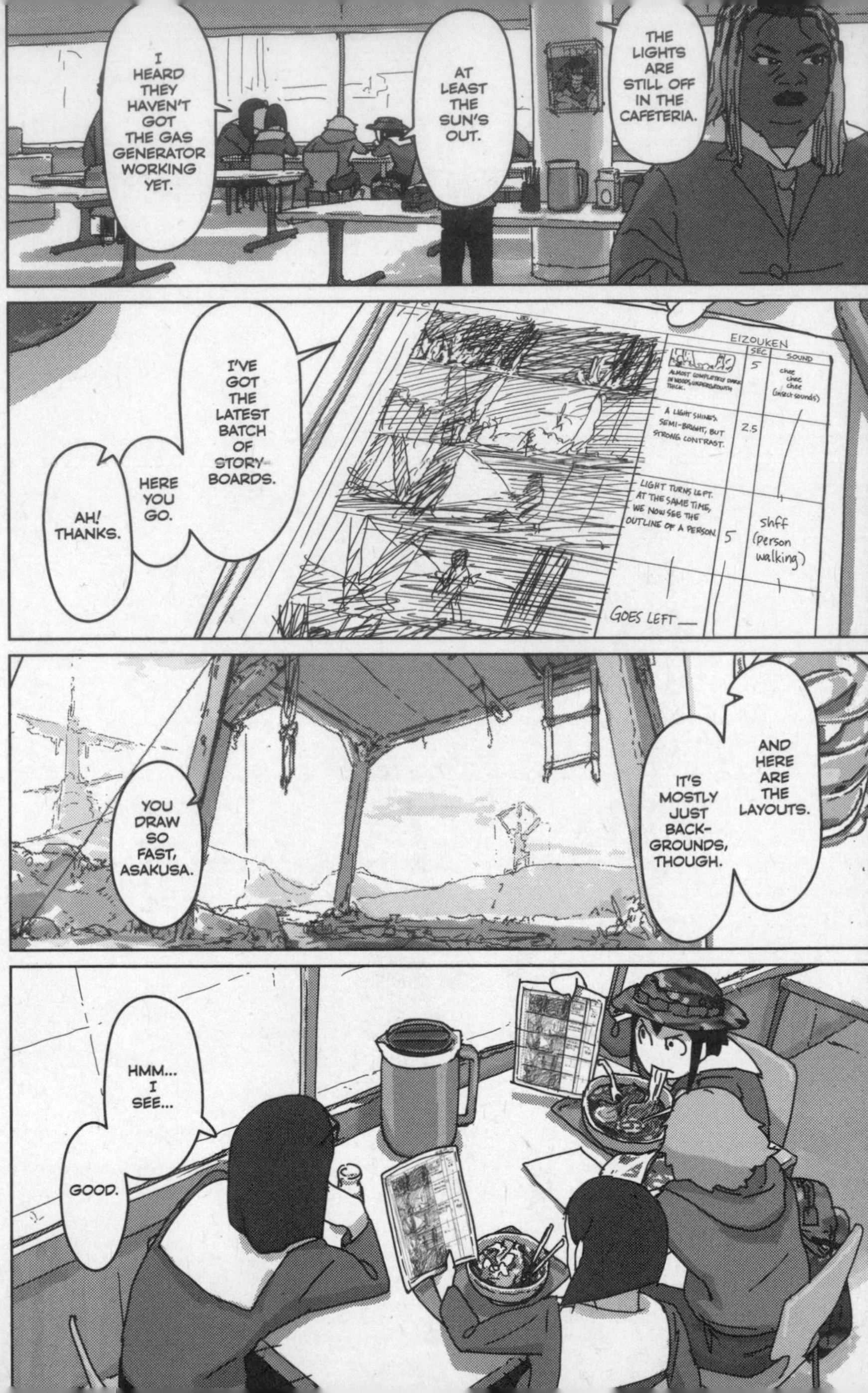
THE LIGHTS ARE STILL OFF IN THE CAFETERIA.
AT LEAST THE SUN'S OUT.
I HEARD THEY HAVEN'T GOT THE GAS GENERATOR WORKING YET.
EIZOUKEN
SEC.
SOUND
ALMOST COMPLETELY DARK IN WOODS, UNDERGROWTH THICK.
5
chee chee chee (insect sounds)
A LIGHT SHINES, SEMI-BRIGHT, BUT STRONG CONTRAST.
2.5
LIGHT TURNS LEFT. AT THE SAME TIME, WE NOW SEE THE OUTLINE OF A PERSON.
5
shff (person walking)
GOES LEFT
I'VE GOT THE LATEST BATCH OF STORY-BOARDS.
HERE YOU GO.
AH! THANKS.
AND HERE ARE THE LAYOUTS.
IT'S MOSTLY JUST BACK-GROUNDS, THOUGH.
YOU DRAW SO FAST, ASAKUSA.
HMM... I SEE...
GOOD.

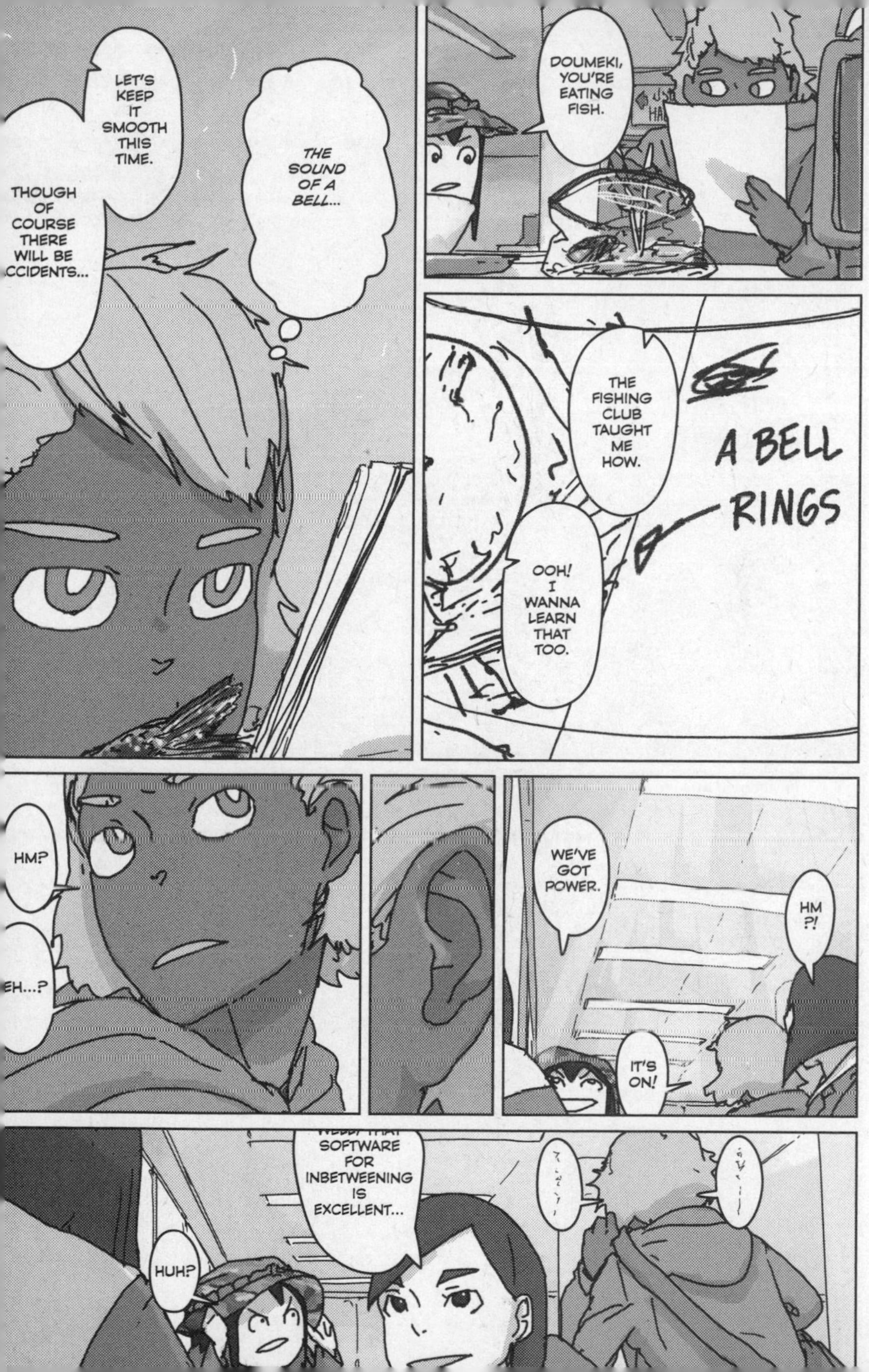
DOUMEKI, YOU'RE EATING FISH.
THE FISHING CLUB TAUGHT ME HOW.
A BELL RINGS
OOH! I WANNA LEARN THAT TOO.
THE SOUND OF A BELL...
LET'S KEEP IT SMOOTH THIS TIME.
THOUGH OF COURSE THERE WILL BE CCIDENTS...
WE'VE GOT POWER.
HM?!
IT'S ON!
HM?
EH...?
SOFTWARE FOR INBETWEENING IS EXCELLENT...
HUH?

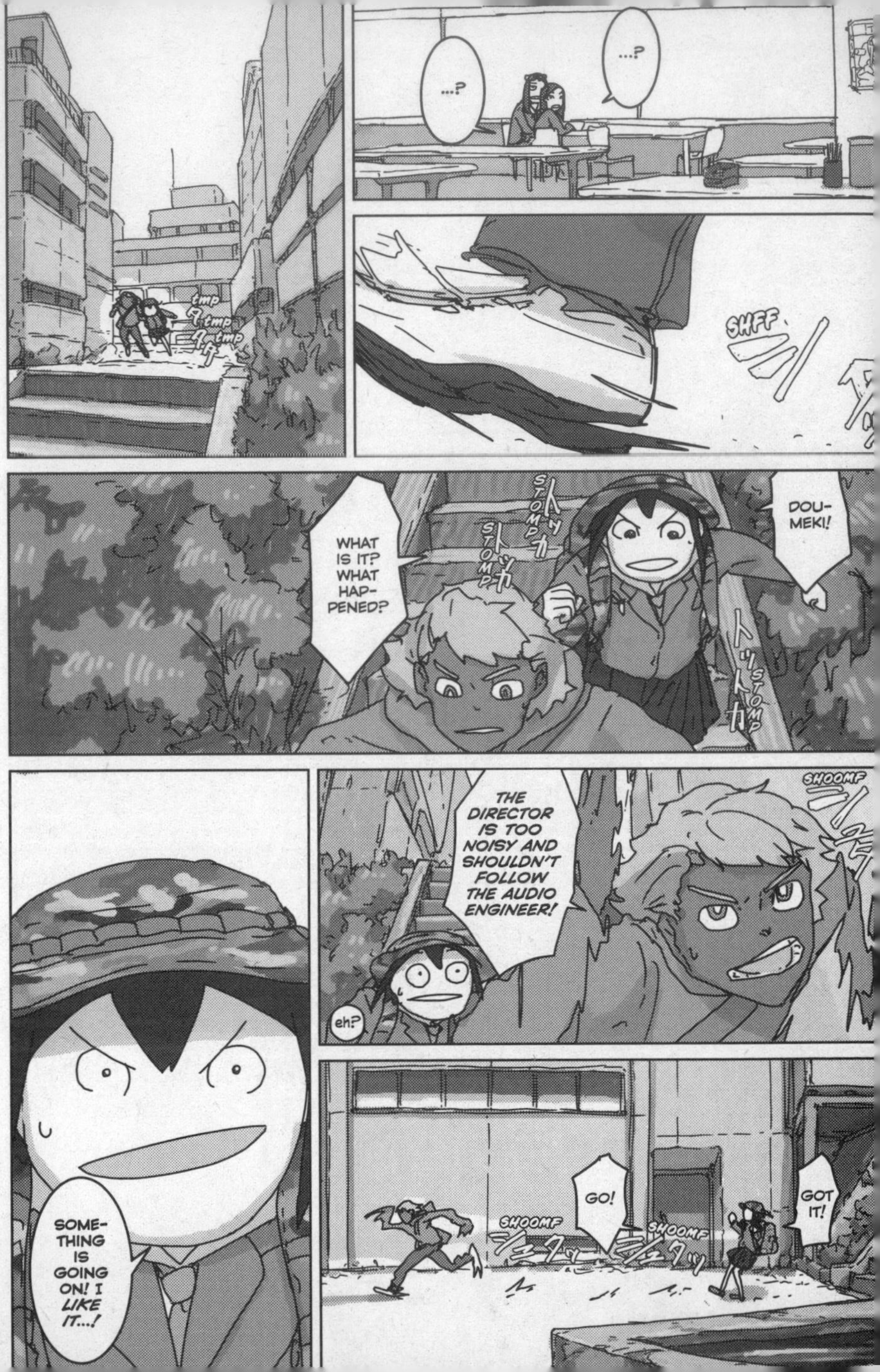
...?
...?
SHFF
tmp
tmp
tmp
DOU-MEKI!
STOMP
STOMP
WHAT IS IT? WHAT HAP-PENED?
STOMP
SHOOMF
THE DIRECTOR IS TOO NOISY AND SHOULDN'T FOLLOW THE AUDIO ENGINEER!
eh?
GOT IT!
GO!
SHOOMF
SHOOMF
SOME-THING IS GOING ON! I *LIKE* IT...!

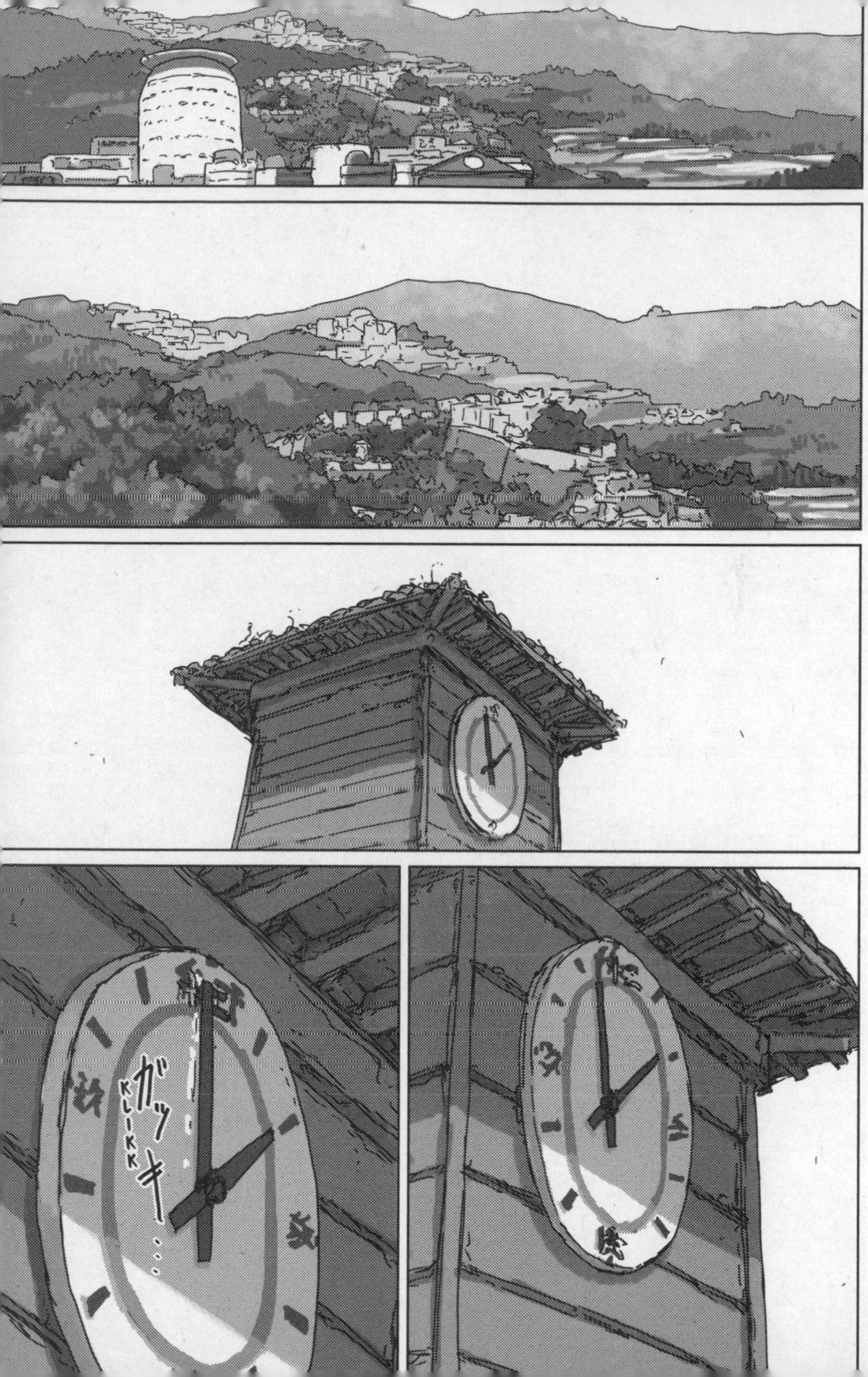
ガッキー…
KLIKK

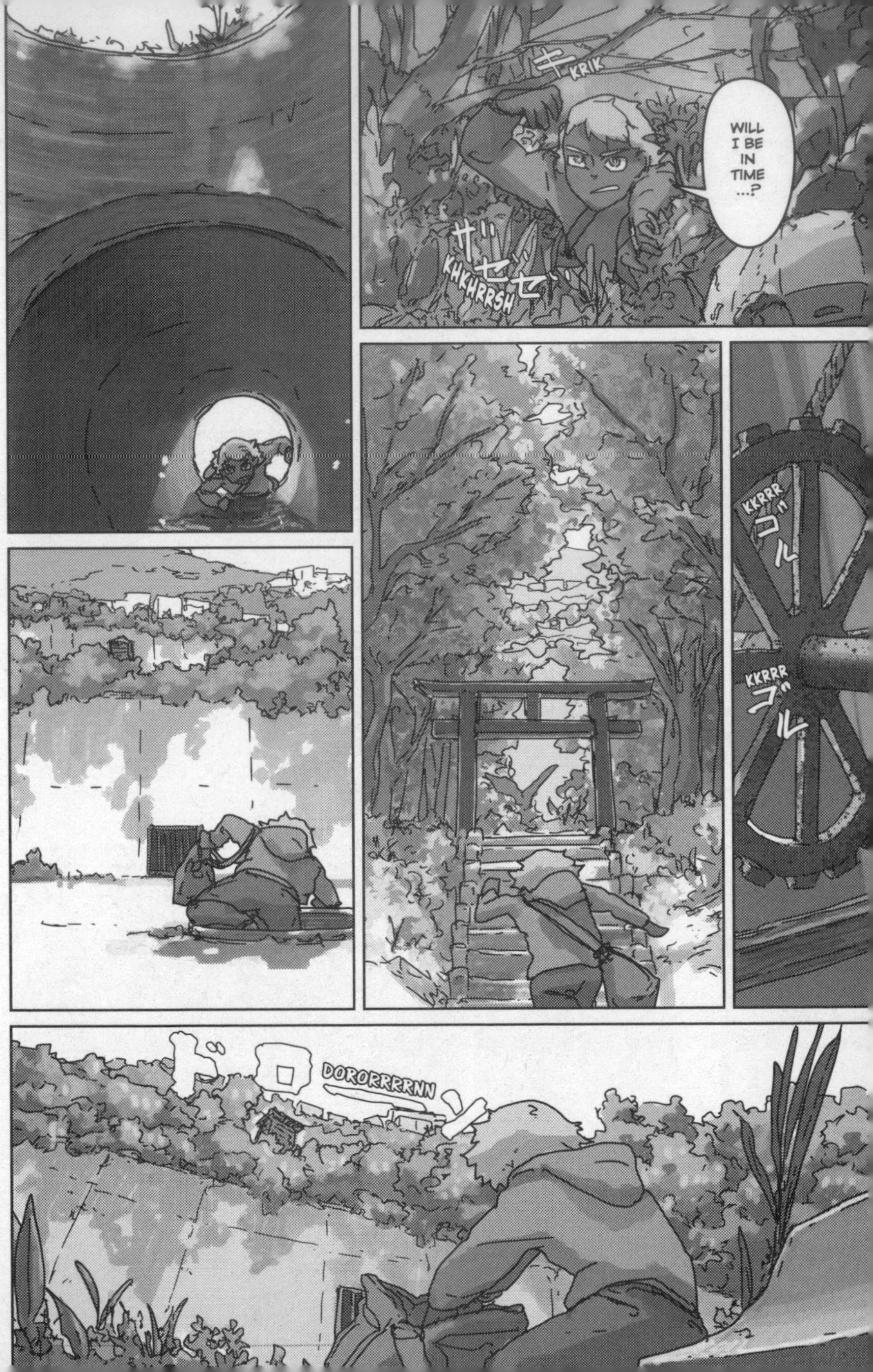
キ
KRIK
WILL I BE IN TIME ...?
ザセセ
KHKHRRSH
KKRRR
ゴル
KKRRR
ゴル
ドロン
DORORRRRNN

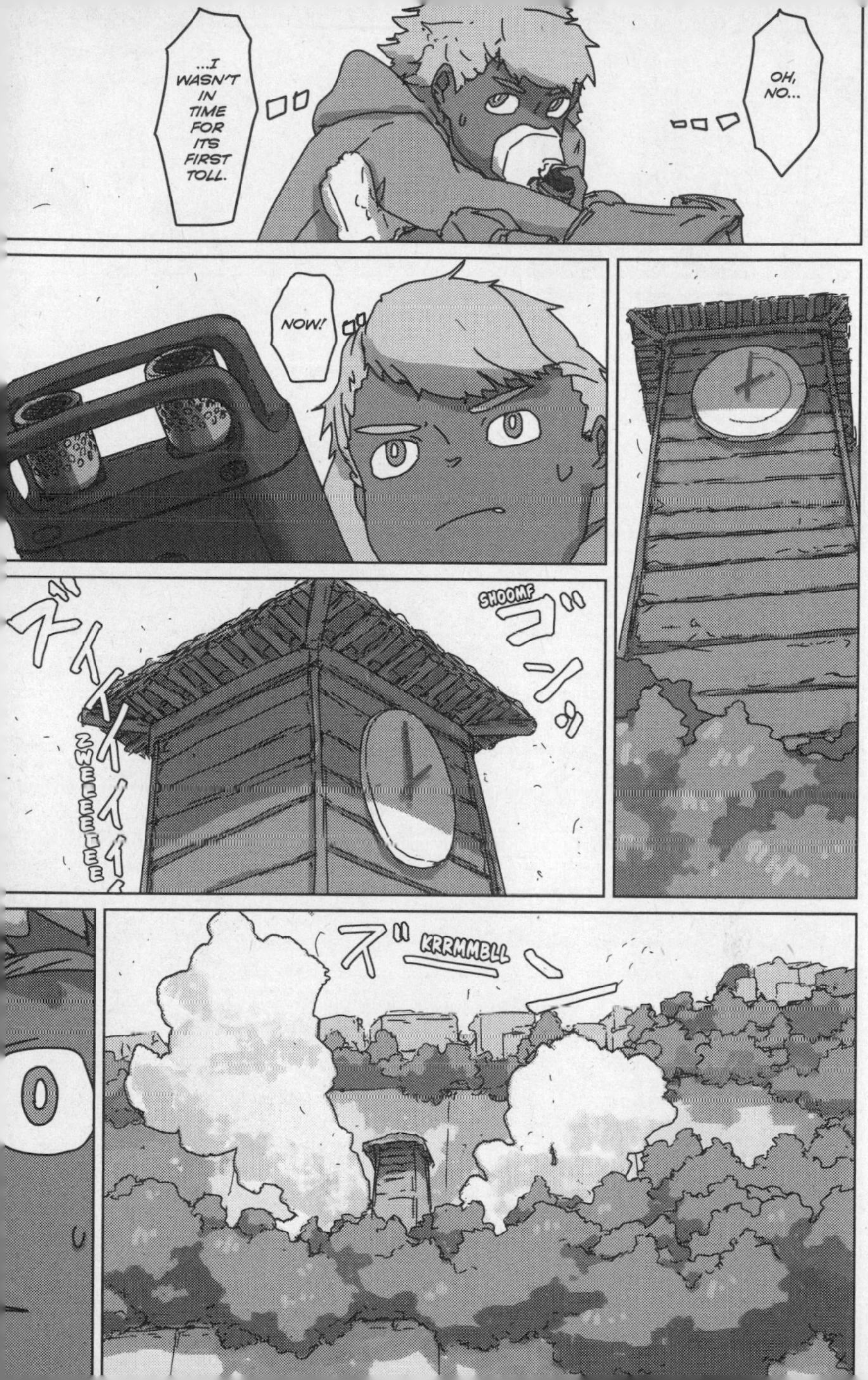
OH, NO...
...I WASN'T IN TIME FOR ITS FIRST TOLL.
NOW!
SHOOMF
ZWEEEEEEE
KRRMMBLL

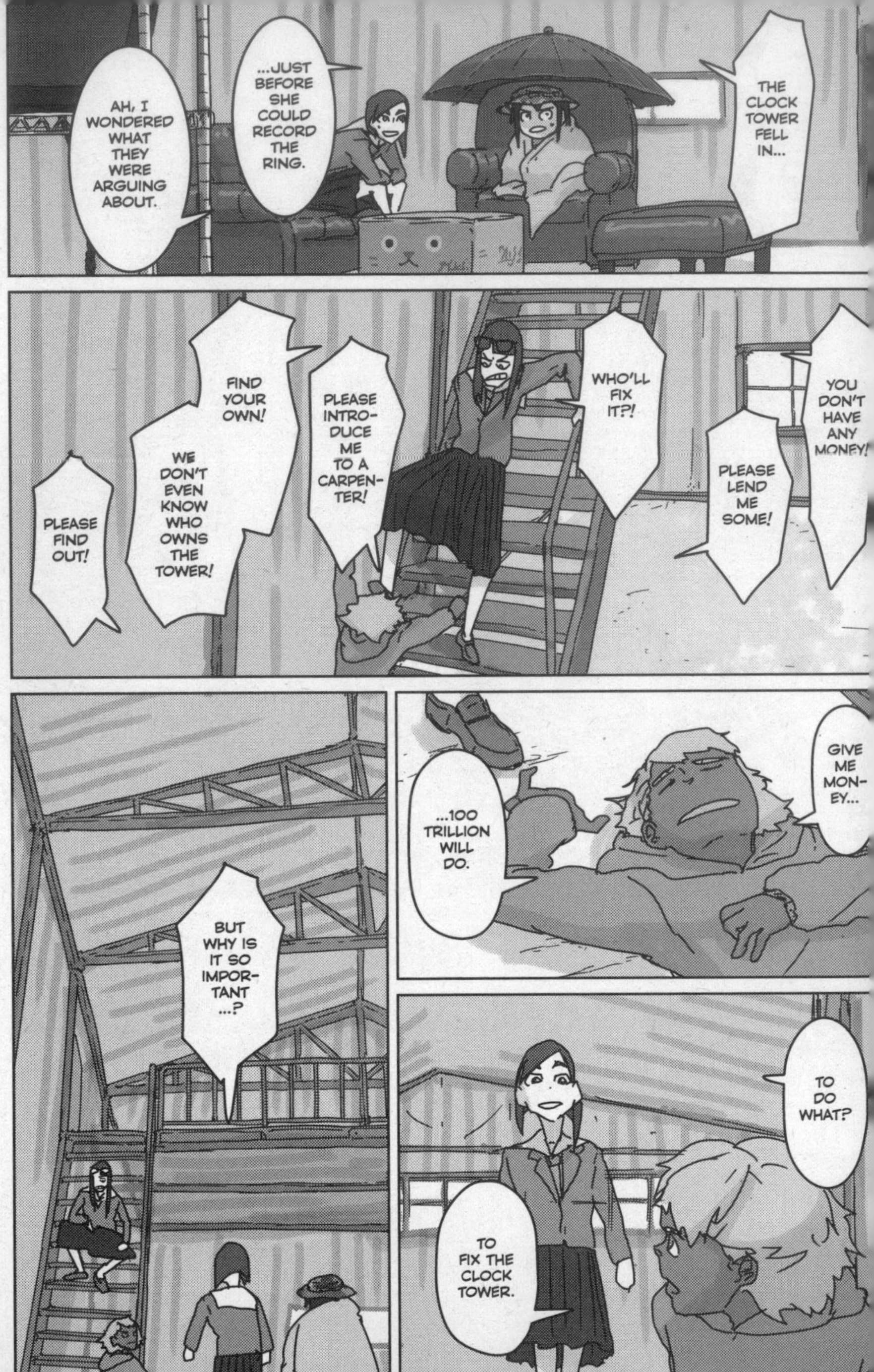
THE CLOCK TOWER FELL IN...
...JUST BEFORE SHE COULD RECORD THE RING.
AH, I WONDERED WHAT THEY WERE ARGUING ABOUT.
YOU DON'T HAVE ANY MONEY!
PLEASE LEND ME SOME!
WHO'LL FIX IT?!
PLEASE INTRODUCE ME TO A CARPENTER!
FIND YOUR OWN!
WE DON'T EVEN KNOW WHO OWNS THE TOWER!
PLEASE FIND OUT!
GIVE ME MONEY...
...100 TRILLION WILL DO.
TO DO WHAT?
TO FIX THE CLOCK TOWER.
BUT WHY IS IT SO IMPORTANT...?

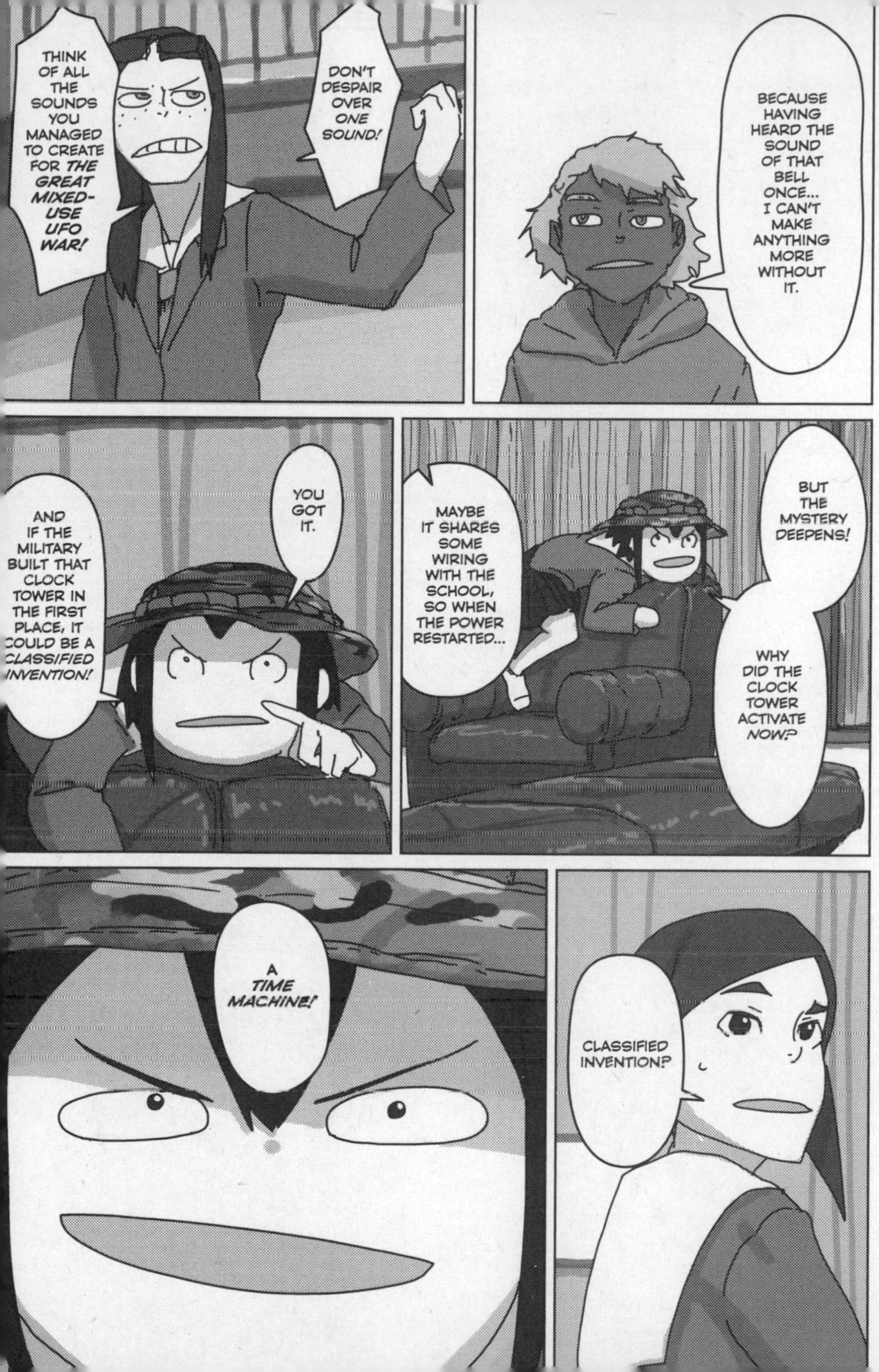
BECAUSE HAVING HEARD THE SOUND OF THAT BELL ONCE... I CAN'T MAKE ANYTHING MORE WITHOUT IT.
DON'T DESPAIR OVER *ONE* SOUND!
THINK OF ALL THE SOUNDS YOU MANAGED TO CREATE FOR ***THE GREAT MIXED-USE UFO WAR!***
BUT THE MYSTERY DEEPENS!
WHY DID THE CLOCK TOWER ACTIVATE *NOW?*
MAYBE IT SHARES SOME WIRING WITH THE SCHOOL, SO WHEN THE POWER RESTARTED...
YOU GOT IT.
AND IF THE MILITARY BUILT THAT CLOCK TOWER IN THE FIRST PLACE, IT COULD BE A *CLASSIFIED INVENTION!*
CLASSIFIED INVENTION?
A *TIME MACHINE!*

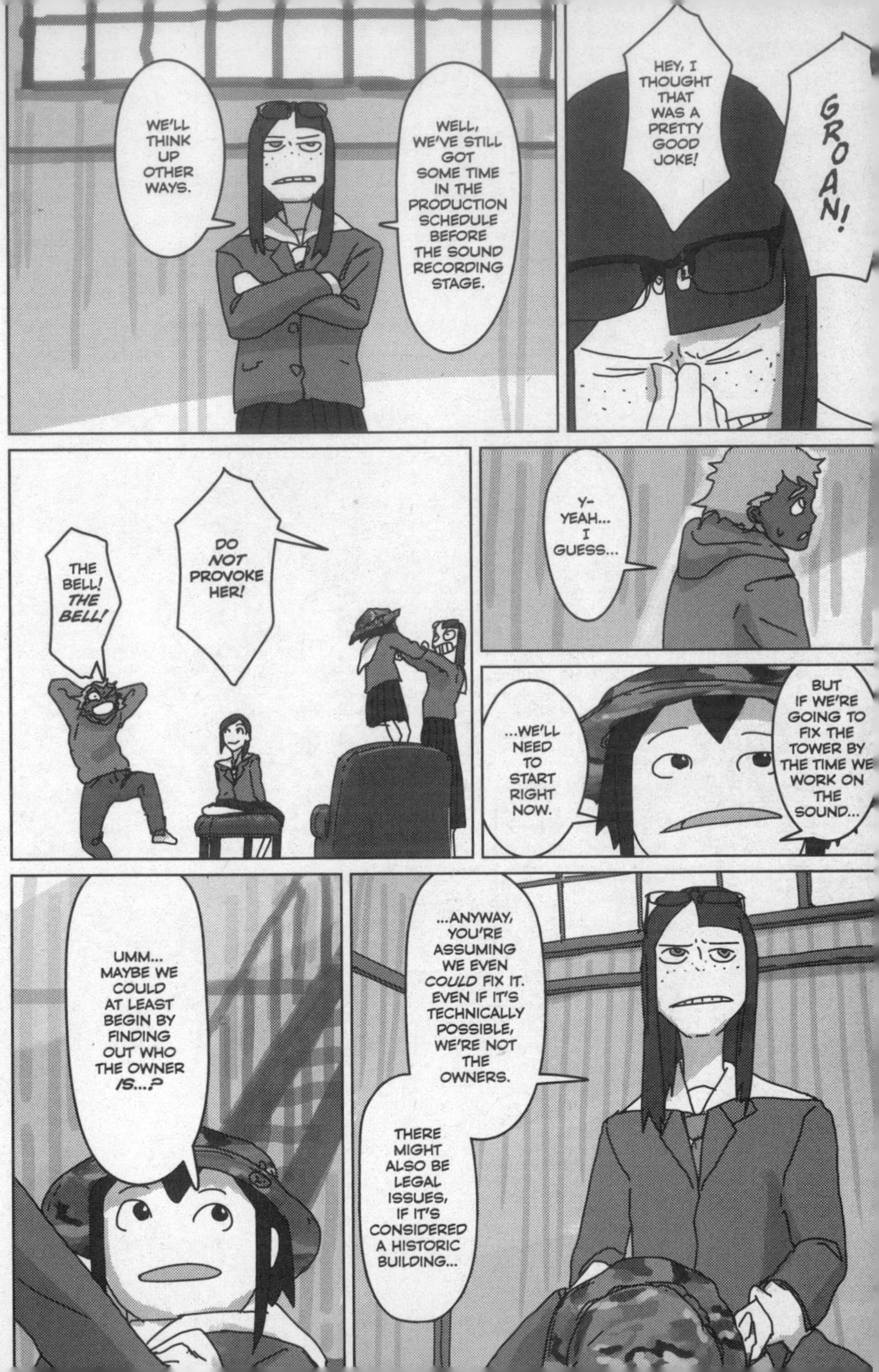
HEY, I THOUGHT THAT WAS A PRETTY GOOD JOKE!
GROAN!
WELL, WE'VE STILL GOT SOME TIME IN THE PRODUCTION SCHEDULE BEFORE THE SOUND RECORDING STAGE.
WE'LL THINK UP OTHER WAYS.
Y-YEAH... I GUESS...
BUT IF WE'RE GOING TO FIX THE TOWER BY THE TIME WE WORK ON THE SOUND...
...WE'LL NEED TO START RIGHT NOW.
DO *NOT* PROVOKE HER!
THE BELL! *THE BELL!*
...ANYWAY, YOU'RE ASSUMING WE EVEN *COULD* FIX IT. EVEN IF IT'S TECHNICALLY POSSIBLE, WE'RE NOT THE OWNERS.
THERE MIGHT ALSO BE LEGAL ISSUES, IF IT'S CONSIDERED A HISTORIC BUILDING...
UMM... MAYBE WE COULD AT LEAST BEGIN BY FINDING OUT WHO THE OWNER *IS*...?

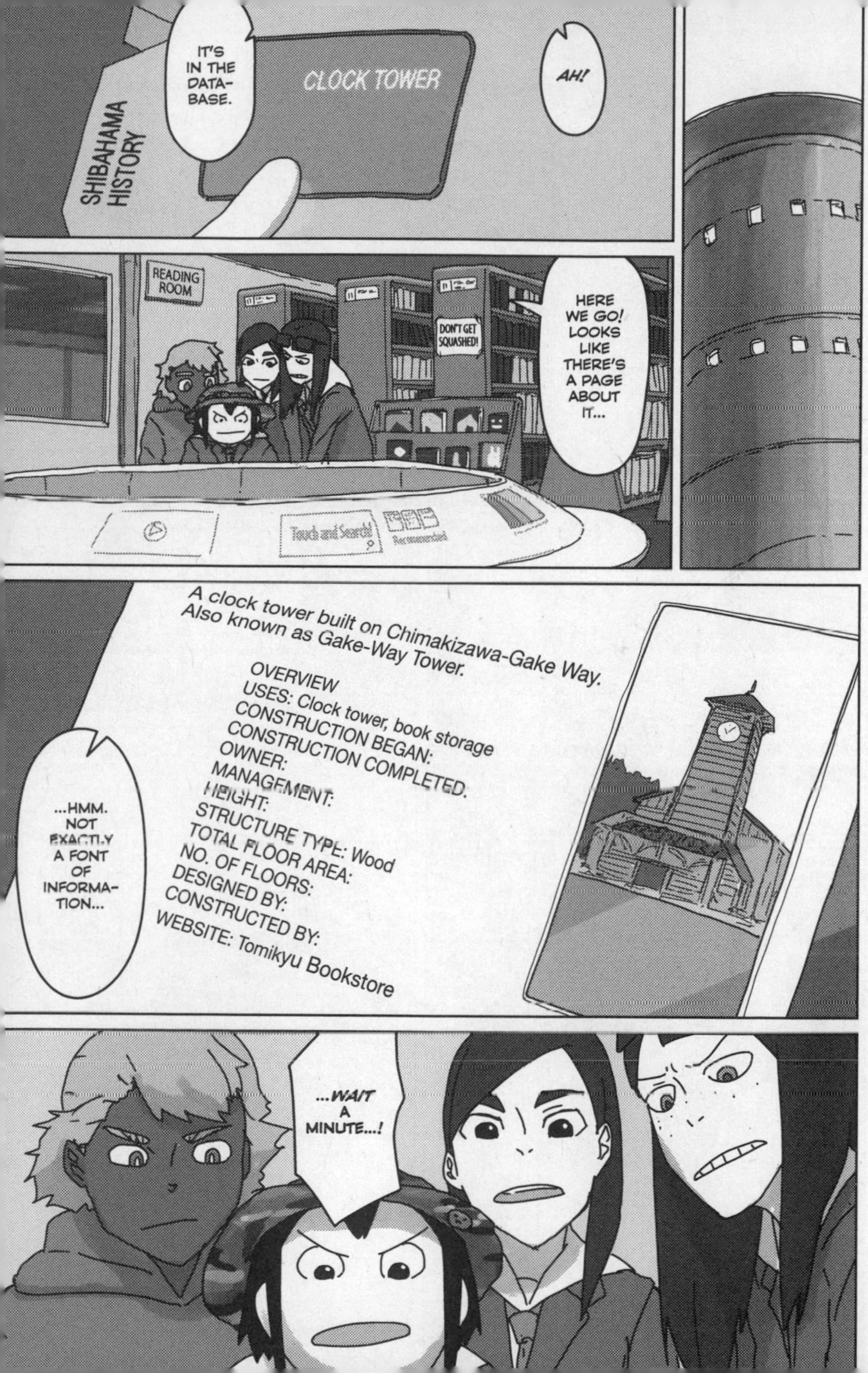
AH!
IT'S IN THE DATA-BASE.
CLOCK TOWER
SHIBAHAMA HISTORY
HERE WE GO! LOOKS LIKE THERE'S A PAGE ABOUT IT...
DON'T GET SQUASHED!
READING ROOM
Touch and Search!
Recommended
A clock tower built on Chimakizawa-Gake Way.
Also known as Gake-Way Tower.
OVERVIEW
USES: Clock tower, book storage
CONSTRUCTION BEGAN:
CONSTRUCTION COMPLETED:
OWNER:
MANAGEMENT:
HEIGHT:
STRUCTURE TYPE: Wood
TOTAL FLOOR AREA:
NO. OF FLOORS:
DESIGNED BY:
CONSTRUCTED BY:
WEBSITE: Tomikyu Bookstore
...HMM. NOT EXACTLY A FONT OF INFORMATION...
...WAIT A MINUTE...!

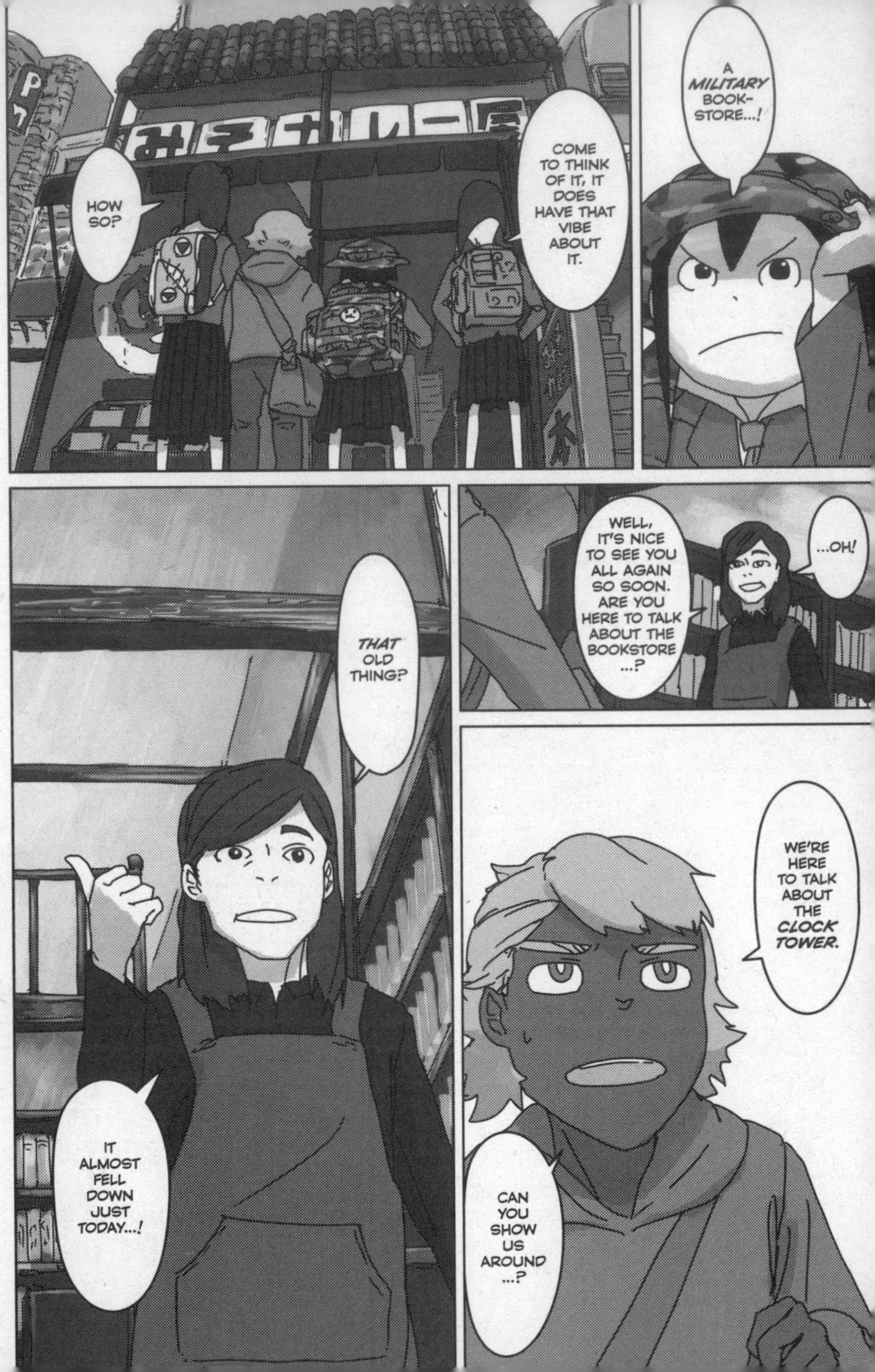
A MILITARY BOOK-STORE...!
COME TO THINK OF IT, IT DOES HAVE THAT VIBE ABOUT IT.
HOW SO?
...OH!
WELL, IT'S NICE TO SEE YOU ALL AGAIN SO SOON. ARE YOU HERE TO TALK ABOUT THE BOOKSTORE ...?
WE'RE HERE TO TALK ABOUT THE CLOCK TOWER.
CAN YOU SHOW US AROUND ...?
THAT OLD THING?
IT ALMOST FELL DOWN JUST TODAY...!

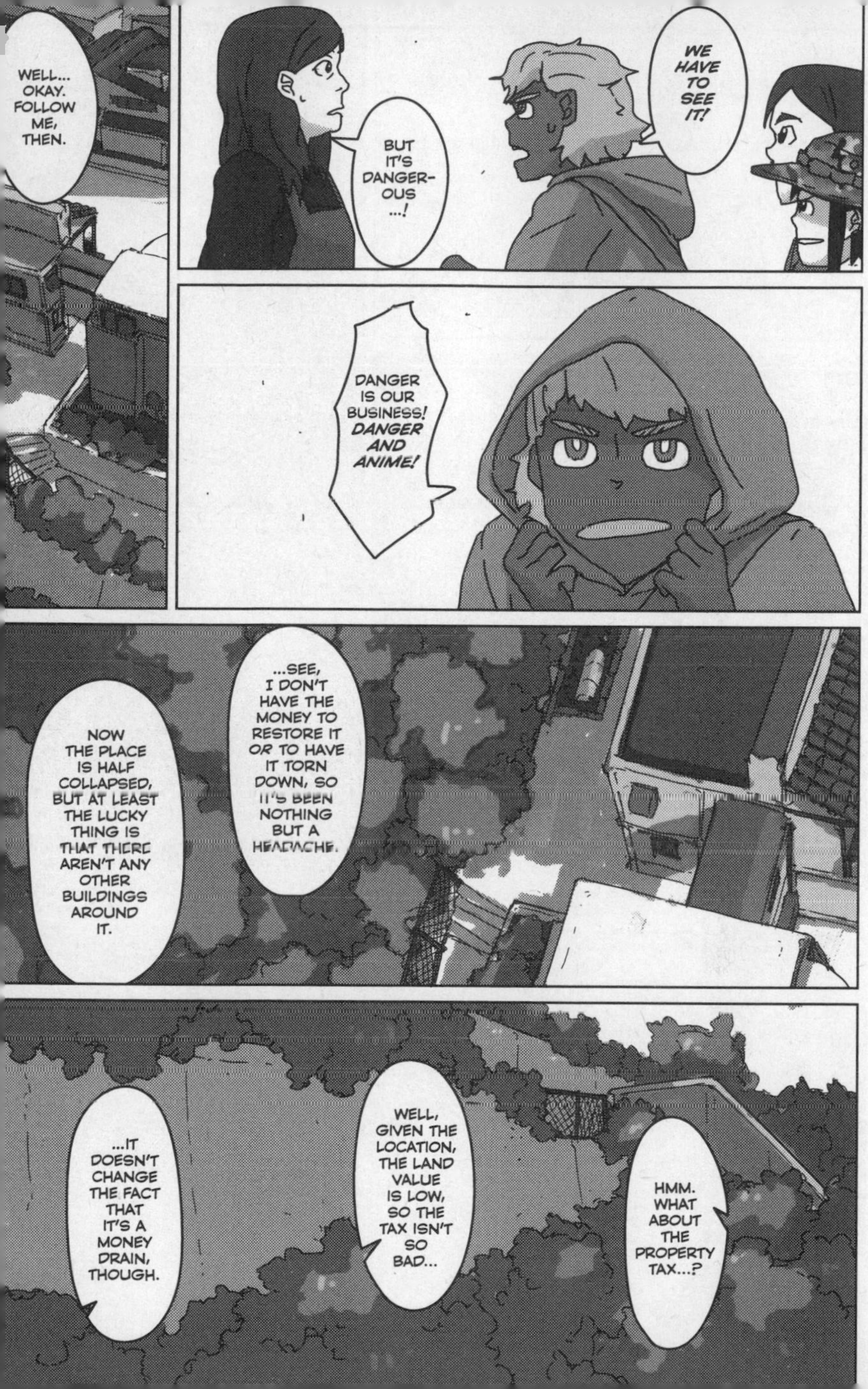
WE HAVE TO SEE IT!
BUT IT'S DANGER-OUS...!
DANGER IS OUR BUSINESS! DANGER AND ANIME!
WELL... OKAY. FOLLOW ME, THEN.
...SEE, I DON'T HAVE THE MONEY TO RESTORE IT OR TO HAVE IT TORN DOWN, SO IT'S BEEN NOTHING BUT A HEADACHE.
NOW THE PLACE IS HALF COLLAPSED, BUT AT LEAST THE LUCKY THING IS THAT THERE AREN'T ANY OTHER BUILDINGS AROUND IT.
HMM. WHAT ABOUT THE PROPERTY TAX...?
WELL, GIVEN THE LOCATION, THE LAND VALUE IS LOW, SO THE TAX ISN'T SO BAD...
...IT DOESN'T CHANGE THE FACT THAT IT'S A MONEY DRAIN, THOUGH.

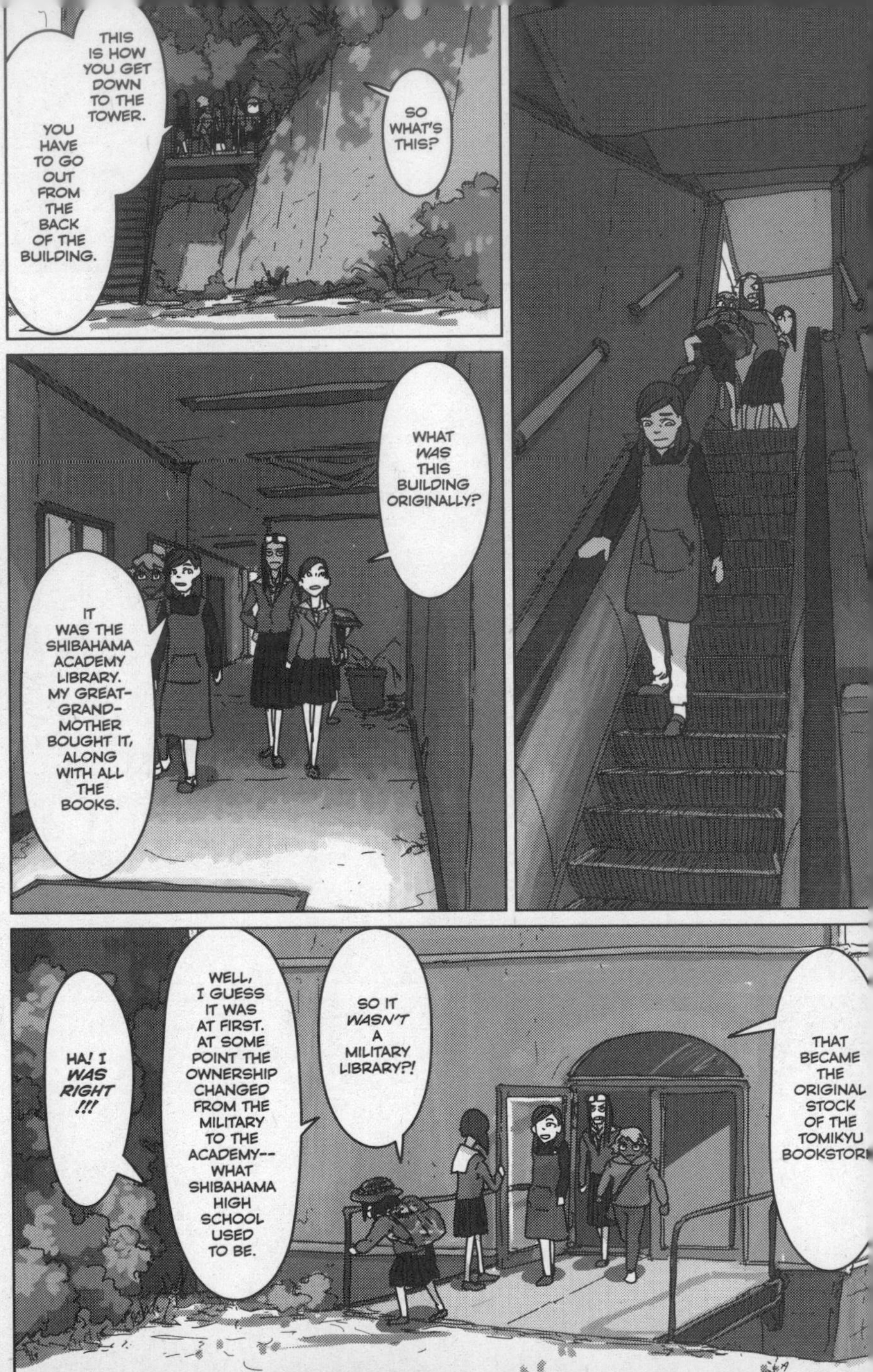
SO WHAT'S THIS?
THIS IS HOW YOU GET DOWN TO THE TOWER. YOU HAVE TO GO OUT FROM THE BACK OF THE BUILDING.
WHAT *WAS* THIS BUILDING ORIGINALLY?
IT WAS THE SHIBAHAMA ACADEMY LIBRARY. MY GREAT-GRAND-MOTHER BOUGHT IT, ALONG WITH ALL THE BOOKS.
THAT BECAME THE ORIGINAL STOCK OF THE TOMIKYU BOOKSTOR
SO IT *WASN'T* A MILITARY LIBRARY?!
WELL, I GUESS IT WAS AT FIRST. AT SOME POINT THE OWNERSHIP CHANGED FROM THE MILITARY TO THE ACADEMY-- WHAT SHIBAHAMA HIGH SCHOOL USED TO BE.
HA! I *WAS RIGHT!!!*

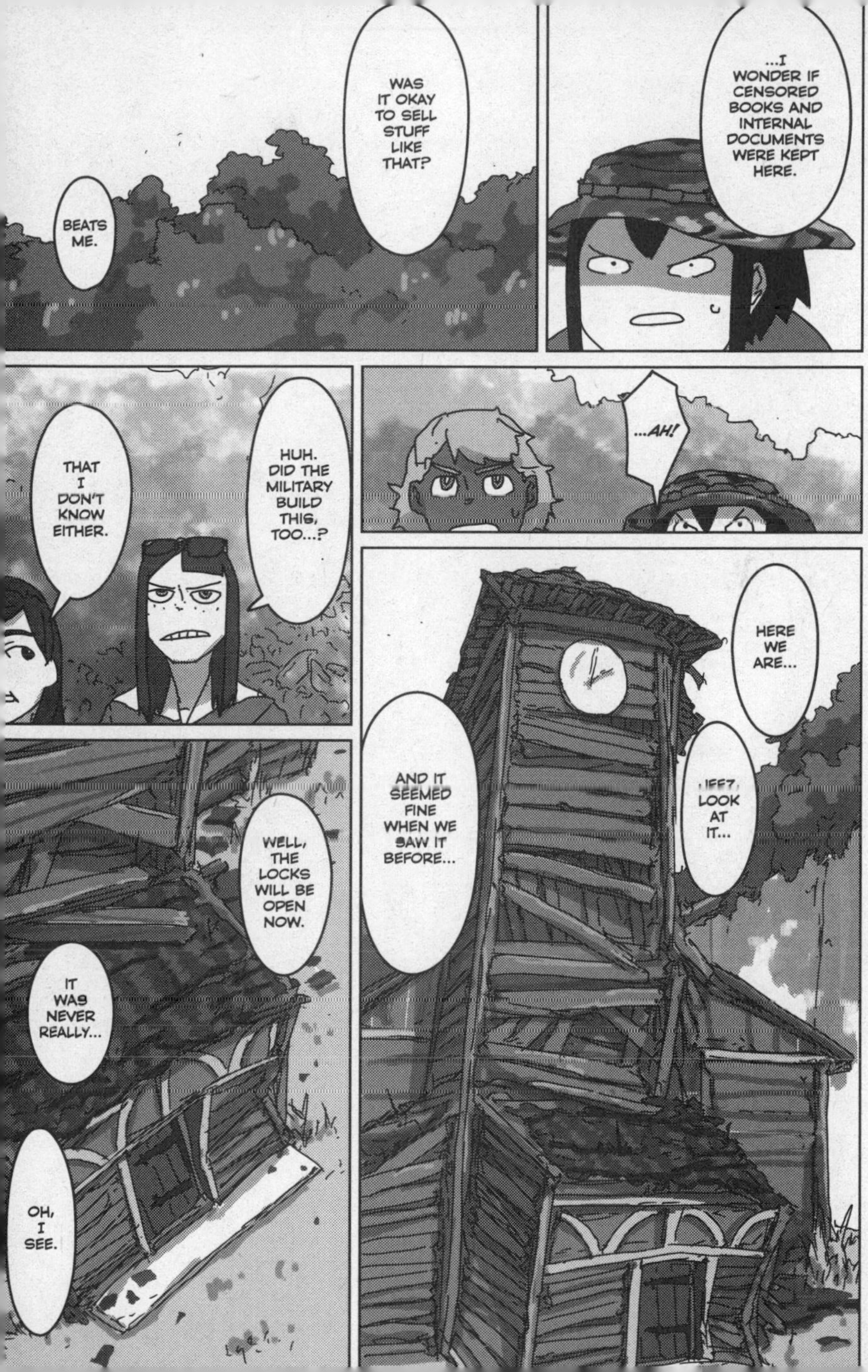
...I WONDER IF CENSORED BOOKS AND INTERNAL DOCUMENTS WERE KEPT HERE.
WAS IT OKAY TO SELL STUFF LIKE THAT?
BEATS ME.
...AH!
HUH. DID THE MILITARY BUILD THIS, TOO...?
THAT I DON'T KNOW EITHER.
HERE WE ARE...
JEEZ, LOOK AT IT...
AND IT SEEMED FINE WHEN WE SAW IT BEFORE...
WELL, THE LOCKS WILL BE OPEN NOW.
IT WAS NEVER REALLY...
OH, I SEE.

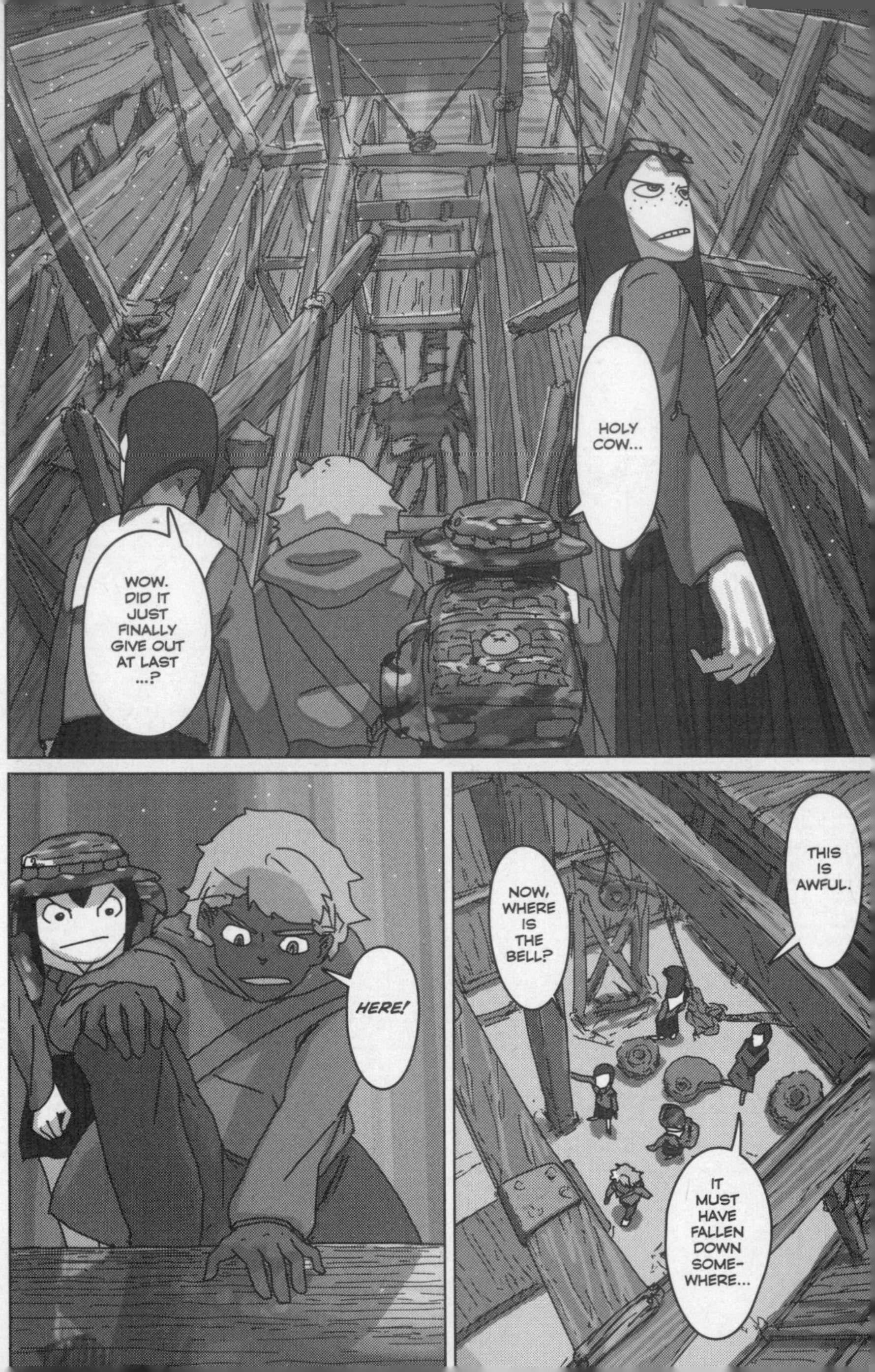
HOLY COW...
WOW. DID IT JUST FINALLY GIVE OUT AT LAST ...?
THIS IS AWFUL.
NOW, WHERE IS THE BELL?
IT MUST HAVE FALLEN DOWN SOME-WHERE...
HERE!

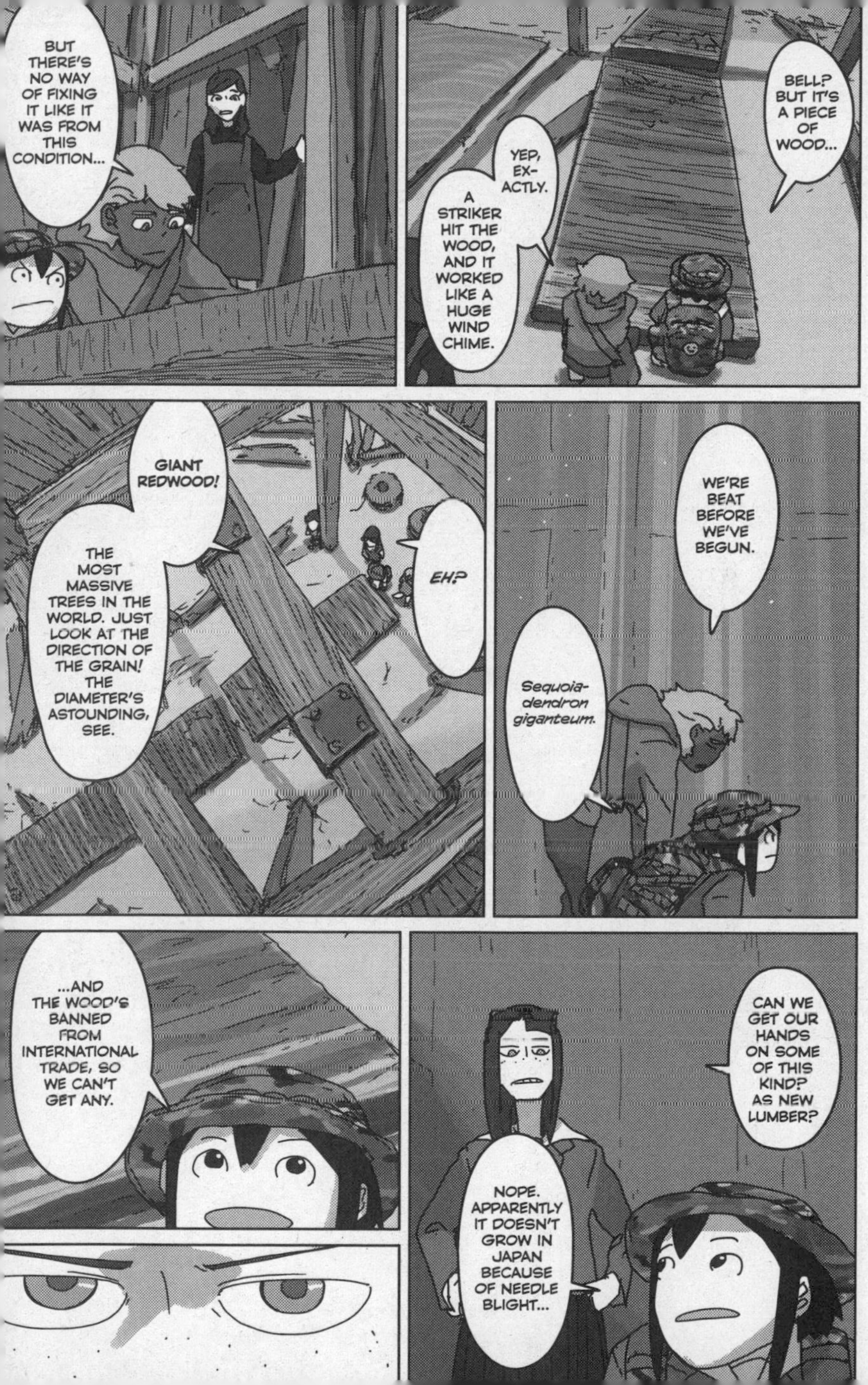
BELL? BUT IT'S A PIECE OF WOOD...
YEP, EXACTLY.
A STRIKER HIT THE WOOD, AND IT WORKED LIKE A HUGE WIND CHIME.
BUT THERE'S NO WAY OF FIXING IT LIKE IT WAS FROM THIS CONDITION...
WE'RE BEAT BEFORE WE'VE BEGUN.
Sequoia-dendron giganteum.
EH?
GIANT REDWOOD!
THE MOST MASSIVE TREES IN THE WORLD. JUST LOOK AT THE DIRECTION OF THE GRAIN! THE DIAMETER'S ASTOUNDING, SEE.
CAN WE GET OUR HANDS ON SOME OF THIS KIND? AS NEW LUMBER?
NOPE. APPARENTLY IT DOESN'T GROW IN JAPAN BECAUSE OF NEEDLE BLIGHT...
...AND THE WOOD'S BANNED FROM INTERNATIONAL TRADE, SO WE CAN'T GET ANY.

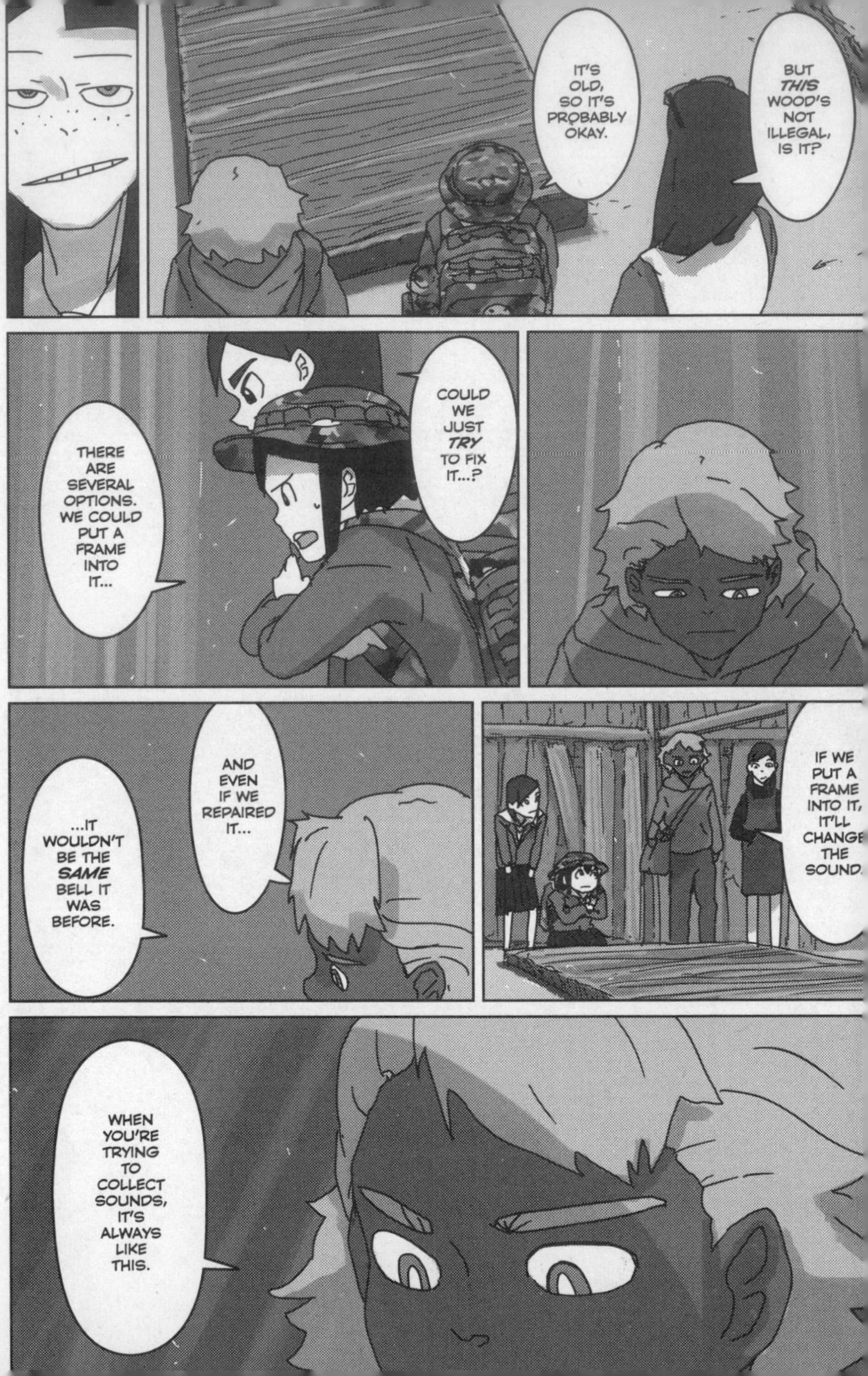
BUT *THIS* WOOD'S NOT ILLEGAL, IS IT?
IT'S OLD, SO IT'S PROBABLY OKAY.
COULD WE JUST *TRY* TO FIX IT...?
THERE ARE SEVERAL OPTIONS. WE COULD PUT A FRAME INTO IT...
IF WE PUT A FRAME INTO IT, IT'LL CHANGE THE SOUND.
AND EVEN IF WE REPAIRED IT...
...IT WOULDN'T BE THE *SAME* BELL IT WAS BEFORE.
WHEN YOU'RE TRYING TO COLLECT SOUNDS, IT'S ALWAYS LIKE THIS.

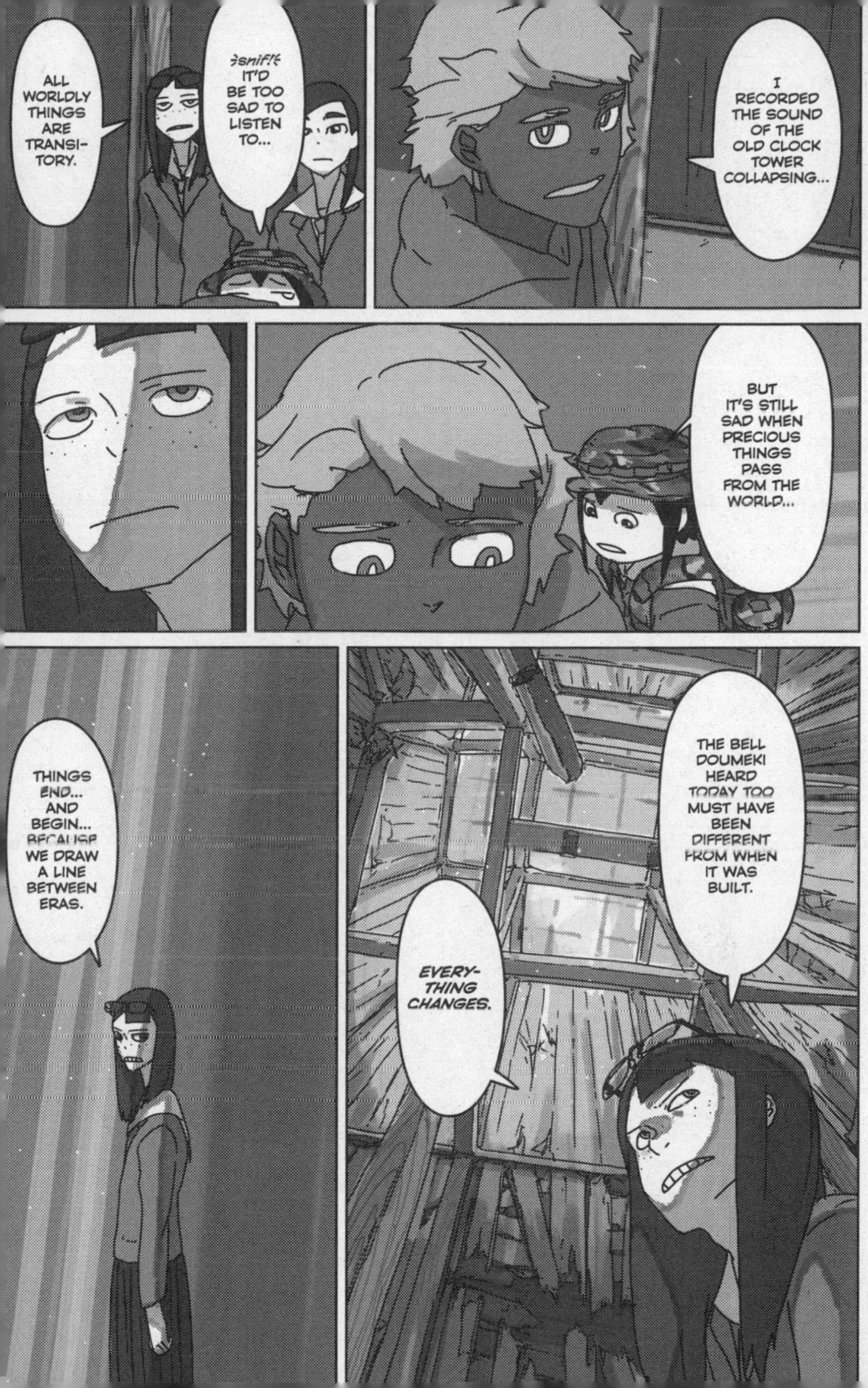
I RECORDED THE SOUND OF THE OLD CLOCK TOWER COLLAPSING...
snif! IT'D BE TOO SAD TO LISTEN TO...
ALL WORLDLY THINGS ARE TRANSI-TORY.
BUT IT'S STILL SAD WHEN PRECIOUS THINGS PASS FROM THE WORLD...
THE BELL DOUMEKI HEARD TODAY TOO MUST HAVE BEEN DIFFERENT FROM WHEN IT WAS BUILT.
EVERY-THING CHANGES.
THINGS END... AND BEGIN... BECAUSE WE DRAW A LINE BETWEEN ERAS.

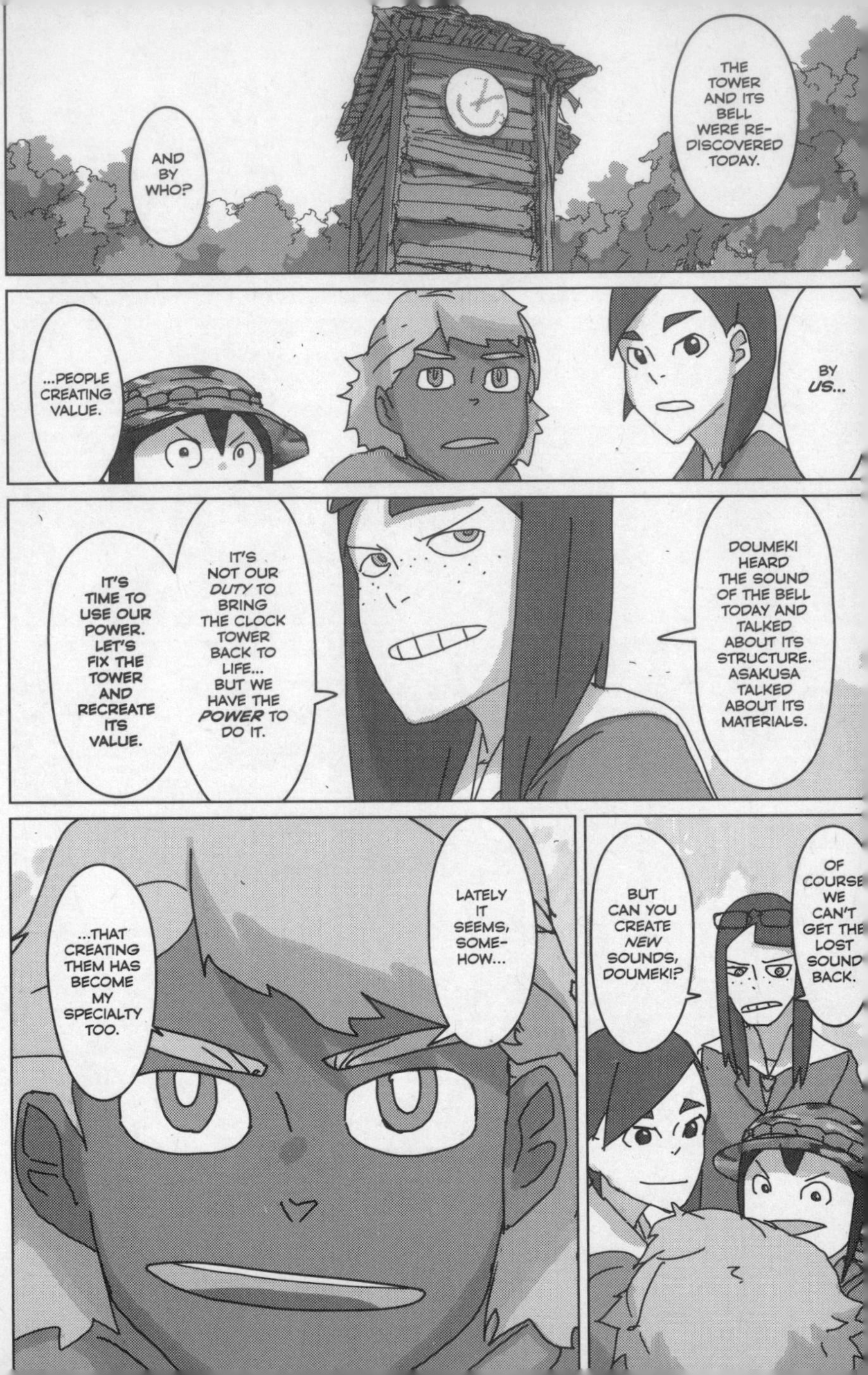
THE TOWER AND ITS BELL WERE RE-DISCOVERED TODAY.
AND BY WHO?
BY *US*...
...PEOPLE CREATING VALUE.
DOUMEKI HEARD THE SOUND OF THE BELL TODAY AND TALKED ABOUT ITS STRUCTURE. ASAKUSA TALKED ABOUT ITS MATERIALS.
IT'S NOT OUR *DUTY* TO BRING THE CLOCK TOWER BACK TO LIFE... BUT WE HAVE THE *POWER* TO DO IT.
IT'S TIME TO USE OUR POWER. LET'S FIX THE TOWER AND RECREATE ITS VALUE.
OF COURSE WE CAN'T GET THE LOST SOUND BACK.
BUT CAN YOU CREATE *NEW* SOUNDS, DOUMEKI!?
LATELY IT SEEMS, SOME-HOW...
...THAT CREATING THEM HAS BECOME MY SPECIALTY TOO.

KEEP YOUR HANDS OFF EIZOUKEN!

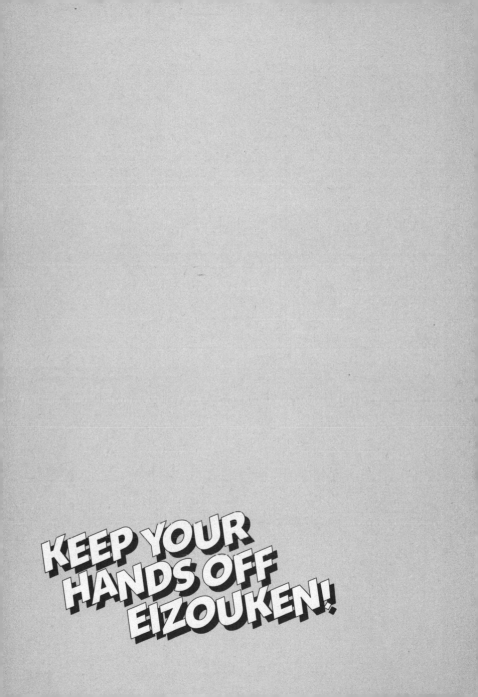

THE CLOCK TOWER'S DE-STROYED?!
APPAR-ENTLY SHE FAILED TO RECORD IT TOO.
SO THAT'S WHY THEY'RE BEING LIKE THAT...
YOU DON'T HAVE ANY MONEY!
PLEASE LEND ME SOME!
WHO'LL FIX IT?!
PLEASE INTRO-DUCE ME TO A CARPEN-TER!
DON'T KNOW ONE!
WE DON'T EVEN KNOW WHO OWNS THE TOWER!
PLEASE FIND OUT!
GIVE ME MONEY!
FIX IT.
FIX IT?!

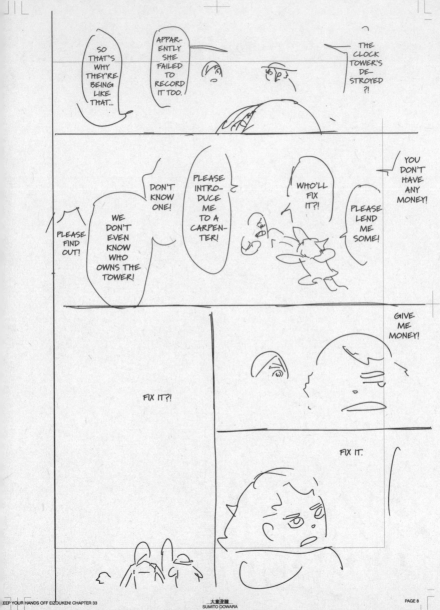

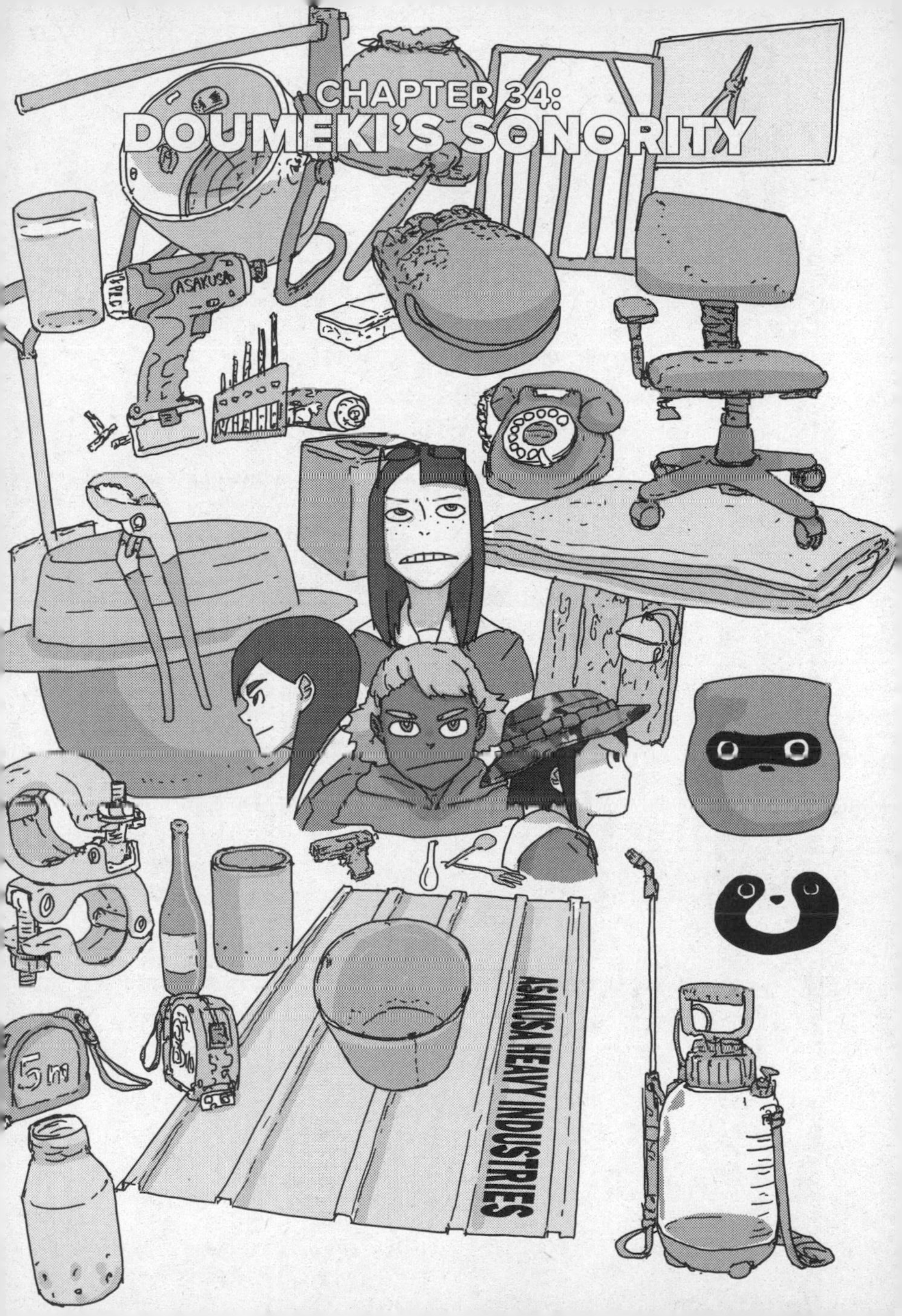
CHAPTER 34:
DOUMEKI'S SONORITY
ASAKUSA
5m
ASAKUSA HEAVY INDUSTRIES

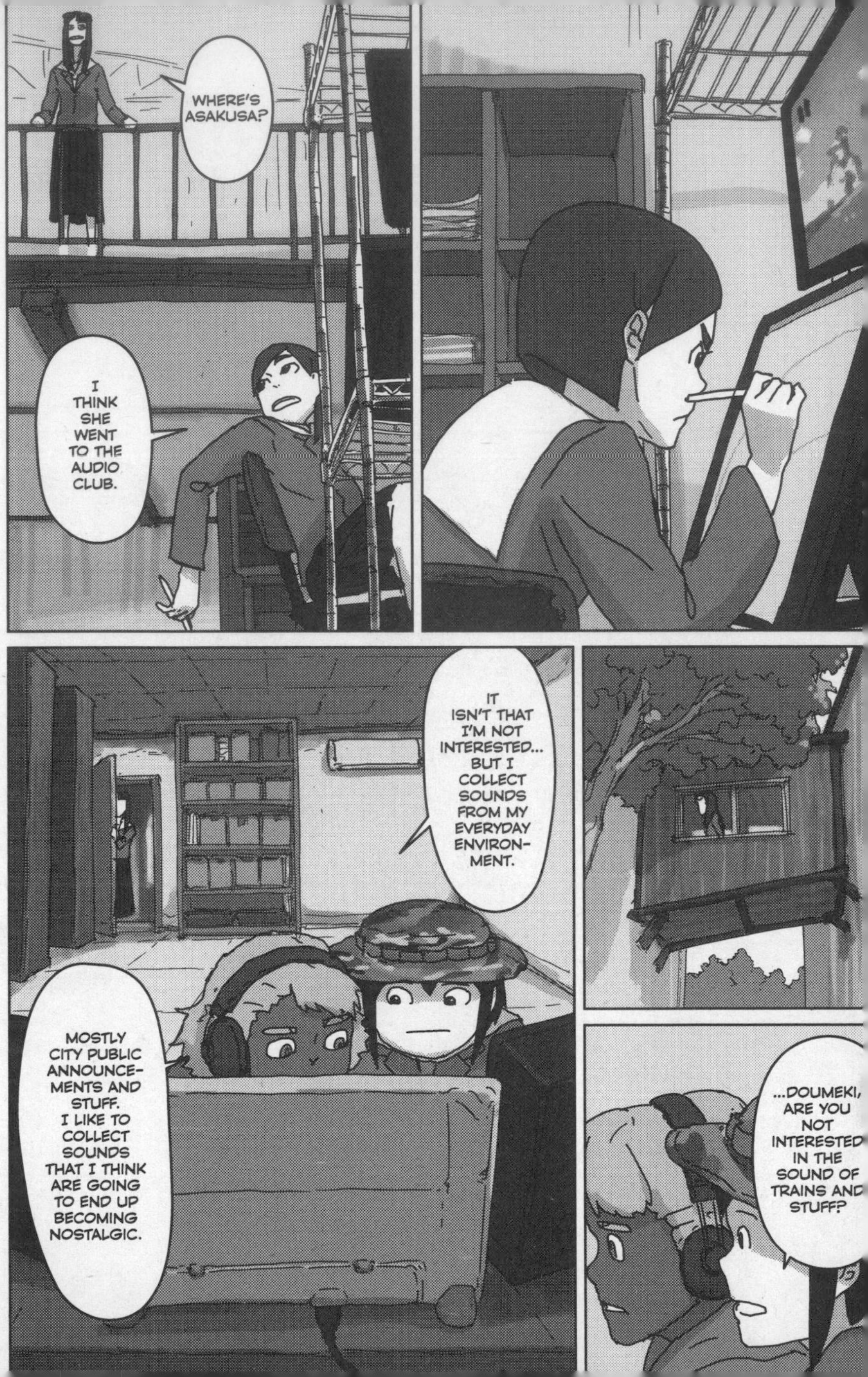
WHERE'S ASAKUSA?
I THINK SHE WENT TO THE AUDIO CLUB.
...DOUMEKI, ARE YOU NOT INTERESTED IN THE SOUND OF TRAINS AND STUFF?
IT ISN'T THAT I'M NOT INTERESTED... BUT I COLLECT SOUNDS FROM MY EVERYDAY ENVIRON-MENT.
MOSTLY CITY PUBLIC ANNOUNCE-MENTS AND STUFF. I LIKE TO COLLECT SOUNDS THAT I THINK ARE GOING TO END UP BECOMING NOSTALGIC.

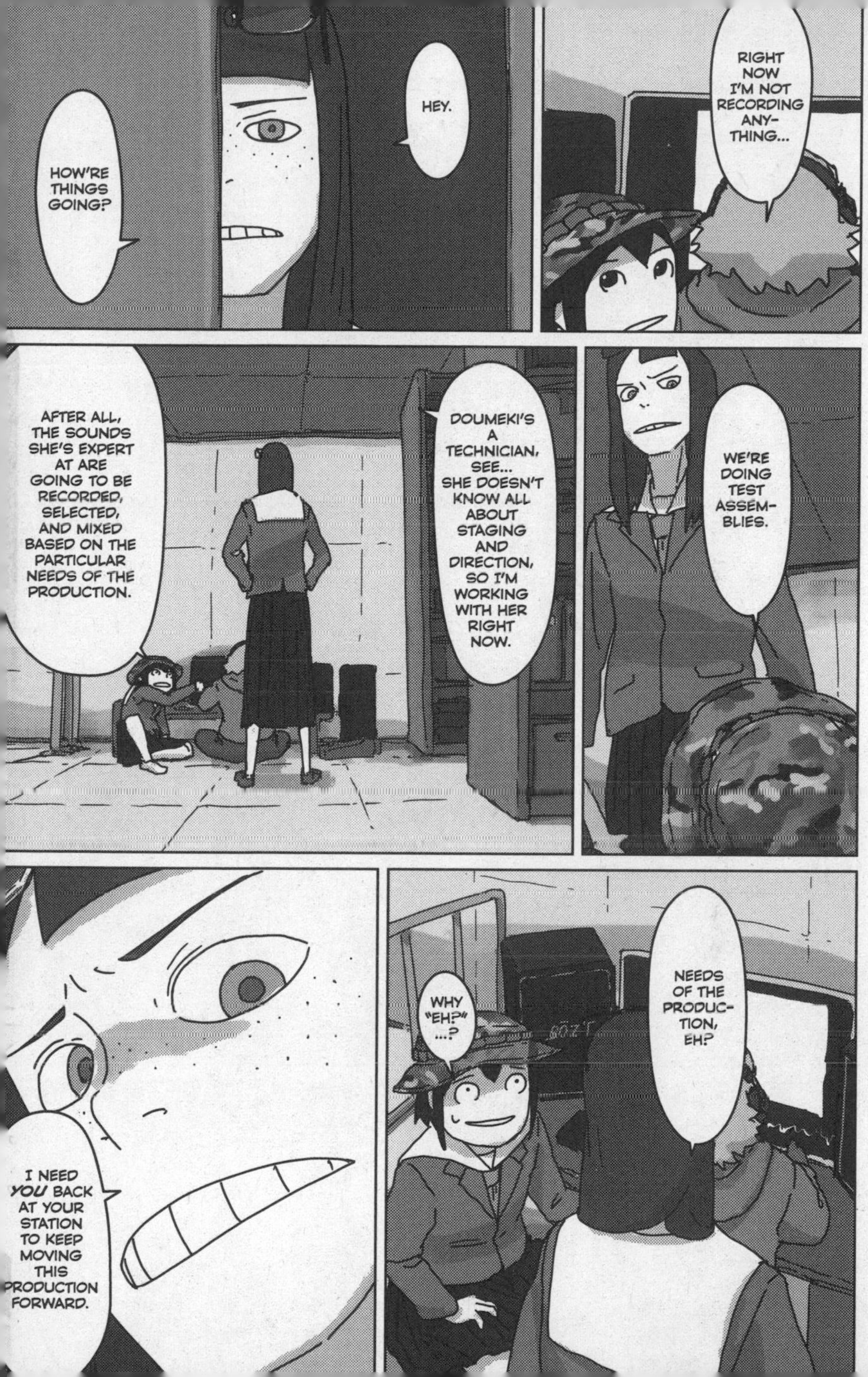
RIGHT NOW I'M NOT RECORDING ANYTHING...
HEY.
HOW'RE THINGS GOING?
WE'RE DOING TEST ASSEMBLIES.
DOUMEKI'S A TECHNICIAN, SEE... SHE DOESN'T KNOW ALL ABOUT STAGING AND DIRECTION, SO I'M WORKING WITH HER RIGHT NOW.
AFTER ALL, THE SOUNDS SHE'S EXPERT AT ARE GOING TO BE RECORDED, SELECTED, AND MIXED BASED ON THE PARTICULAR NEEDS OF THE PRODUCTION.
NEEDS OF THE PRODUCTION, EH?
WHY "EH?" ...?
I NEED *YOU* BACK AT YOUR STATION TO KEEP MOVING THIS PRODUCTION FORWARD.

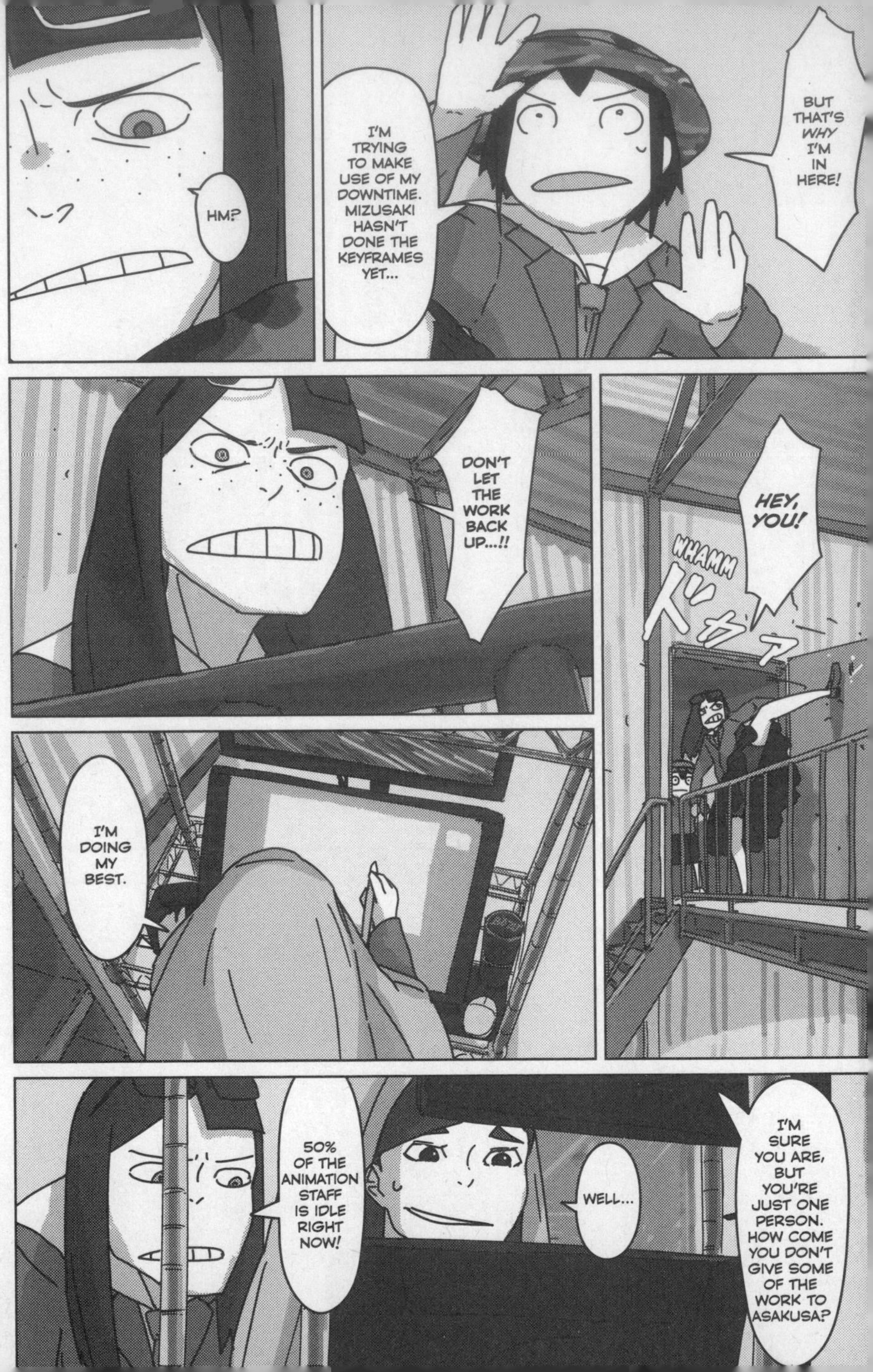
BUT THAT'S *WHY* I'M IN HERE!
I'M TRYING TO MAKE USE OF MY DOWNTIME. MIZUSAKI HASN'T DONE THE KEYFRAMES YET...
HM?
HEY, YOU!
WHAMM
DON'T LET THE WORK BACK UP...!!
I'M DOING MY BEST.
I'M SURE YOU ARE, BUT YOU'RE JUST ONE PERSON. HOW COME YOU DON'T GIVE SOME OF THE WORK TO ASAKUSA?
WELL...
50% OF THE ANIMATION STAFF IS IDLE RIGHT NOW!

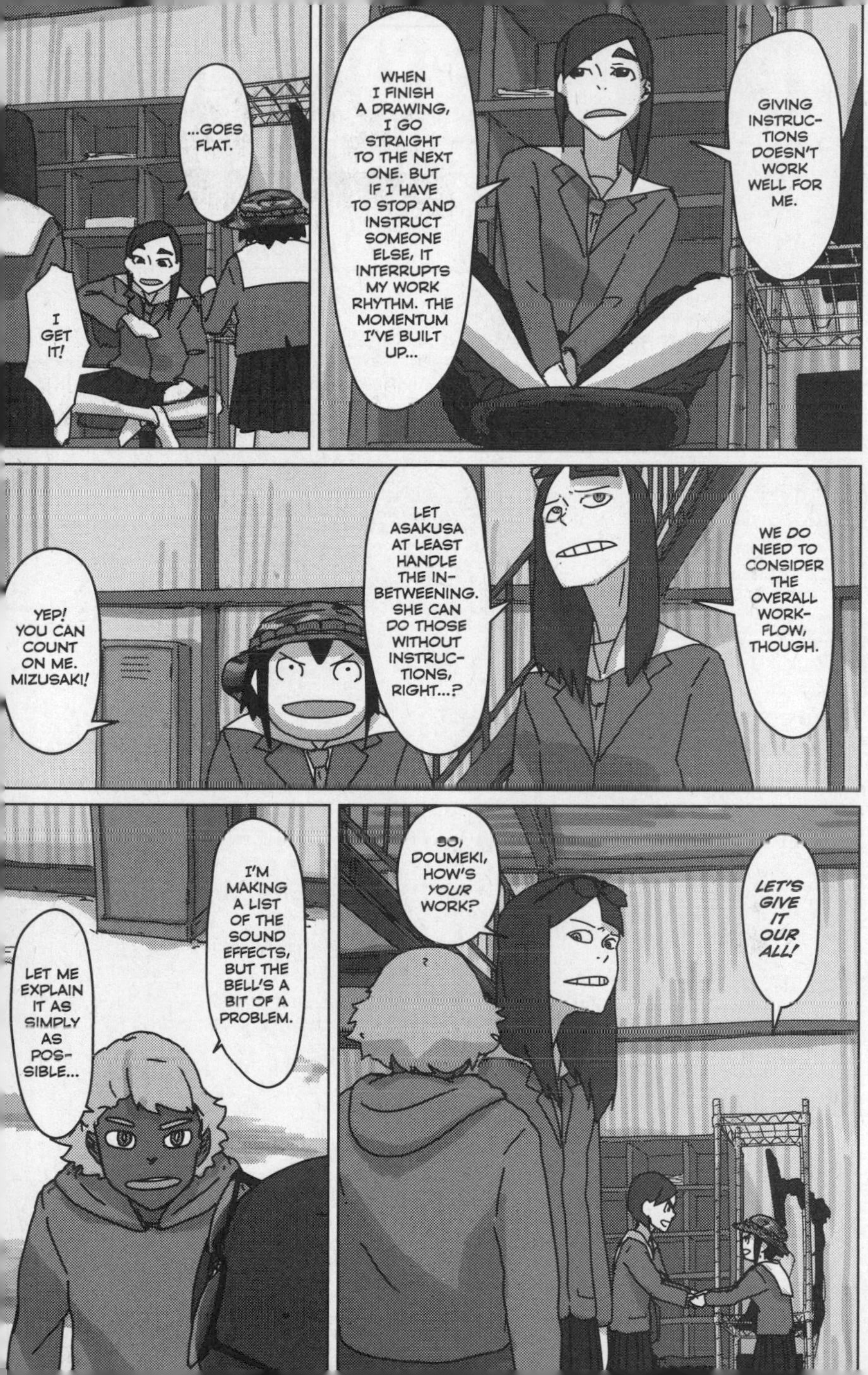
GIVING INSTRUCTIONS DOESN'T WORK WELL FOR ME.
WHEN I FINISH A DRAWING, I GO STRAIGHT TO THE NEXT ONE. BUT IF I HAVE TO STOP AND INSTRUCT SOMEONE ELSE, IT INTERRUPTS MY WORK RHYTHM. THE MOMENTUM I'VE BUILT UP...
...GOES FLAT.
I GET IT!
WE *DO* NEED TO CONSIDER THE OVERALL WORKFLOW, THOUGH.
LET ASAKUSA AT LEAST HANDLE THE IN-BETWEENING. SHE CAN DO THOSE WITHOUT INSTRUCTIONS, RIGHT...?
YEP! YOU CAN COUNT ON ME. MIZUSAKI!
LET'S GIVE IT OUR ALL!
SO, DOUMEKI, HOW'S *YOUR* WORK?
I'M MAKING A LIST OF THE SOUND EFFECTS, BUT THE BELL'S A BIT OF A PROBLEM.
LET ME EXPLAIN IT AS SIMPLY AS POSSIBLE...

DOUMEKI'S SONORITY

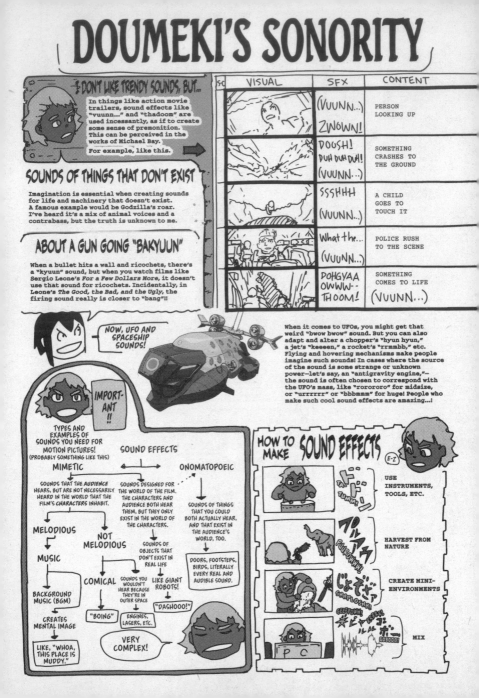

I DON'T LIKE TRENDY SOUNDS, BUT...

In things like action movie trailers, sound effects like "vuunn..." and "thadoom" are used incessantly, as if to create some sense of premonition. This can be perceived in the works of Michael Bay.

For example, like this.

SC	VISUAL	SFX	CONTENT
		(VUUNN...) ZWOWN!	PERSON LOOKING UP
		DOOSH! DUH DUH DUH! (VUUNN...)	SOMETHING CRASHES TO THE GROUND
		SSSHHH (VUUNN...)	A CHILD GOES TO TOUCH IT
		What the... (VUUNN...)	POLICE RUSH TO THE SCENE
		DOHGYAA OWWW- THOOM!	SOMETHING COMES TO LIFE (VUUNN...)

SOUNDS OF THINGS THAT DON'T EXIST

Imagination is essential when creating sounds for life and machinery that doesn't exist. A famous example would be Godzilla's roar. I've heard it's a mix of animal voices and a contrabass, but the truth is unknown to me.

ABOUT A GUN GOING "BAKYUUN"

When a bullet hits a wall and ricochets, there's a "kyuun" sound, but when you watch films like Sergio Leone's *For a Few Dollars More*, it doesn't use that sound for ricochets. Incidentally, in Leone's *The Good, the Bad, and the Ugly*, the firing sound really is closer to "bang"!!

NOW, UFO AND SPACESHIP SOUNDS!

When it comes to UFOs, you might get that weird "bwow bwow" sound. But you can also adapt and alter a chopper's "hyun hyun," a jet's "keeeen," a rocket's "rrmmbb," etc. Flying and hovering mechanisms make people imagine such sounds! In cases where the source of the sound is some strange or unknown power—let's say, an "antigravity engine,"—the sound is often chosen to correspond with the UFO's mass, like "rorororo" for midsize, or "urrrrrr" or "bbbmmm" for huge! People who make such cool sound effects are amazing...!

IMPORTANT!!

TYPES AND EXAMPLES OF SOUNDS YOU NEED FOR MOTION PICTURES!
(PROBABLY SOMETHING LIKE THIS)

SOUND EFFECTS

MIMETIC

- SOUNDS THAT THE *AUDIENCE* HEARS, BUT ARE NOT NECESSARILY HEARD IN THE WORLD THAT THE FILM'S *CHARACTERS* INHABIT.
  - MELODIOUS
    - MUSIC
      - BACKGROUND MUSIC (BGM)
        - CREATES MENTAL IMAGE
          - LIKE, "WHOA, THIS PLACE IS MUDDY."
  - NOT MELODIOUS
    - COMICAL
      - "BOING"
    - SOUNDS YOU WOULDN'T HEAR BECAUSE THEY'RE IN OUTER SPACE
      - ENGINES, LASERS, ETC.
- SOUNDS DESIGNED FOR THE WORLD OF THE FILM. THE CHARACTERS AND AUDIENCE BOTH HEAR THEM, BUT THEY ONLY EXIST IN THE WORLD OF THE CHARACTERS.
  - SOUNDS OF OBJECTS THAT DON'T EXIST IN REAL LIFE
    - LIKE GIANT ROBOTS!
      - "DASHOOO!"

ONOMATOPOEIC

- SOUNDS OF THINGS THAT YOU COULD BOTH ACTUALLY HEAR, AND THAT EXIST IN THE AUDIENCE'S WORLD, TOO.
  - DOORS, FOOTSTEPS, BIRDS, LITERALLY EVERY REAL AND AUDIBLE SOUND.

VERY COMPLEX!

HOW TO MAKE SOUND EFFECTS

E-Z
TA-TUMM!
USE INSTRUMENTS, TOOLS, ETC.
FWROWWH!
HARVEST FROM NATURE
SHRPLOSHH!
CREATE MINI-ENVIRONMENTS
GEEEPONK!
GOBOOO!
PC
MIX

GIANT REDWOOD BELL

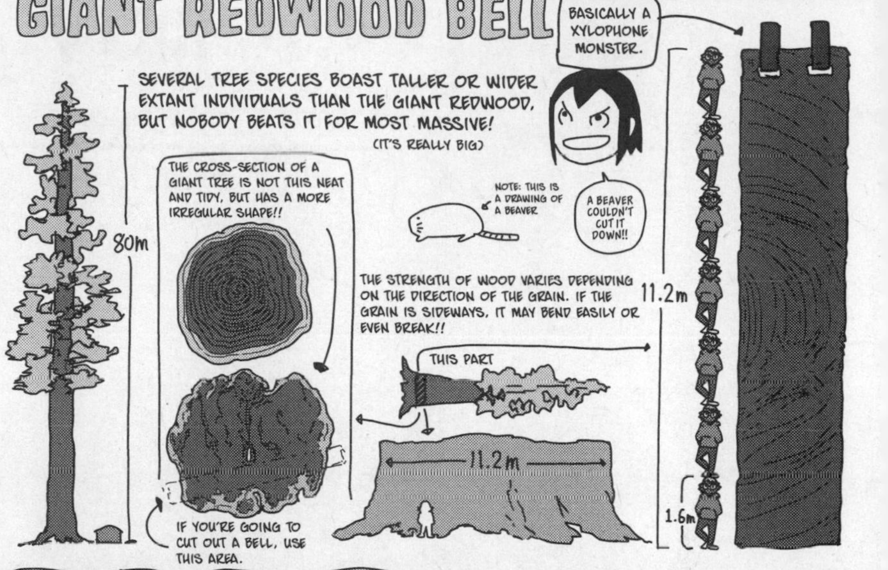
BASICALLY A XYLOPHONE MONSTER.
SEVERAL TREE SPECIES BOAST TALLER OR WIDER EXTANT INDIVIDUALS THAN THE GIANT REDWOOD, BUT NOBODY BEATS IT FOR MOST MASSIVE!
(IT'S REALLY BIG)
80m
THE CROSS-SECTION OF A GIANT TREE IS NOT THIS NEAT AND TIDY, BUT HAS A MORE IRREGULAR SHAPE!!
NOTE: THIS IS A DRAWING OF A BEAVER
A BEAVER COULDN'T CUT IT DOWN!!
THE STRENGTH OF WOOD VARIES DEPENDING ON THE DIRECTION OF THE GRAIN. IF THE GRAIN IS SIDEWAYS, IT MAY BEND EASILY OR EVEN BREAK!!
THIS PART
11.2m
11.2m
1.6m
IF YOU'RE GOING TO CUT OUT A BELL, USE THIS AREA.

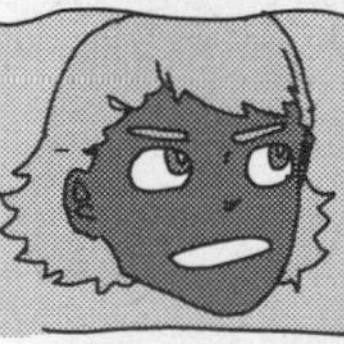

ON AN UNRELATED SUBJECT...
YOU CAN'T HEAR THE SOUND OF A TREE SUCKING UP WATER EVEN WITH A STETHOSCOPE. THE SOUND IS THERE AND EXISTS, BUT IT'S AT TOO HIGH A FREQUENCY FOR HUMAN BEINGS TO HEAR. YOU MAY HEAR OTHER NOISES FROM THE TREE, SUCH AS ITS MOTIONS FROM THE WIND, BUT AS FOR THE WATER, YOU'LL HAVE TO BE METAPHORICAL, LIKE PUTTING A SEASHELL TO YOUR EAR AND SAYING YOU CAN HEAR "THE SOUND OF WAVES".

THE SOUND OF A GIANT TREE BELL

HOW TO MAKE IT

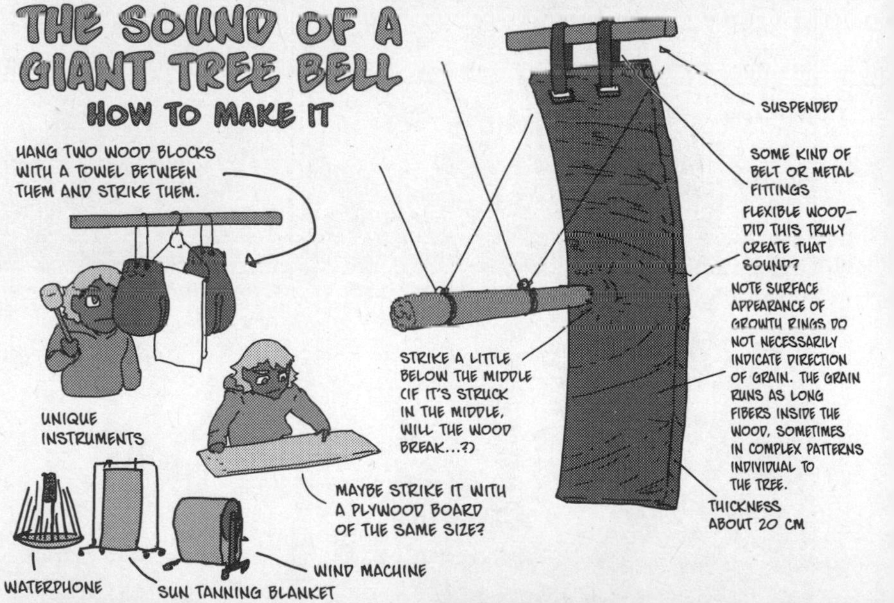
HANG TWO WOOD BLOCKS WITH A TOWEL BETWEEN THEM AND STRIKE THEM.
UNIQUE INSTRUMENTS
MAYBE STRIKE IT WITH A PLYWOOD BOARD OF THE SAME SIZE?
WATERPHONE
SUN TANNING BLANKET
WIND MACHINE
SUSPENDED
SOME KIND OF BELT OR METAL FITTINGS
FLEXIBLE WOOD—DID THIS TRULY CREATE THAT SOUND?
NOTE SURFACE APPEARANCE OF GROWTH RINGS DO NOT NECESSARILY INDICATE DIRECTION OF GRAIN. THE GRAIN RUNS AS LONG FIBERS INSIDE THE WOOD, SOMETIMES IN COMPLEX PATTERNS INDIVIDUAL TO THE TREE.
STRIKE A LITTLE BELOW THE MIDDLE (IF IT'S STRUCK IN THE MIDDLE, WILL THE WOOD BREAK...?)
THICKNESS ABOUT 20 CM

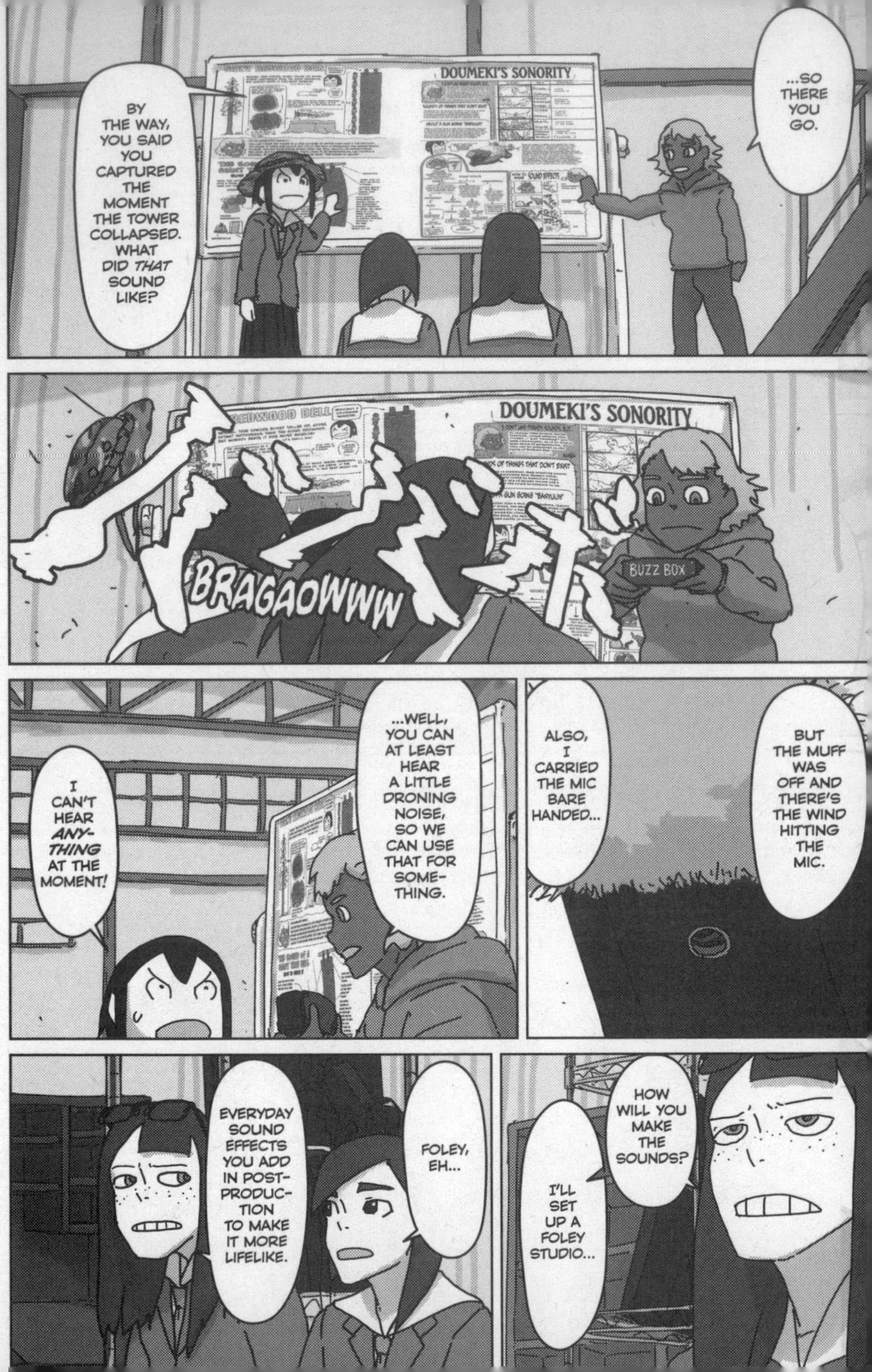

...SO THERE YOU GO.
DOUMEKI'S SONORITY
BY THE WAY, YOU SAID YOU CAPTURED THE MOMENT THE TOWER COLLAPSED. WHAT DID *THAT* SOUND LIKE?
DOUMEKI'S SONORITY
BUZZ BOX
BRAGAOWWW
BUT THE MUFF WAS OFF AND THERE'S THE WIND HITTING THE MIC.
ALSO, I CARRIED THE MIC BARE HANDED...
...WELL, YOU CAN AT LEAST HEAR A LITTLE DRONING NOISE, SO WE CAN USE THAT FOR SOME-THING.
I CAN'T HEAR *ANY-THING* AT THE MOMENT!
HOW WILL YOU MAKE THE SOUNDS?
I'LL SET UP A FOLEY STUDIO...
FOLEY, EH...
EVERYDAY SOUND EFFECTS YOU ADD IN POST-PRODUC-TION TO MAKE IT MORE LIFELIKE.

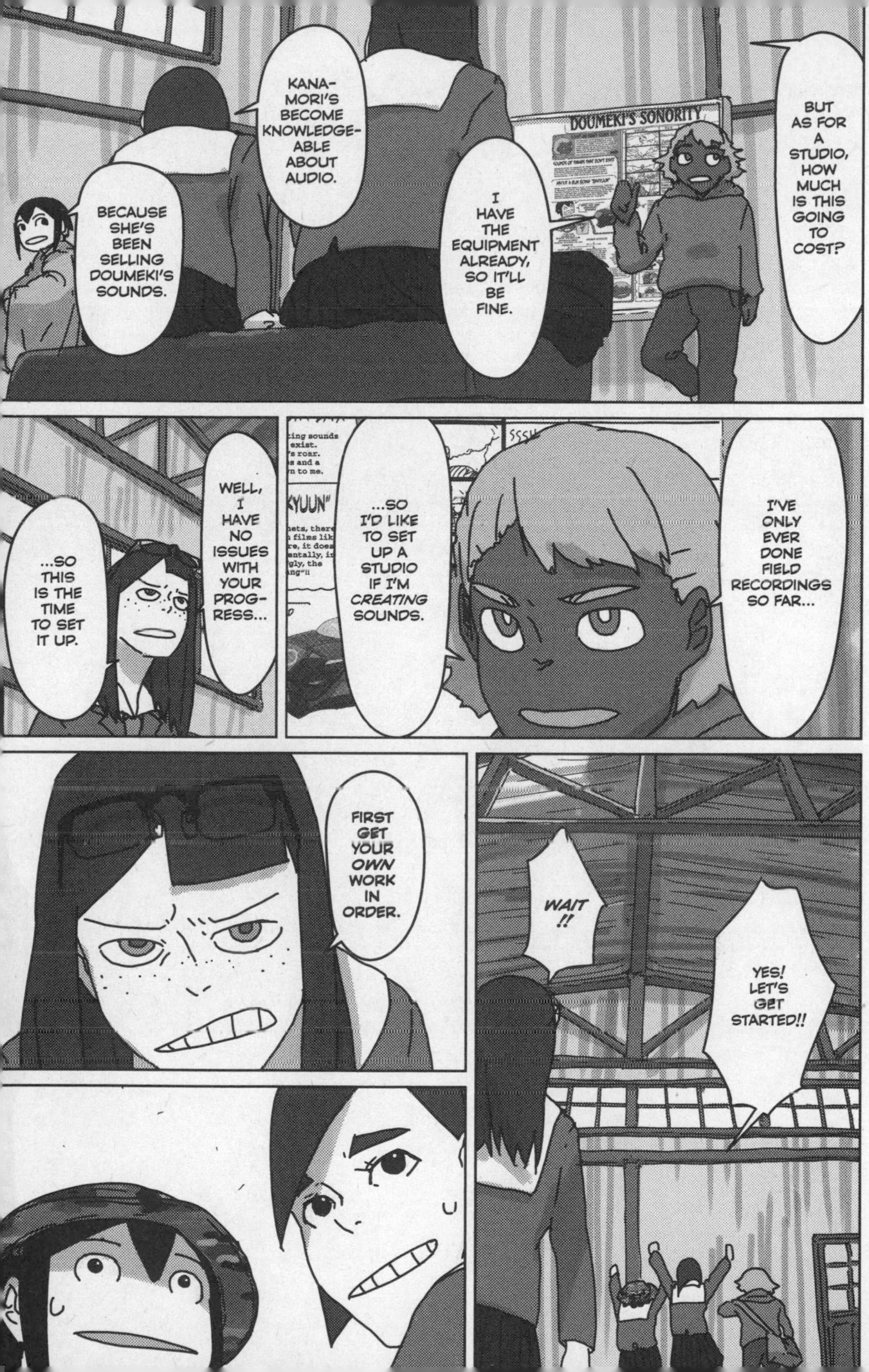
DOUMEKI'S SONORITY
BUT AS FOR A STUDIO, HOW MUCH IS THIS GOING TO COST?
I HAVE THE EQUIPMENT ALREADY, SO IT'LL BE FINE.
KANA-MORI'S BECOME KNOWLEDGE-ABLE ABOUT AUDIO.
BECAUSE SHE'S BEEN SELLING DOUMEKI'S SOUNDS.
I'VE ONLY EVER DONE FIELD RECORDINGS SO FAR...
...SO I'D LIKE TO SET UP A STUDIO IF I'M *CREATING* SOUNDS.
WELL, I HAVE NO ISSUES WITH YOUR PROG-RESS...
...SO THIS IS THE TIME TO SET IT UP.
YES! LET'S GET STARTED!!
WAIT!!
FIRST GET YOUR *OWN* WORK IN ORDER.

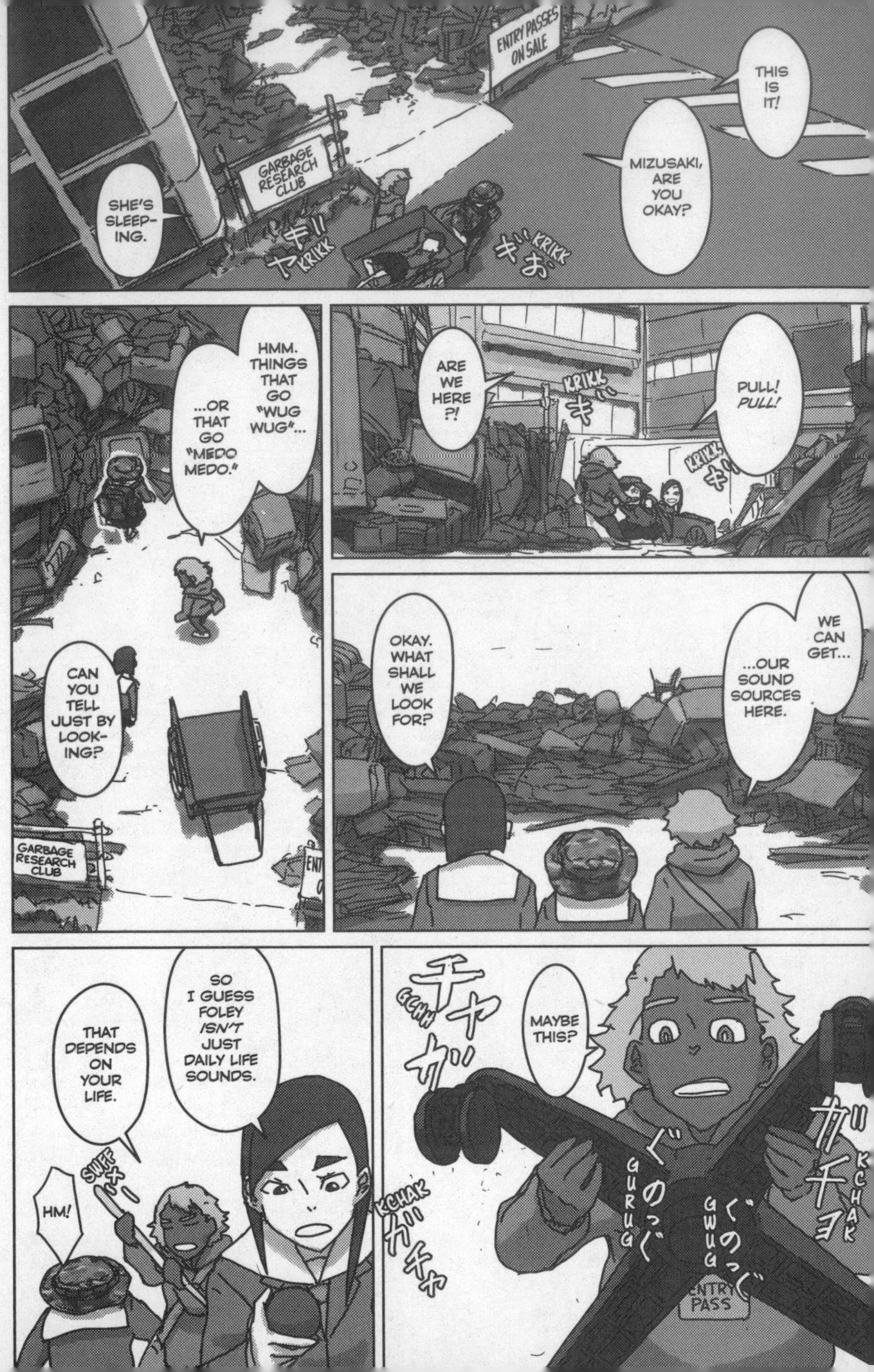
ENTRY PASSES ON SALE
THIS IS IT!
MIZUSAKI, ARE YOU OKAY?
KRIKK
KRIKK
GARBAGE RESEARCH CLUB
SHE'S SLEEPING.
PULL! *PULL!*
KRIKK
ARE WE HERE?!
KRIKK
WE CAN GET...
...OUR SOUND SOURCES HERE.
OKAY. WHAT SHALL WE LOOK FOR?
HMM. THINGS THAT GO "WUG WUG"...
...OR THAT GO "MEDO MEDO."
CAN YOU TELL JUST BY LOOKING?
GARBAGE RESEARCH CLUB
GCHH
MAYBE THIS?
KCHAK
GURUG
GWUG
ENTRY PASS
SO I GUESS FOLEY *ISN'T* JUST DAILY LIFE SOUNDS.
THAT DEPENDS ON YOUR LIFE.
KCHAK
SWFF
HM!

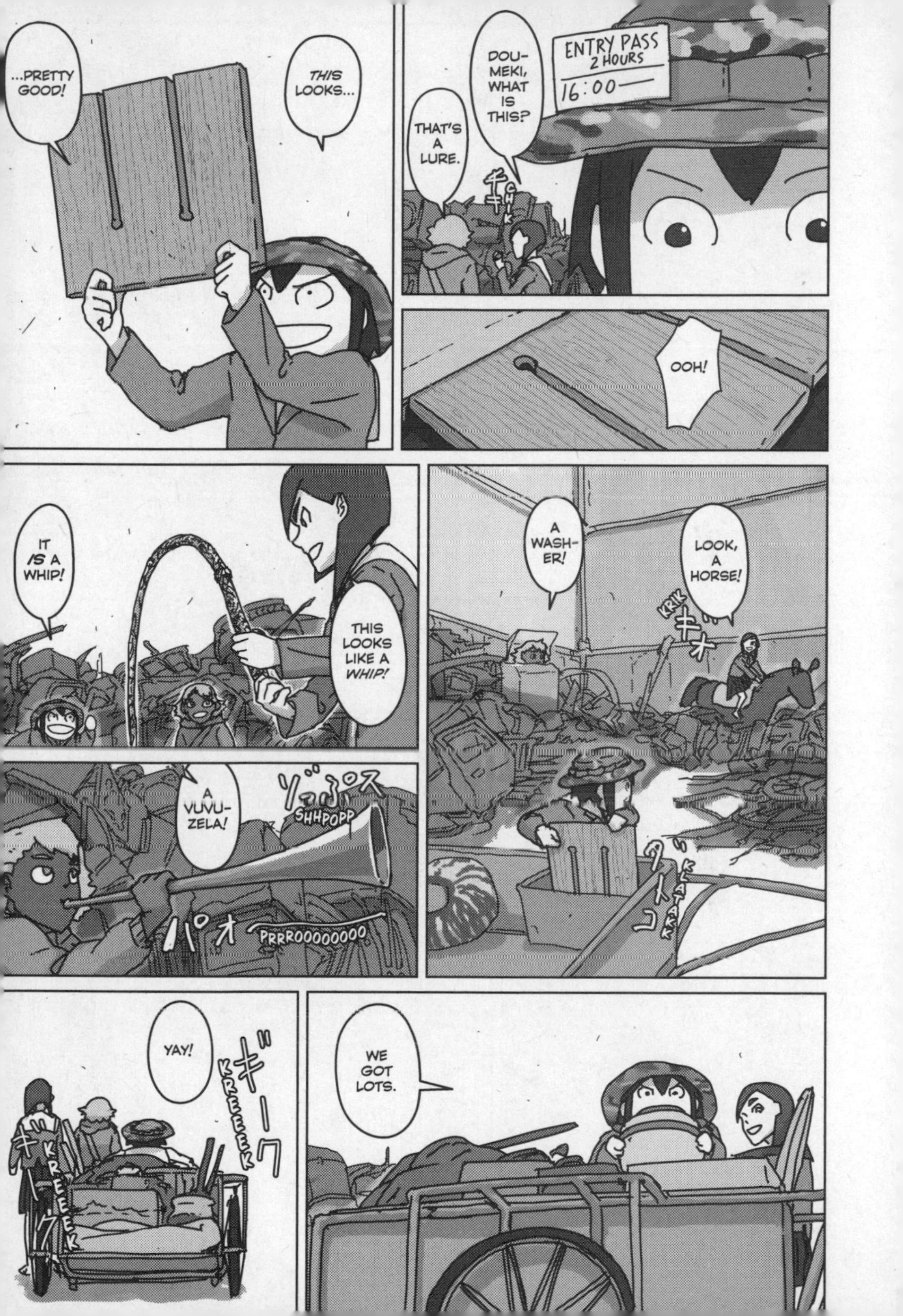
ENTRY PASS
2 HOURS
16:00
DOU-MEKI, WHAT IS THIS?
THAT'S A LURE.
CHIK
OOH!
THIS LOOKS...
...PRETTY GOOD!
LOOK, A HORSE!
KRIK
A WASHER!
KLATAKK
THIS LOOKS LIKE A *WHIP!*
IT *IS* A WHIP!
SHHPOPP
A VUVUZELA!
PRRROOOOOOOO
WE GOT LOTS.
YAY!
KREEEEK
KREEEK

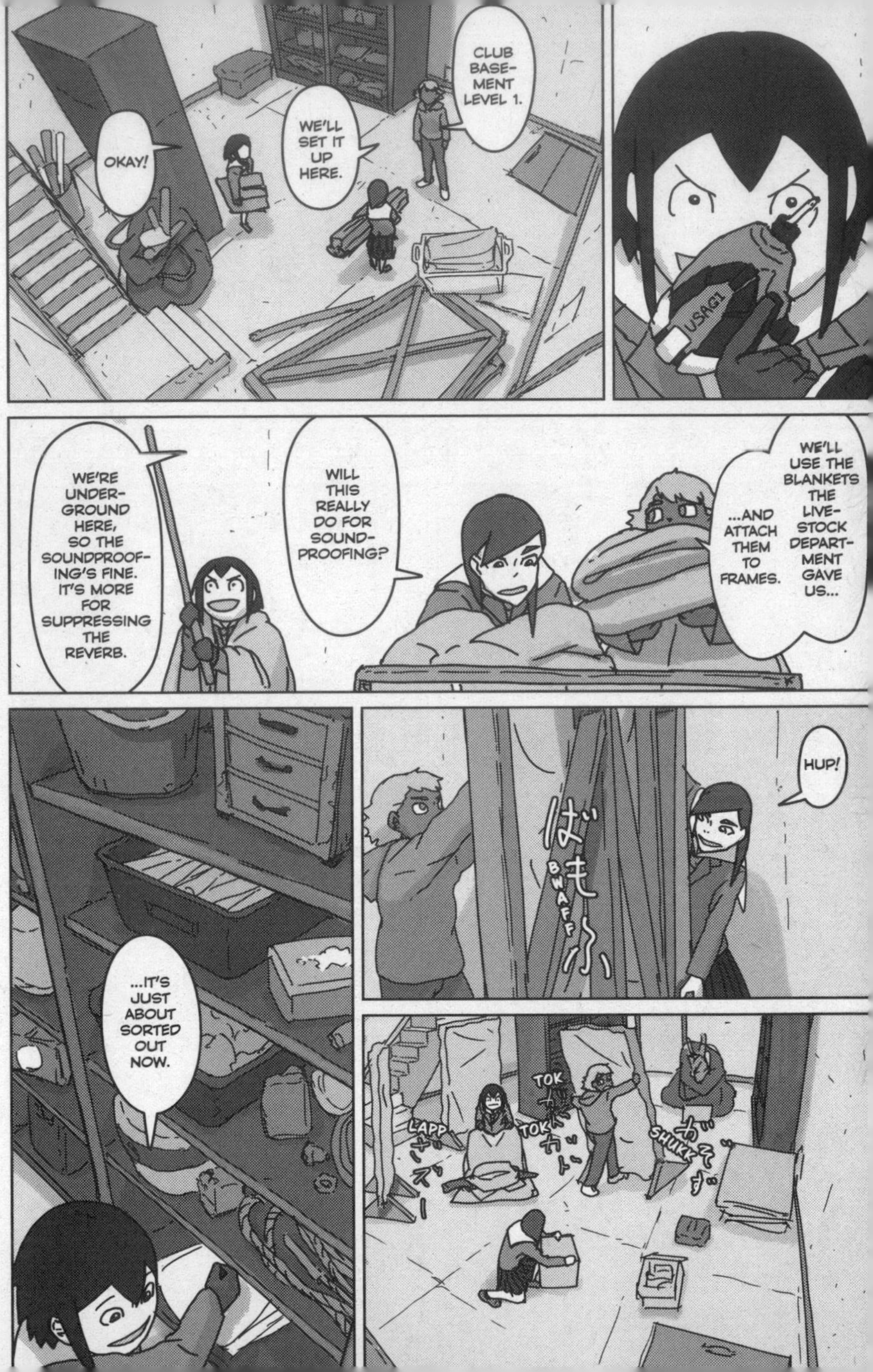
USAGI
CLUB BASEMENT LEVEL 1.
WE'LL SET IT UP HERE.
OKAY!
WE'LL USE THE BLANKETS THE LIVESTOCK DEPARTMENT GAVE US...
...AND ATTACH THEM TO FRAMES.
WILL THIS REALLY DO FOR SOUNDPROOFING?
WE'RE UNDERGROUND HERE, SO THE SOUNDPROOFING'S FINE. IT'S MORE FOR SUPPRESSING THE REVERB.
HUP!
BWAFF
TOK
SHUKK
TOK
LAPP
...IT'S JUST ABOUT SORTED OUT NOW.

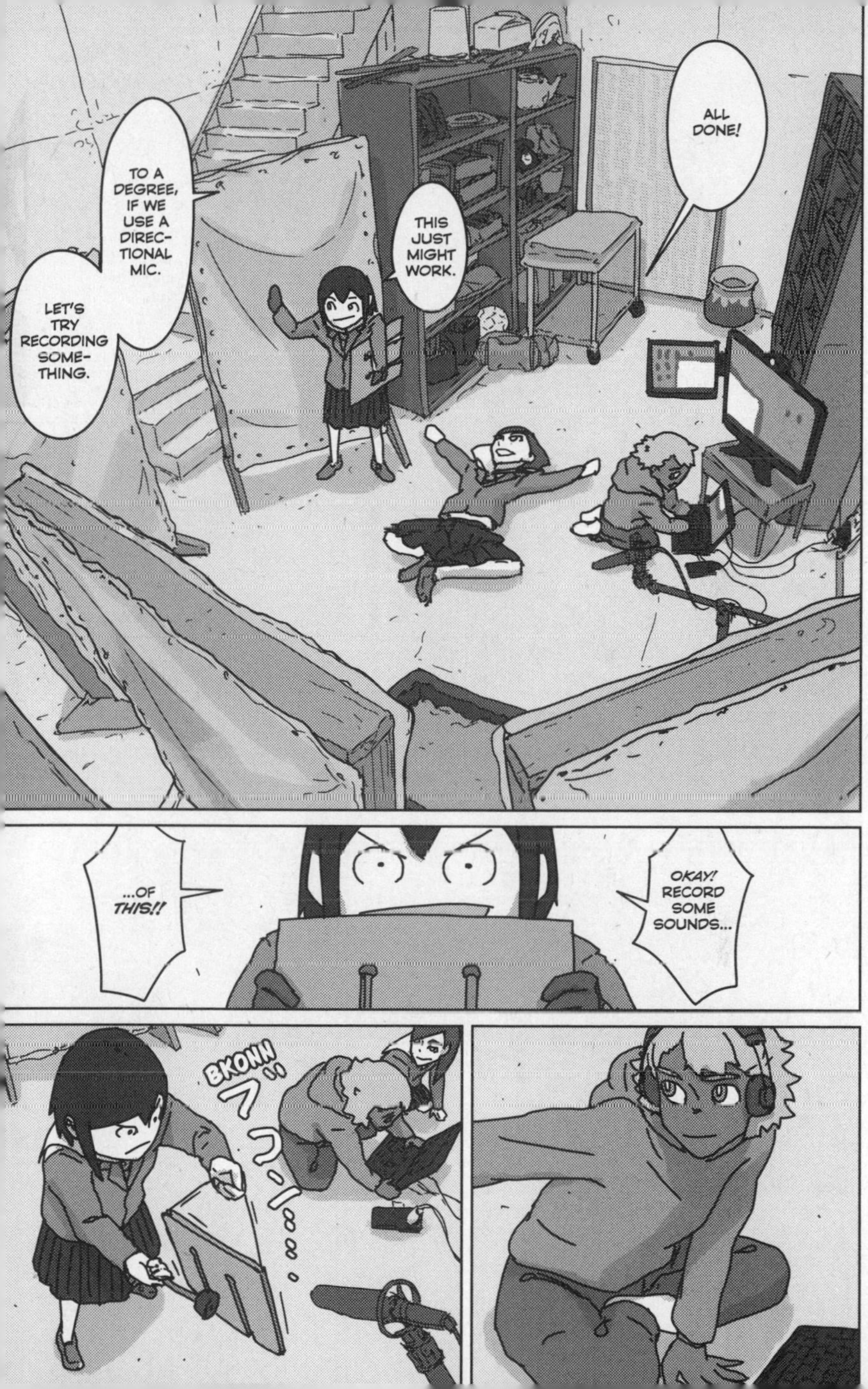
ALL DONE!
THIS JUST MIGHT WORK.
TO A DEGREE, IF WE USE A DIREC-TIONAL MIC.
LET'S TRY RECORDING SOME-THING.
OKAY! RECORD SOME SOUNDS...
...OF *THIS!!*
BKONN

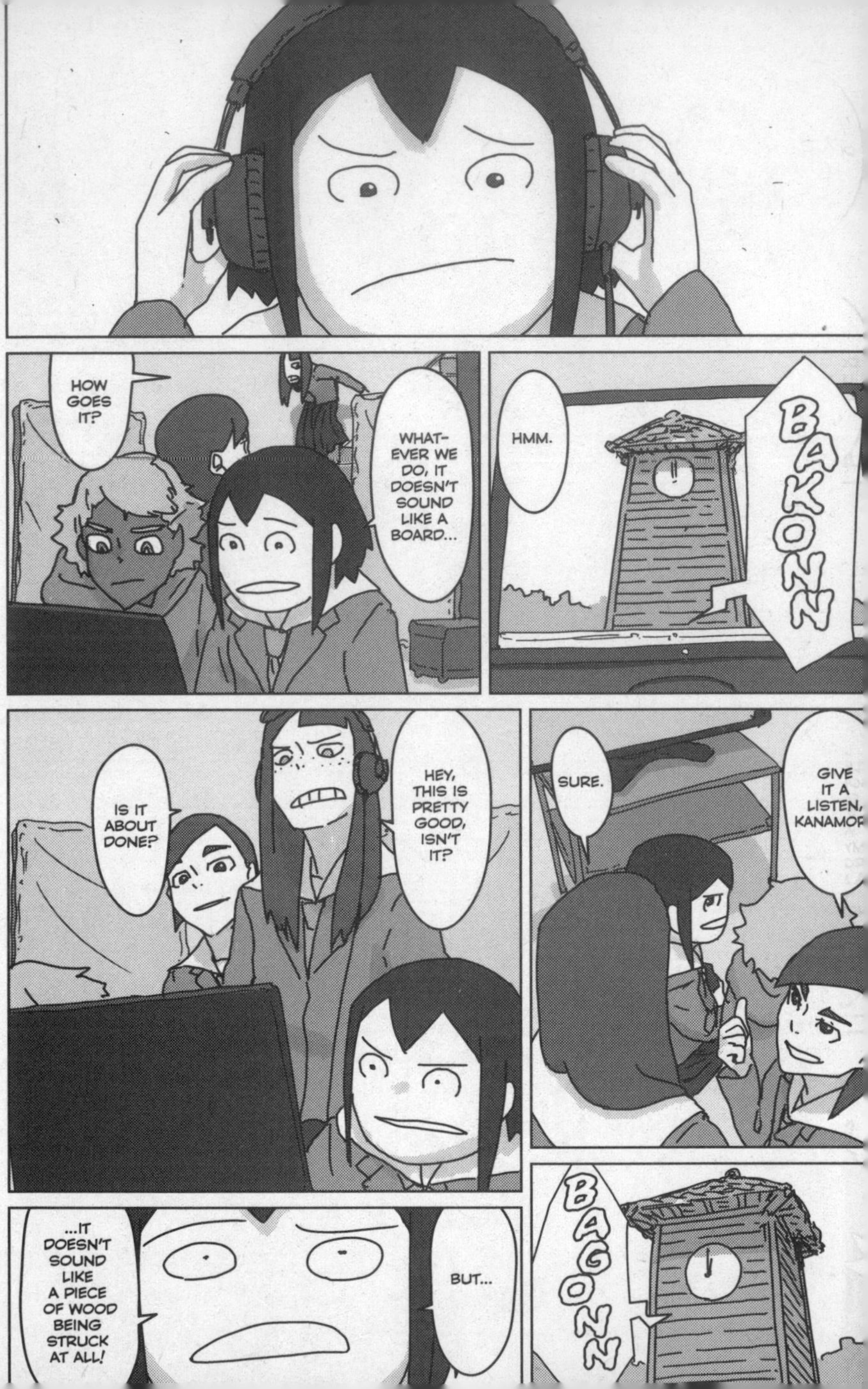
BAKONN
HMM.
WHATEVER WE DO, IT DOESN'T SOUND LIKE A BOARD...
HOW GOES IT?
GIVE IT A LISTEN, KANAMOR
SURE.
HEY, THIS IS PRETTY GOOD, ISN'T IT?
IS IT ABOUT DONE?
BAGONN
BUT...
...IT DOESN'T SOUND LIKE A PIECE OF WOOD BEING STRUCK AT ALL!

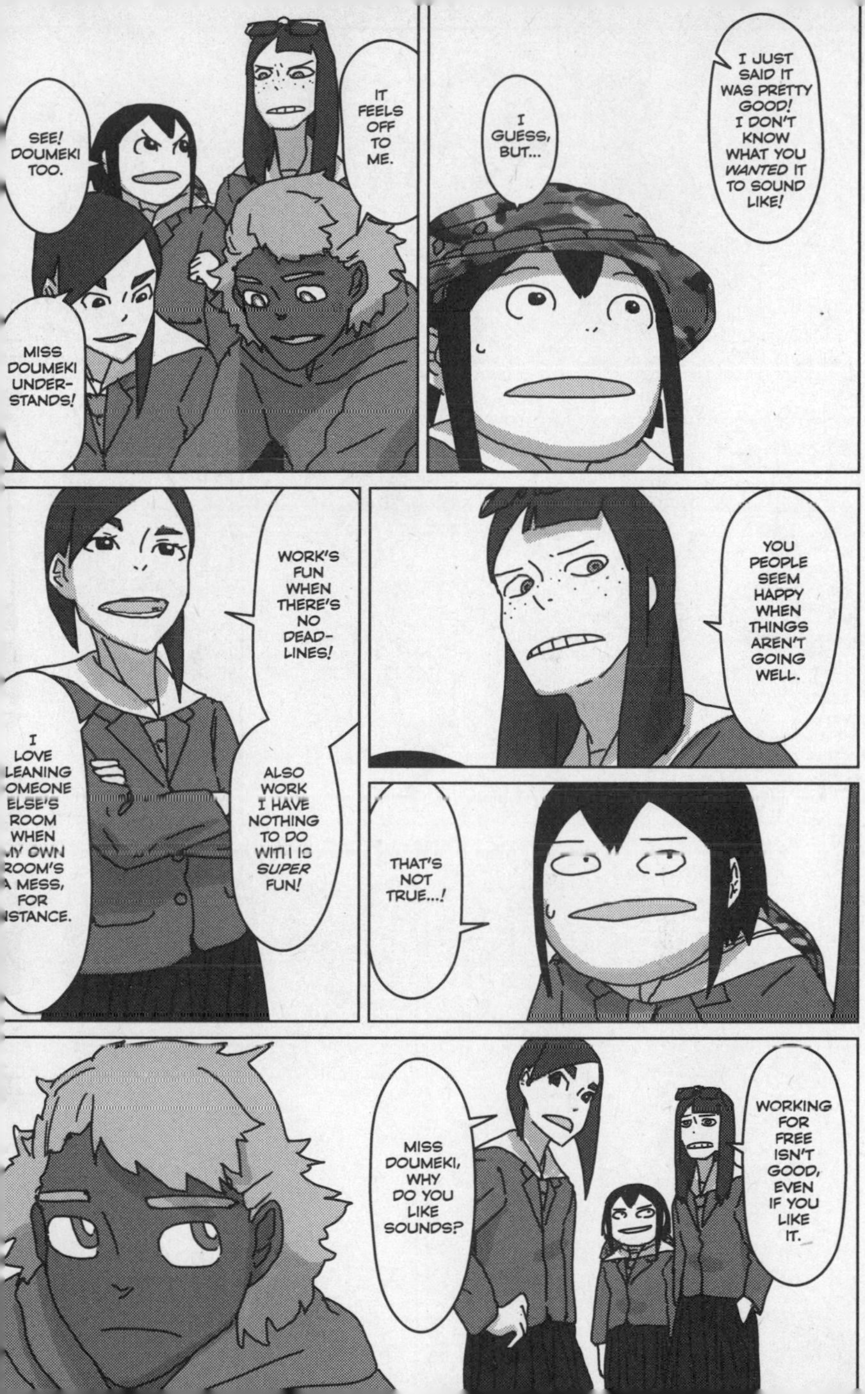
I JUST SAID IT WAS PRETTY GOOD! I DON'T KNOW WHAT YOU *WANTED* IT TO SOUND LIKE!
I GUESS, BUT...
IT FEELS OFF TO ME.
SEE! DOUMEKI TOO.
MISS DOUMEKI UNDERSTANDS!
YOU PEOPLE SEEM HAPPY WHEN THINGS AREN'T GOING WELL.
THAT'S NOT TRUE...!
WORK'S FUN WHEN THERE'S NO DEADLINES!
ALSO WORK I HAVE NOTHING TO DO WITH IS *SUPER* FUN!
I LOVE LEANING OMEONE ELSE'S ROOM WHEN MY OWN ROOM'S A MESS, FOR NSTANCE.
WORKING FOR FREE ISN'T GOOD, EVEN IF YOU LIKE IT.
MISS DOUMEKI, WHY DO YOU LIKE SOUNDS?

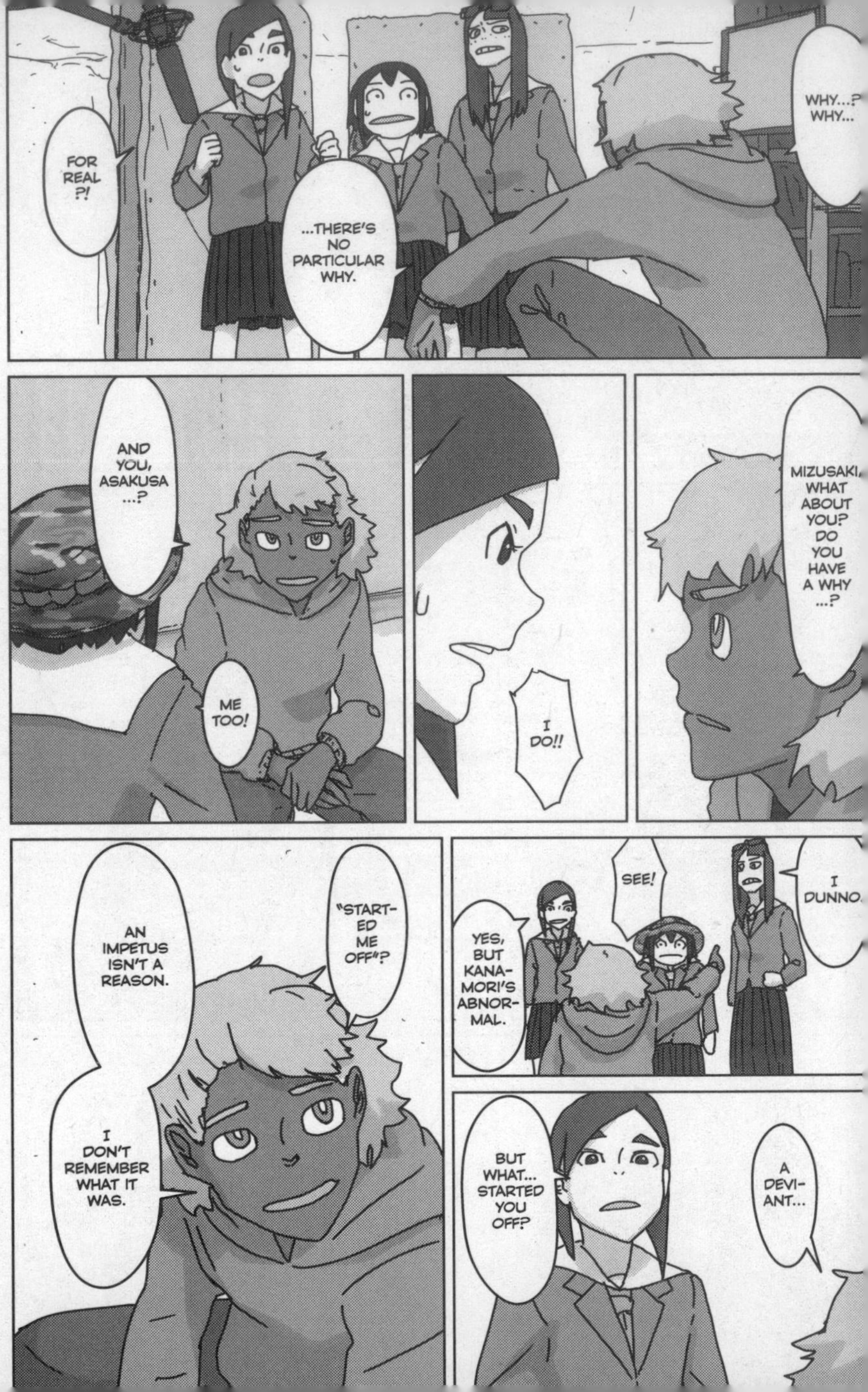
WHY...? WHY...
...THERE'S NO PARTICULAR WHY.
FOR REAL?!
MIZUSAKI, WHAT ABOUT YOU? DO YOU HAVE A WHY ...?
I DO!!
AND YOU, ASAKUSA ...?
ME TOO!
I DUNNO.
SEE!
YES, BUT KANAMORI'S ABNORMAL.
A DEVIANT...
BUT WHAT... STARTED YOU OFF?
"STARTED ME OFF"?
AN IMPETUS ISN'T A REASON.
I DON'T REMEMBER WHAT IT WAS.

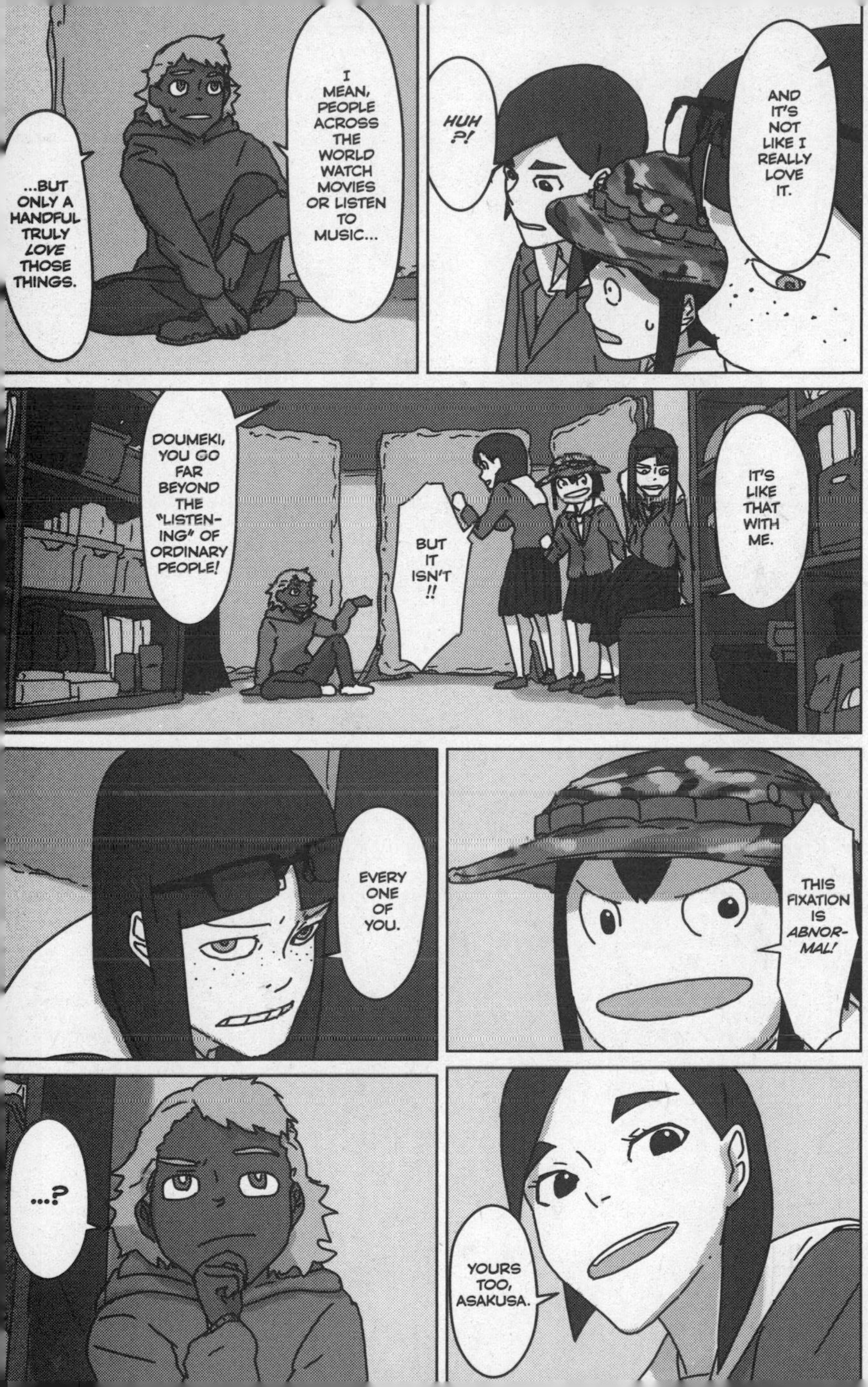
AND IT'S NOT LIKE I REALLY LOVE IT.
HUH?!
I MEAN, PEOPLE ACROSS THE WORLD WATCH MOVIES OR LISTEN TO MUSIC...
...BUT ONLY A HANDFUL TRULY *LOVE* THOSE THINGS.
IT'S LIKE THAT WITH ME.
BUT IT ISN'T!!
DOUMEKI, YOU GO FAR BEYOND THE "LISTENING" OF ORDINARY PEOPLE!
THIS FIXATION IS *ABNORMAL!*
EVERY ONE OF YOU.
YOURS TOO, ASAKUSA.
...?

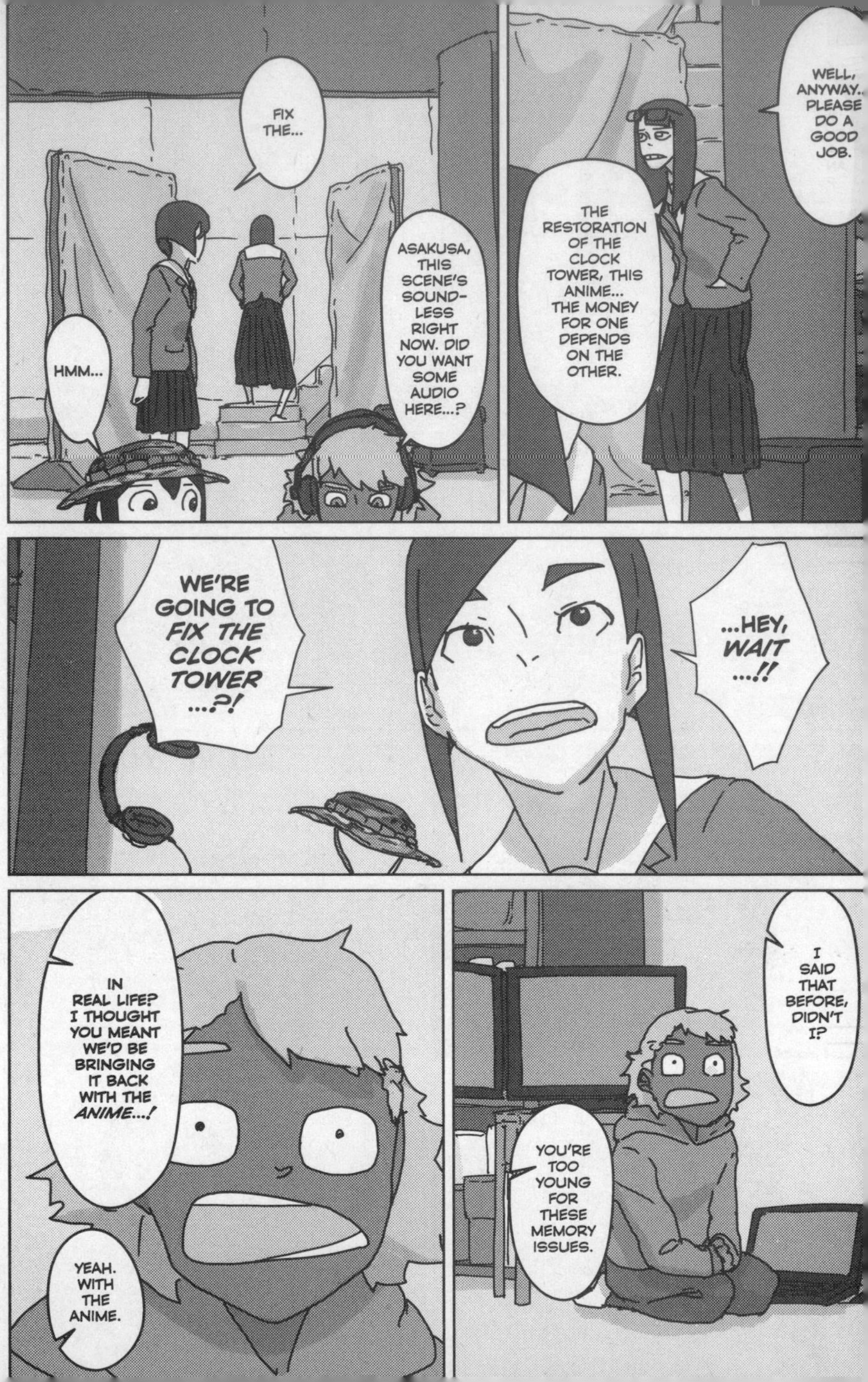
WELL, ANYWAY... PLEASE DO A GOOD JOB.
THE RESTORATION OF THE CLOCK TOWER, THIS ANIME... THE MONEY FOR ONE DEPENDS ON THE OTHER.
FIX THE...
ASAKUSA, THIS SCENE'S SOUND-LESS RIGHT NOW. DID YOU WANT SOME AUDIO HERE...?
HMM...
...HEY, *WAIT* ...!!
WE'RE GOING TO *FIX THE CLOCK TOWER* ...?!
I SAID THAT BEFORE, DIDN'T I?
YOU'RE TOO YOUNG FOR THESE MEMORY ISSUES.
IN REAL LIFE? I THOUGHT YOU MEANT WE'D BE BRINGING IT BACK WITH THE *ANIME*...!
YEAH. WITH THE ANIME.

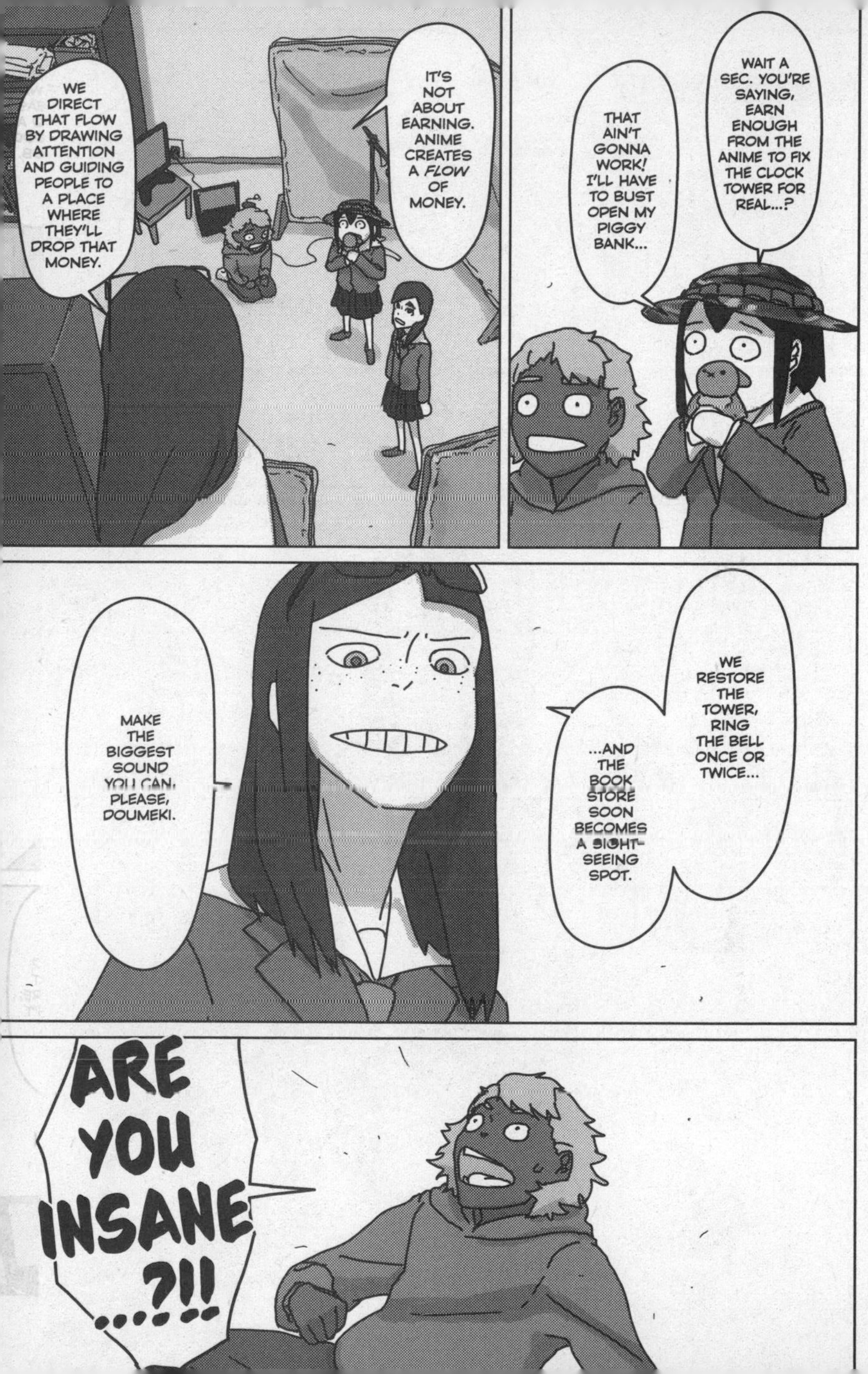
WAIT A SEC. YOU'RE SAYING, EARN ENOUGH FROM THE ANIME TO FIX THE CLOCK TOWER FOR REAL...?
THAT AIN'T GONNA WORK! I'LL HAVE TO BUST OPEN MY PIGGY BANK...
IT'S NOT ABOUT EARNING. ANIME CREATES A *FLOW* OF MONEY.
WE DIRECT THAT FLOW BY DRAWING ATTENTION AND GUIDING PEOPLE TO A PLACE WHERE THEY'LL DROP THAT MONEY.
WE RESTORE THE TOWER, RING THE BELL ONCE OR TWICE...
...AND THE BOOK STORE SOON BECOMES A SIGHT-SEEING SPOT.
MAKE THE BIGGEST SOUND YOU CAN, PLEASE, DOUMEKI.
ARE YOU INSANE...?!!

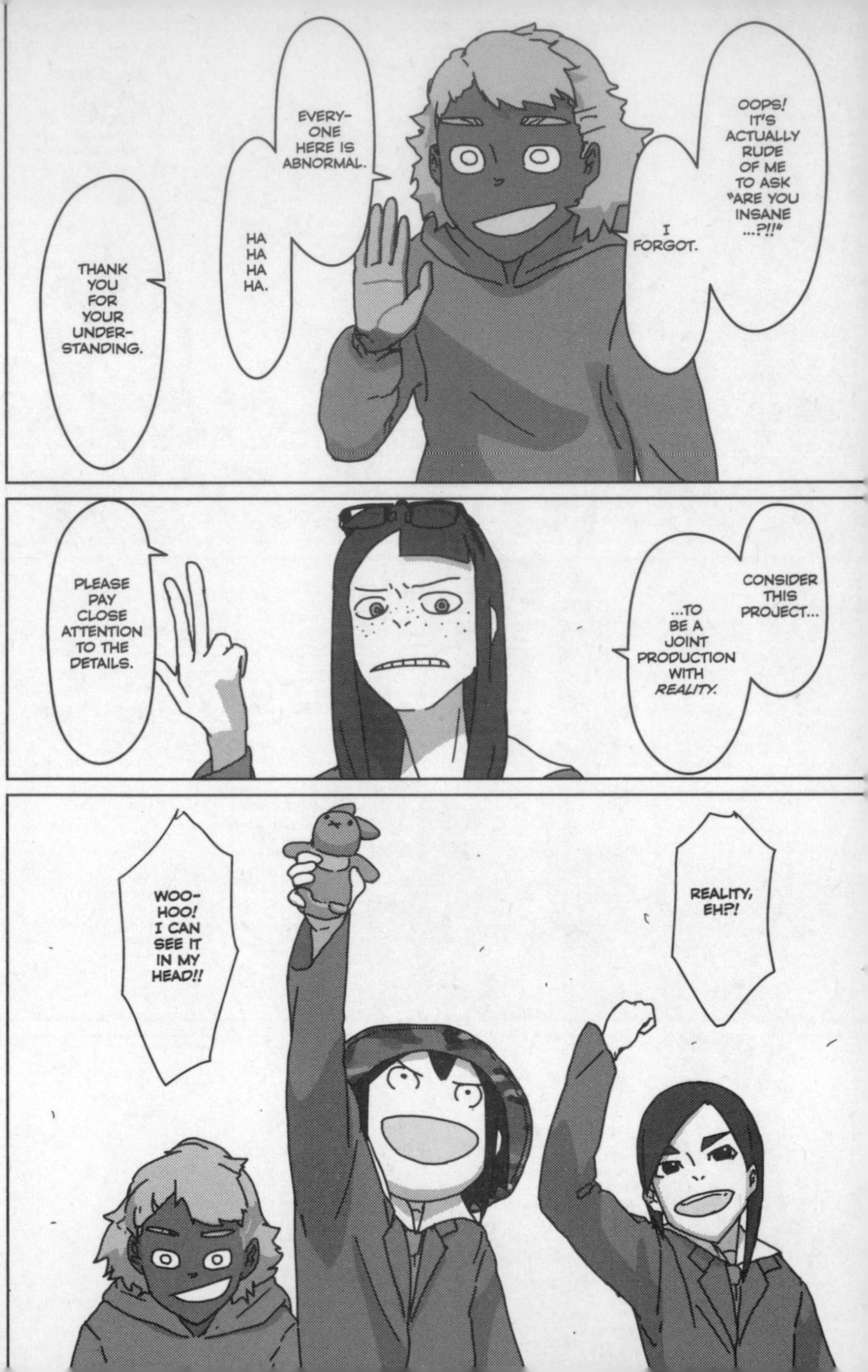
OOPS! IT'S ACTUALLY RUDE OF ME TO ASK "ARE YOU INSANE ...?!"
I FORGOT.
EVERYONE HERE IS ABNORMAL.
HA HA HA HA.
THANK YOU FOR YOUR UNDERSTANDING.
CONSIDER THIS PROJECT...
...TO BE A JOINT PRODUCTION WITH *REALITY*.
PLEASE PAY CLOSE ATTENTION TO THE DETAILS.
REALITY, EH?!
WOO-HOO! I CAN SEE IT IN MY HEAD!!

KEEP YOUR HANDS OFF EIZOUKEN!

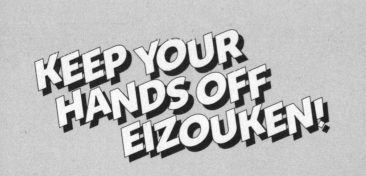

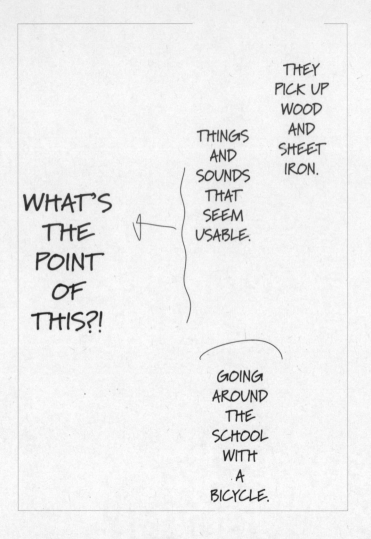

THEY PICK UP WOOD AND SHEET IRON.

THINGS AND SOUNDS THAT SEEM USABLE.

WHAT'S THE POINT OF THIS?!

GOING AROUND THE SCHOOL WITH A BICYCLE.

1

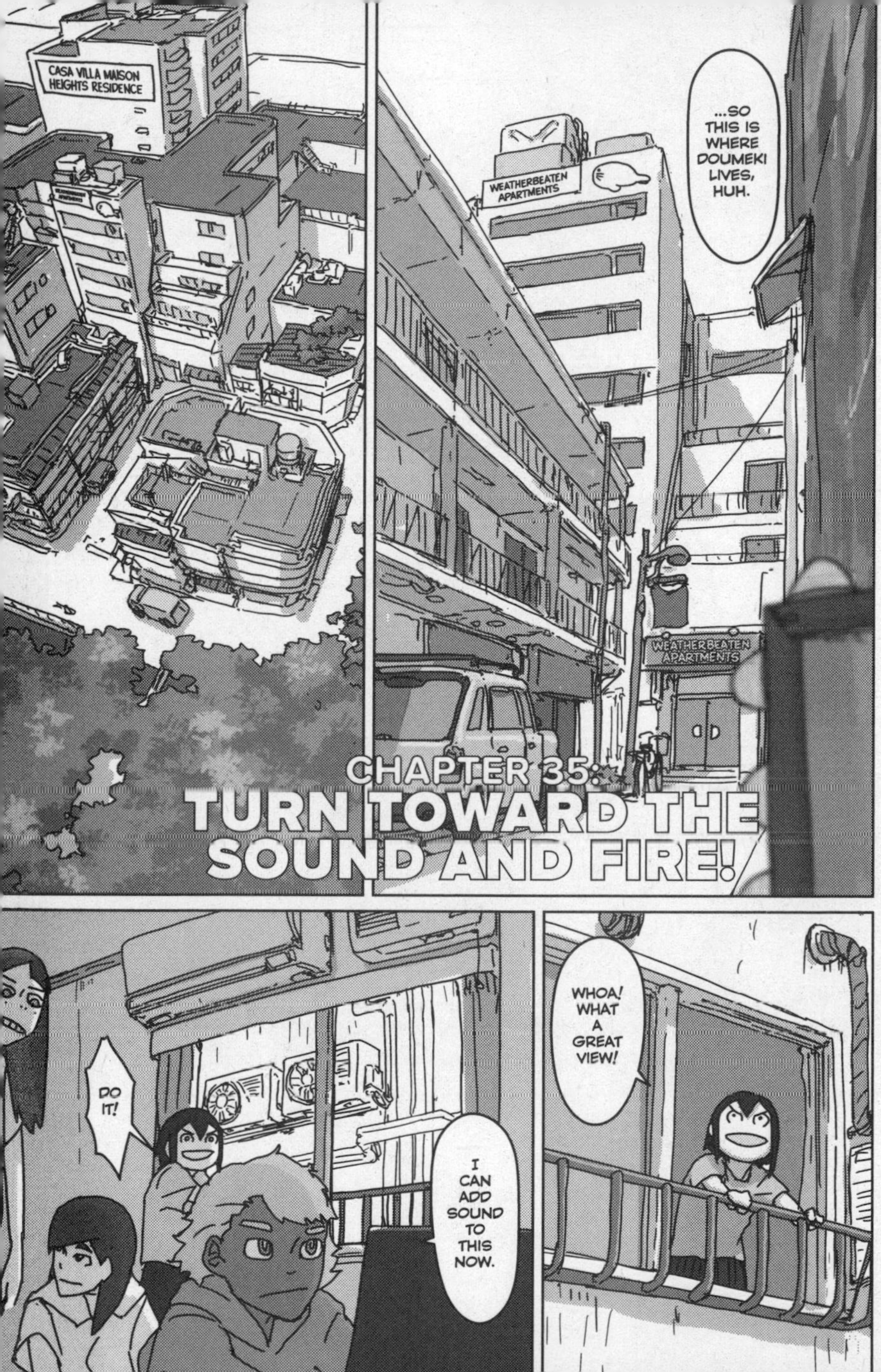
...SO THIS IS WHERE DOUMEKI LIVES, HUH.
WEATHERBEATEN APARTMENTS
WEATHERBEATEN APARTMENTS
CASA VILLA MAISON HEIGHTS RESIDENCE
CHAPTER 35:
TURN TOWARD THE SOUND AND FIRE!
WHOA! WHAT A GREAT VIEW!
I CAN ADD SOUND TO THIS NOW.
DO IT!

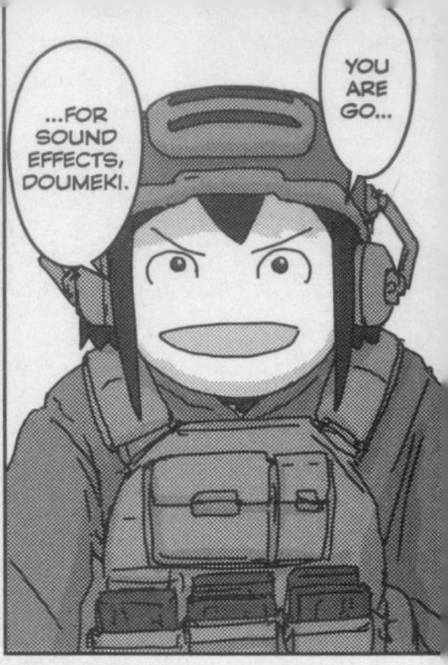
YOU ARE GO...
...FOR SOUND EFFECTS, DOUMEKI.
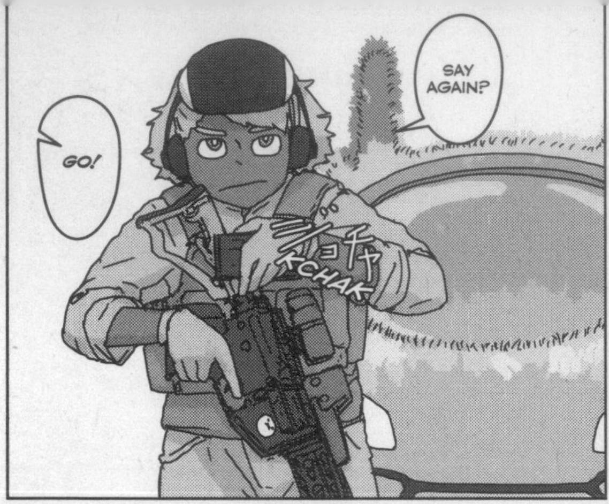
SAY AGAIN?
GO!
KCHAK
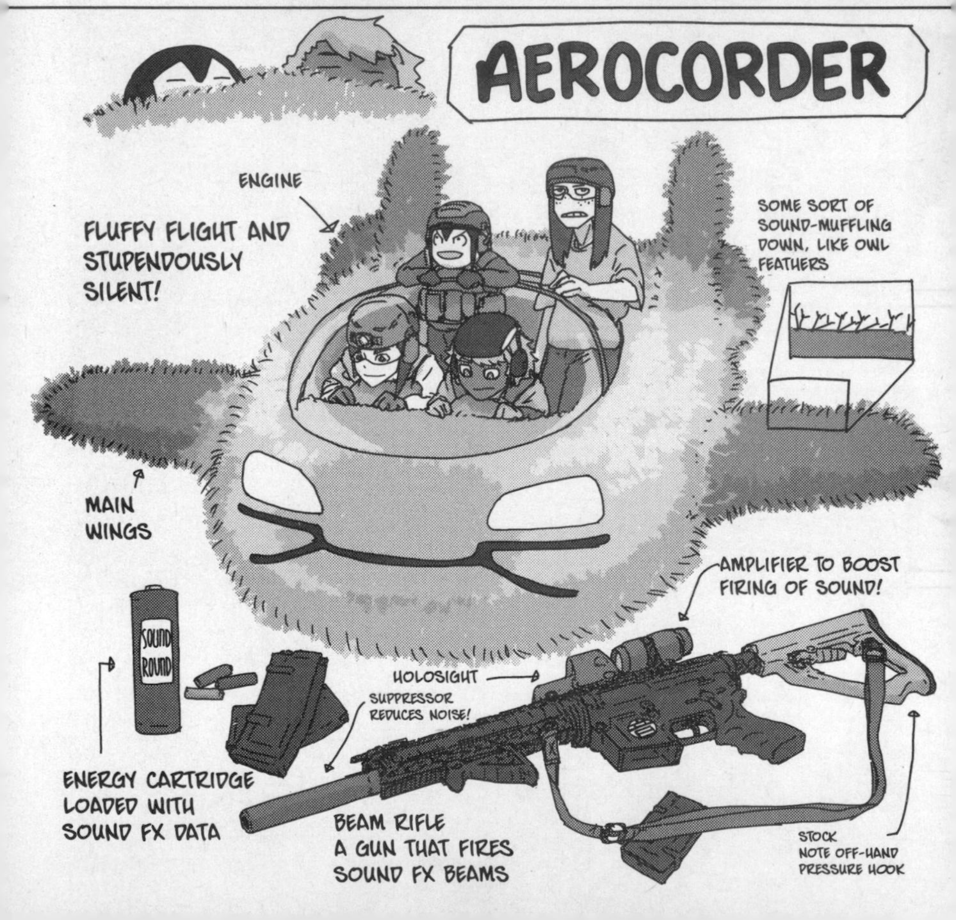
AEROCORDER
SOME SORT OF SOUND-MUFFLING DOWN, LIKE OWL FEATHERS
ENGINE
FLUFFY FLIGHT AND STUPENDOUSLY SILENT!
MAIN WINGS
AMPLIFIER TO BOOST FIRING OF SOUND!
SOUND ROUND
HOLOSIGHT
SUPPRESSOR REDUCES NOISE!
ENERGY CARTRIDGE LOADED WITH SOUND FX DATA
BEAM RIFLE A GUN THAT FIRES SOUND FX BEAMS
STOCK NOTE OFF-HAND PRESSURE HOOK

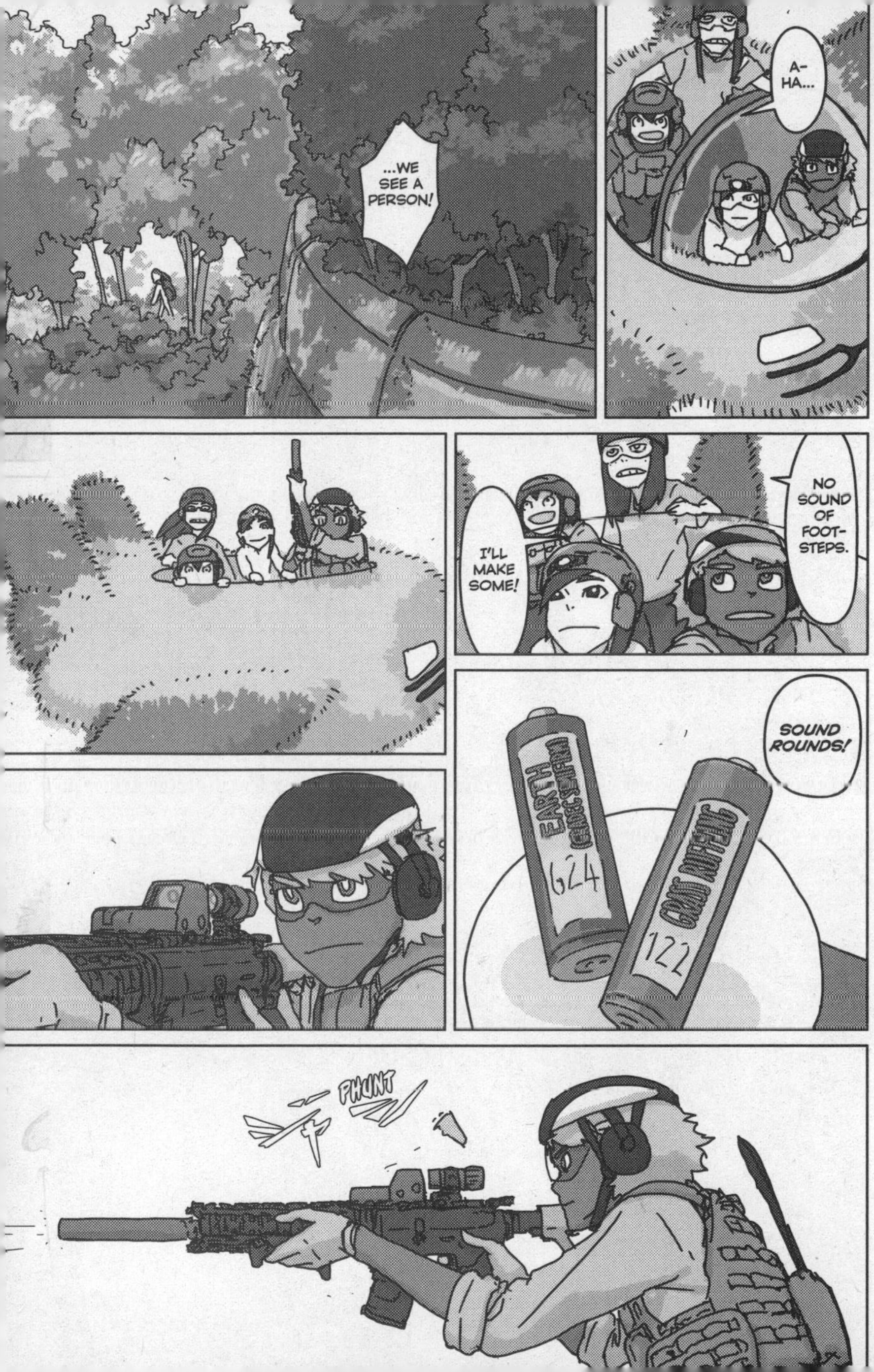
A-HA...
...WE SEE A PERSON!
NO SOUND OF FOOT-STEPS.
I'LL MAKE SOME!
SOUND ROUNDS!
EARTH
624
122
PHUNT

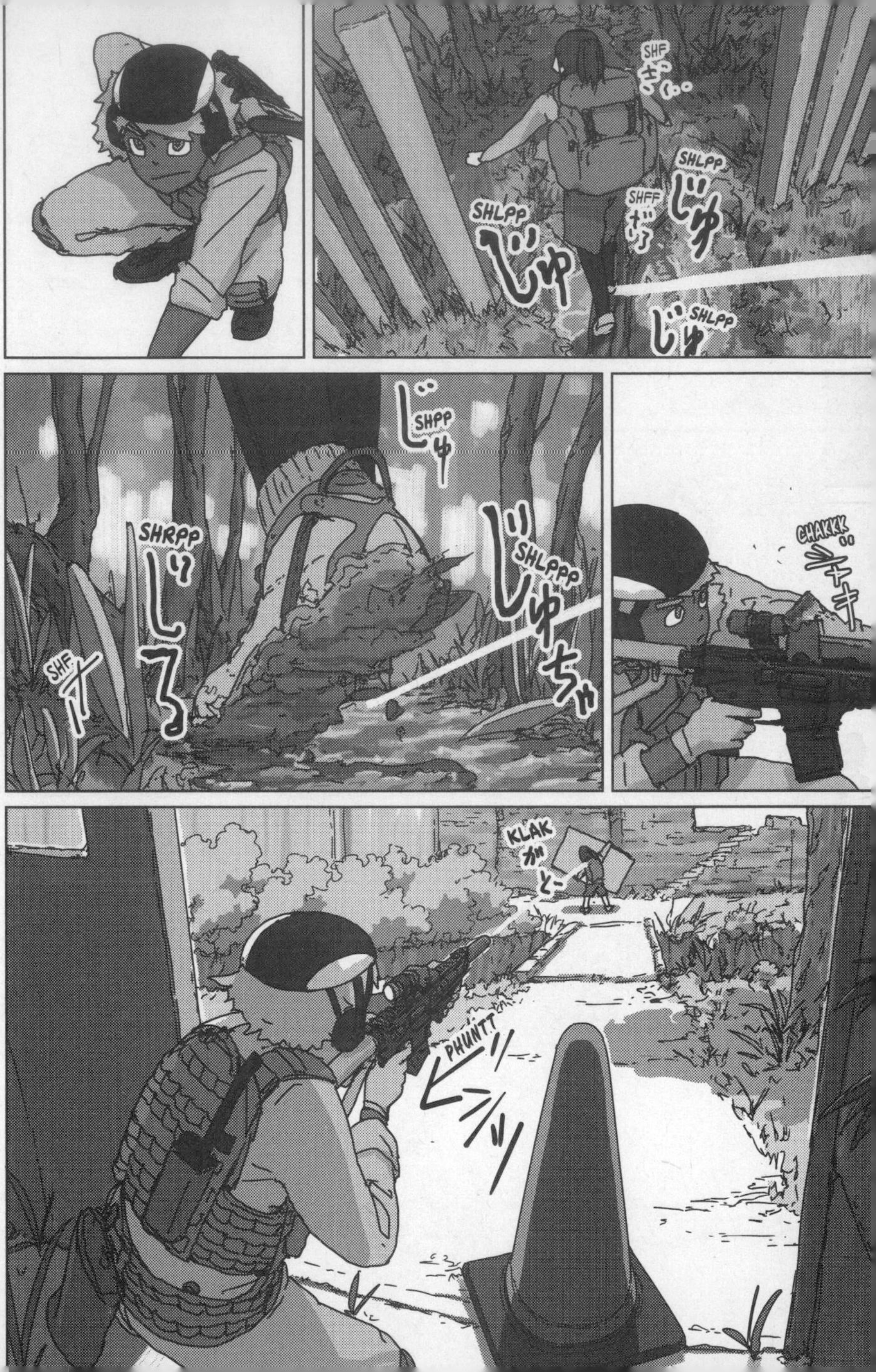

SHF
SHLPP
じゅ
SHFF
SHLPP
じゅ
SHLPP
じゅ
CHAKKK
SHPP
じゅ
SHLPPP
SHRPP
SHF
KLAK
PHUNTT

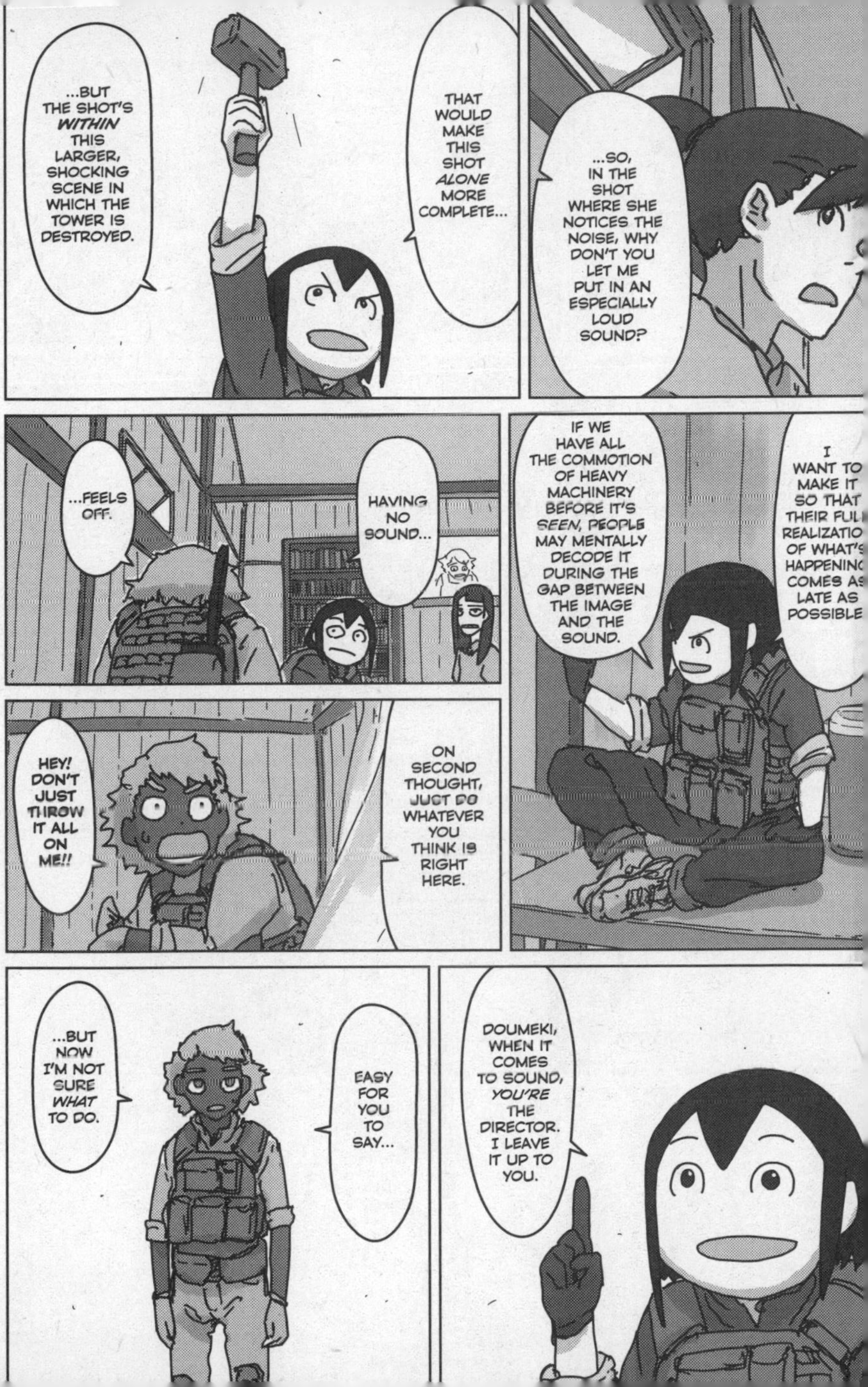
...SO, IN THE SHOT WHERE SHE NOTICES THE NOISE, WHY DON'T YOU LET ME PUT IN AN ESPECIALLY LOUD SOUND?
THAT WOULD MAKE THIS SHOT *ALONE* MORE COMPLETE...
...BUT THE SHOT'S *WITHIN* THIS LARGER, SHOCKING SCENE IN WHICH THE TOWER IS DESTROYED.
I WANT TO MAKE IT SO THAT THEIR FUL REALIZATIO OF WHAT'S HAPPENIN COMES AS LATE AS POSSIBLE
IF WE HAVE ALL THE COMMOTION OF HEAVY MACHINERY BEFORE IT'S *SEEN*, PEOPLE MAY MENTALLY DECODE IT DURING THE GAP BETWEEN THE IMAGE AND THE SOUND.
HAVING NO SOUND...
...FEELS OFF.
ON SECOND THOUGHT, JUST DO WHATEVER YOU THINK IS RIGHT HERE.
HEY! DON'T JUST THROW IT ALL ON ME!!
DOUMEKI, WHEN IT COMES TO SOUND, *YOU'RE* THE DIRECTOR. I LEAVE IT UP TO YOU.
EASY FOR YOU TO SAY...
...BUT NOW I'M NOT SURE *WHAT* TO DO.

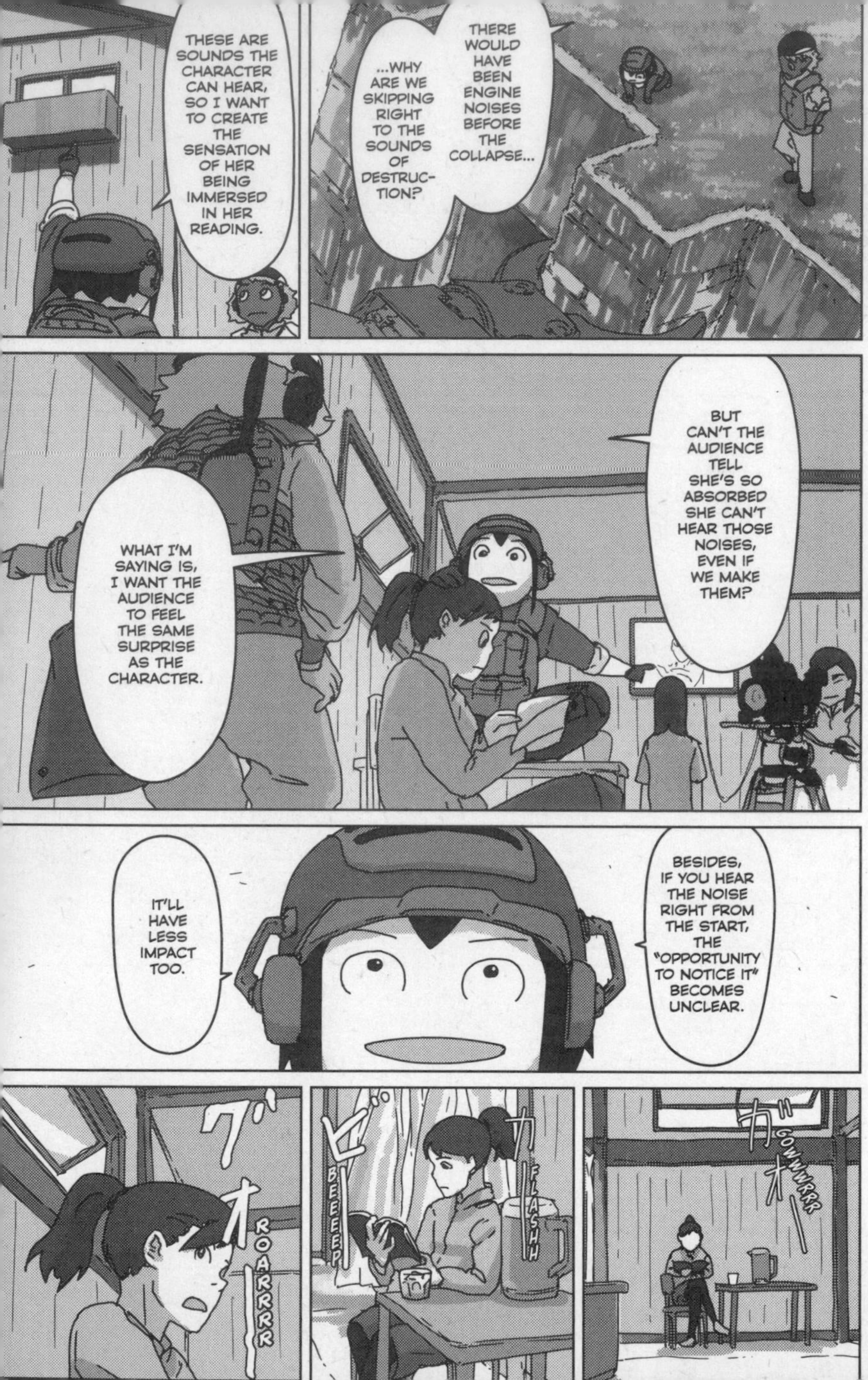
THERE WOULD HAVE BEEN ENGINE NOISES BEFORE THE COLLAPSE...
...WHY ARE WE SKIPPING RIGHT TO THE SOUNDS OF DESTRUC- TION?
THESE ARE SOUNDS THE CHARACTER CAN HEAR, SO I WANT TO CREATE THE SENSATION OF HER BEING IMMERSED IN HER READING.
BUT CAN'T THE AUDIENCE TELL SHE'S SO ABSORBED SHE CAN'T HEAR THOSE NOISES, EVEN IF WE MAKE THEM?
WHAT I'M SAYING IS, I WANT THE AUDIENCE TO FEEL THE SAME SURPRISE AS THE CHARACTER.
BESIDES, IF YOU HEAR THE NOISE RIGHT FROM THE START, THE "OPPORTUNITY TO NOTICE IT" BECOMES UNCLEAR.
IT'LL HAVE LESS IMPACT TOO.
GOWWRRR
FLASHH
BEEEEP
ROARRRR

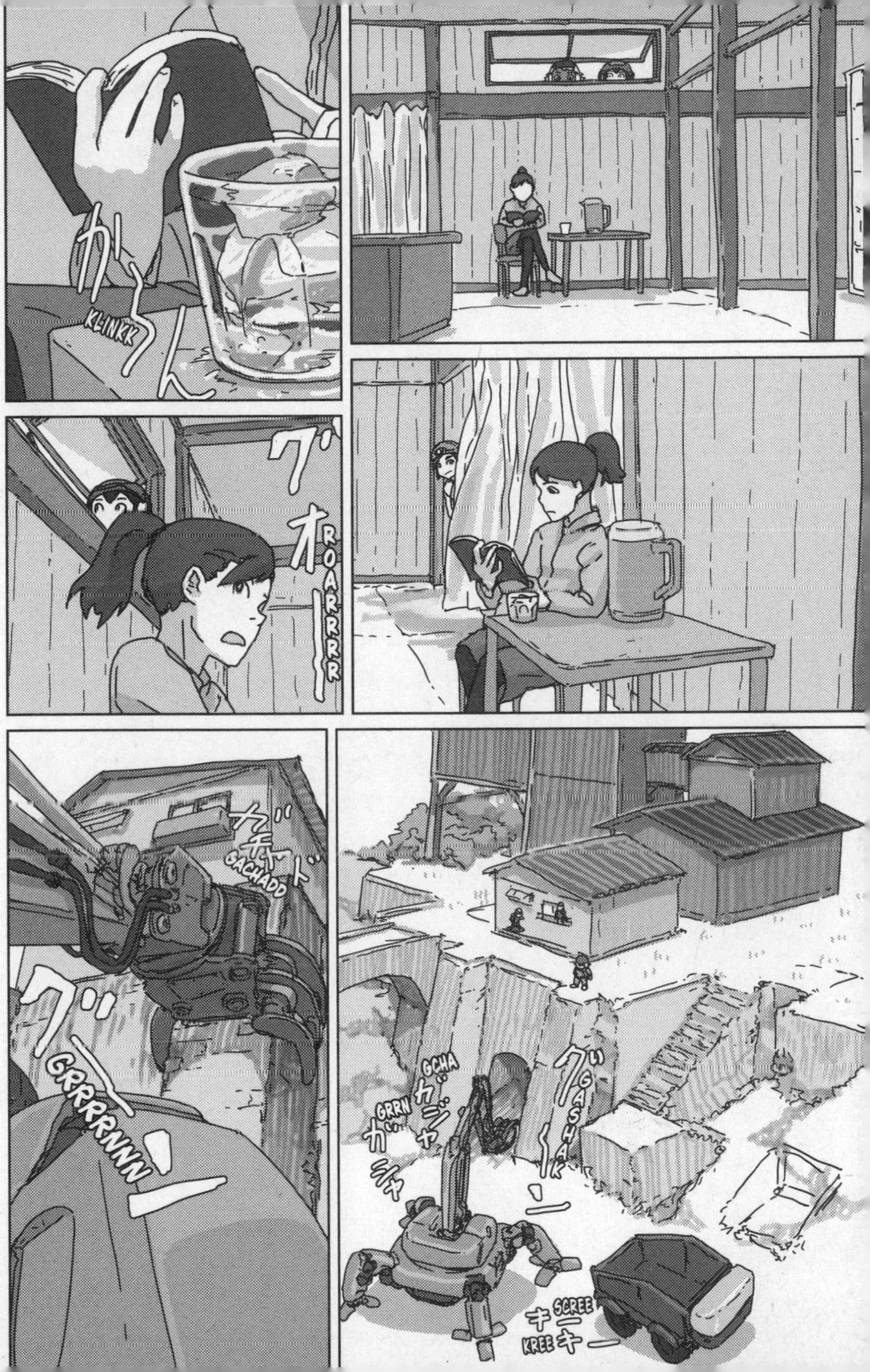
からん
KLINKK
グオー
ROARRRR
GCHA
ガジャ
GRRN
カシャ
GASHAK
SCREE
キー
KREE
キー
ガチャド
SACHADD
グー
GRRRRNNN

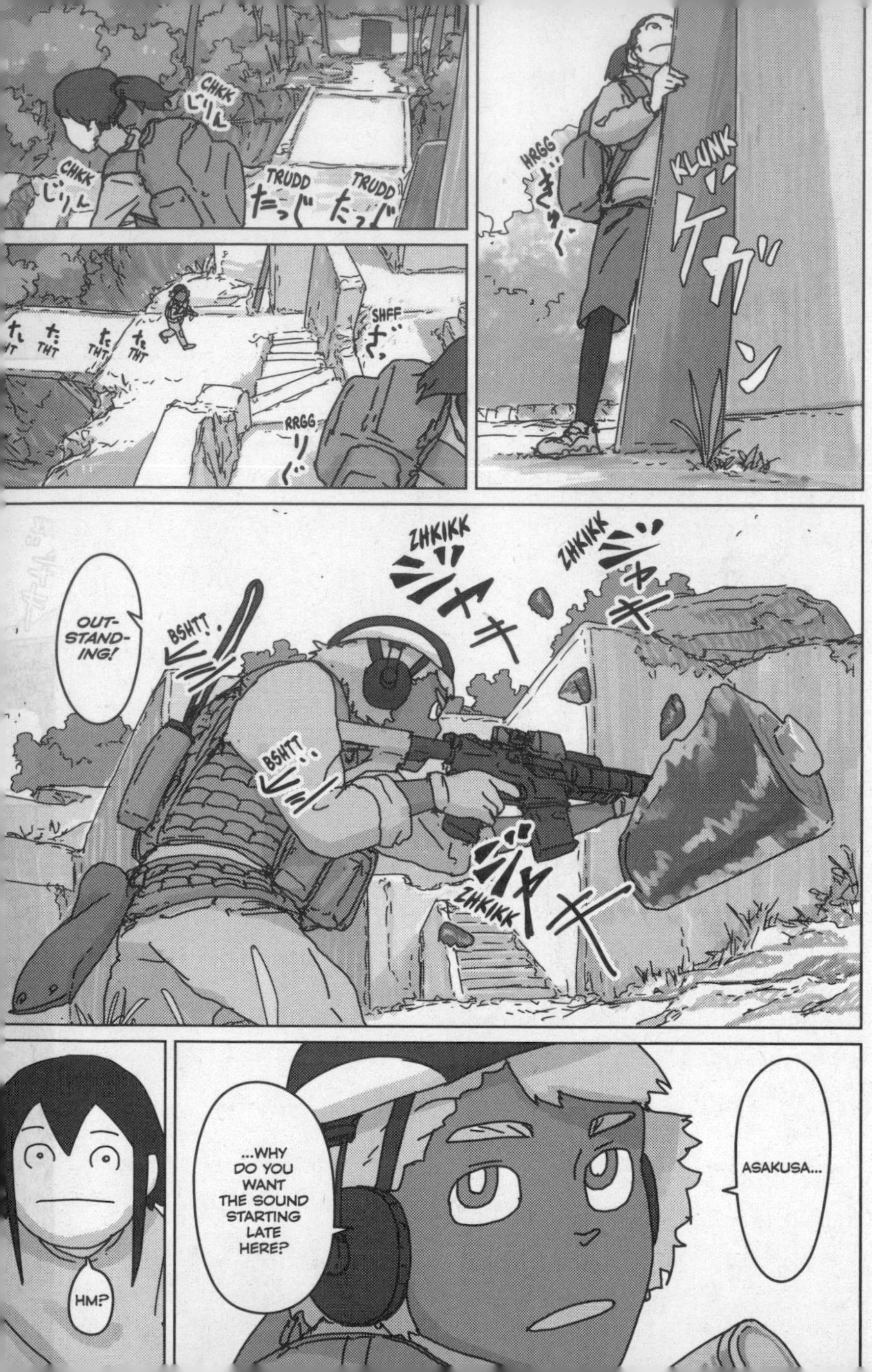
KLUNK
HRGG
CHKK
CHKK
TRUDD
TRUDD
SHFF
THT
THT
THT
THT
RRGG
ZHKIKK
ZHKIKK
OUT-STANDING!
BSHTT!
BSHTT!
ZHKIKK
ASAKUSA...
...WHY DO YOU WANT THE SOUND STARTING LATE HERE?
HM?

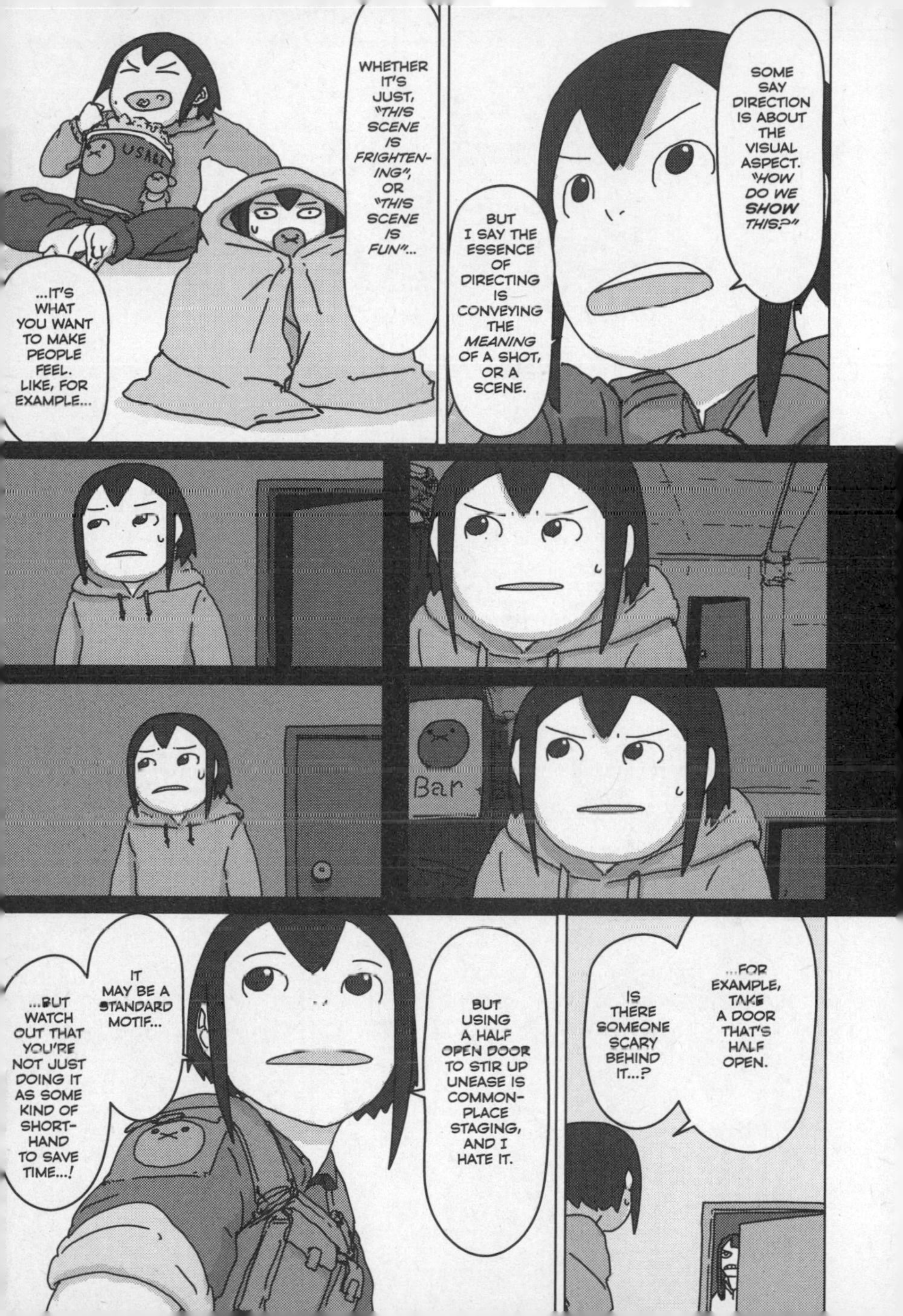
SOME SAY DIRECTION IS ABOUT THE VISUAL ASPECT. *"HOW DO WE* **SHOW** *THIS?"*
BUT I SAY THE ESSENCE OF DIRECTING IS CONVEYING THE *MEANING* OF A SHOT, OR A SCENE.
WHETHER IT'S JUST, *"THIS SCENE IS FRIGHTENING"*, OR *"THIS SCENE IS FUN"*...
...IT'S WHAT YOU WANT TO MAKE PEOPLE FEEL. LIKE, FOR EXAMPLE...
Bar
...FOR EXAMPLE, TAKE A DOOR THAT'S HALF OPEN.
IS THERE SOMEONE SCARY BEHIND IT...?
BUT USING A HALF OPEN DOOR TO STIR UP UNEASE IS COMMONPLACE STAGING, AND I HATE IT.
IT MAY BE A STANDARD MOTIF...
...BUT WATCH OUT THAT YOU'RE NOT JUST DOING IT AS SOME KIND OF SHORTHAND TO SAVE TIME...!

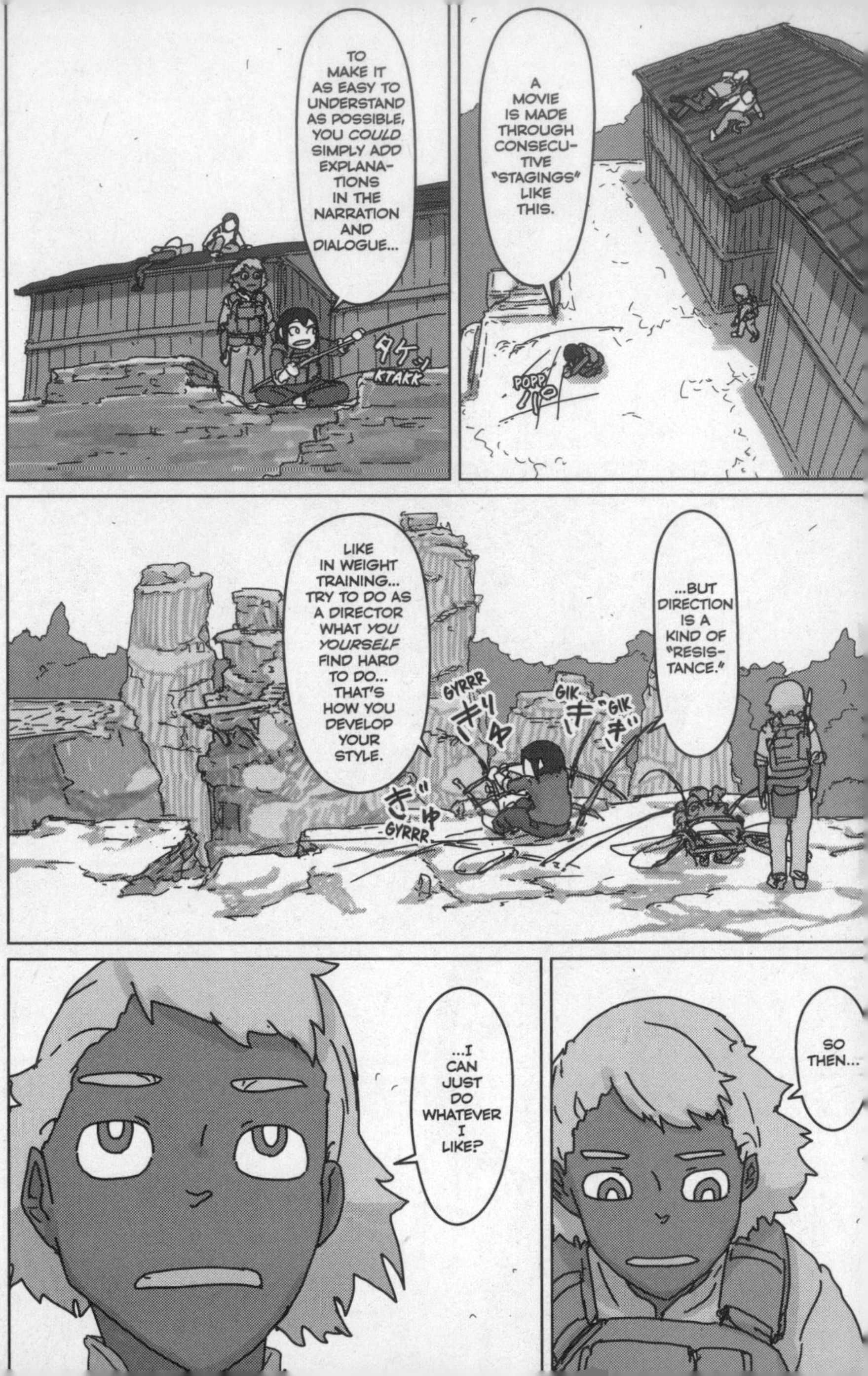
A MOVIE IS MADE THROUGH CONSECUTIVE "STAGINGS" LIKE THIS.
POPP
TO MAKE IT AS EASY TO UNDERSTAND AS POSSIBLE, YOU *COULD* SIMPLY ADD EXPLANATIONS IN THE NARRATION AND DIALOGUE...
KTAKK
...BUT DIRECTION IS A KIND OF "RESISTANCE."
GIK
GIK
LIKE IN WEIGHT TRAINING... TRY TO DO AS A DIRECTOR WHAT *YOU YOURSELF* FIND HARD TO DO... THAT'S HOW YOU DEVELOP YOUR STYLE.
GYRRR
GYRRR
SO THEN...
...I CAN JUST DO WHATEVER I LIKE?

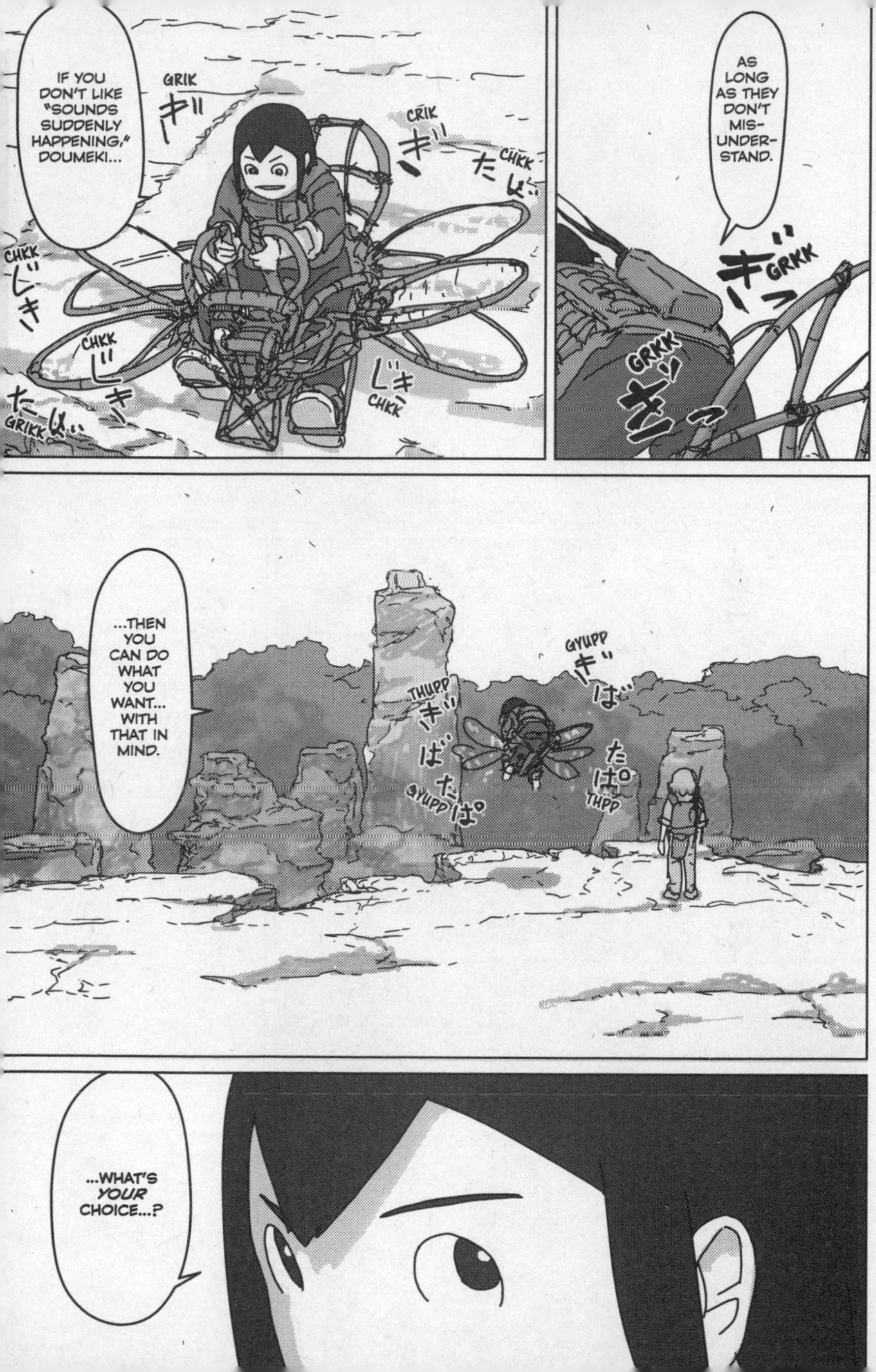
AS LONG AS THEY DON'T MIS-UNDER-STAND.
GRKK
GRKK
IF YOU DON'T LIKE "SOUNDS SUDDENLY HAPPENING," DOUMEKI...
GRIK
CRIK
CHKK
CHKK
CHKK
CHKK
GRIKK
...THEN YOU CAN DO WHAT YOU WANT... WITH THAT IN MIND.
GYUPP
THPP
GYUPP
THPP
...WHAT'S *YOUR* CHOICE...?

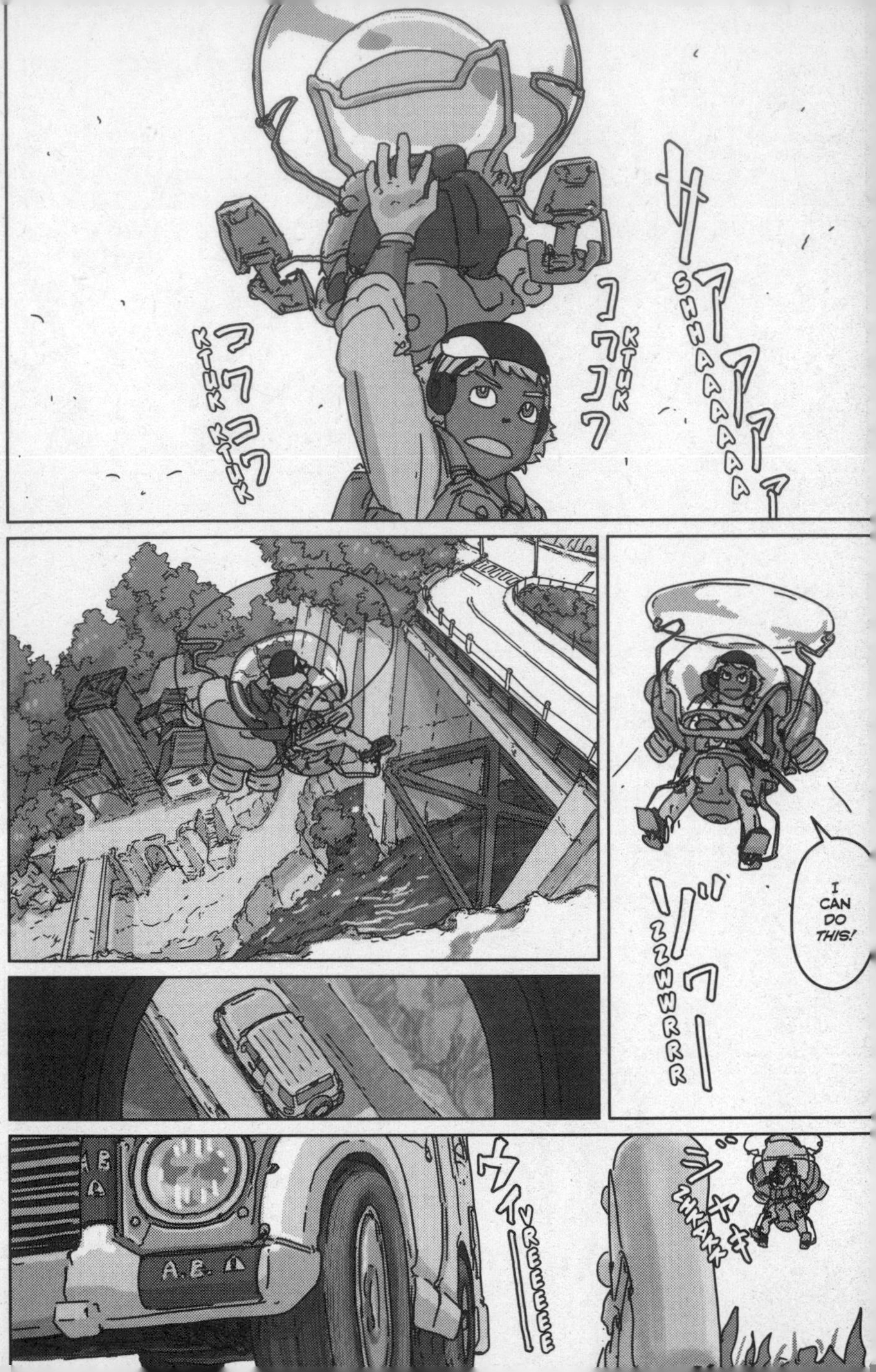
SHHAAAAAAA
KTUK
KTUK KTUK KTUK
I CAN DO *THIS!*
ZZWWRRR
ZHKAKK
VREEEEEE

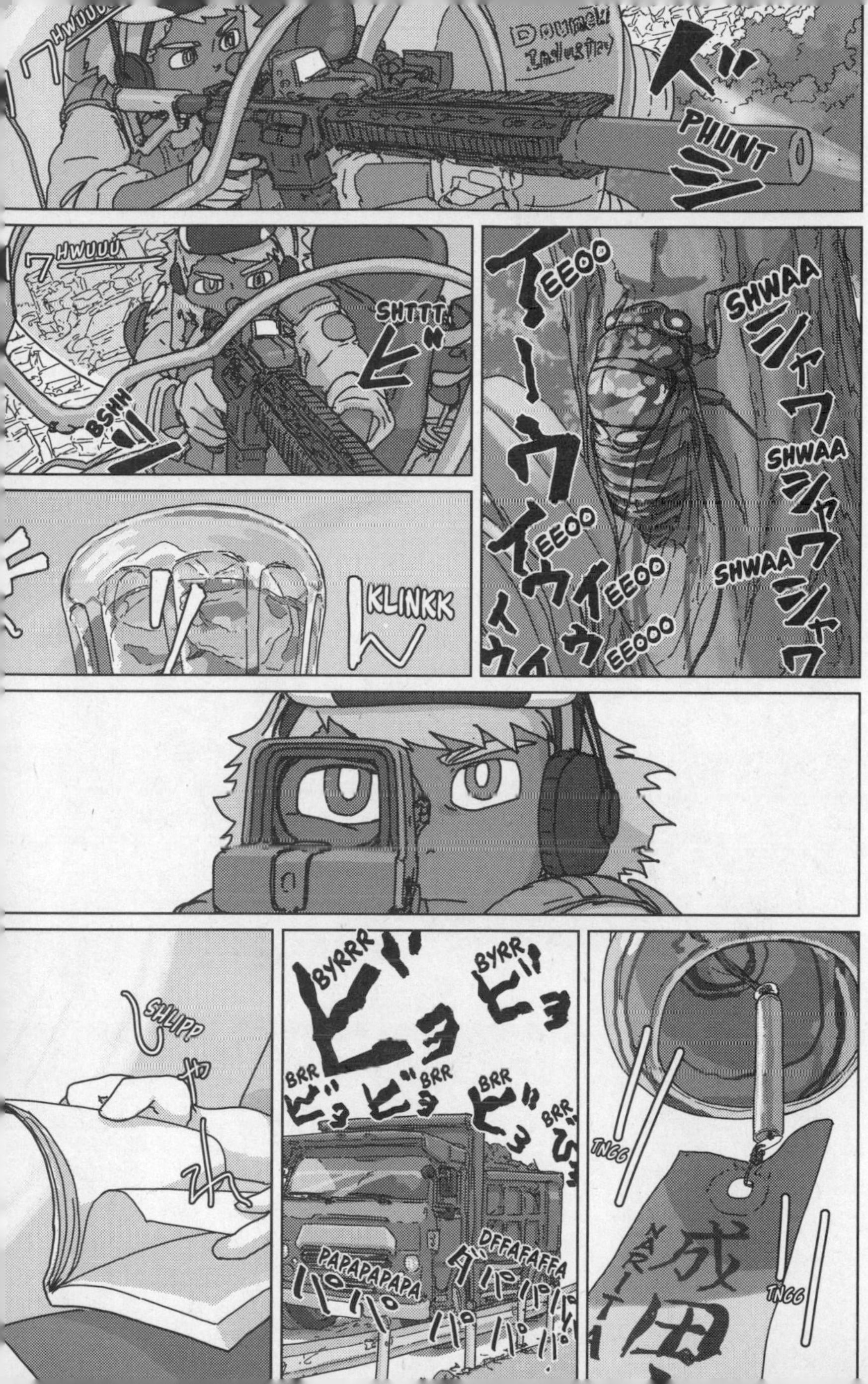
HWUUU
ズッ
PHUNT
EEOO
SHWAA
シャワ
SHWAA
シャワ
EEOO
EEOO
SHWAA
EEOOO
HWUUU
SHTTT
ビッ
BSHH
KLINKK
TNGG
NARITA
成田
TNGG
BYRRR
ビョ
BYRR
ビョ
BRR
ビョ
BRR
ビョ
BRR
ビョ
BRR
ビョ
PAPAPAPAPA
パパ
DFFAFAFFA
SHLIPP

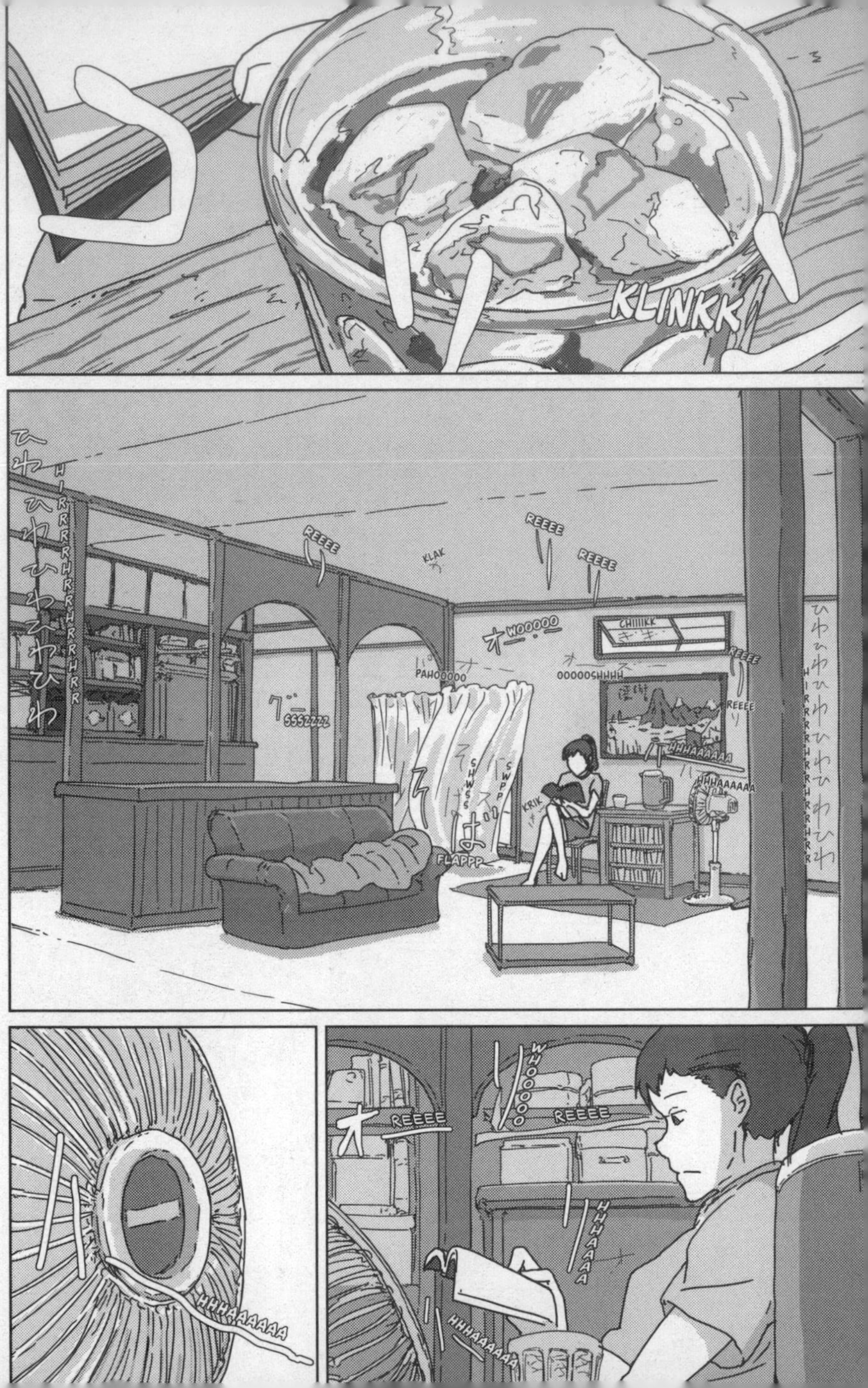
KLINKK
REEEE
HRRRRHRRRHRRRRHRR
REEEE
REEEE
CHIIIIKK
WOOOOO
OOOOOSHHHH
KLAK
REEEE
PAHOOOOO
HHHAAAAAAA
HHHAAAAAAA
HRRRRHRRRRHRRRHRR
SSSZZZZ
SWPP
SHWSS
KRIK
FLAPPP
REEEE
WHOOOOOO
REEEE
HHHAAAA
HHHAAAAAAA
HHHAAAAAAA

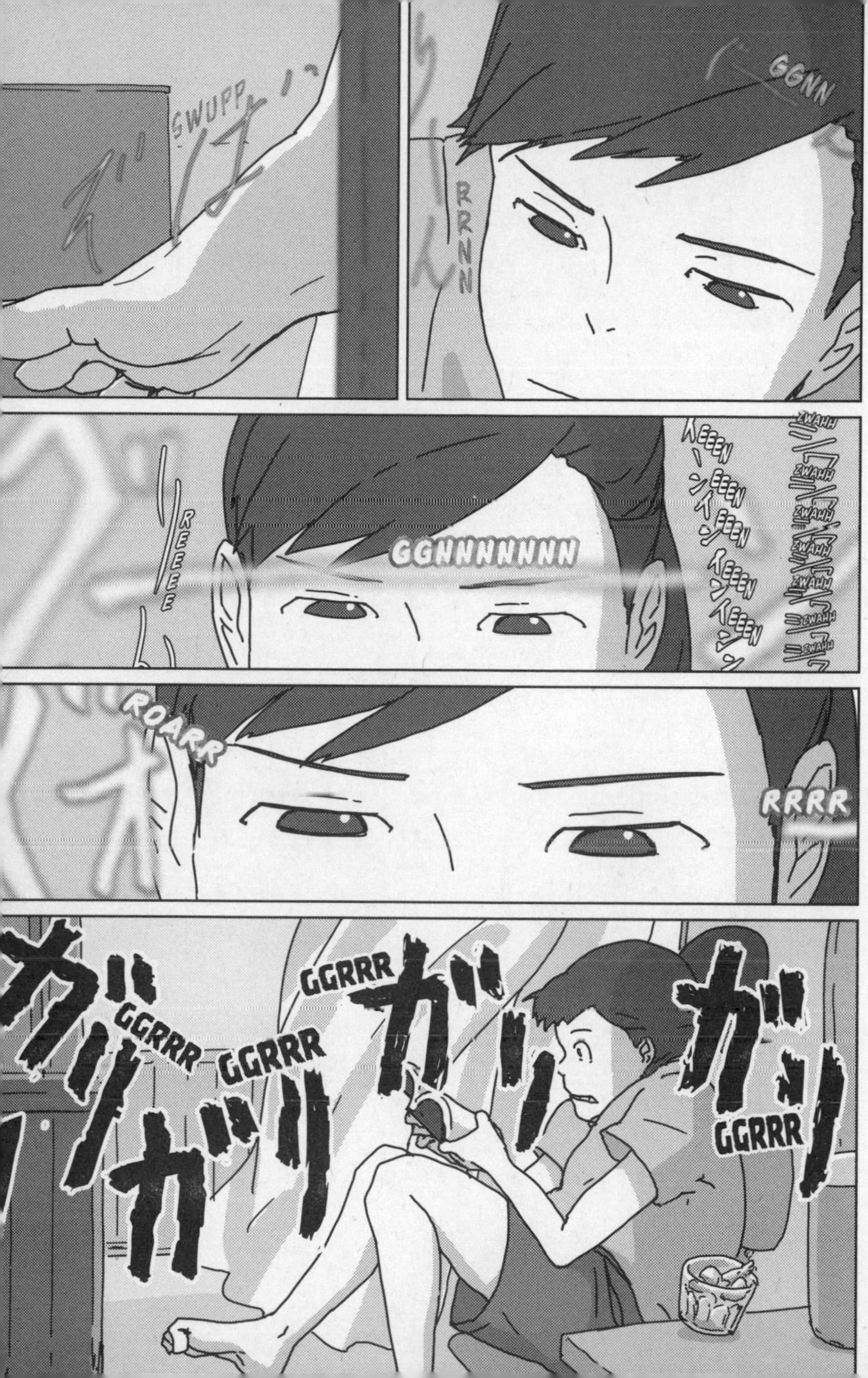
GGNN
RRNN
SWUPP
ZWAHH ZWAHH ZWAHH ZWAHH ZWAHH ZWAHH ZWAHH
KEEEN EEEN EEEN KEEEN KEEEN
GGNNNNNNNN
REEEE
RRRR
ROARR
GGRRR
ガリガリ
GGRRR
GGRRR
ガリガリ
GGRRR

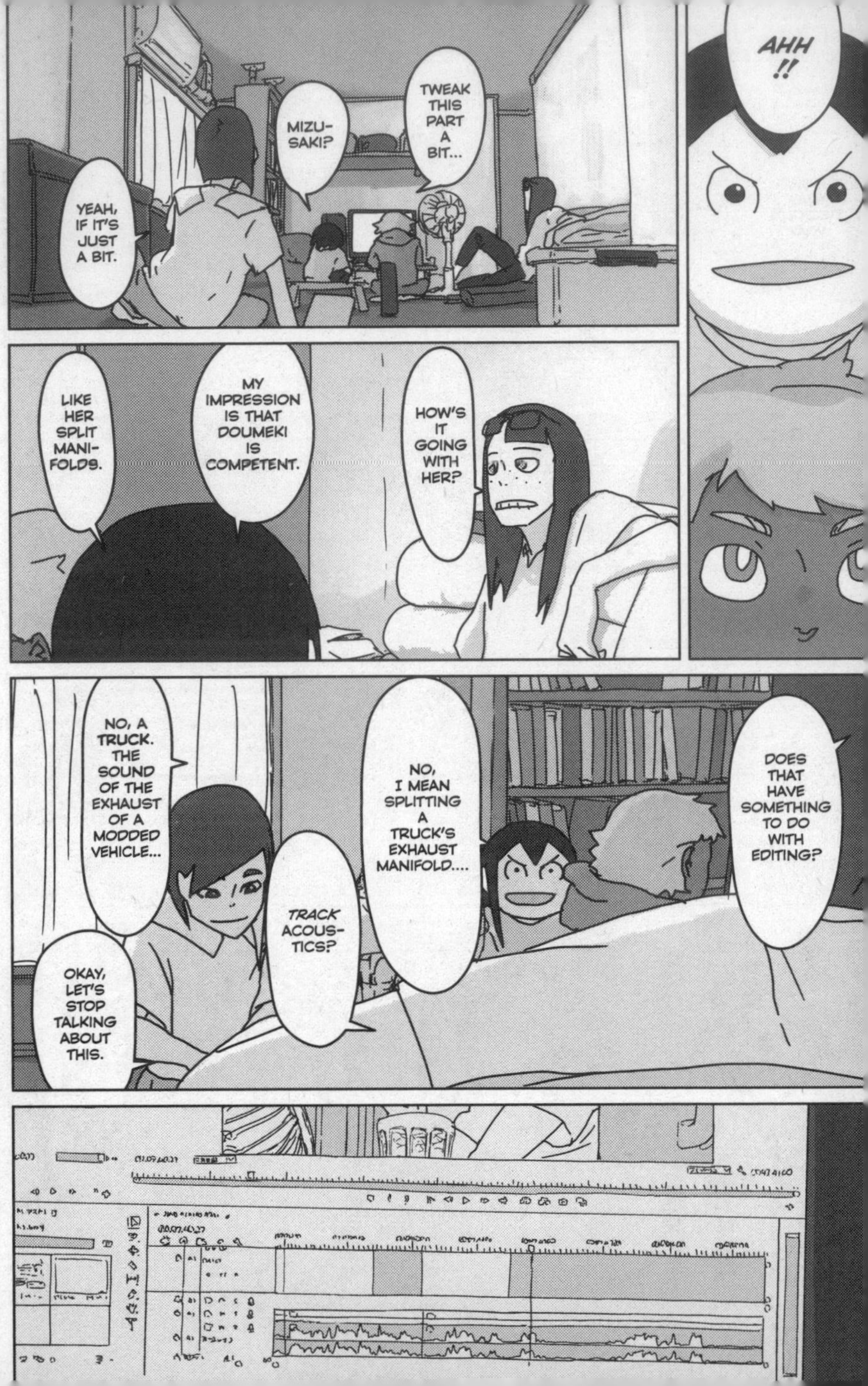
AHH!!
TWEAK THIS PART A BIT...
MIZU-SAKI?
YEAH, IF IT'S JUST A BIT.
HOW'S IT GOING WITH HER?
MY IMPRESSION IS THAT DOUMEKI IS COMPETENT.
LIKE HER SPLIT MANI-FOLDS.
DOES THAT HAVE SOMETHING TO DO WITH EDITING?
NO, I MEAN SPLITTING A TRUCK'S EXHAUST MANIFOLD....
TRACK ACOUS-TICS?
NO, A TRUCK. THE SOUND OF THE EXHAUST OF A MODDED VEHICLE...
OKAY, LET'S STOP TALKING ABOUT THIS.

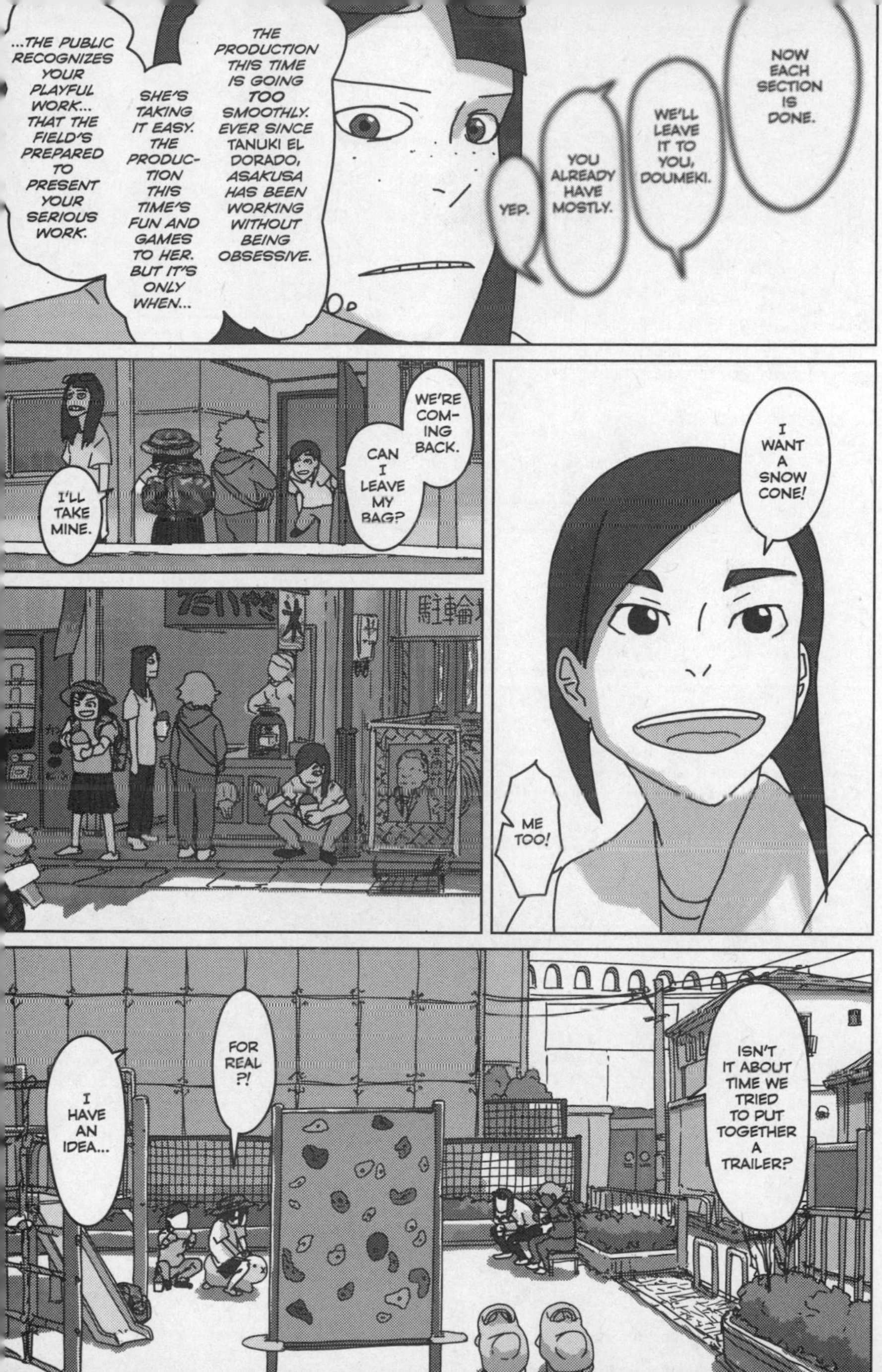
NOW EACH SECTION IS DONE.
WE'LL LEAVE IT TO YOU, DOUMEKI.
YOU ALREADY HAVE MOSTLY.
YEP.
THE PRODUCTION THIS TIME IS GOING TOO SMOOTHLY. EVER SINCE TANUKI EL DORADO, ASAKUSA HAS BEEN WORKING WITHOUT BEING OBSESSIVE.
SHE'S TAKING IT EASY. THE PRODUCTION THIS TIME'S FUN AND GAMES TO HER. BUT IT'S ONLY WHEN...
...THE PUBLIC RECOGNIZES YOUR PLAYFUL WORK... THAT THE FIELD'S PREPARED TO PRESENT YOUR SERIOUS WORK.
I WANT A SNOW CONE!
ME TOO!
WE'RE COMING BACK.
CAN I LEAVE MY BAG?
I'LL TAKE MINE.
ISN'T IT ABOUT TIME WE TRIED TO PUT TOGETHER A TRAILER?
FOR REAL?!
I HAVE AN IDEA...

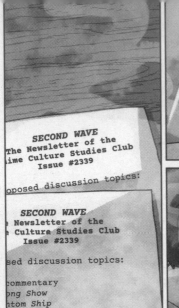

SECOND WAVE
The Newsletter of the
ime Culture Studies Club
Issue #2339

oposed discussion topics:

SECOND WAVE
e Newsletter of the
Culture Studies Club
Issue #2339

sed discussion topics:

commentary
ng Show
ntom Ship
ll works)

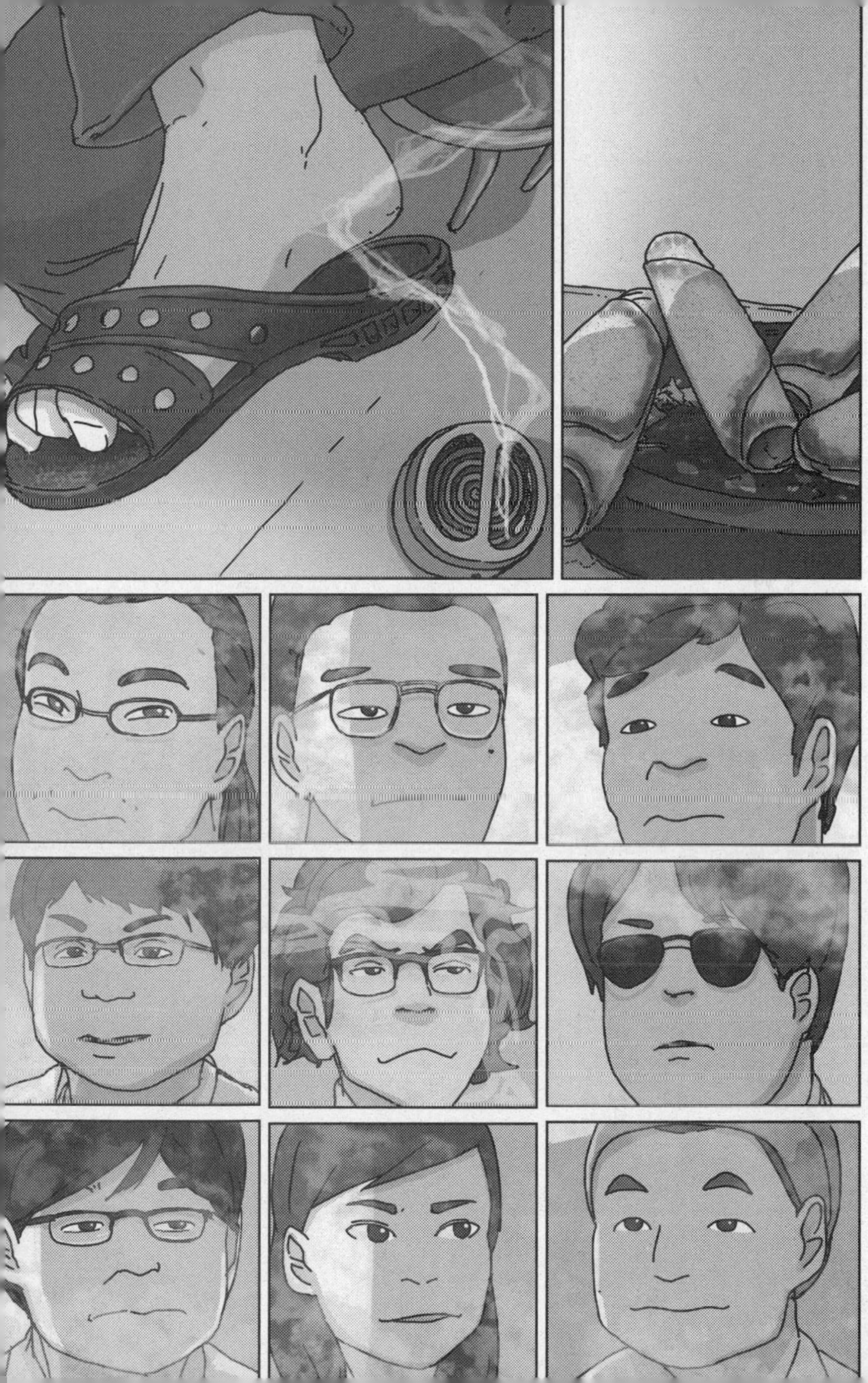

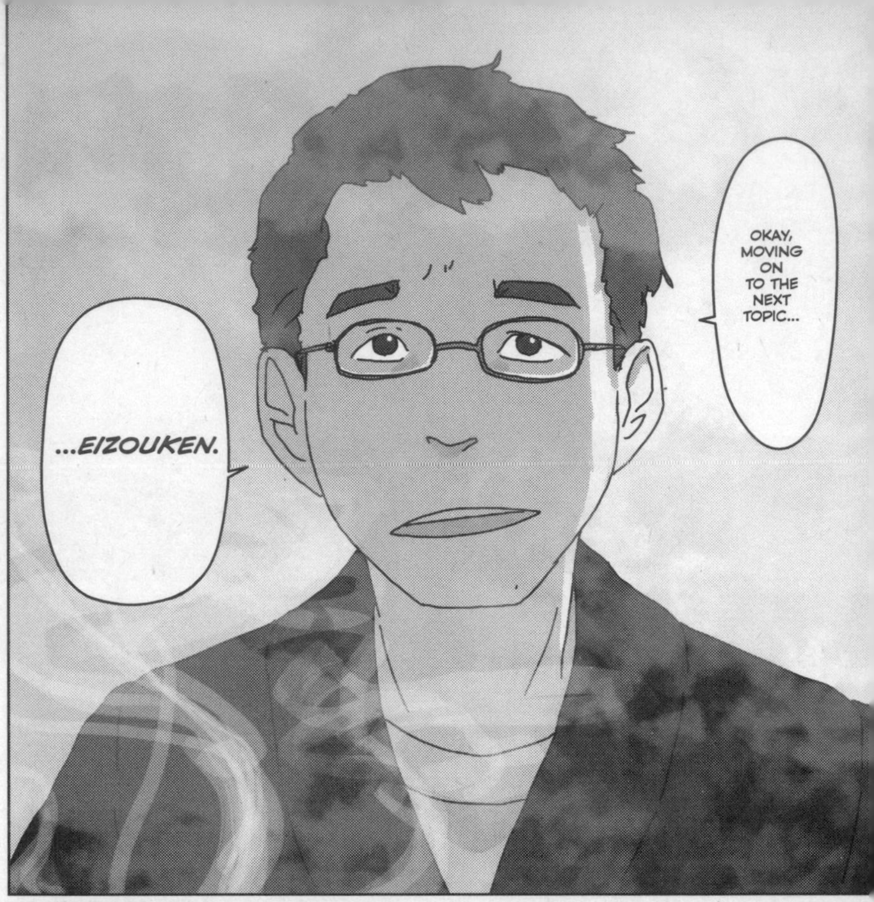
OKAY, MOVING ON TO THE NEXT TOPIC...
...EIZOUKEN.

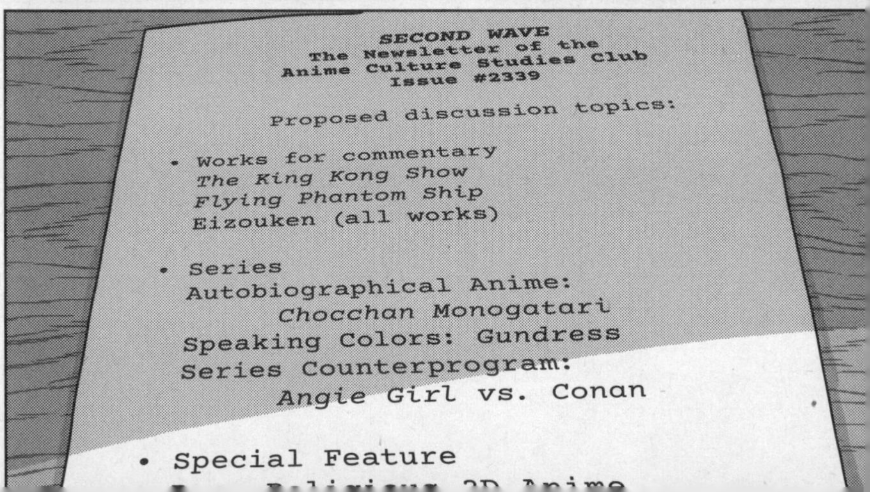
SECOND WAVE
The Newsletter of the
Anime Culture Studies Club
Issue #2339
Proposed discussion topics:
• Works for commentary
The King Kong Show
Flying Phantom Ship
Eizouken (all works)
• Series
Autobiographical Anime:
Chocchan Monogatari
Speaking Colors: Gundress
Series Counterprogram:
Angie Girl vs. Conan
• Special Feature

KEEP YOUR HANDS OFF EIZOUKEN!

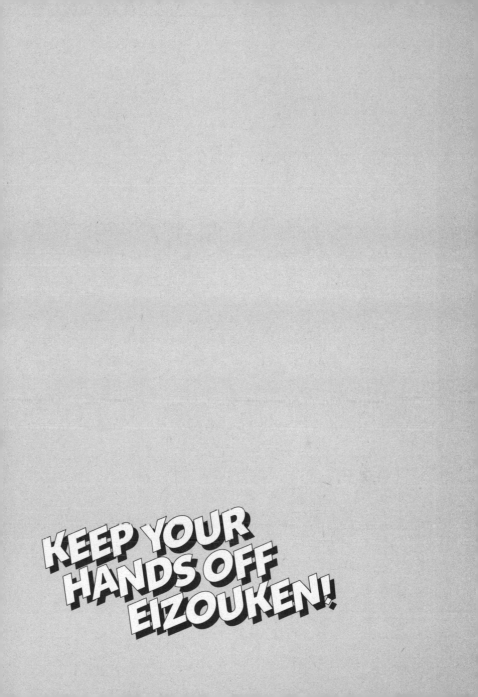

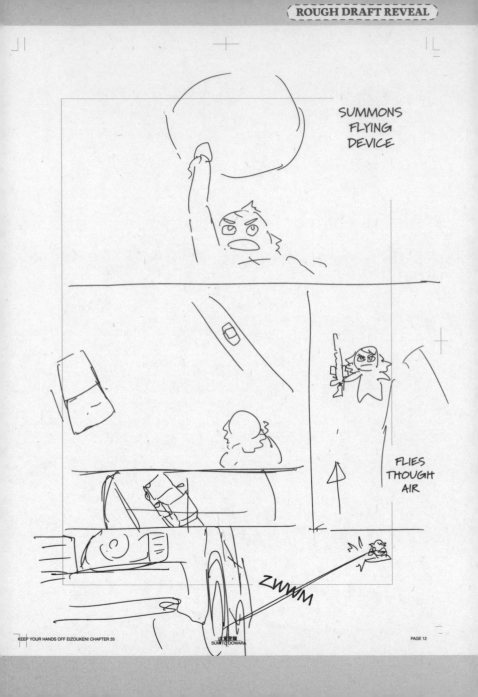

SUMMONS
FLYING
DEVICE

FLIES
THOUGH
AIR

ZWWM

CHAPTER 36: PREPARE FOR SCREENING

Q: How would you describe your normal thought process?

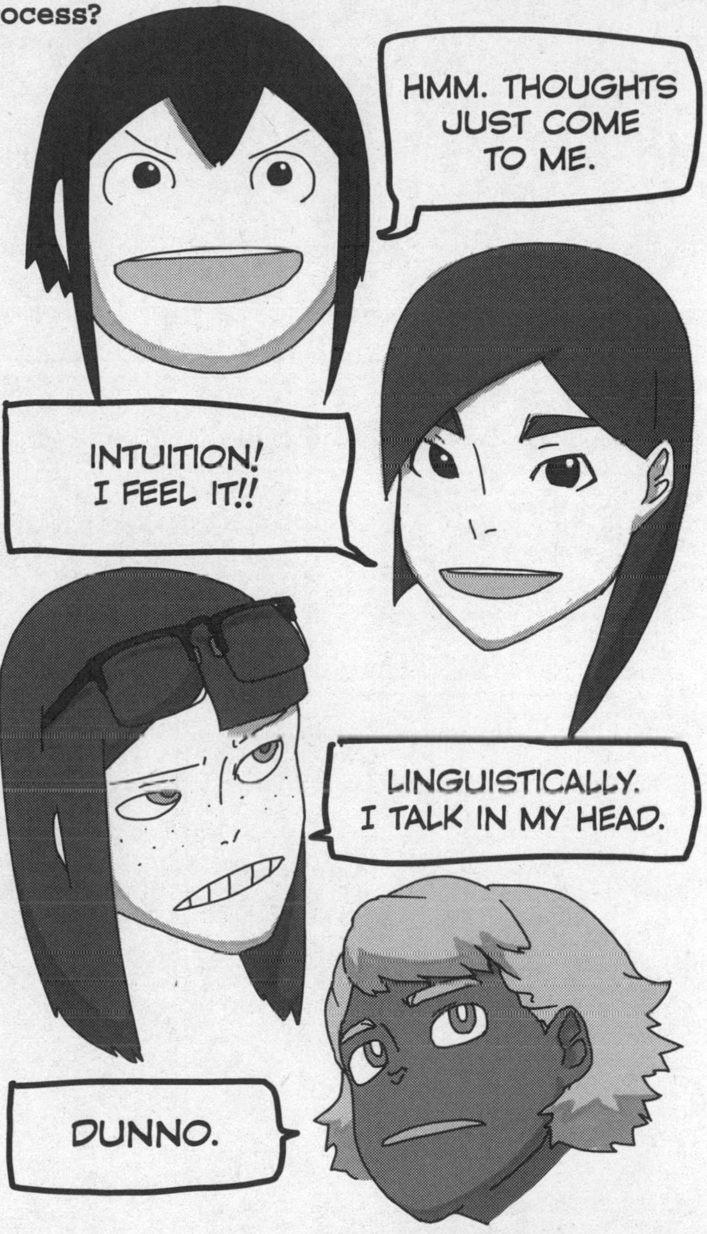
HMM. THOUGHTS JUST COME TO ME.
INTUITION! I FEEL IT!!
LINGUISTICALLY. I TALK IN MY HEAD.
DUNNO.

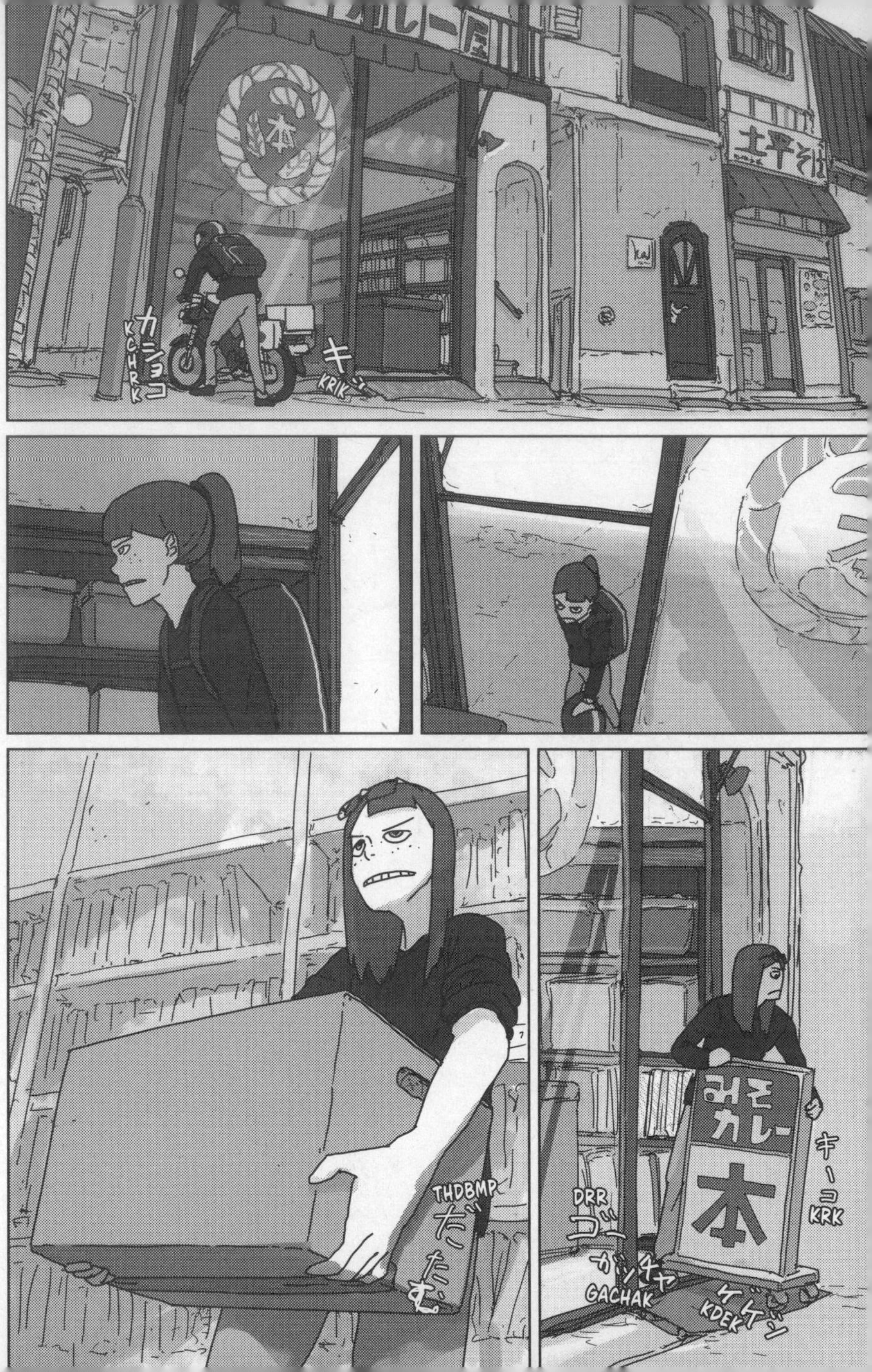
カショコ
KCHRK
キ
KRIK
キーコ
KRK
DRR
ゴー
みそ
カレー
本
ガッチャ
GACHAK
ゲゲン
KDEK
THDBMP
だたむ

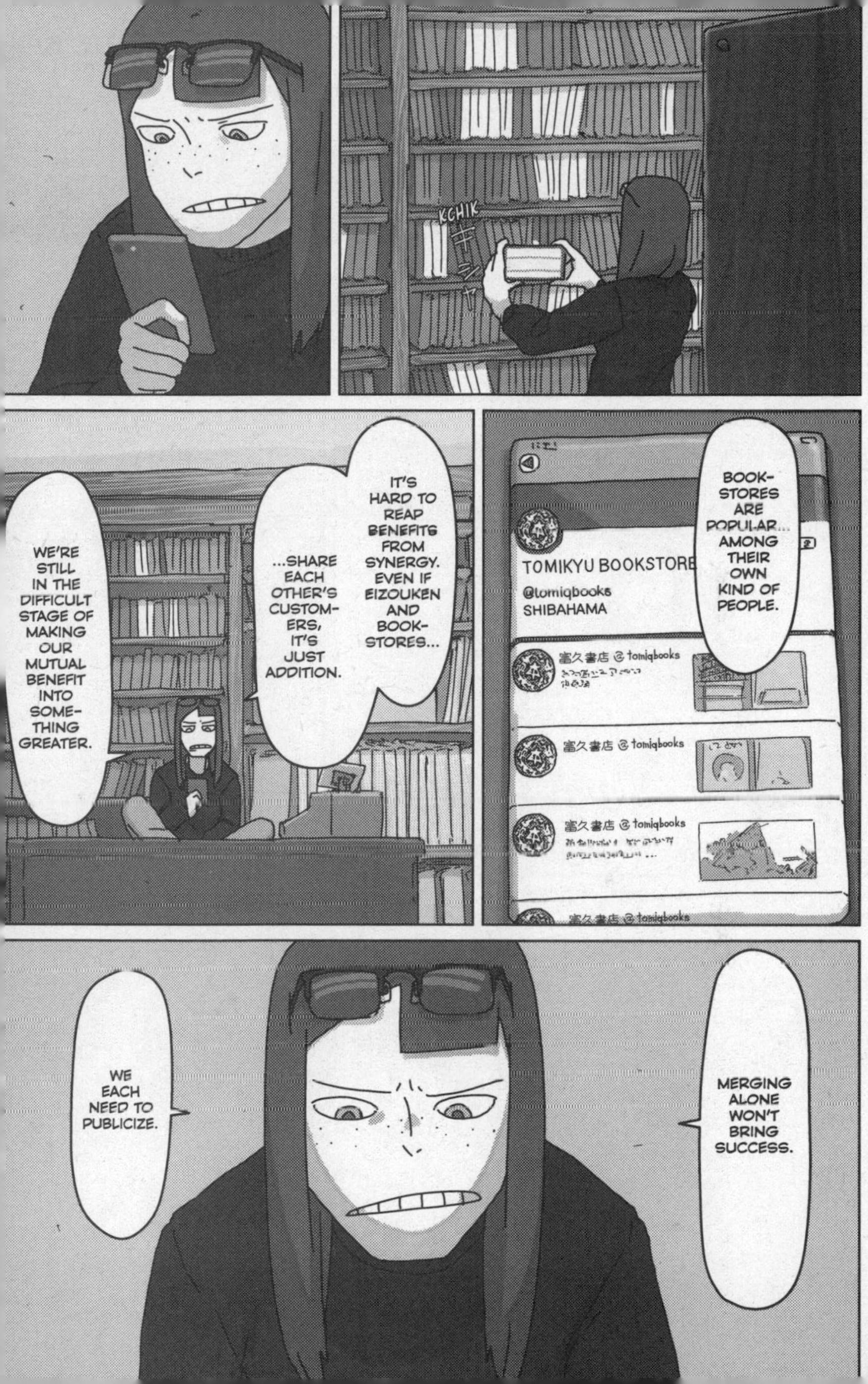
KCHIK
TOMIKYU BOOKSTORE
@tomiqbooks
SHIBAHAMA
富久書店 @ tomiqbooks
富久書店 @ tomiqbooks
富久書店 @ tomiqbooks
富久書店 @ tomiqbooks
BOOKSTORES ARE POPULAR... AMONG THEIR OWN KIND OF PEOPLE.
IT'S HARD TO REAP BENEFITS FROM SYNERGY. EVEN IF EIZOUKEN AND BOOKSTORES...
...SHARE EACH OTHER'S CUSTOMERS, IT'S JUST ADDITION.
WE'RE STILL IN THE DIFFICULT STAGE OF MAKING OUR MUTUAL BENEFIT INTO SOMETHING GREATER.
MERGING ALONE WON'T BRING SUCCESS.
WE EACH NEED TO PUBLICIZE.

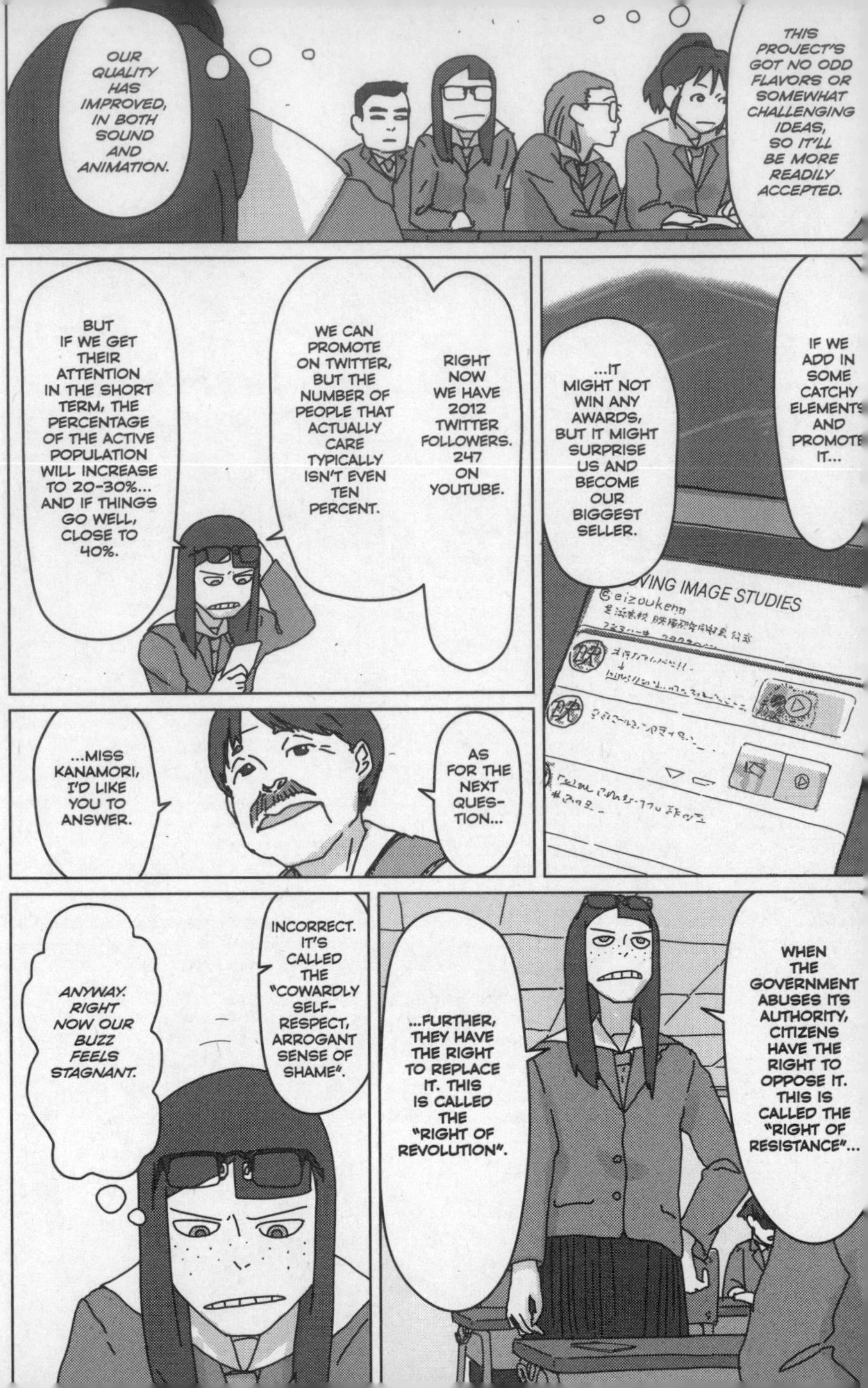
THIS PROJECT'S GOT NO ODD FLAVORS OR SOMEWHAT CHALLENGING IDEAS, SO IT'LL BE MORE READILY ACCEPTED.
OUR QUALITY HAS IMPROVED, IN BOTH SOUND AND ANIMATION.
IF WE ADD IN SOME CATCHY ELEMENTS AND PROMOTE IT...
...IT MIGHT NOT WIN ANY AWARDS, BUT IT MIGHT SURPRISE US AND BECOME OUR BIGGEST SELLER.
VING IMAGE STUDIES
@eizouken
RIGHT NOW WE HAVE 2012 TWITTER FOLLOWERS. 247 ON YOUTUBE.
WE CAN PROMOTE ON TWITTER, BUT THE NUMBER OF PEOPLE THAT ACTUALLY CARE TYPICALLY ISN'T EVEN TEN PERCENT.
BUT IF WE GET THEIR ATTENTION IN THE SHORT TERM, THE PERCENTAGE OF THE ACTIVE POPULATION WILL INCREASE TO 20-30%... AND IF THINGS GO WELL, CLOSE TO 40%.
AS FOR THE NEXT QUES-TION...
...MISS KANAMORI, I'D LIKE YOU TO ANSWER.
WHEN THE GOVERNMENT ABUSES ITS AUTHORITY, CITIZENS HAVE THE RIGHT TO OPPOSE IT. THIS IS CALLED THE "RIGHT OF RESISTANCE"...
...FURTHER, THEY HAVE THE RIGHT TO REPLACE IT. THIS IS CALLED THE "RIGHT OF REVOLUTION".
INCORRECT. IT'S CALLED THE "COWARDLY SELF-RESPECT, ARROGANT SENSE OF SHAME".
ANYWAY. RIGHT NOW OUR BUZZ FEELS STAGNANT.

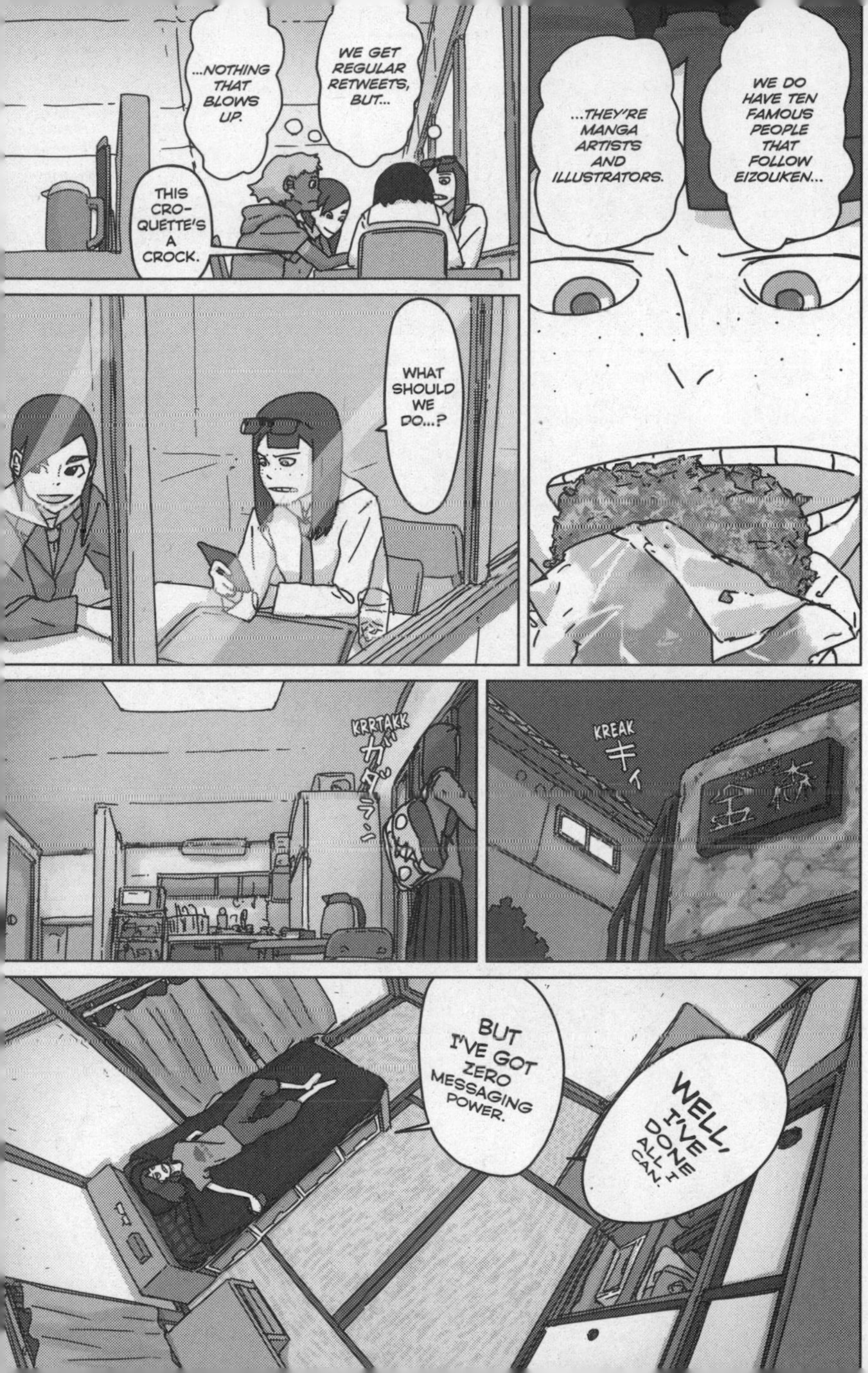
WE DO HAVE TEN FAMOUS PEOPLE THAT FOLLOW EIZOUKEN...
...THEY'RE MANGA ARTISTS AND ILLUSTRATORS.
WE GET REGULAR RETWEETS, BUT...
...NOTHING THAT BLOWS UP.
THIS CROQUETTE'S A CROCK.
WHAT SHOULD WE DO...?
KREAK
KRRTAKK
WELL, I'VE DONE ALL I CAN.
BUT I'VE GOT ZERO MESSAGING POWER.

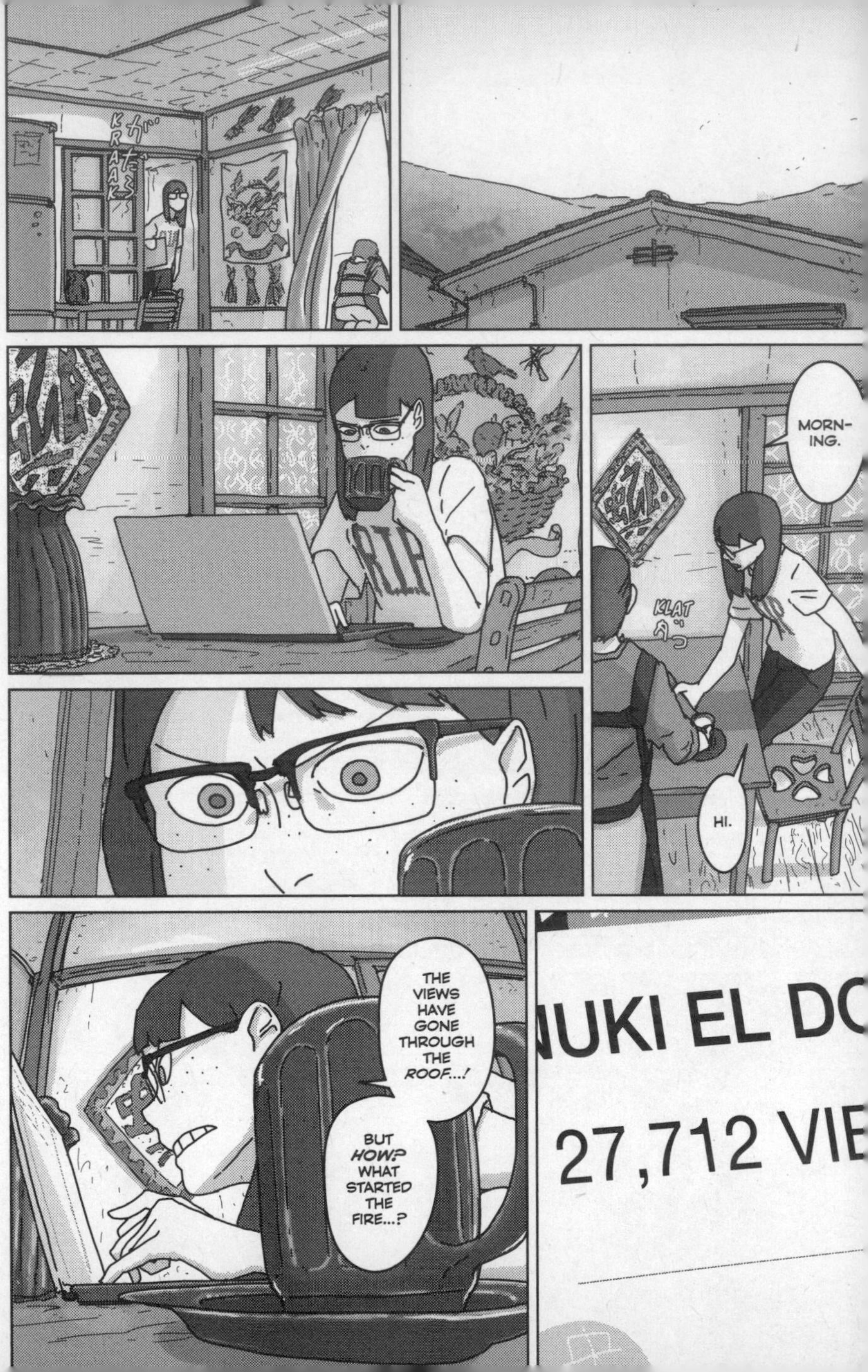
KRAAK
MORNING.
KLAT
HI.
NUKI EL DO
27,712 VIE
THE VIEWS HAVE GONE THROUGH THE *ROOF*...!
BUT *HOW?* WHAT STARTED THE FIRE...?

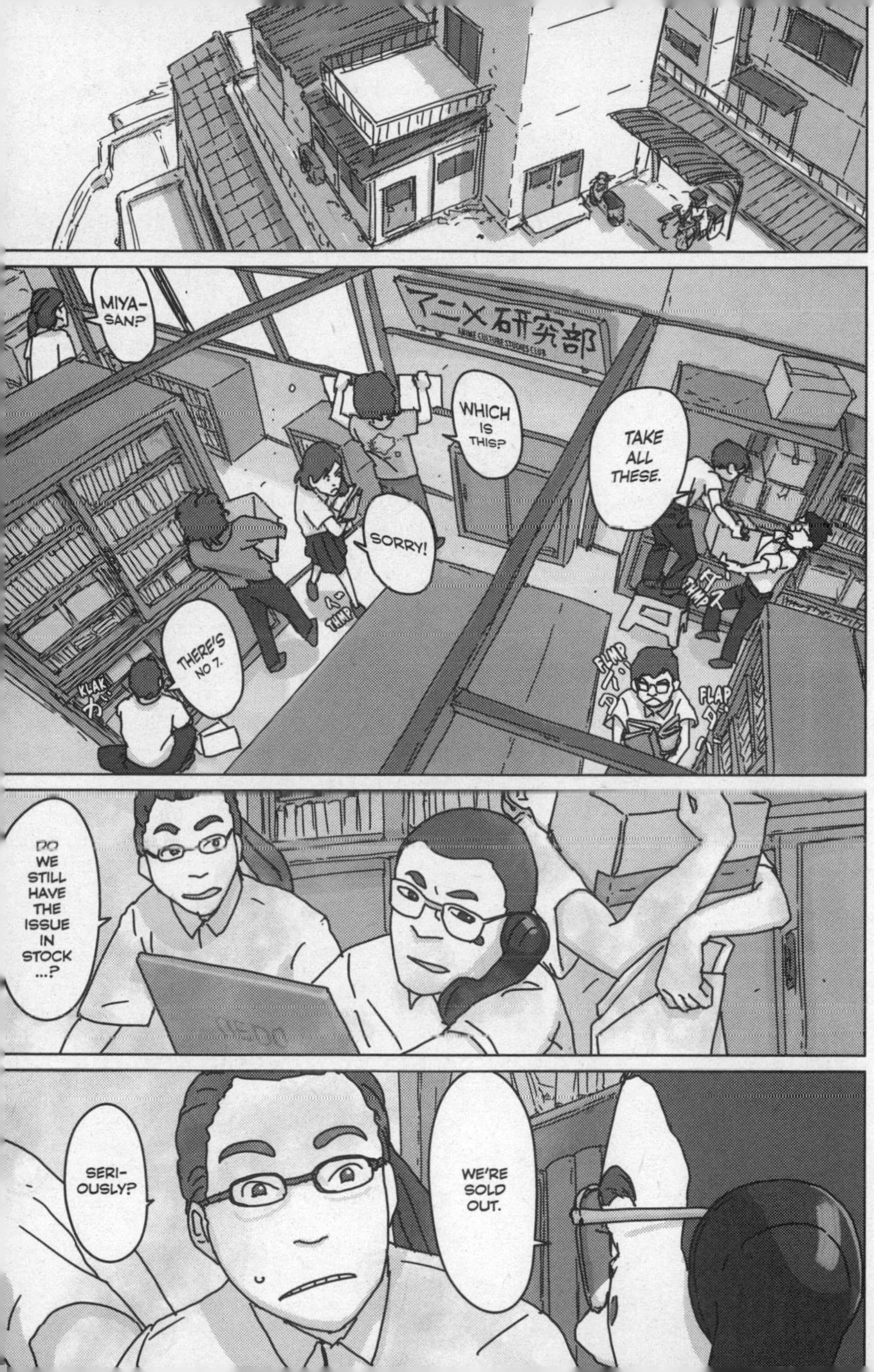
アニメ研究部
ANIME CULTURE STUDIES CLUB
TAKE ALL THESE.
THMP
FLAP
FLMP
WHICH IS THIS?
MIYA-SAN?
SORRY!
THMP
THERE'S NO 7.
KLAK
DO WE STILL HAVE THE ISSUE IN STOCK...?
WE'RE SOLD OUT.
SERIOUSLY?

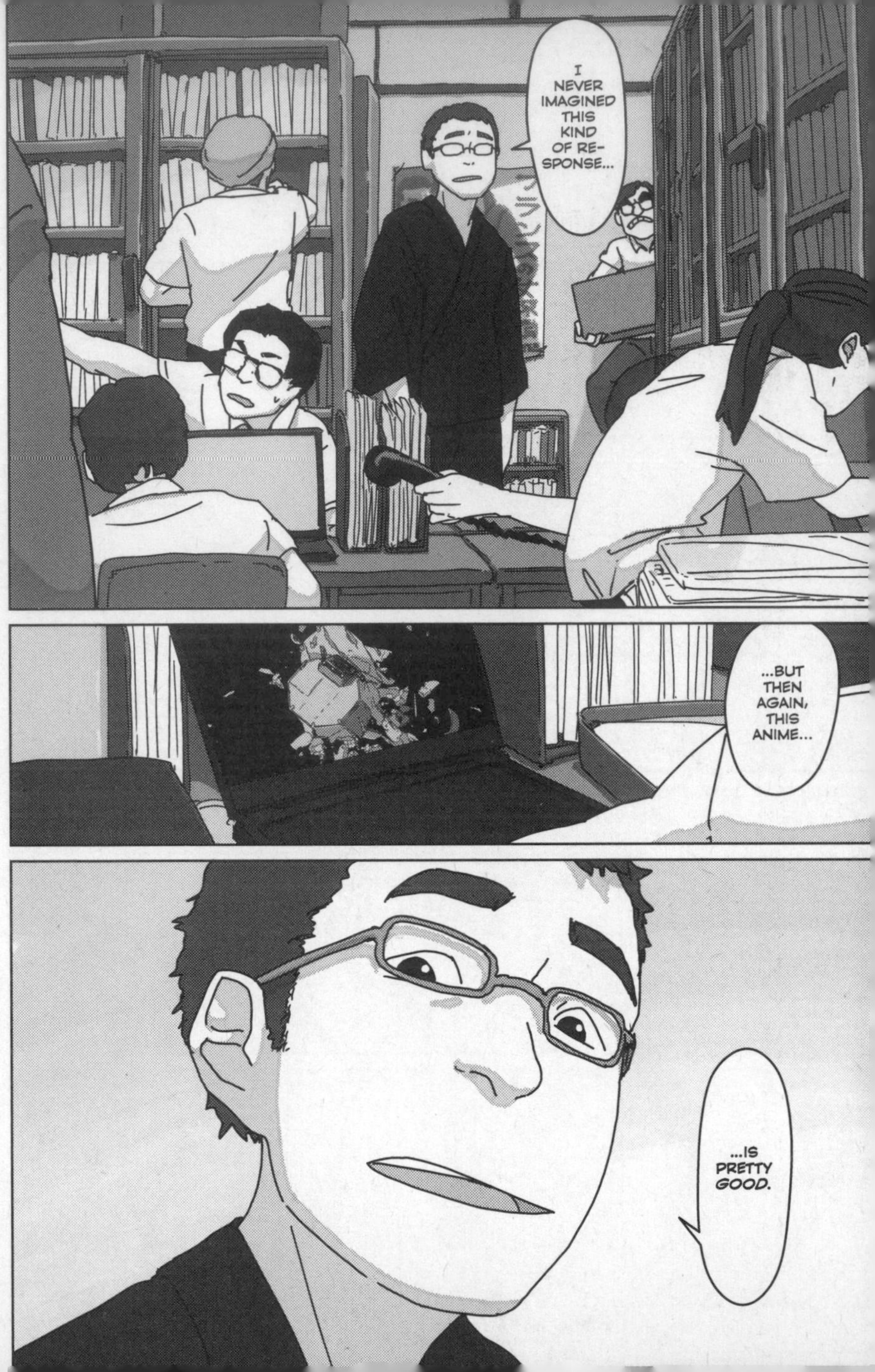
I NEVER IMAGINED THIS KIND OF RE-SPONSE...
...BUT THEN AGAIN, THIS ANIME...
...IS PRETTY GOOD.

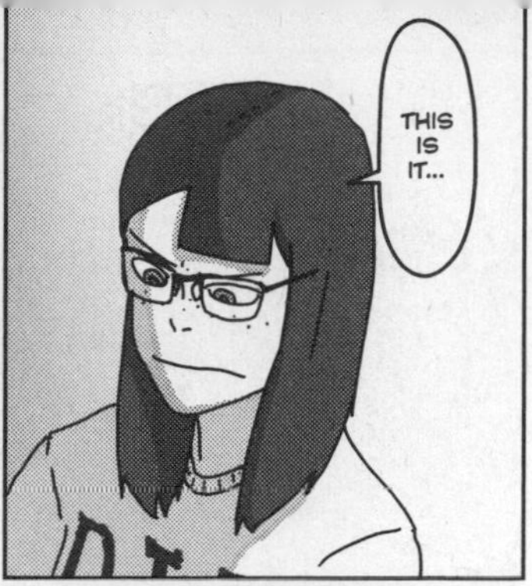
THIS IS IT...

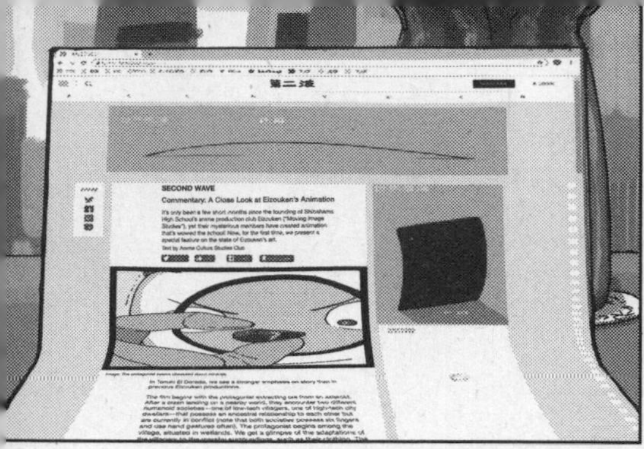
SECOND WAVE
Commentary: A Close Look at Eizouken's Animation

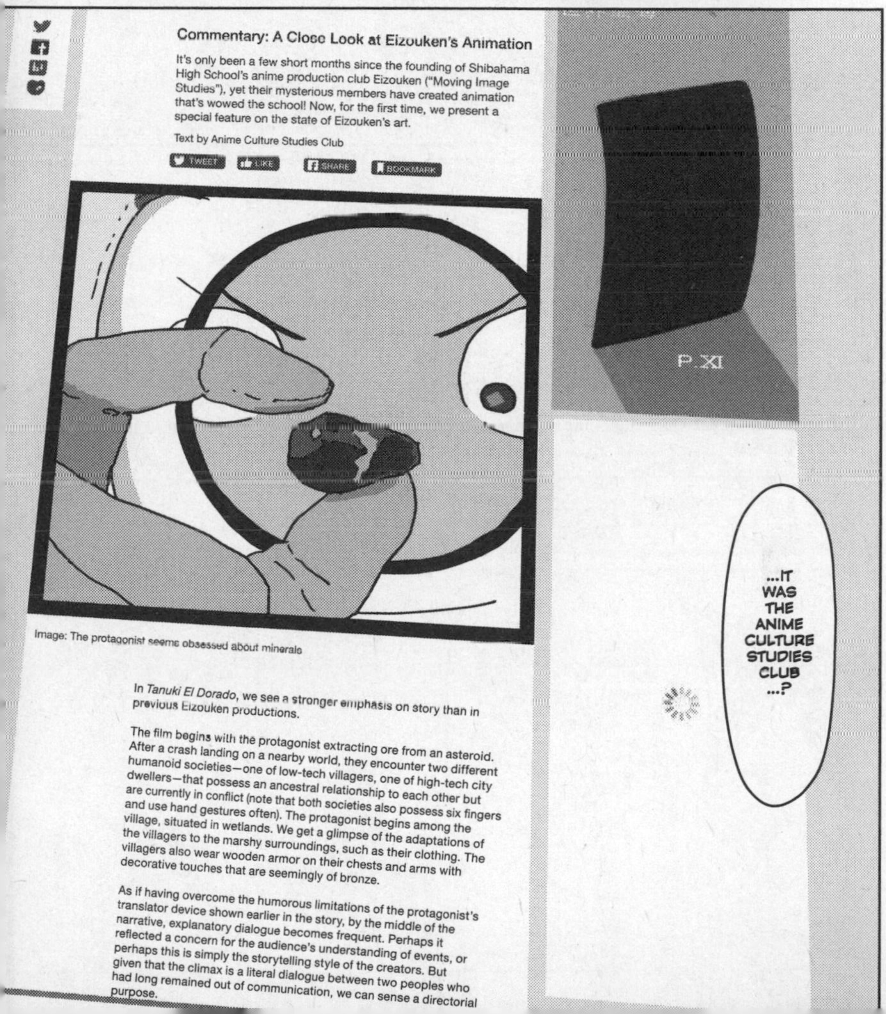
P.XI
Commentary: A Close Look at Eizouken's Animation
It's only been a few short months since the founding of Shibahama High School's anime production club Eizouken ("Moving Image Studies"), yet their mysterious members have created animation that's wowed the school! Now, for the first time, we present a special feature on the state of Eizouken's art.
Text by Anime Culture Studies Club
TWEET
LIKE
SHARE
BOOKMARK
Image: The protagonist seems obsessed about minerals
In Tanuki El Dorado, we see a stronger emphasis on story than in previous Eizouken productions.
The film begins with the protagonist extracting ore from an asteroid. After a crash landing on a nearby world, they encounter two different humanoid societies—one of low-tech villagers, one of high-tech city dwellers—that possess an ancestral relationship to each other but are currently in conflict (note that both societies also possess six fingers and use hand gestures often). The protagonist begins among the village, situated in wetlands. We get a glimpse of the adaptations of the villagers to the marshy surroundings, such as their clothing. The villagers also wear wooden armor on their chests and arms with decorative touches that are seemingly of bronze.
As if having overcome the humorous limitations of the protagonist's translator device shown earlier in the story, by the middle of the narrative, explanatory dialogue becomes frequent. Perhaps it reflected a concern for the audience's understanding of events, or perhaps this is simply the storytelling style of the creators. But given that the climax is a literal dialogue between two peoples who had long remained out of communication, we can sense a directorial purpose.
...IT WAS THE ANIME CULTURE STUDIES CLUB...?

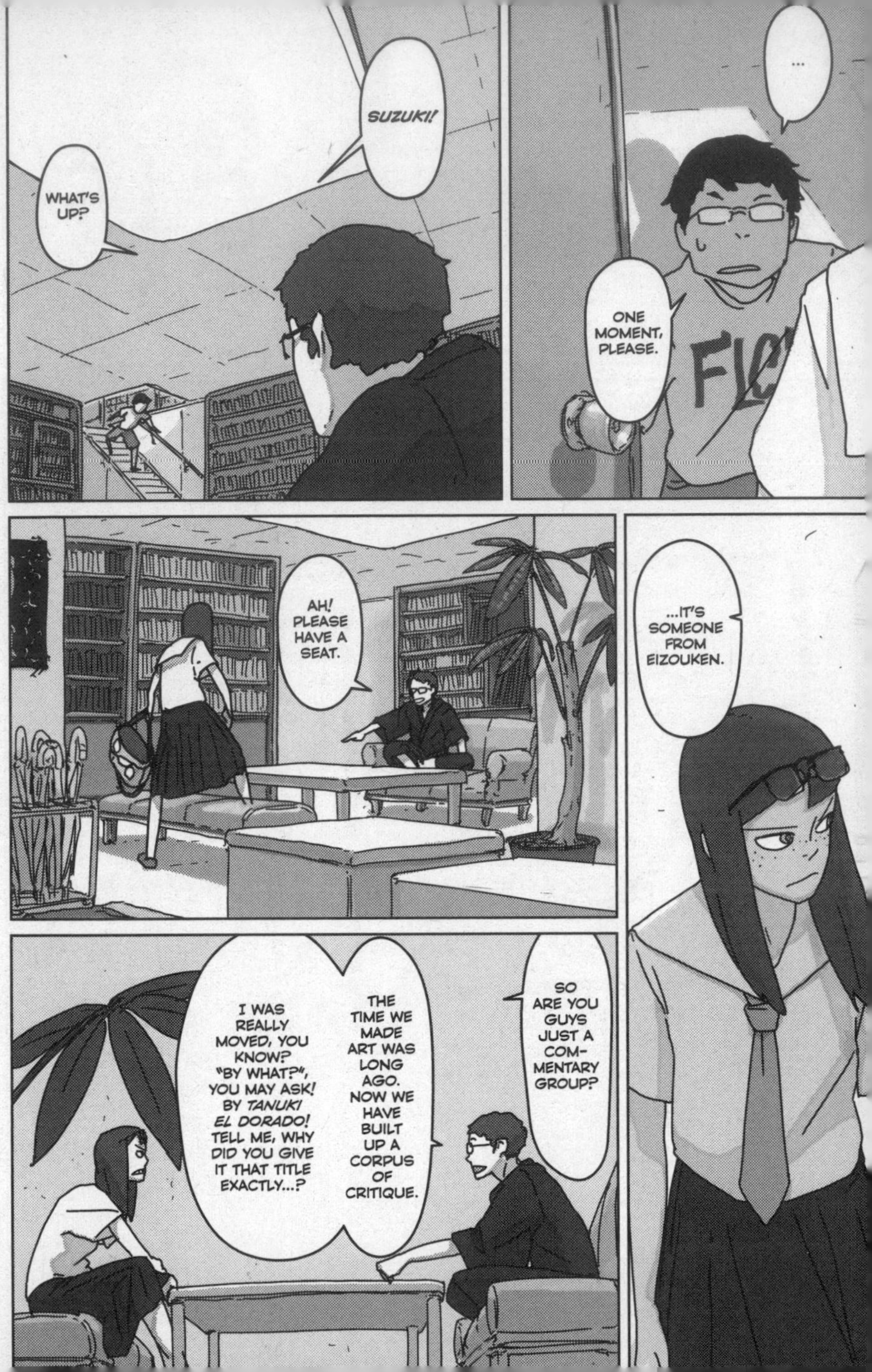
...
ONE MOMENT, PLEASE.
SUZUKI!
WHAT'S UP?
...IT'S SOMEONE FROM EIZOUKEN.
AH! PLEASE HAVE A SEAT.
SO ARE YOU GUYS JUST A COMMENTARY GROUP?
THE TIME WE MADE ART WAS LONG AGO. NOW WE HAVE BUILT UP A CORPUS OF CRITIQUE.
I WAS REALLY MOVED, YOU KNOW? "BY WHAT?", YOU MAY ASK! BY *TANUKI EL DORADO*! TELL ME, WHY DID YOU GIVE IT THAT TITLE EXACTLY...?

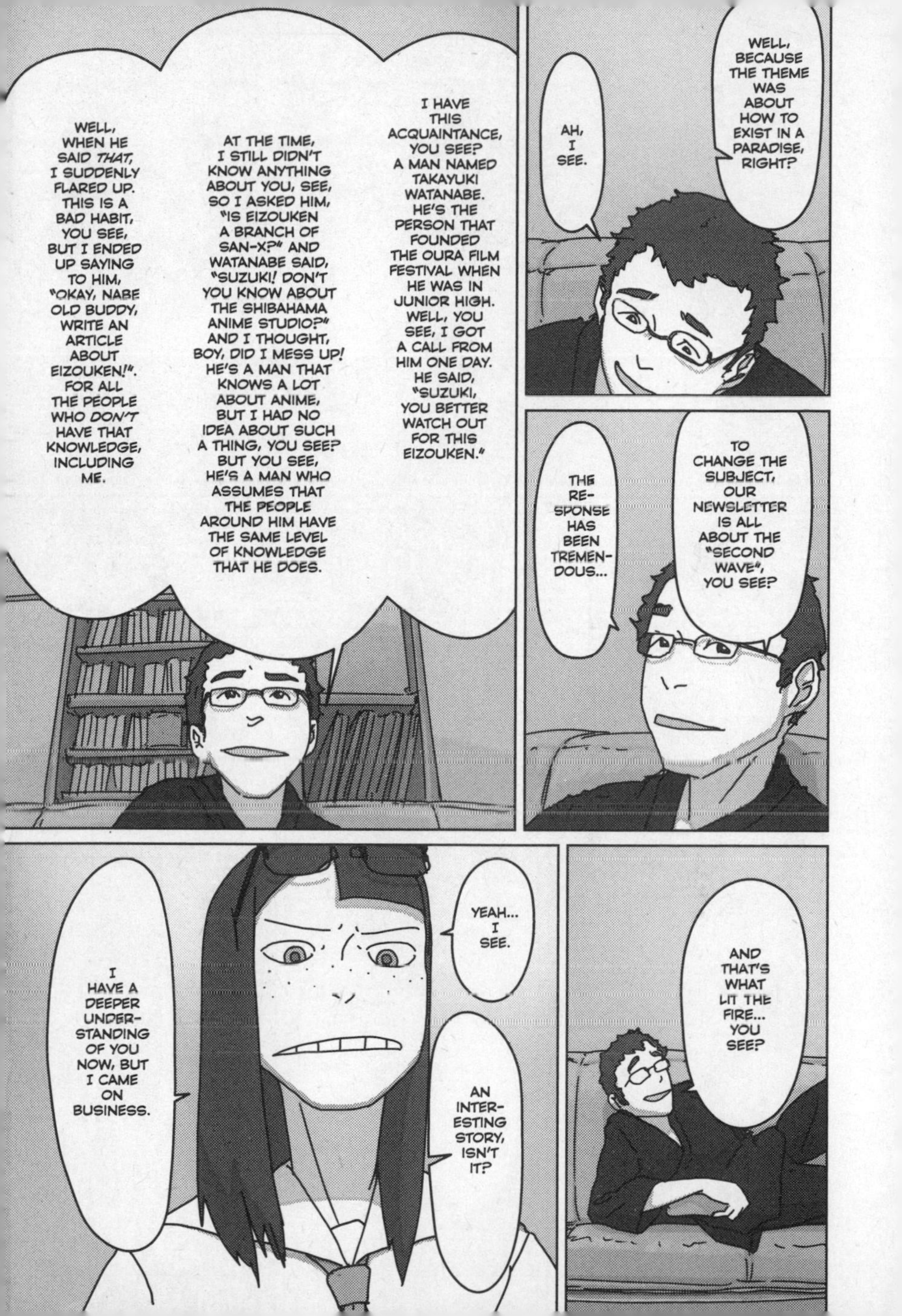
WELL, BECAUSE THE THEME WAS ABOUT HOW TO EXIST IN A PARADISE, RIGHT?
AH, I SEE.
TO CHANGE THE SUBJECT, OUR NEWSLETTER IS ALL ABOUT THE "SECOND WAVE", YOU SEE?
THE RESPONSE HAS BEEN TREMENDOUS...
I HAVE THIS ACQUAINTANCE, YOU SEE? A MAN NAMED TAKAYUKI WATANABE. HE'S THE PERSON THAT FOUNDED THE OURA FILM FESTIVAL WHEN HE WAS IN JUNIOR HIGH. WELL, YOU SEE, I GOT A CALL FROM HIM ONE DAY. HE SAID, "SUZUKI, YOU BETTER WATCH OUT FOR THIS EIZOUKEN."
AT THE TIME, I STILL DIDN'T KNOW ANYTHING ABOUT YOU, SEE, SO I ASKED HIM, "IS EIZOUKEN A BRANCH OF SAN-X?" AND WATANABE SAID, "SUZUKI! DON'T YOU KNOW ABOUT THE SHIBAHAMA ANIME STUDIO?" AND I THOUGHT, BOY, DID I MESS UP! HE'S A MAN THAT KNOWS A LOT ABOUT ANIME, BUT I HAD NO IDEA ABOUT SUCH A THING, YOU SEE? BUT YOU SEE, HE'S A MAN WHO ASSUMES THAT THE PEOPLE AROUND HIM HAVE THE SAME LEVEL OF KNOWLEDGE THAT HE DOES.
WELL, WHEN HE SAID *THAT*, I SUDDENLY FLARED UP. THIS IS A BAD HABIT, YOU SEE, BUT I ENDED UP SAYING TO HIM, "OKAY, NABE OLD BUDDY, WRITE AN ARTICLE ABOUT EIZOUKEN!". FOR ALL THE PEOPLE WHO *DON'T* HAVE THAT KNOWLEDGE, INCLUDING ME.
AND THAT'S WHAT LIT THE FIRE... YOU SEE?
YEAH... I SEE.
AN INTERESTING STORY, ISN'T IT?
I HAVE A DEEPER UNDERSTANDING OF YOU NOW, BUT I CAME ON BUSINESS.

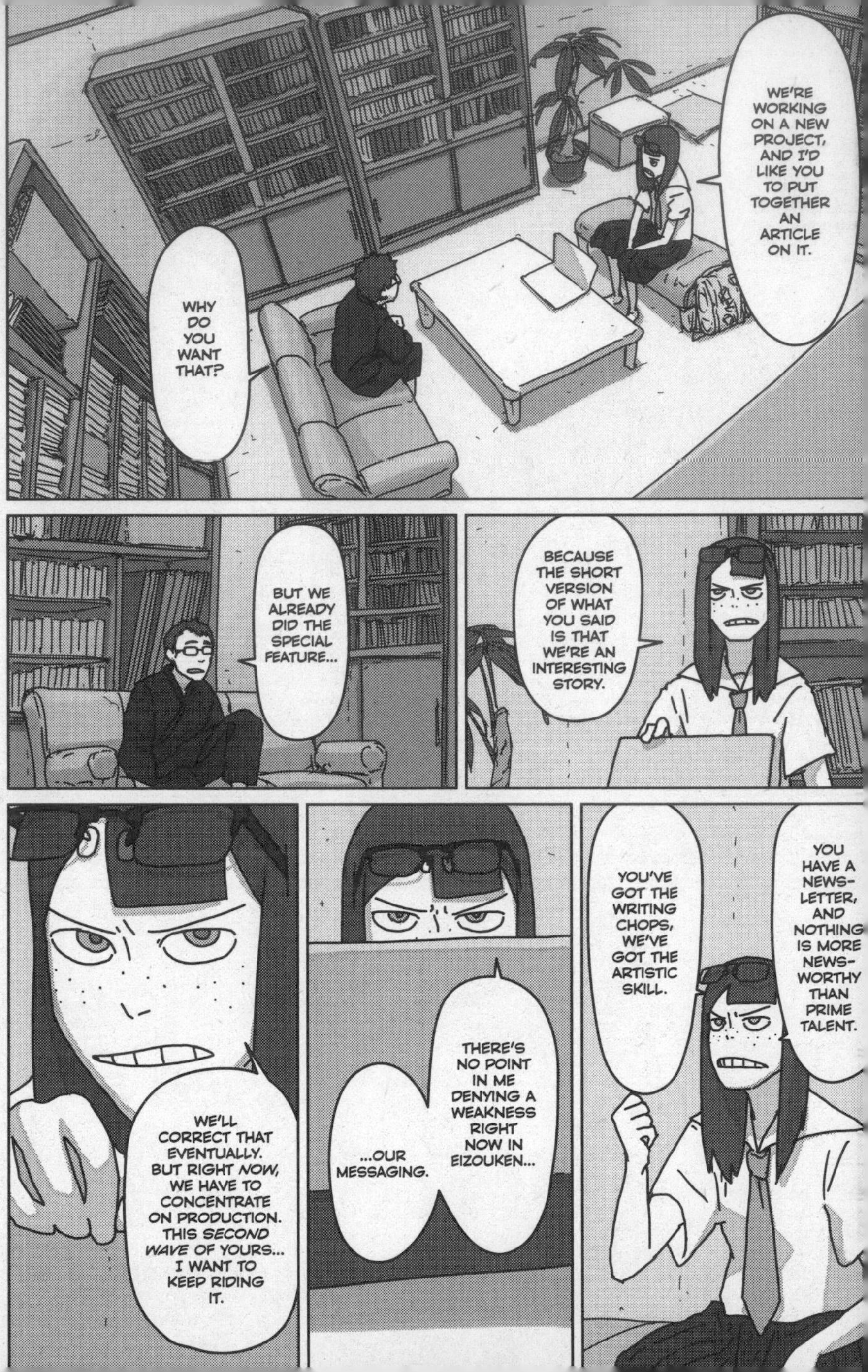
WE'RE WORKING ON A NEW PROJECT, AND I'D LIKE YOU TO PUT TOGETHER AN ARTICLE ON IT.
WHY DO YOU WANT THAT?
BECAUSE THE SHORT VERSION OF WHAT YOU SAID IS THAT WE'RE AN INTERESTING STORY.
BUT WE ALREADY DID THE SPECIAL FEATURE...
YOU HAVE A NEWSLETTER, AND NOTHING IS MORE NEWSWORTHY THAN PRIME TALENT.
YOU'VE GOT THE WRITING CHOPS, WE'VE GOT THE ARTISTIC SKILL.
THERE'S NO POINT IN ME DENYING A WEAKNESS RIGHT NOW IN EIZOUKEN...
...OUR MESSAGING.
WE'LL CORRECT THAT EVENTUALLY. BUT RIGHT *NOW*, WE HAVE TO CONCENTRATE ON PRODUCTION. THIS *SECOND WAVE* OF YOURS... I WANT TO KEEP RIDING IT.

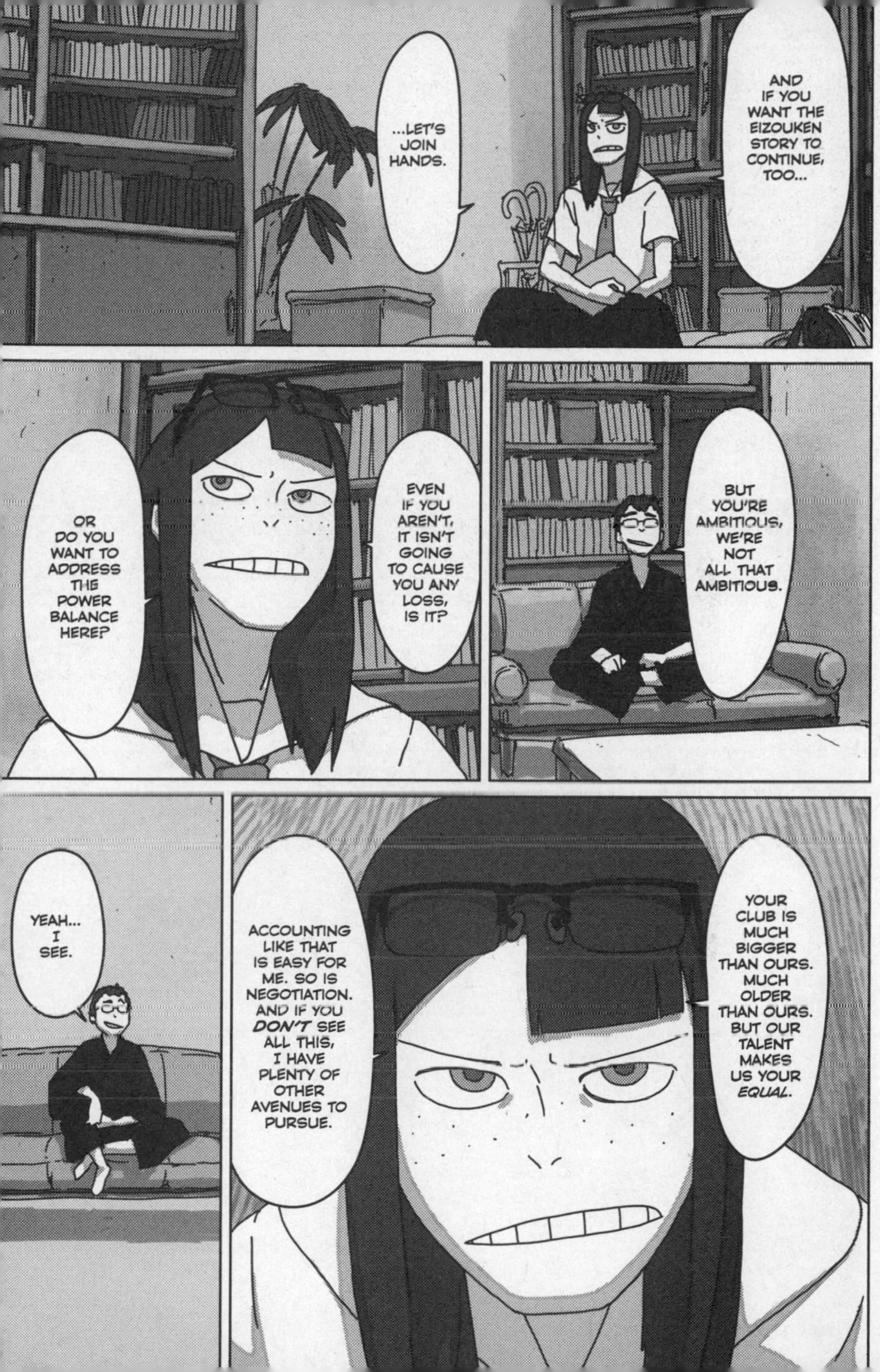
AND IF YOU WANT THE EIZOUKEN STORY TO CONTINUE, TOO...
...LET'S JOIN HANDS.
BUT YOU'RE AMBITIOUS, WE'RE NOT ALL THAT AMBITIOUS.
EVEN IF YOU AREN'T, IT ISN'T GOING TO CAUSE YOU ANY LOSS, IS IT?
OR DO YOU WANT TO ADDRESS THE POWER BALANCE HERE?
YOUR CLUB IS MUCH BIGGER THAN OURS. MUCH OLDER THAN OURS. BUT OUR TALENT MAKES US YOUR *EQUAL*.
ACCOUNTING LIKE THAT IS EASY FOR ME. SO IS NEGOTIATION. AND IF YOU *DON'T* SEE ALL THIS, I HAVE PLENTY OF OTHER AVENUES TO PURSUE.
YEAH... I SEE.

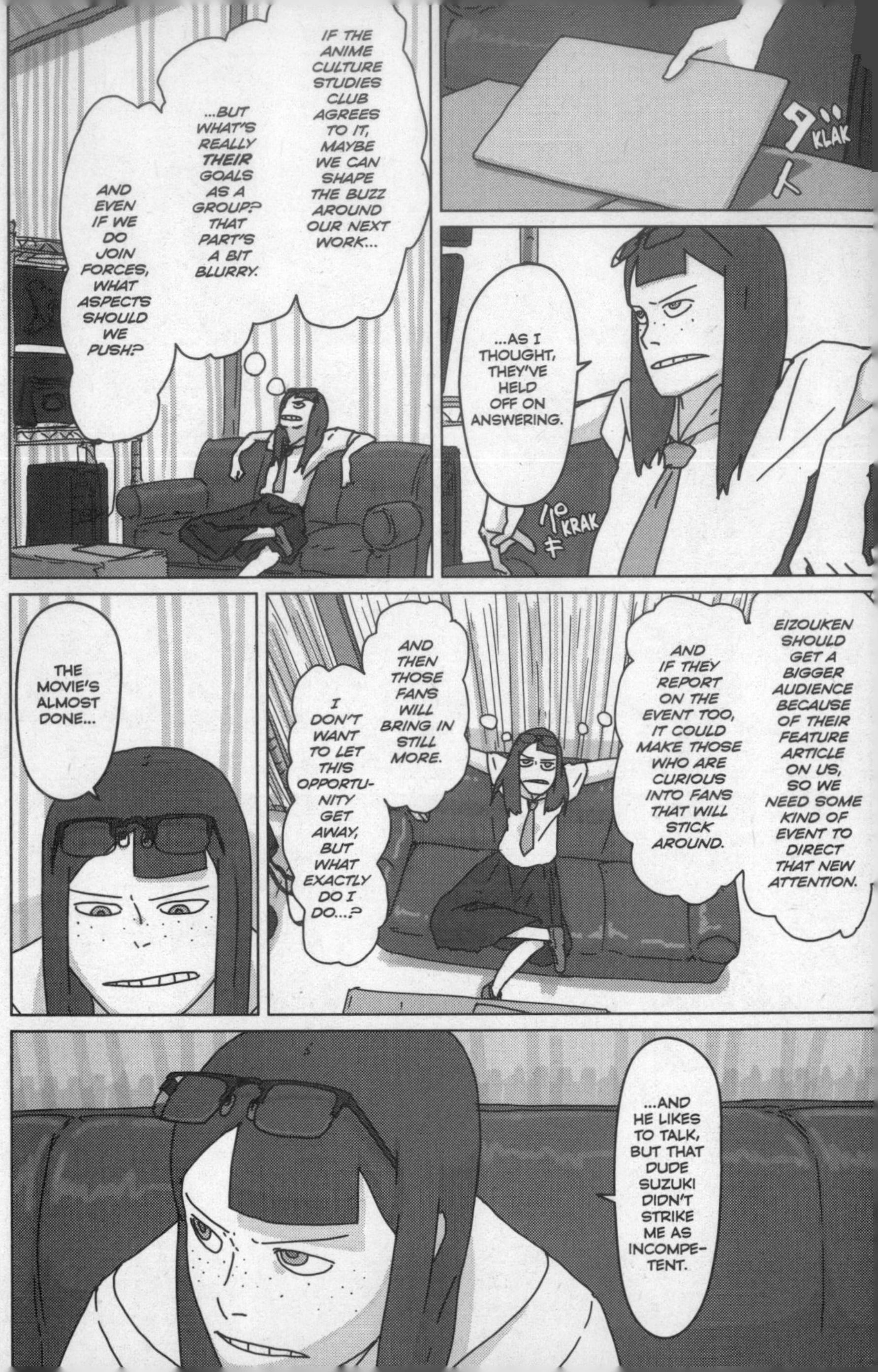
KLAK
...AS I THOUGHT, THEY'VE HELD OFF ON ANSWERING.
KRAK
IF THE ANIME CULTURE STUDIES CLUB AGREES TO IT, MAYBE WE CAN SHAPE THE BUZZ AROUND OUR NEXT WORK...
...BUT WHAT'S REALLY *THEIR* GOALS AS A GROUP? THAT PART'S A BIT BLURRY.
AND EVEN IF WE DO JOIN FORCES, WHAT ASPECTS SHOULD WE PUSH?
EIZOUKEN SHOULD GET A BIGGER AUDIENCE BECAUSE OF THEIR FEATURE ARTICLE ON US, SO WE NEED SOME KIND OF EVENT TO DIRECT THAT NEW ATTENTION.
AND IF THEY REPORT ON THE EVENT TOO, IT COULD MAKE THOSE WHO ARE CURIOUS INTO FANS THAT WILL STICK AROUND.
AND THEN THOSE FANS WILL BRING IN STILL MORE.
I DON'T WANT TO LET THIS OPPORTUNITY GET AWAY, BUT WHAT EXACTLY DO I DO...?
THE MOVIE'S ALMOST DONE...
...AND HE LIKES TO TALK, BUT THAT DUDE SUZUKI DIDN'T STRIKE ME AS INCOMPETENT.

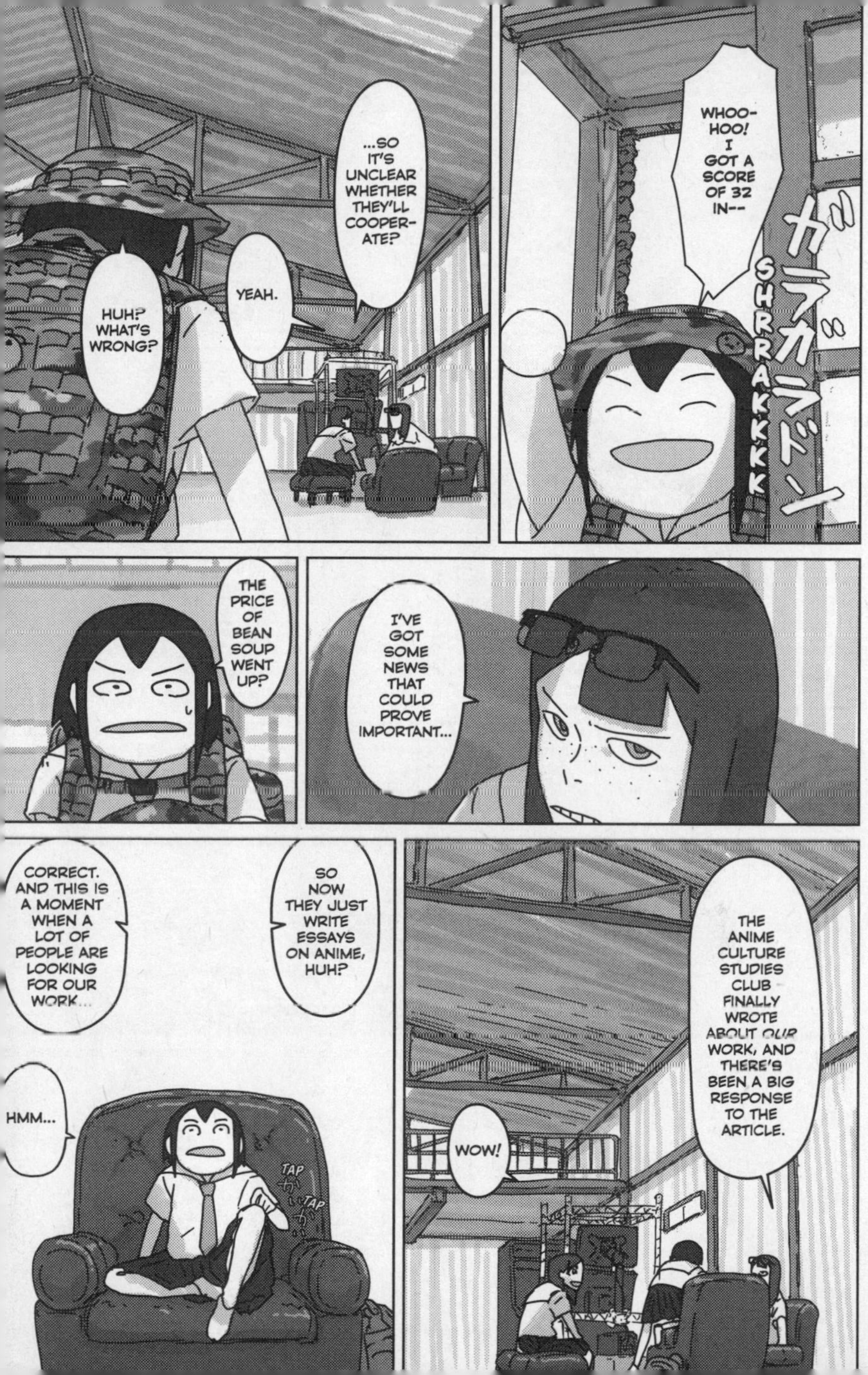
WHOO-HOO! I GOT A SCORE OF 32 IN--
SHRRAKKKK
...SO IT'S UNCLEAR WHETHER THEY'LL COOPER-ATE?
YEAH.
HUH? WHAT'S WRONG?
I'VE GOT SOME NEWS THAT COULD PROVE IMPORTANT...
THE PRICE OF BEAN SOUP WENT UP?
THE ANIME CULTURE STUDIES CLUB FINALLY WROTE ABOUT OUR WORK, AND THERE'S BEEN A BIG RESPONSE TO THE ARTICLE.
WOW!
SO NOW THEY JUST WRITE ESSAYS ON ANIME, HUH?
CORRECT. AND THIS IS A MOMENT WHEN A LOT OF PEOPLE ARE LOOKING FOR OUR WORK...
HMM...
TAP
TAP

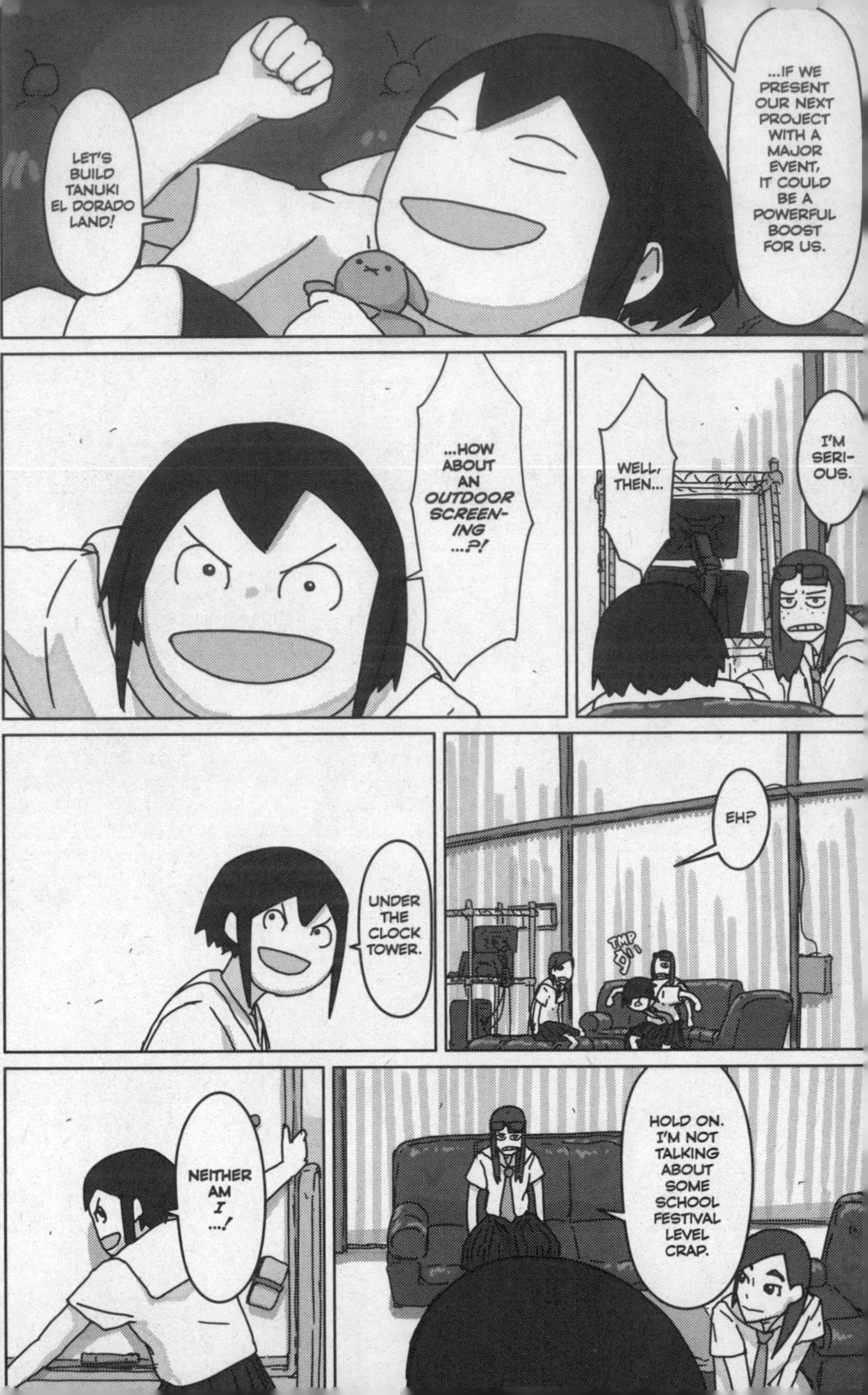
...IF WE PRESENT OUR NEXT PROJECT WITH A MAJOR EVENT, IT COULD BE A POWERFUL BOOST FOR US.
LET'S BUILD TANUKI EL DORADO LAND!
I'M SERI-OUS.
WELL, THEN...
...HOW ABOUT AN *OUTDOOR SCREEN-ING* ...?!
EH?
UNDER THE CLOCK TOWER.
HOLD ON. I'M NOT TALKING ABOUT SOME SCHOOL FESTIVAL LEVEL CRAP.
NEITHER AM *I* ...!

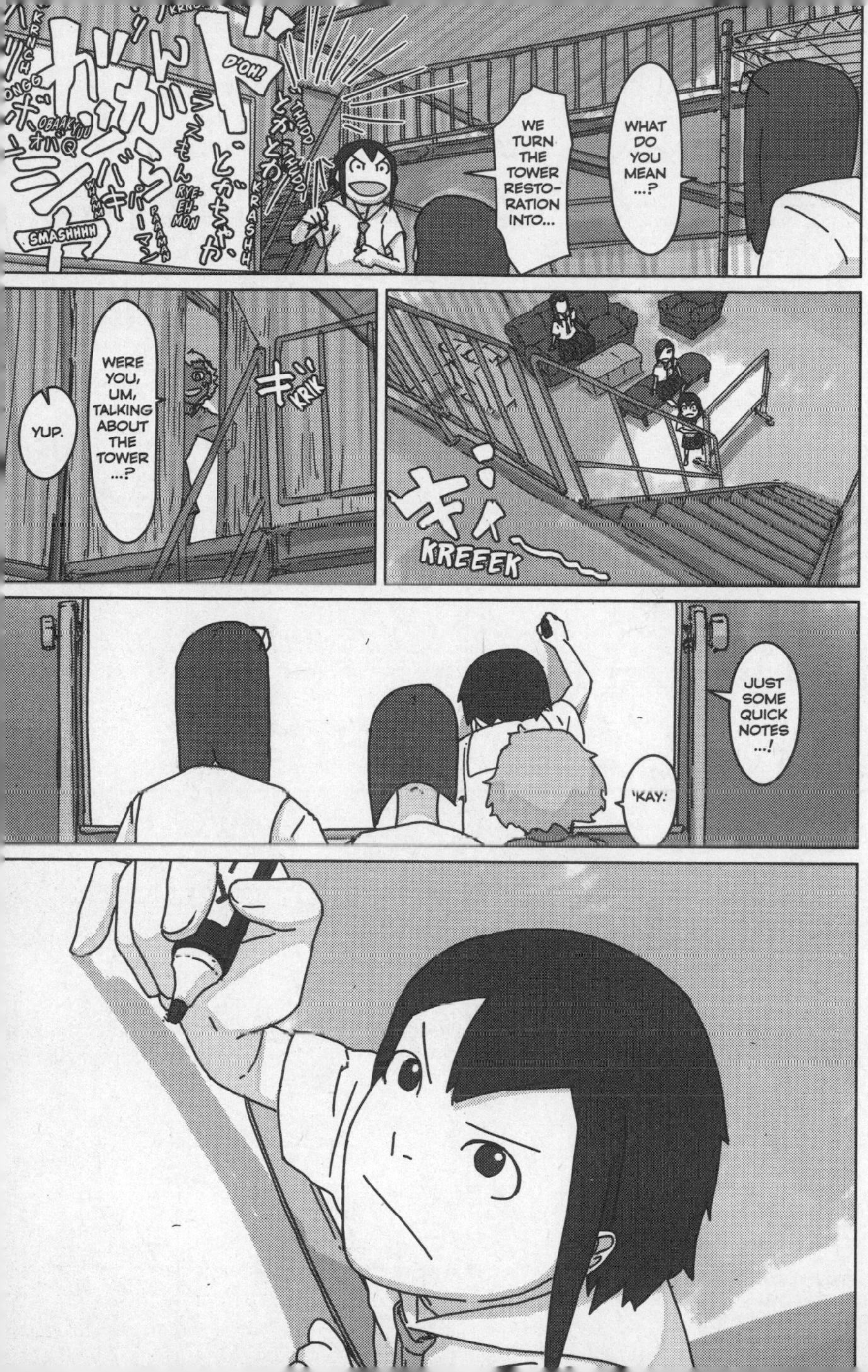
WHAT DO YOU MEAN ...?
WE TURN THE TOWER RESTORATION INTO...
とかとか
THUDD THUDD
D'OH!
とかちゃか、
KRASHH
えもん
RYE-EH-MON
パーマン
PAAAMAN
WHAMM
オバQ
OBAAKYUU
SMASHHHH
KRNCH
WERE YOU, UM, TALKING ABOUT THE TOWER ...?
YUP.
キ
KRIK
キィ
KREEEK
JUST SOME QUICK NOTES ...!
'KAY.

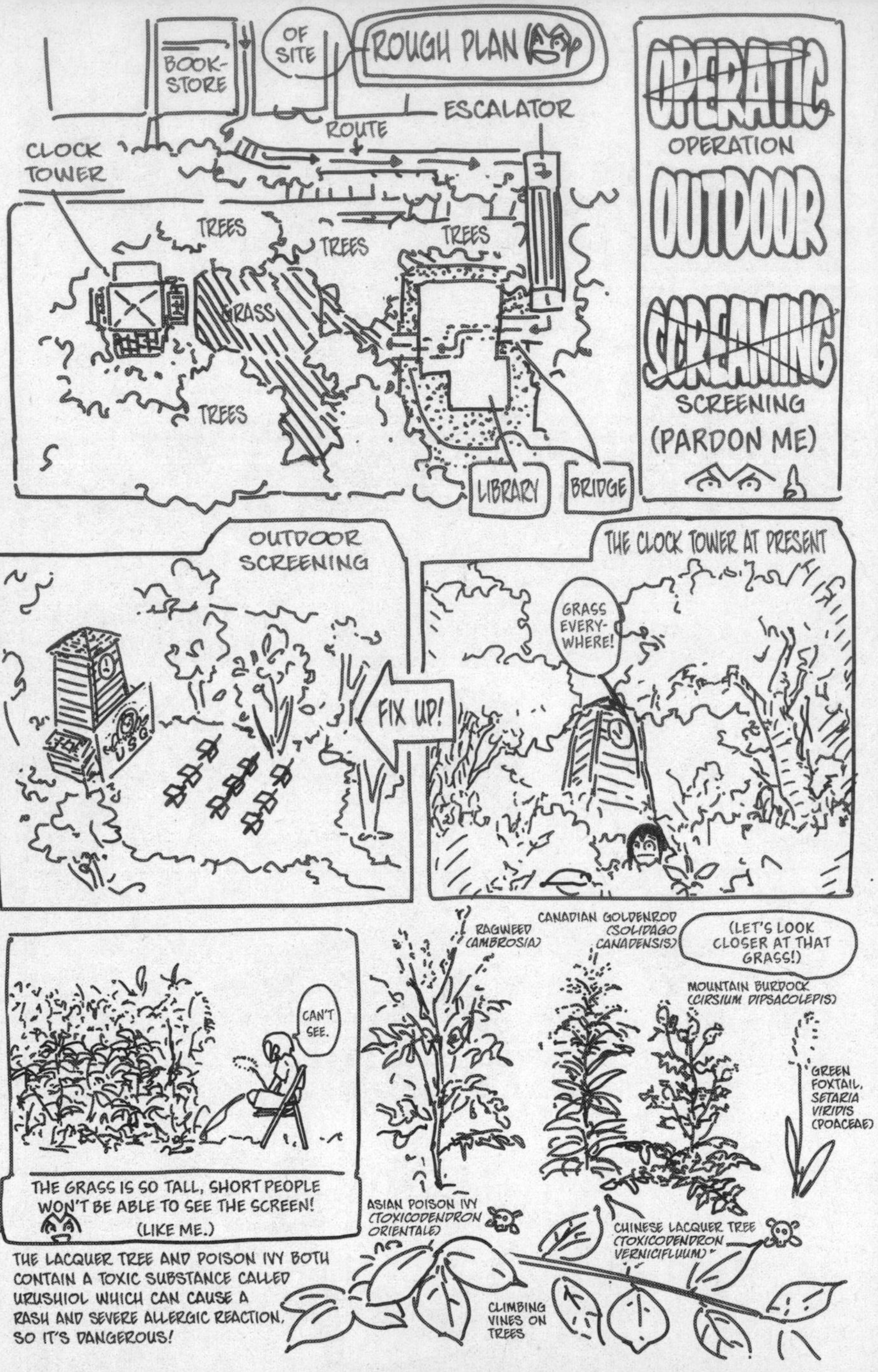
OPERATIC
OPERATION
OUTDOOR
SCREAMING
SCREENING
(PARDON ME)
ROUGH PLAN
OF SITE
BOOK-STORE
ESCALATOR
ROUTE
CLOCK TOWER
TREES
TREES
TREES
GRASS
TREES
LIBRARY
BRIDGE
THE CLOCK TOWER AT PRESENT
GRASS EVERY-WHERE!
FIX UP!
OUTDOOR SCREENING
(LET'S LOOK CLOSER AT THAT GRASS!)
MOUNTAIN BURDOCK (CIRSIUM DIPSACOLEPIS)
GREEN FOXTAIL, SETARIA VIRIDIS (POACEAE)
CANADIAN GOLDENROD (SOLIDAGO CANADENSIS)
RAGWEED (AMBROSIA)
CHINESE LACQUER TREE (TOXICODENDRON VERNICIFLUUM)
ASIAN POISON IVY (TOXICODENDRON ORIENTALE)
CLIMBING VINES ON TREES
CAN'T SEE.
THE GRASS IS SO TALL, SHORT PEOPLE WON'T BE ABLE TO SEE THE SCREEN!
(LIKE ME.)
THE LACQUER TREE AND POISON IVY BOTH CONTAIN A TOXIC SUBSTANCE CALLED URUSHIOL WHICH CAN CAUSE A RASH AND SEVERE ALLERGIC REACTION, SO IT'S DANGEROUS!

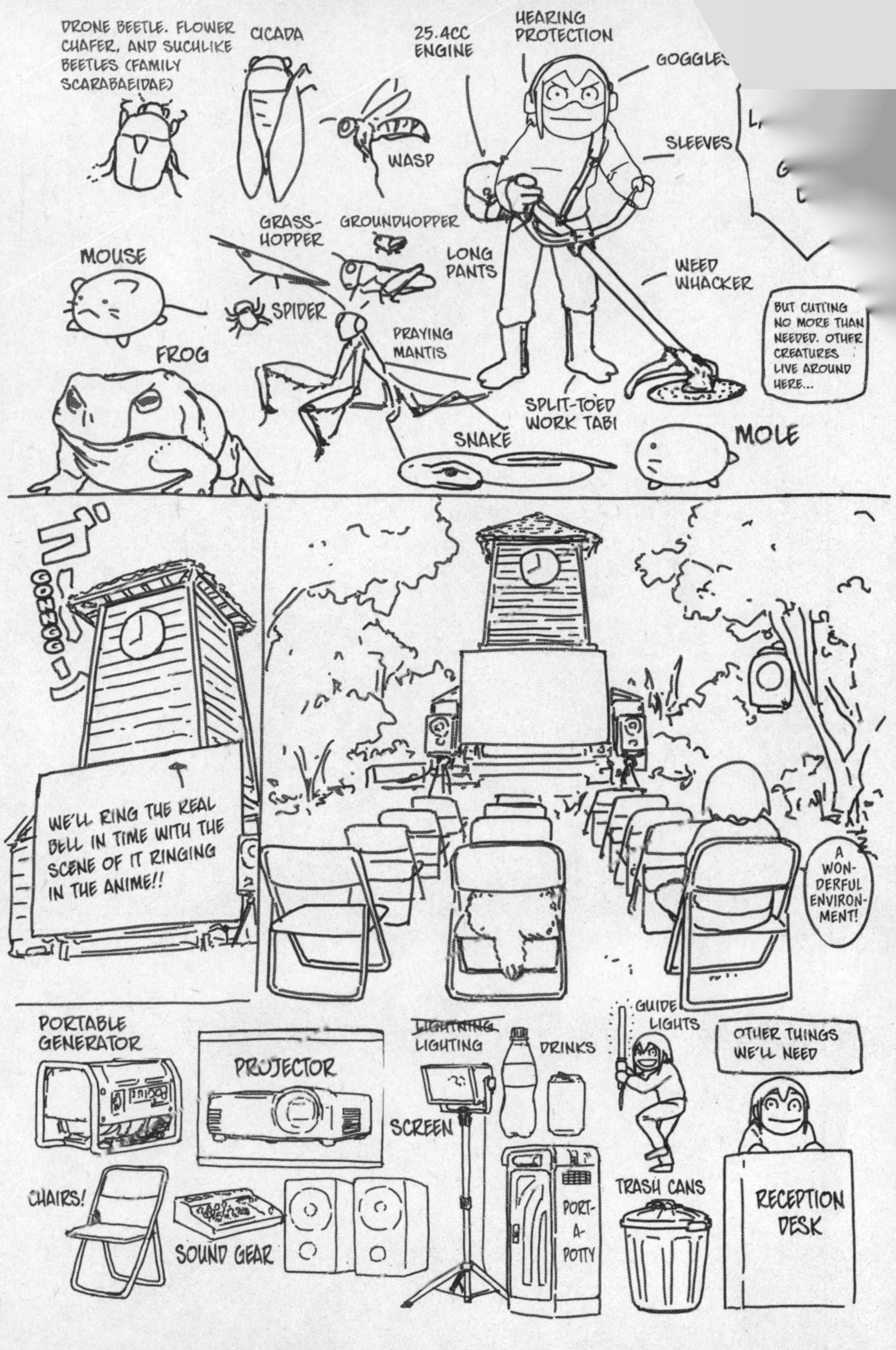

HEARING PROTECTION
GOGGLES
25.4CC ENGINE
SLEEVES
WEED WHACKER
BUT CUTTING NO MORE THAN NEEDED. OTHER CREATURES LIVE AROUND HERE...
LONG PANTS
SPLIT-TOED WORK TABI
CICADA
DRONE BEETLE, FLOWER CHAFER, AND SUCHLIKE BEETLES (FAMILY SCARABAEIDAE)
WASP
GROUNDHOPPER
GRASS-HOPPER
MOUSE
SPIDER
PRAYING MANTIS
FROG
MOLE
SNAKE
A WONDERFUL ENVIRONMENT!
ゴーン
GONNGG
WE'LL RING THE REAL BELL IN TIME WITH THE SCENE OF IT RINGING IN THE ANIME!!
OTHER THINGS WE'LL NEED
GUIDE LIGHTS
RECEPTION DESK
TRASH CANS
DRINKS
PORT-A-POTTY
~~LIGHTNING~~ LIGHTING
SCREEN
PROJECTOR
PORTABLE GENERATOR
SOUND GEAR
CHAIRS!

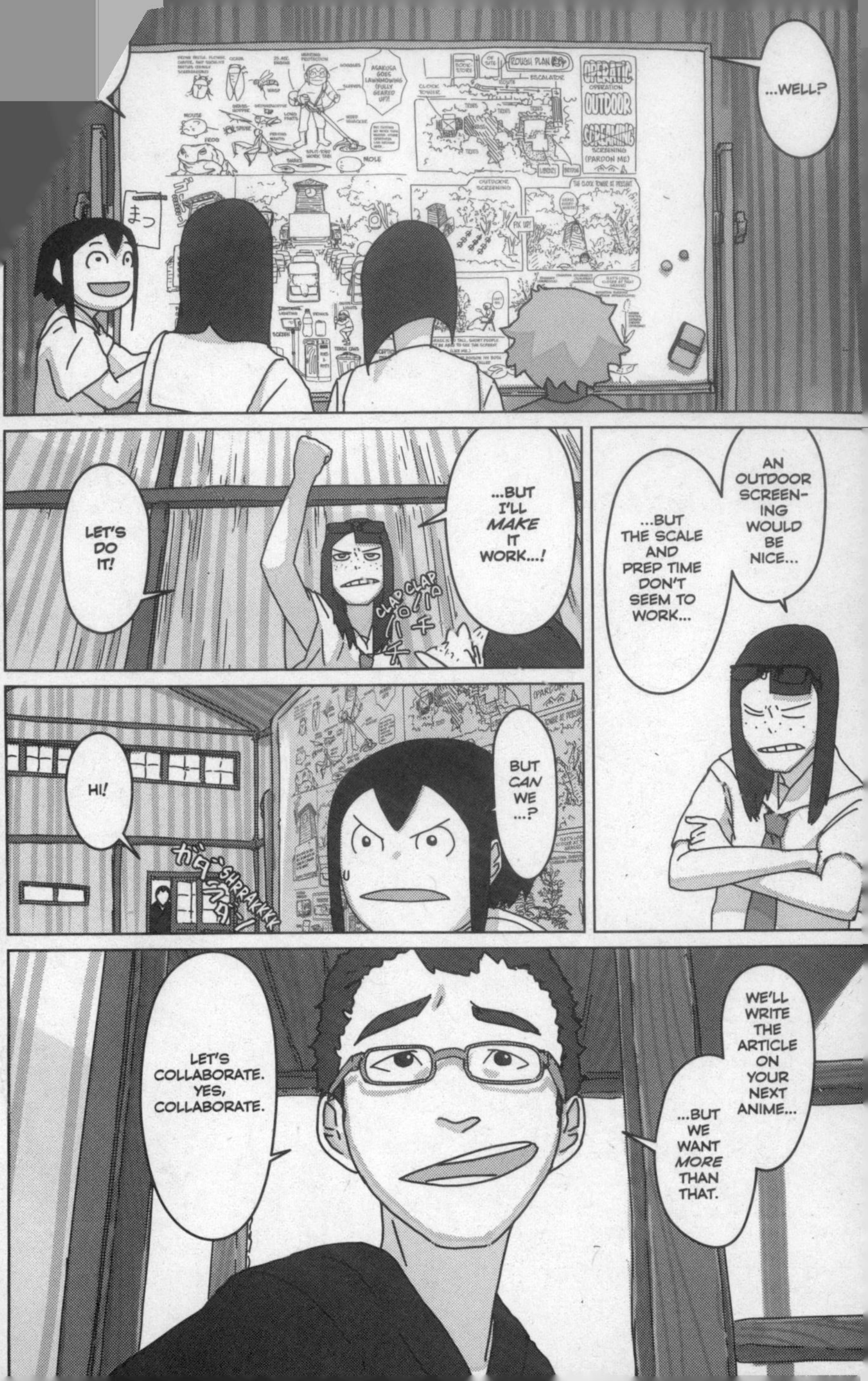
...WELL?
ROUGH PLAN
OPERATIC
OPERATION
OUTDOOR
SCREAMING
SCREENING
(PARDON ME)
AN OUTDOOR SCREEN-ING WOULD BE NICE...
...BUT THE SCALE AND PREP TIME DON'T SEEM TO WORK...
...BUT I'LL *MAKE* IT WORK...!
CLAP CLAP
LET'S DO IT!
BUT *CAN* WE ...?
SHRRAKKKK
HI!
WE'LL WRITE THE ARTICLE ON YOUR NEXT ANIME...
...BUT WE WANT *MORE* THAN THAT.
LET'S COLLABORATE. YES, COLLABORATE.

KEEP YOUR HANDS OFF EIZOUKEN!

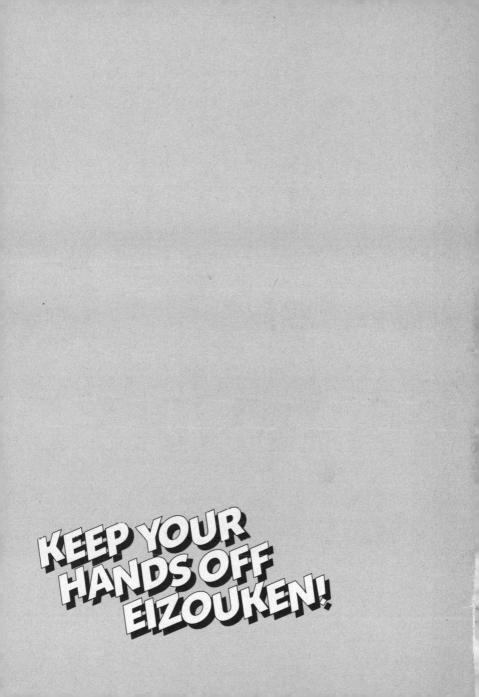

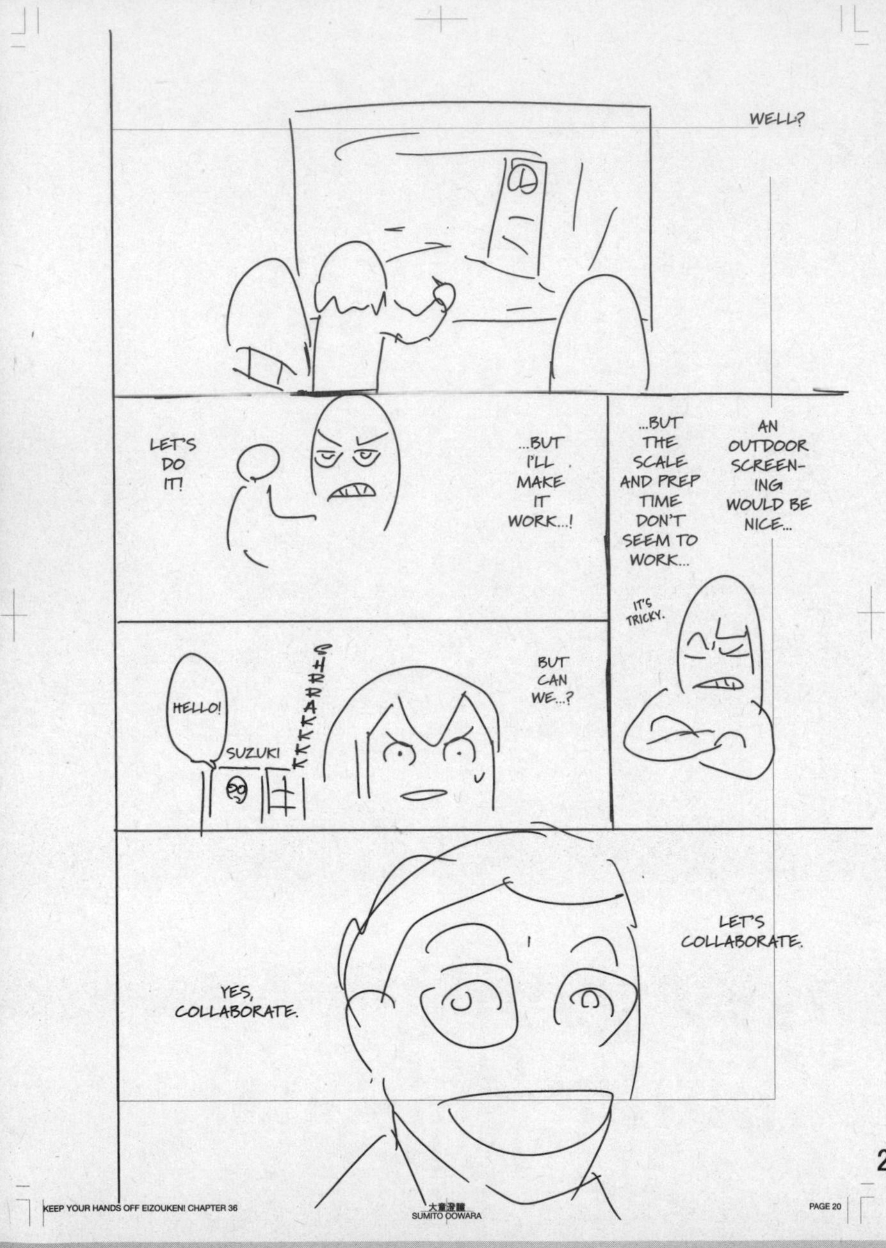
WELL?
AN OUTDOOR SCREEN-ING WOULD BE NICE...
...BUT THE SCALE AND PREP TIME DON'T SEEM TO WORK...
IT'S TRICKY.
...BUT I'LL MAKE IT WORK...!
LET'S DO IT!
BUT CAN WE...?
SHRRAKKKKKK
HELLO!
SUZUKI
LET'S COLLABORATE.
YES, COLLABORATE.
KEEP YOUR HANDS OFF EIZOUKEN! CHAPTER 36
大童澄瞳
SUMITO OOWARA
PAGE 20

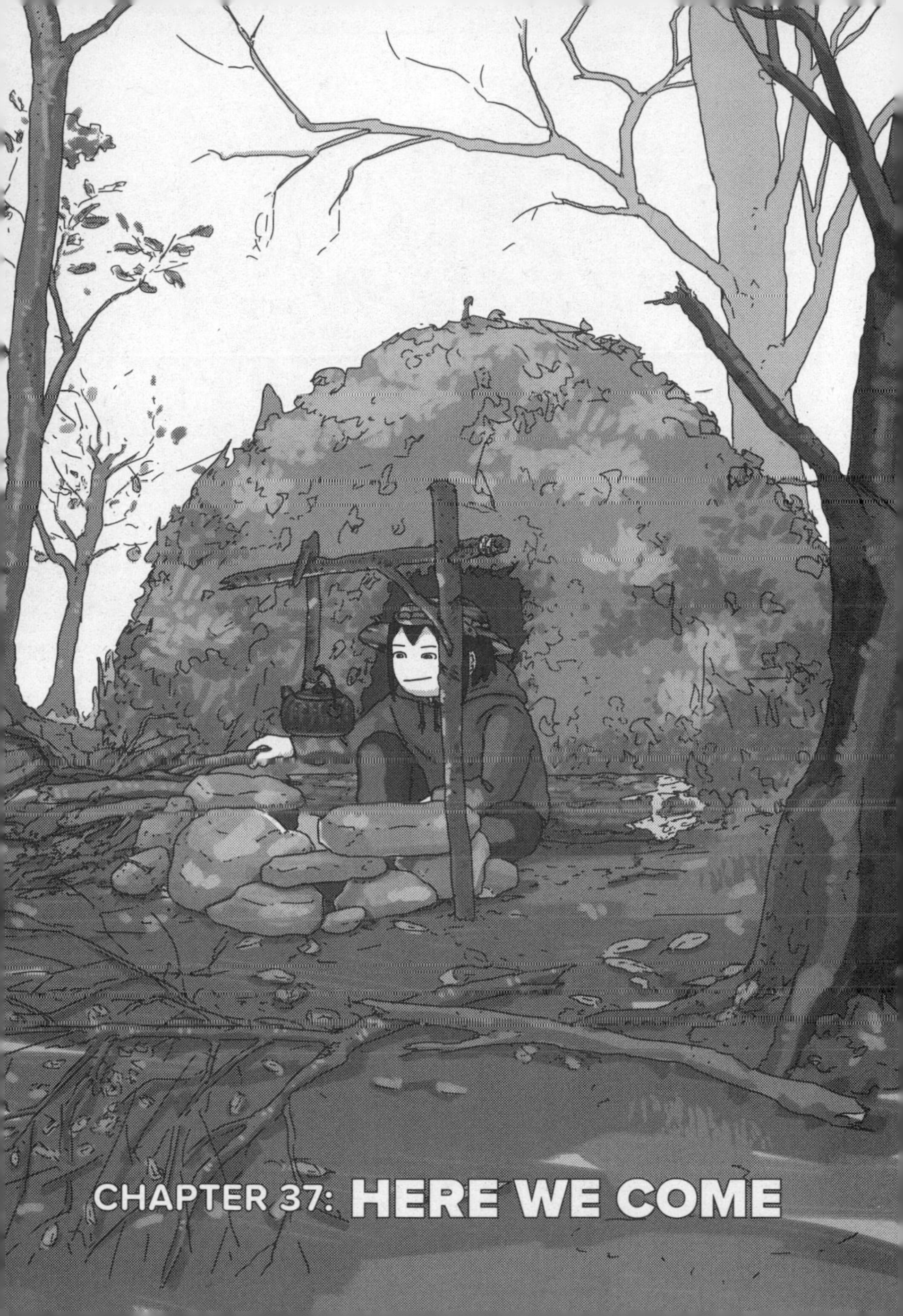

CHAPTER 37: HERE WE COME

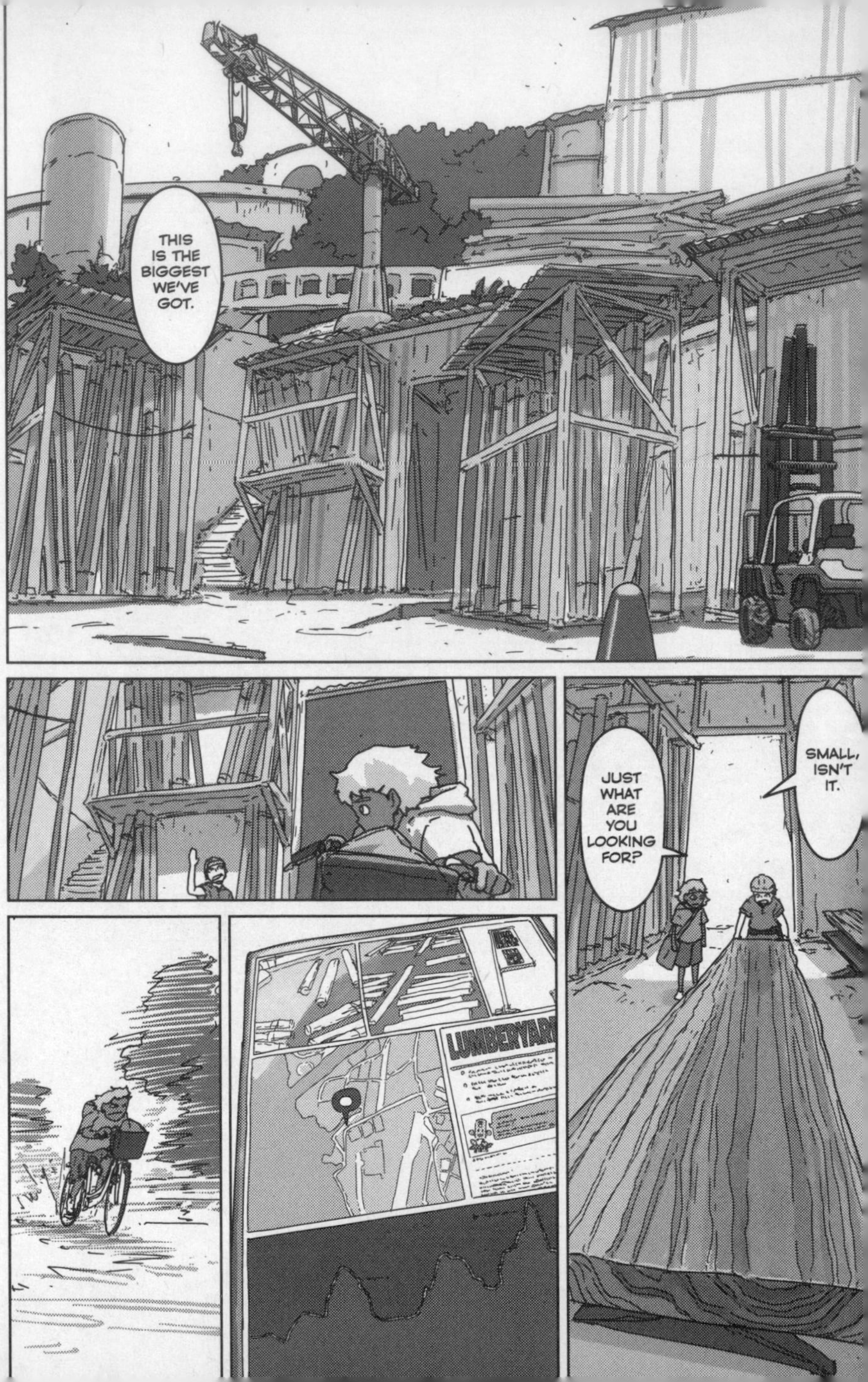
THIS IS THE BIGGEST WE'VE GOT.
SMALL, ISN'T IT.
JUST WHAT ARE YOU LOOKING FOR?

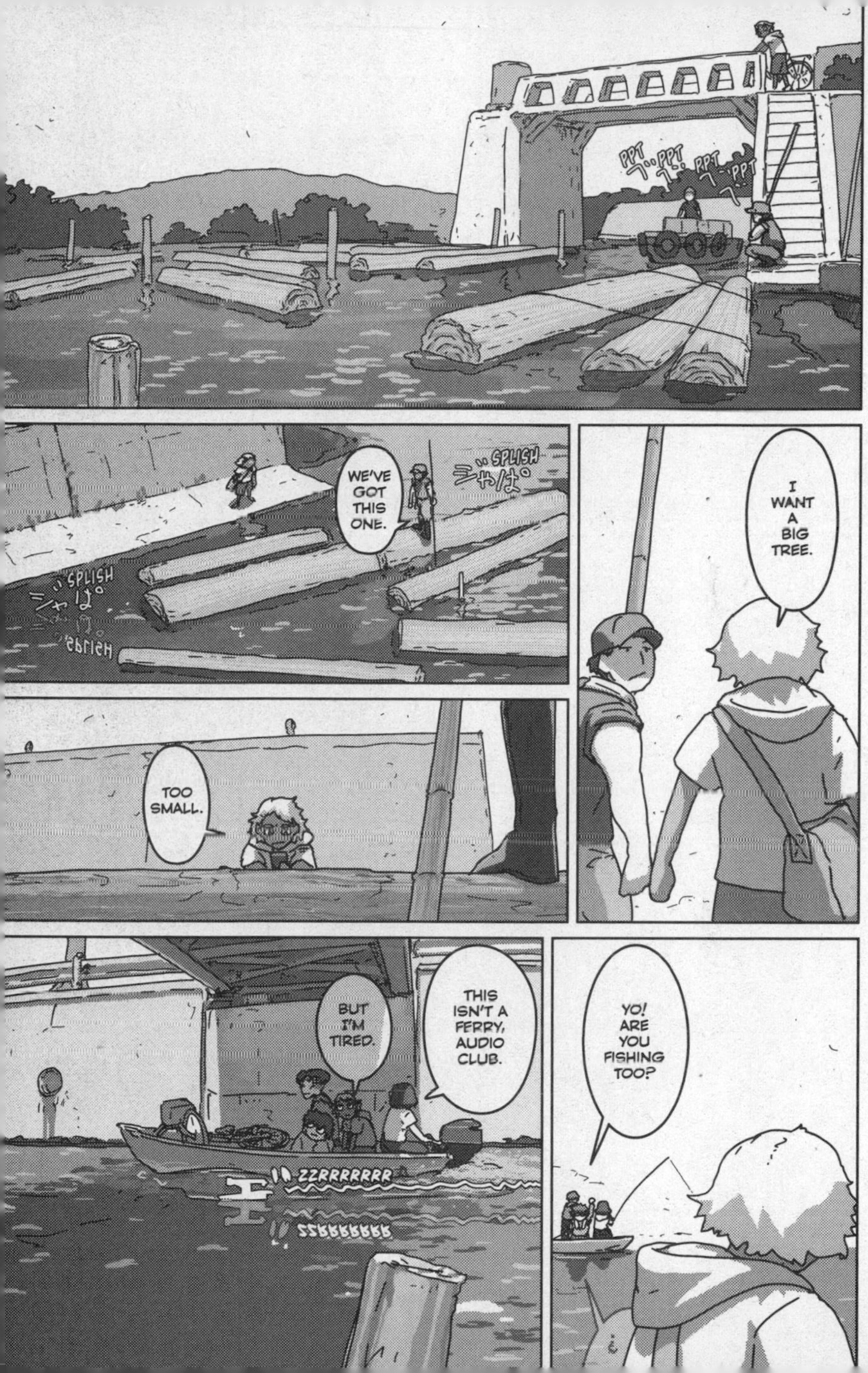
PPT PPT PPT PPT
I WANT A BIG TREE.
SPLISH
WE'VE GOT THIS ONE.
SPLISH
TOO SMALL.
YO! ARE YOU FISHING TOO?
THIS ISN'T A FERRY, AUDIO CLUB.
BUT I'M TIRED.
ZZRRRRRRR

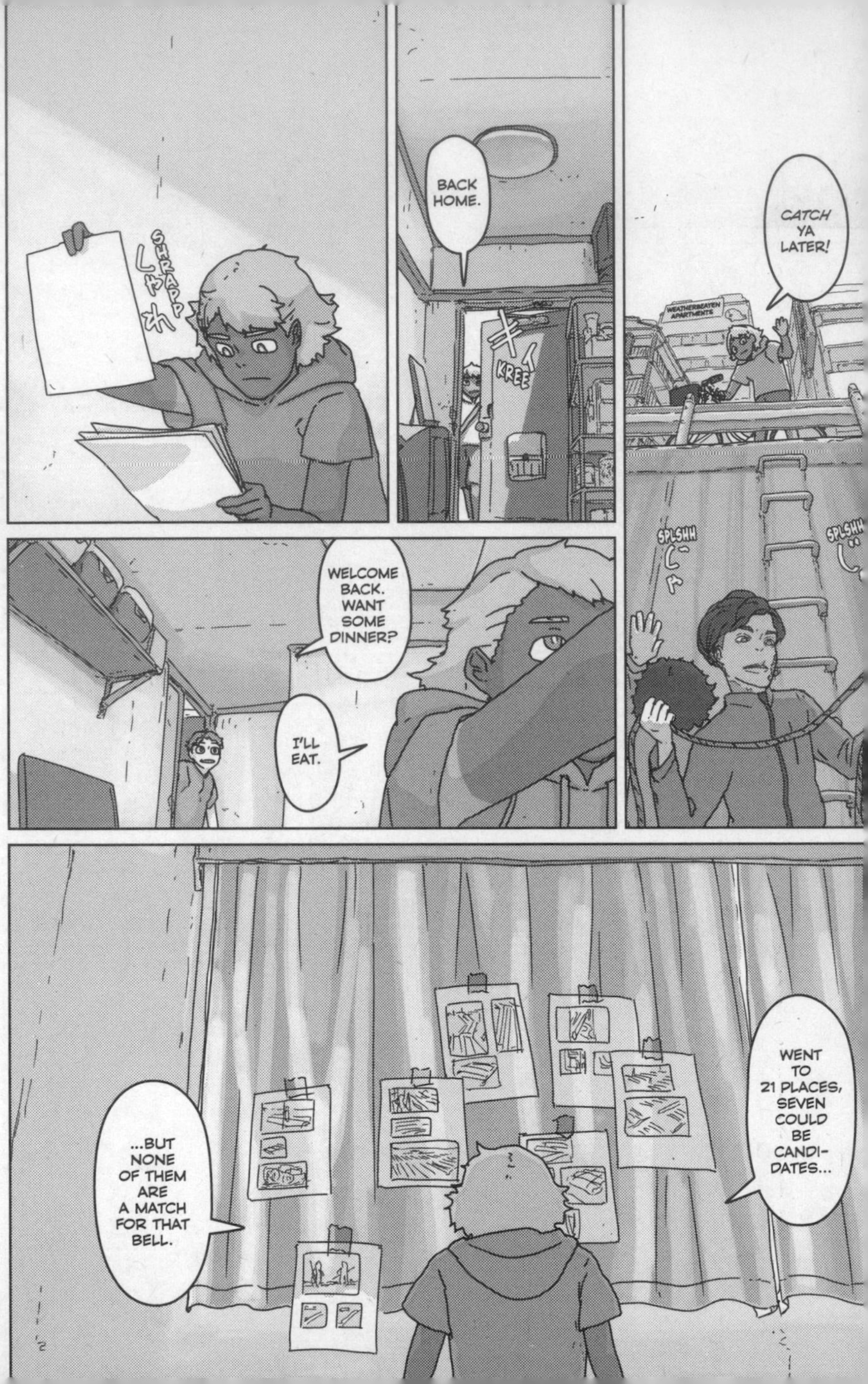
CATCH YA LATER!
WEATHERBEATEN APARTMENTS
SPLSHH
SPLSHH
BACK HOME.
KREE
SHRAPP
WELCOME BACK. WANT SOME DINNER?
I'LL EAT.
WENT TO 21 PLACES, SEVEN COULD BE CANDI- DATES...
...BUT NONE OF THEM ARE A MATCH FOR THAT BELL.

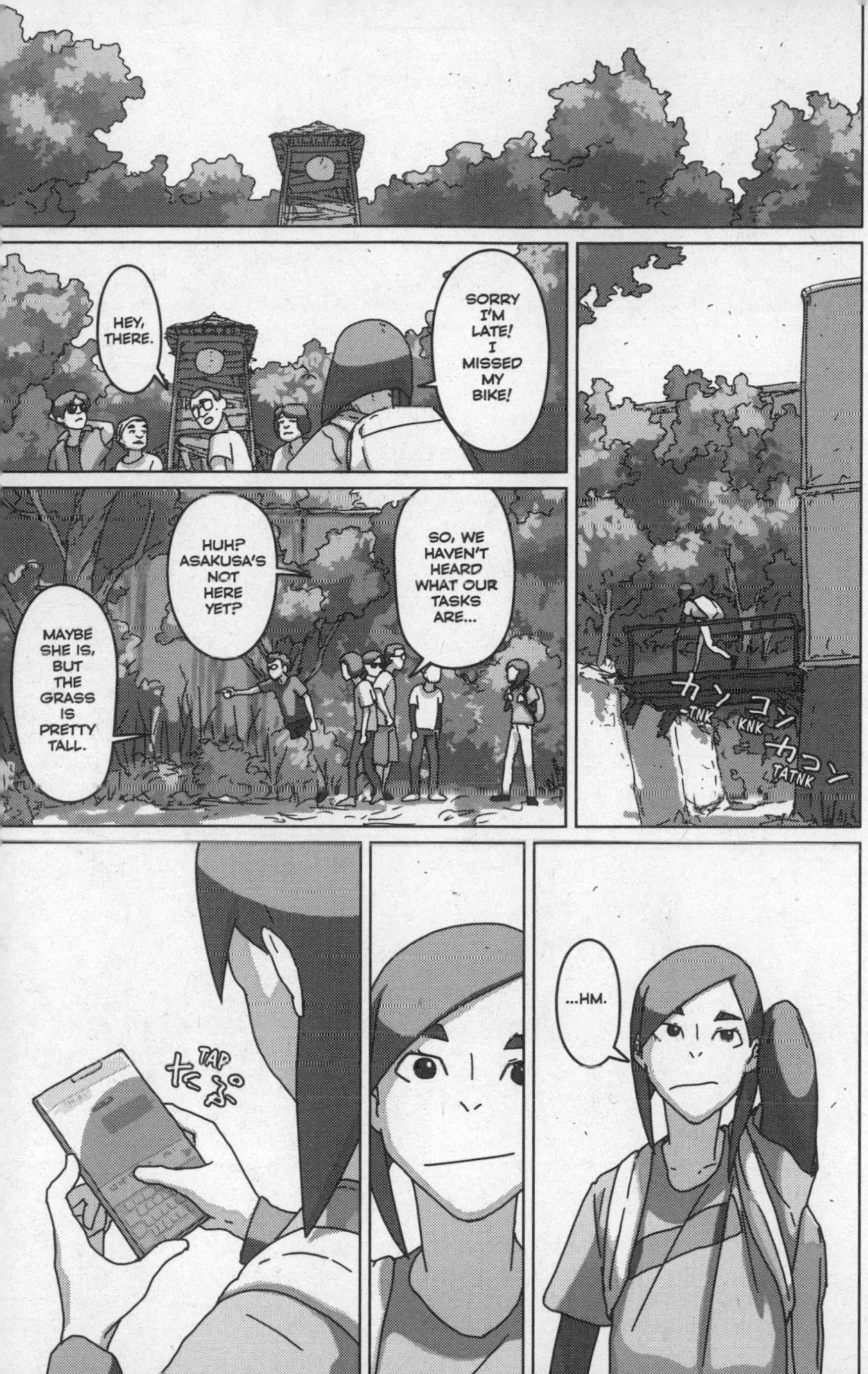
カン
TNK
コン
KNK
カコン
TATNK
SORRY I'M LATE! I MISSED MY BIKE!
HEY, THERE.
SO, WE HAVEN'T HEARD WHAT OUR TASKS ARE...
HUH? ASAKUSA'S NOT HERE YET?
MAYBE SHE IS, BUT THE GRASS IS PRETTY TALL.
...HM.
たぷ
TAP

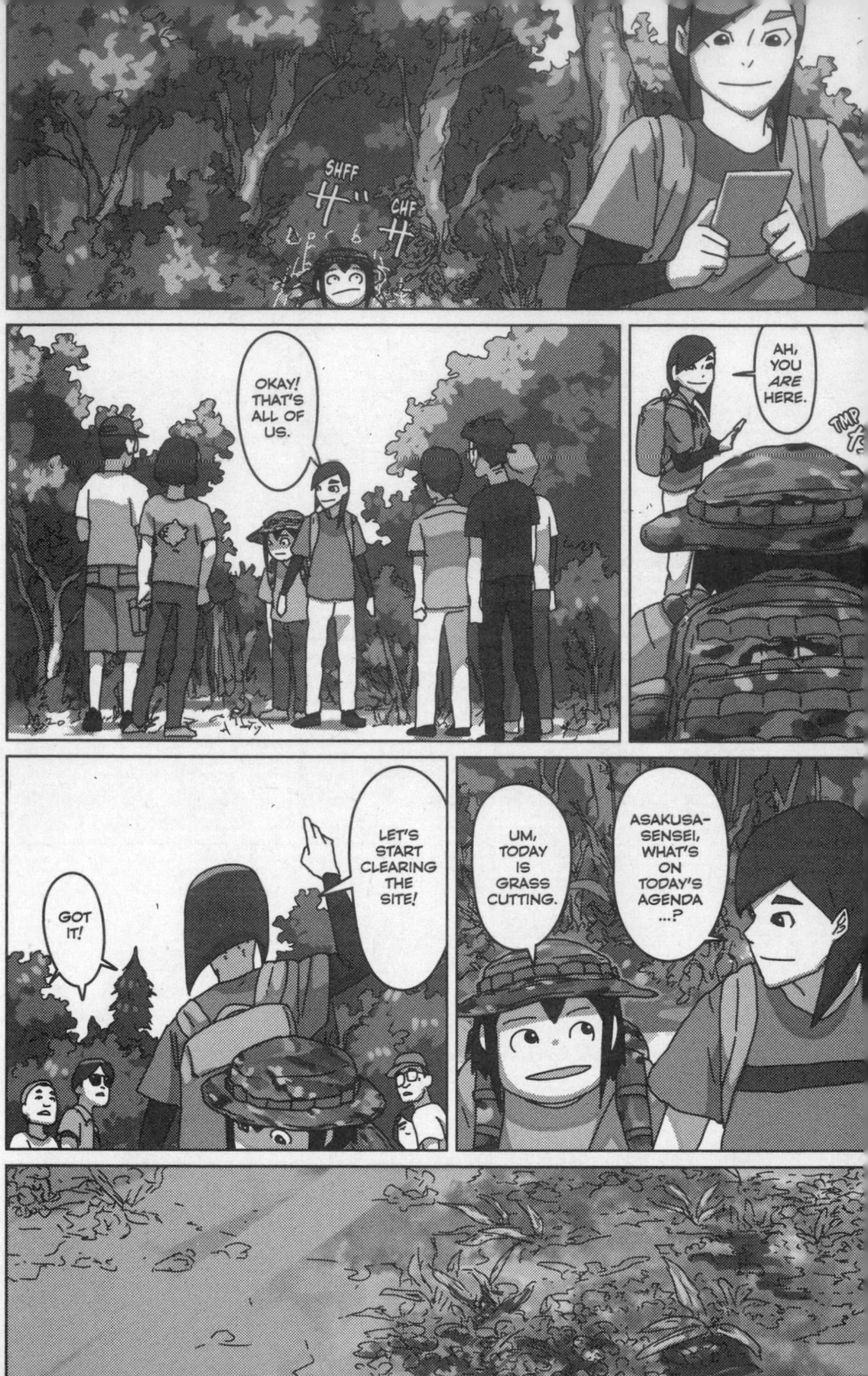
SHFF
CHF
AH, YOU *ARE* HERE.
TMP
OKAY! THAT'S ALL OF US.
ASAKUSA-SENSEI, WHAT'S ON TODAY'S AGENDA ...?
UM, TODAY IS GRASS CUTTING.
LET'S START CLEARING THE SITE!
GOT IT!

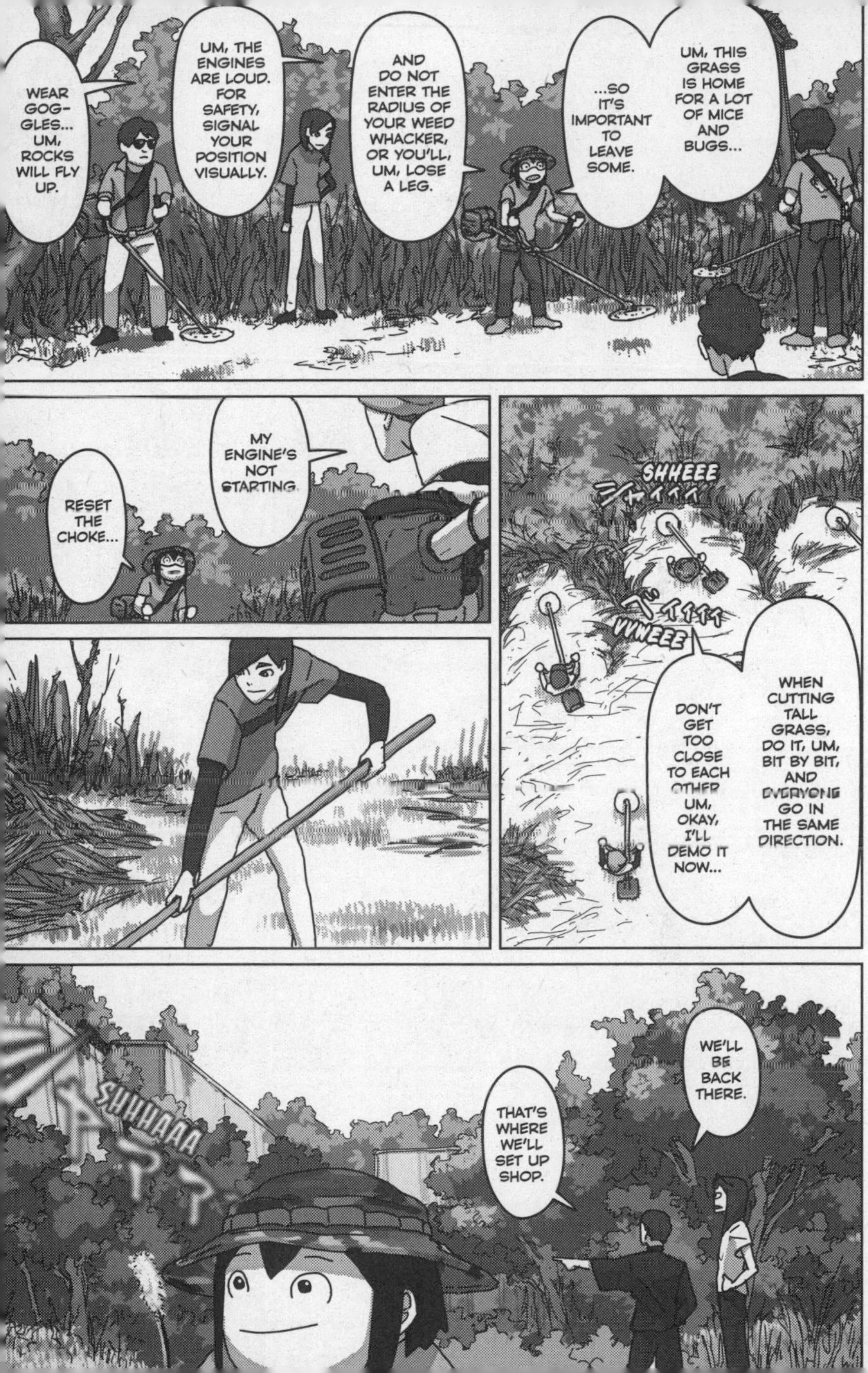
UM, THIS GRASS IS HOME FOR A LOT OF MICE AND BUGS...
...SO IT'S IMPORTANT TO LEAVE SOME.
AND DO NOT ENTER THE RADIUS OF YOUR WEED WHACKER, OR YOU'LL, UM, LOSE A LEG.
UM, THE ENGINES ARE LOUD. FOR SAFETY, SIGNAL YOUR POSITION VISUALLY.
WEAR GOG-GLES... UM, ROCKS WILL FLY UP.
SHHEEE
VVWEEE
WHEN CUTTING TALL GRASS, DO IT, UM, BIT BY BIT, AND EVERYONE GO IN THE SAME DIRECTION.
DON'T GET TOO CLOSE TO EACH OTHER. UM, OKAY, I'LL DEMO IT NOW...
MY ENGINE'S NOT STARTING.
RESET THE CHOKE...
WE'LL BE BACK THERE.
THAT'S WHERE WE'LL SET UP SHOP.
SHHHAAA

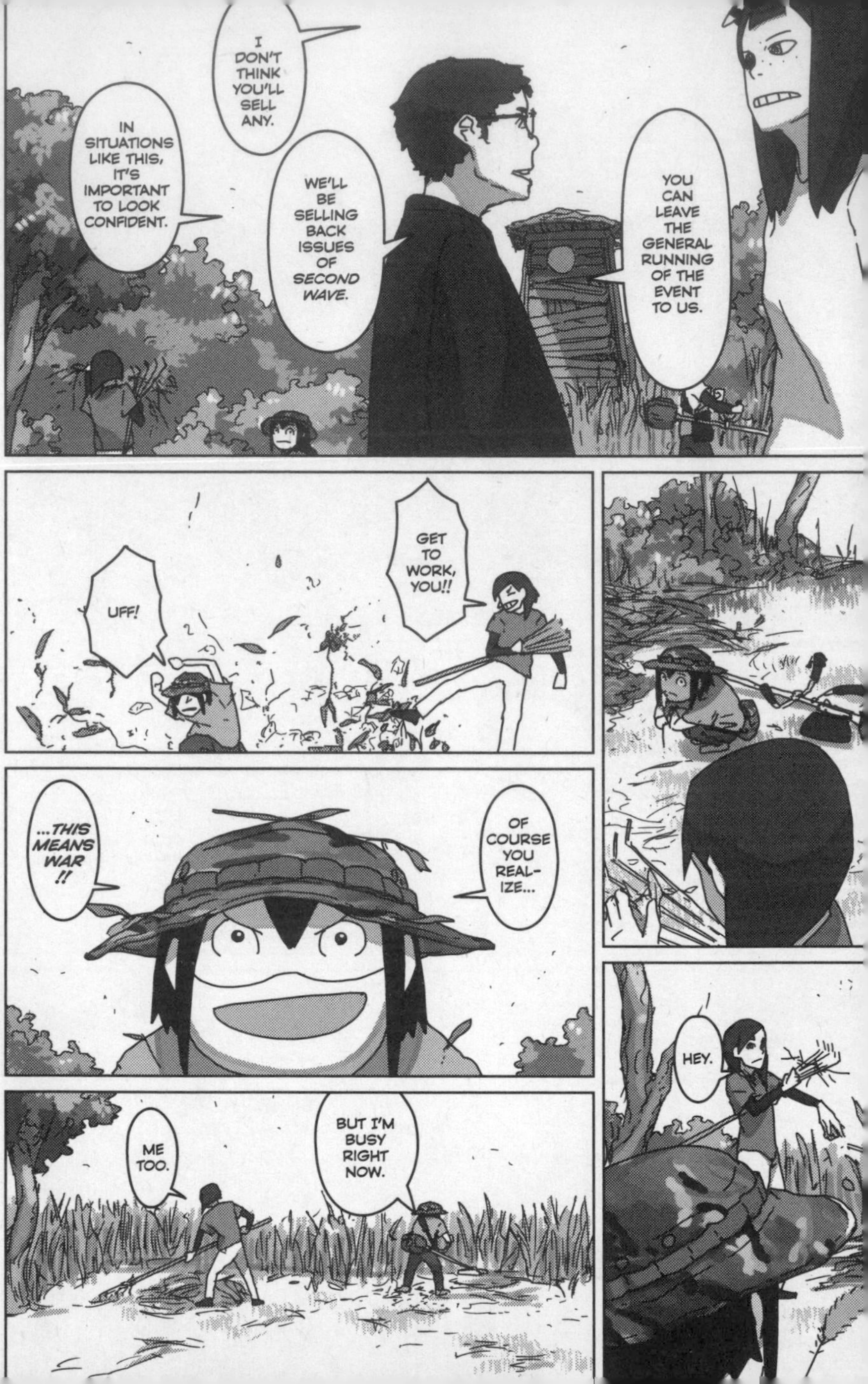
YOU CAN LEAVE THE GENERAL RUNNING OF THE EVENT TO US.
WE'LL BE SELLING BACK ISSUES OF *SECOND WAVE.*
I DON'T THINK YOU'LL SELL ANY.
IN SITUATIONS LIKE THIS, IT'S IMPORTANT TO LOOK CONFIDENT.
HEY.
GET TO WORK, YOU!!
UFF!
OF COURSE YOU REAL-IZE...
...THIS MEANS WAR!!
BUT I'M BUSY RIGHT NOW.
ME TOO.

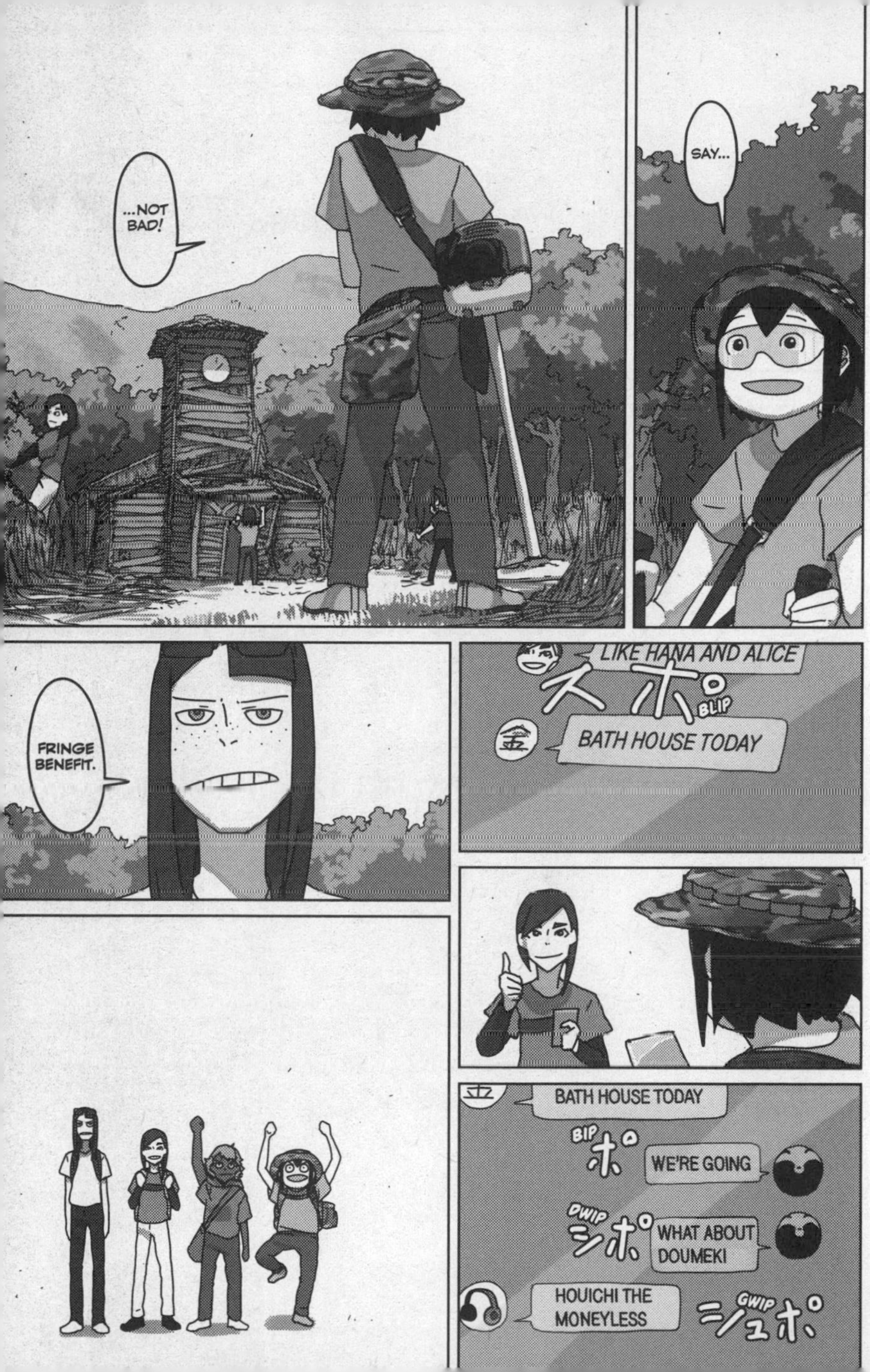
SAY...
...NOT BAD!
LIKE HANA AND ALICE
スポ
BLIP
BATH HOUSE TODAY
FRINGE BENEFIT.
BATH HOUSE TODAY
BIP
ポ
WE'RE GOING
DWIP
シポ
WHAT ABOUT DOUMEKI
HOUICHI THE MONEYLESS
GWIP
ニュポ

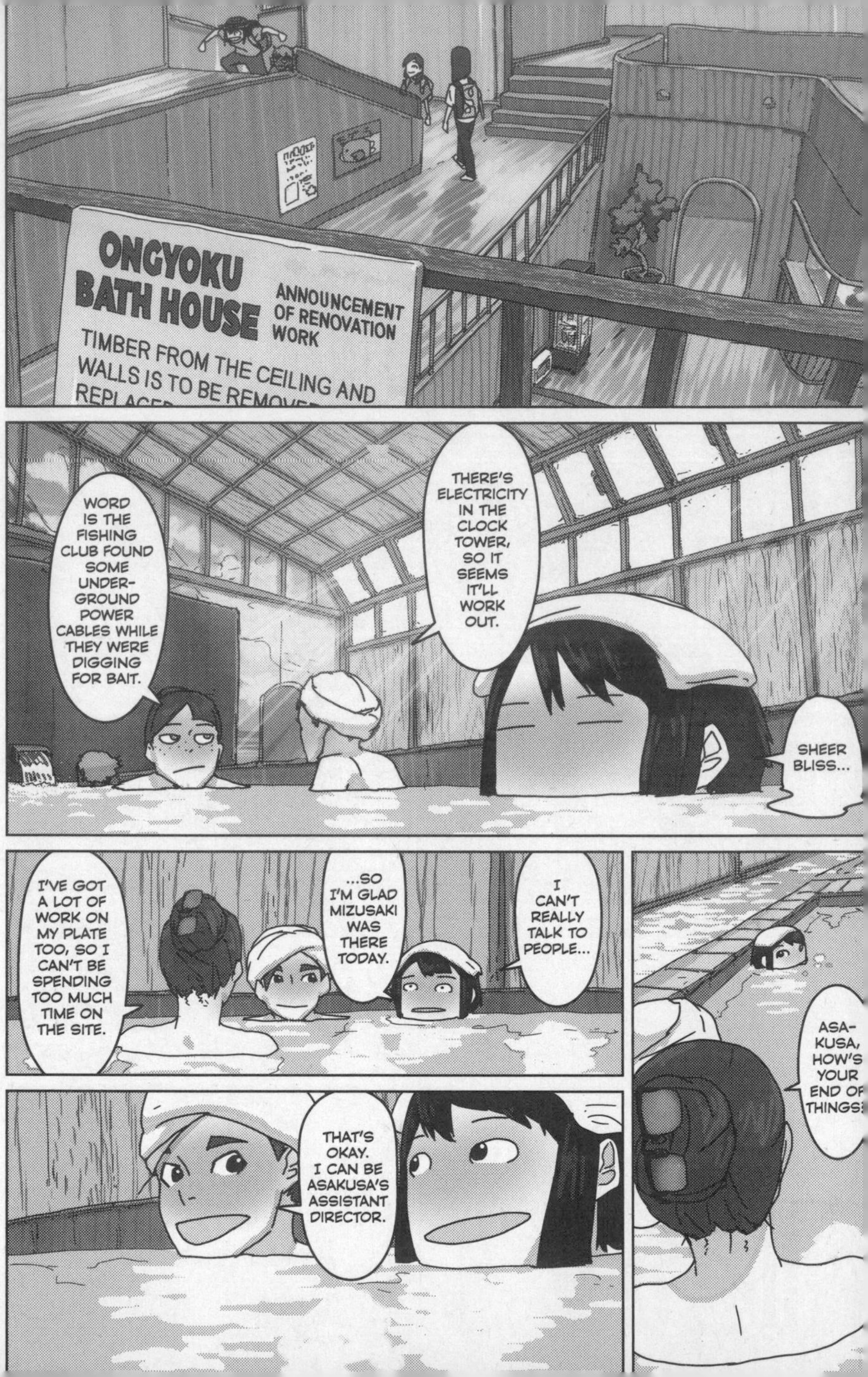
ONGYOKU BATH HOUSE
ANNOUNCEMENT OF RENOVATION WORK
TIMBER FROM THE CEILING AND WALLS IS TO BE REMOV
SHEER BLISS...
THERE'S ELECTRICITY IN THE CLOCK TOWER, SO IT SEEMS IT'LL WORK OUT.
WORD IS THE FISHING CLUB FOUND SOME UNDER-GROUND POWER CABLES WHILE THEY WERE DIGGING FOR BAIT.
ASA-KUSA, HOW'S YOUR END OF THINGS
I CAN'T REALLY TALK TO PEOPLE...
...SO I'M GLAD MIZUSAKI WAS THERE TODAY.
I'VE GOT A LOT OF WORK ON MY PLATE TOO, SO I CAN'T BE SPENDING TOO MUCH TIME ON THE SITE.
THAT'S OKAY. I CAN BE ASAKUSA'S ASSISTANT DIRECTOR.

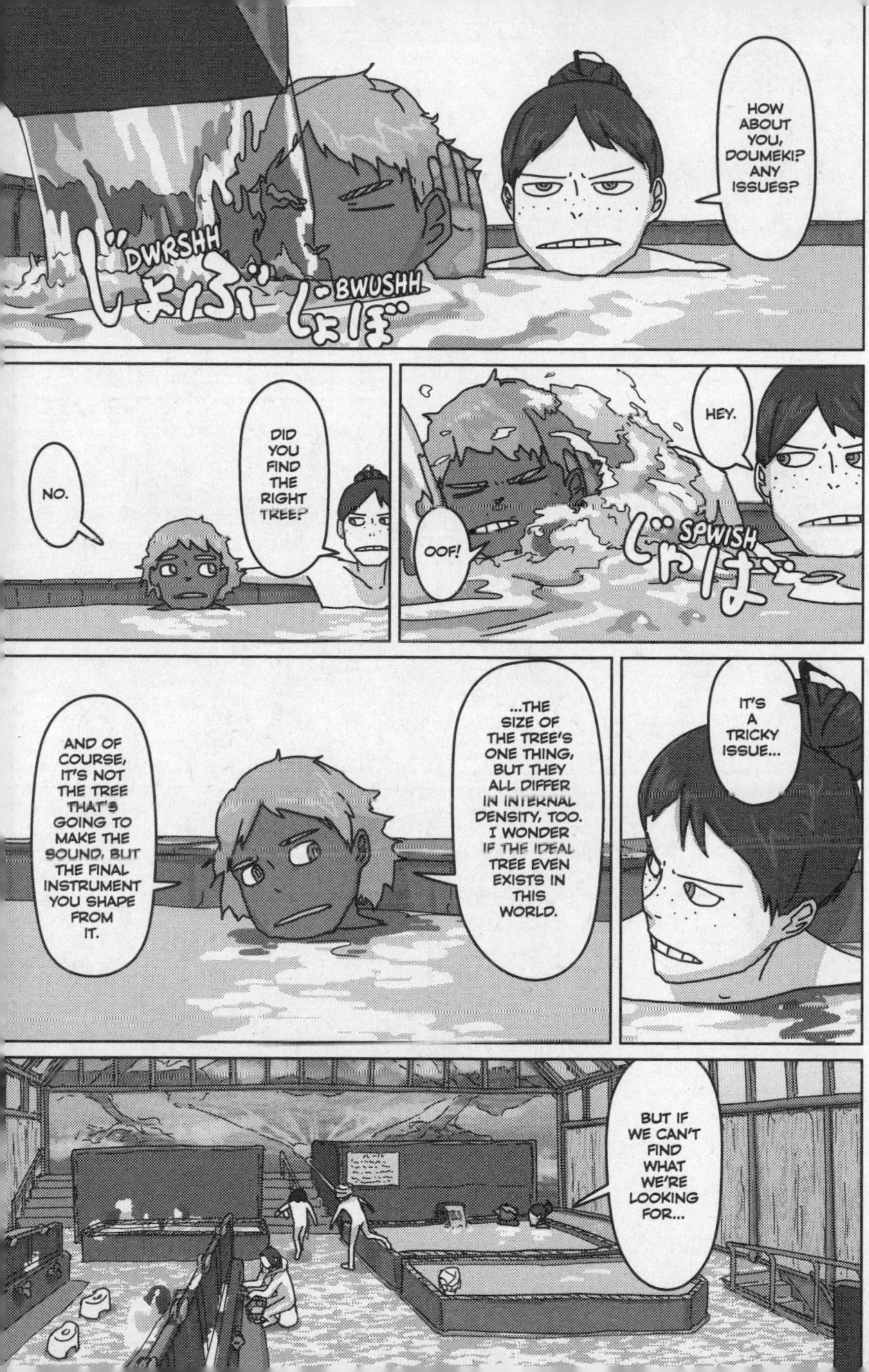
HOW ABOUT YOU, DOUMEKI? ANY ISSUES?
じょぶ DWRSHH
じょぼ BWUSHH
HEY.
OOF!
じゃばー SPWISH
DID YOU FIND THE RIGHT TREE?
NO.
IT'S A TRICKY ISSUE...
...THE SIZE OF THE TREE'S ONE THING, BUT THEY ALL DIFFER IN INTERNAL DENSITY, TOO. I WONDER IF THE IDEAL TREE EVEN EXISTS IN THIS WORLD.
AND OF COURSE, IT'S NOT THE TREE THAT'S GOING TO MAKE THE SOUND, BUT THE FINAL INSTRUMENT YOU SHAPE FROM IT.
BUT IF WE CAN'T FIND WHAT WE'RE LOOKING FOR...

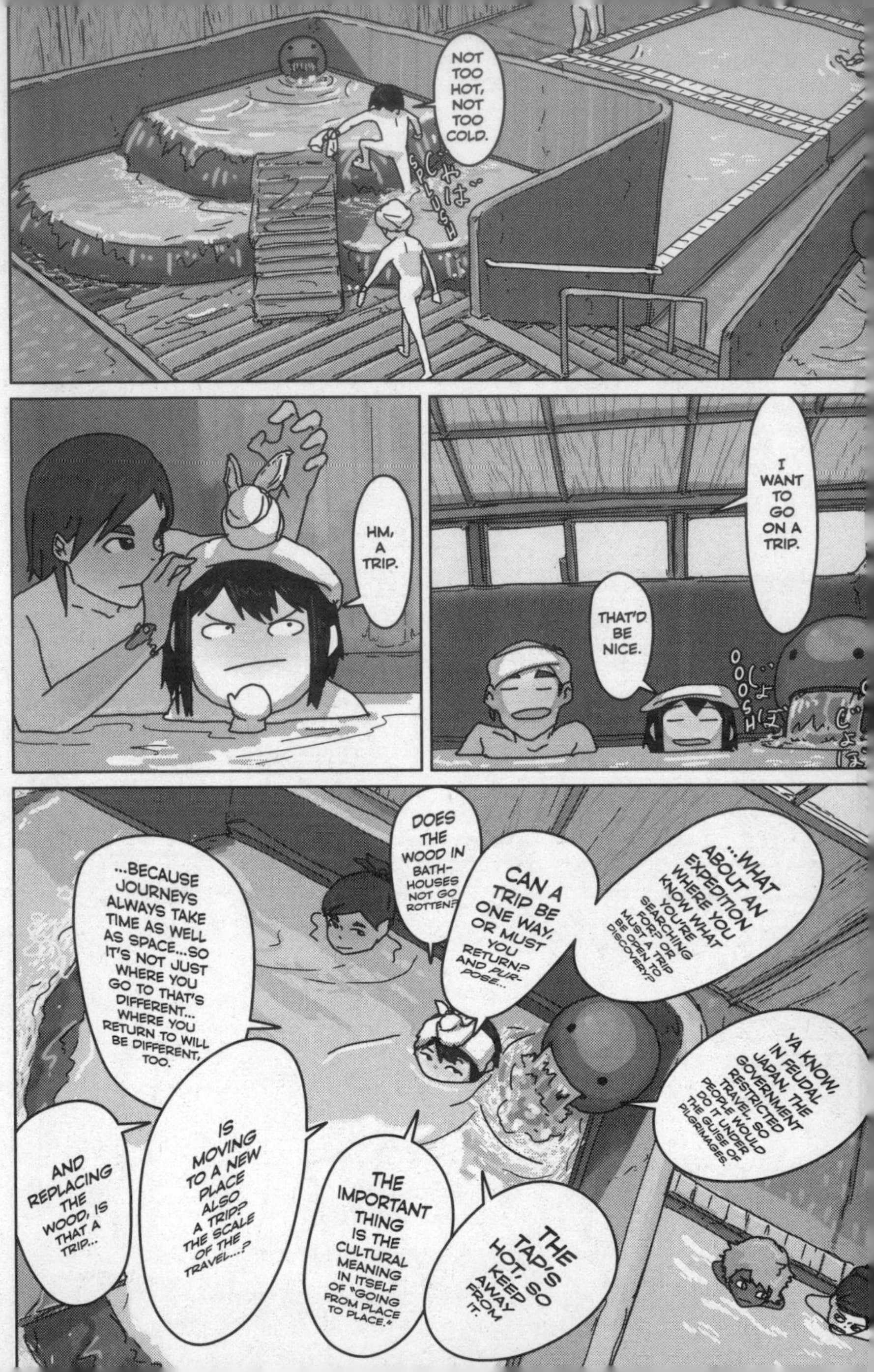
NOT TOO HOT, NOT TOO COLD.
SPLOOSH
I WANT TO GO ON A TRIP.
THAT'D BE NICE.
HM, A TRIP.
...WHAT ABOUT AN EXPEDITION WHERE YOU KNOW WHAT YOU'RE SEARCHING FOR? OR MUST A TRIP BE OPEN TO DISCOVERY?
CAN A TRIP BE ONE WAY, OR MUST YOU RETURN? AND PUR-POSE...
DOES THE WOOD IN BATH-HOUSES NOT GO ROTTEN?
...BECAUSE JOURNEYS ALWAYS TAKE TIME AS WELL AS SPACE...SO IT'S NOT JUST WHERE YOU GO TO THAT'S DIFFERENT... WHERE YOU RETURN TO WILL BE DIFFERENT, TOO.
YA KNOW, IN FEUDAL JAPAN, THE GOVERNMENT RESTRICTED TRAVEL, SO PEOPLE WOULD DO IT UNDER THE GUISE OF PILGRIMAGES.
THE TAP'S HOT, SO KEEP AWAY FROM IT.
THE IMPORTANT THING IS THE CULTURAL MEANING IN ITSELF OF "GOING FROM PLACE TO PLACE."
IS MOVING TO A NEW PLACE ALSO A TRIP? THE SCALE OF THE TRAVEL...?
AND REPLACING THE WOOD, IS THAT A TRIP...

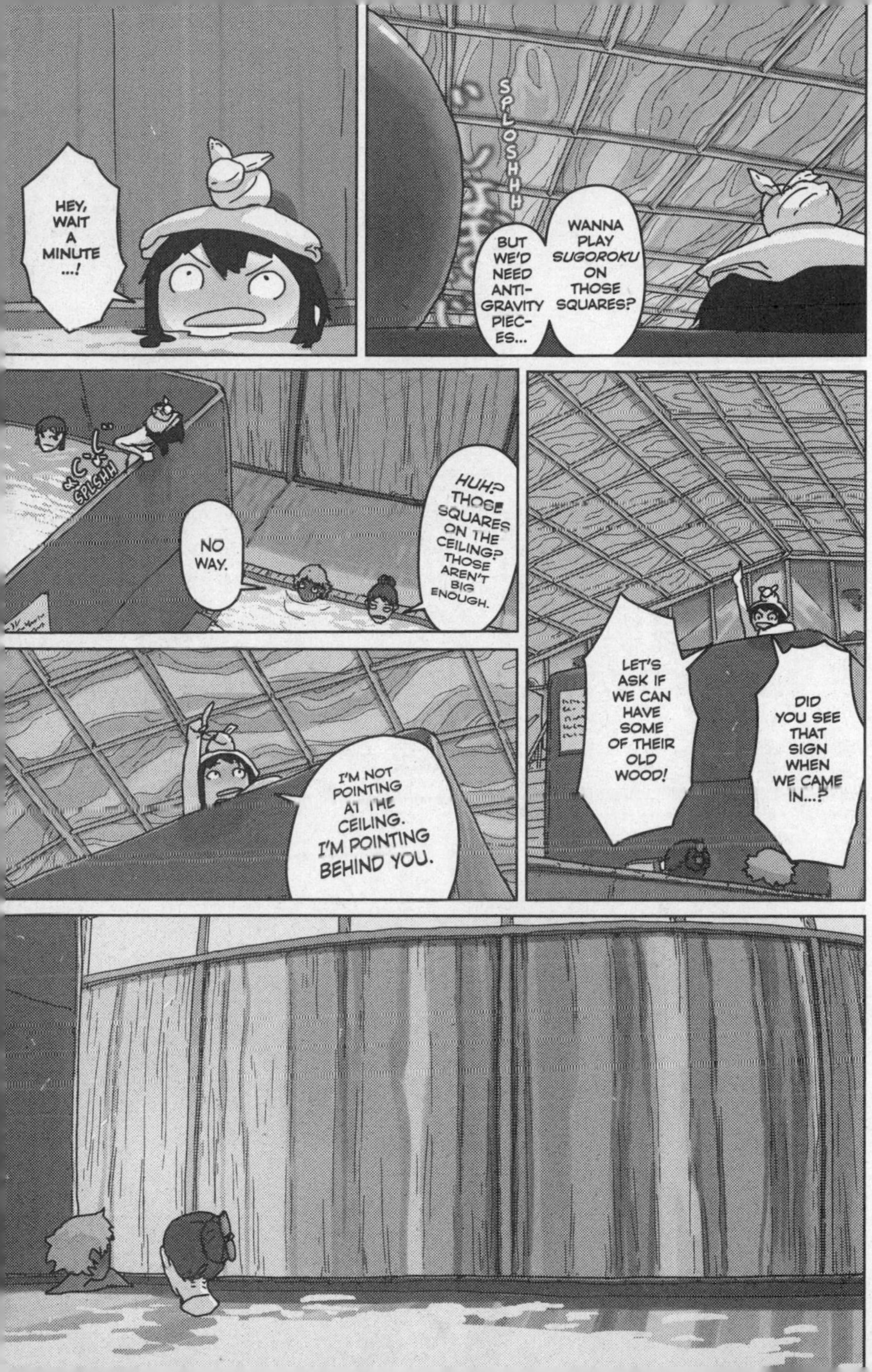
SPLOSHHH
WANNA PLAY SUGOROKU ON THOSE SQUARES?
BUT WE'D NEED ANTI-GRAVITY PIECES...
HEY, WAIT A MINUTE ...!
DID YOU SEE THAT SIGN WHEN WE CAME IN...?
LET'S ASK IF WE CAN HAVE SOME OF THEIR OLD WOOD!
HUH? THOSE SQUARES ON THE CEILING? THOSE AREN'T BIG ENOUGH.
NO WAY.
SPLSHH
I'M NOT POINTING AT THE CEILING. I'M POINTING BEHIND YOU.

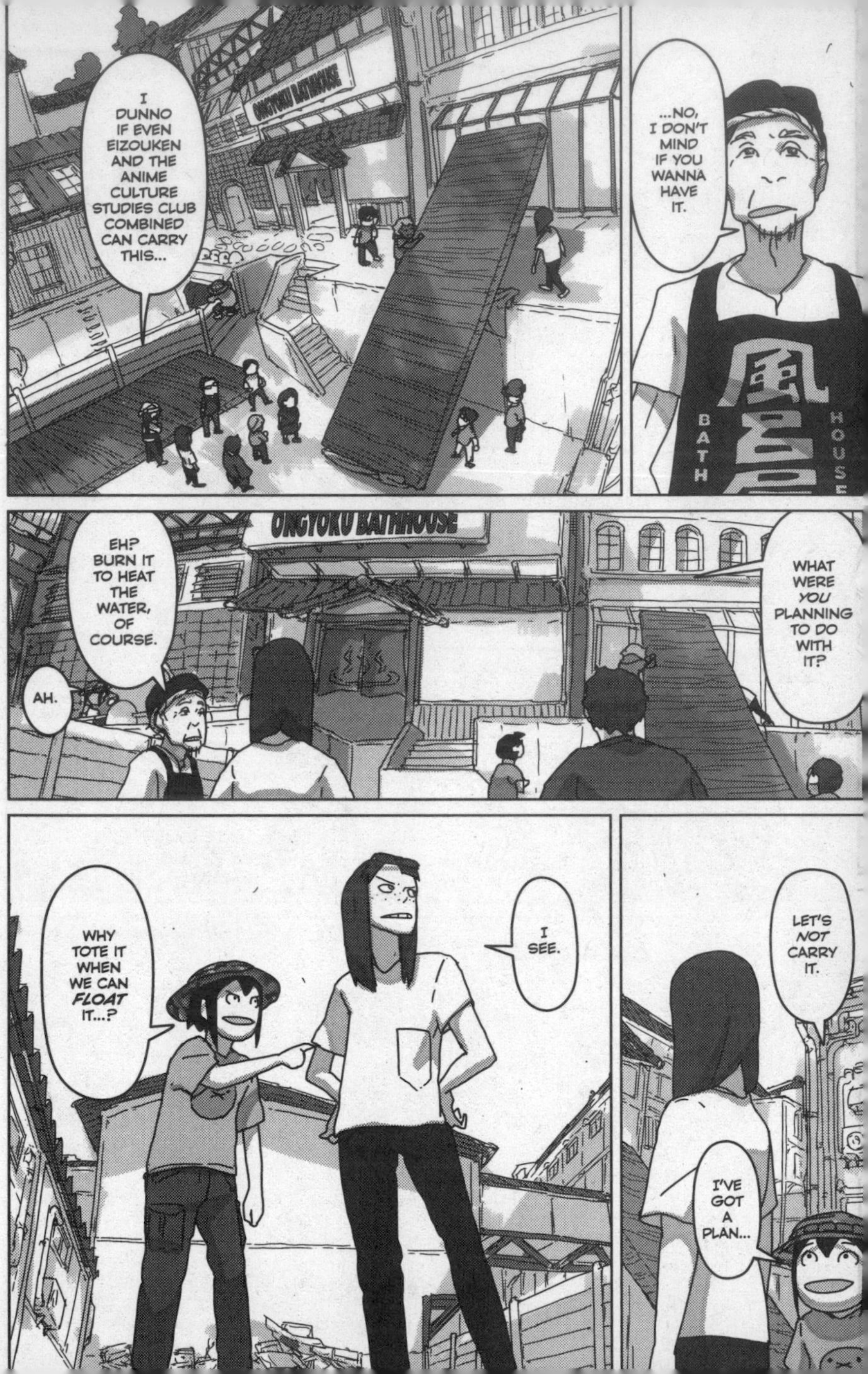
...NO, I DON'T MIND IF YOU WANNA HAVE IT.
BATH HOUSE
ONGYOKU BATHHOUSE
I DUNNO IF EVEN EIZOUKEN AND THE ANIME CULTURE STUDIES CLUB COMBINED CAN CARRY THIS...
WHAT WERE *YOU* PLANNING TO DO WITH IT?
ONGYOKU BATHHOUSE
EH? BURN IT TO HEAT THE WATER, OF COURSE.
AH.
LET'S *NOT* CARRY IT.
I'VE GOT A PLAN...
I SEE.
WHY TOTE IT WHEN WE CAN *FLOAT* IT...?

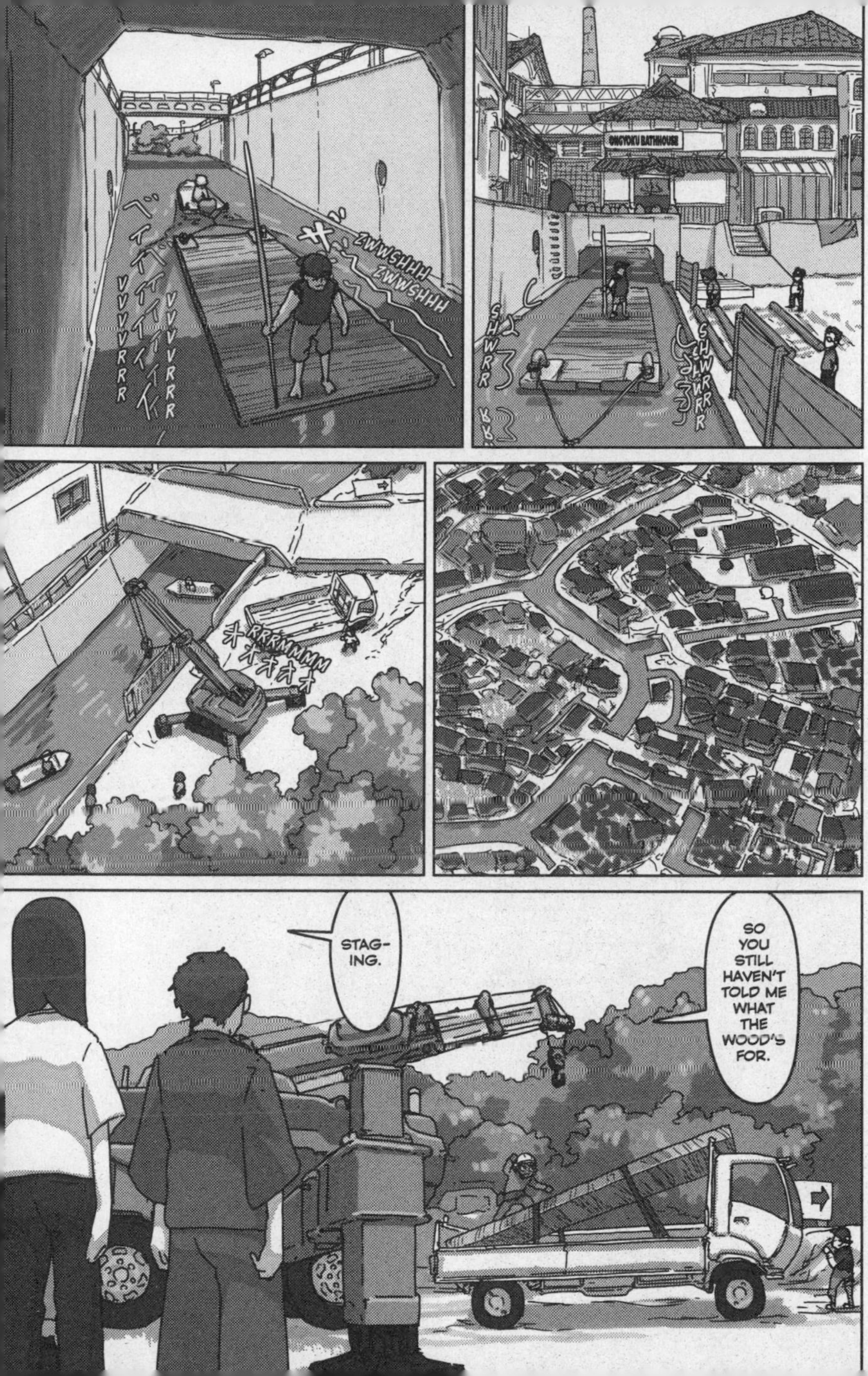
ONGYOKU BATHHOUSE
SHWRR
SHWRRR
ZWWSHHH
ZWWSHHH
VVVVVRRR
VVVVVRRR
RRRMMMM
SO YOU STILL HAVEN'T TOLD ME WHAT THE WOOD'S FOR.
STAG-ING.

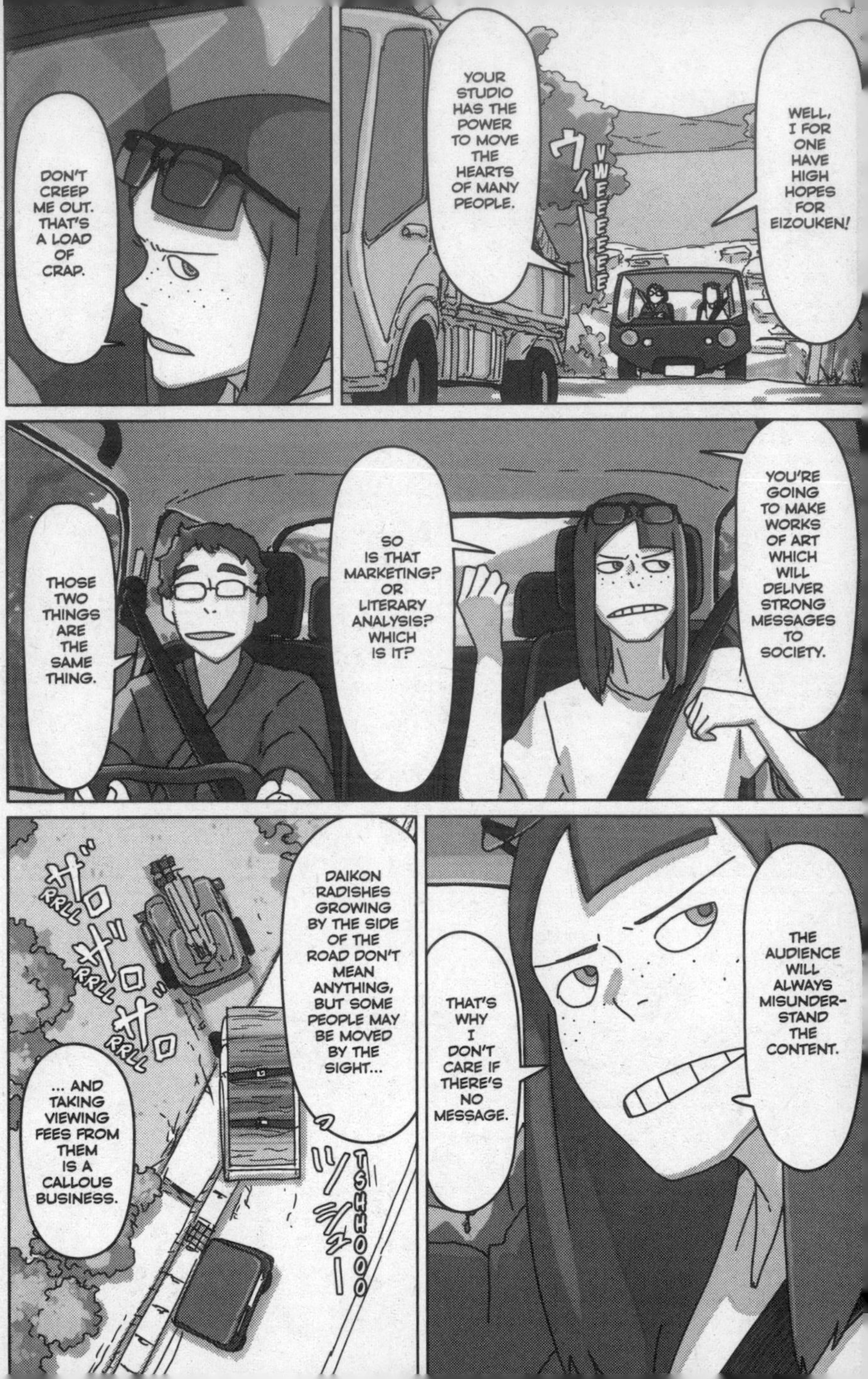
WELL, I FOR ONE HAVE HIGH HOPES FOR EIZOUKEN!
YOUR STUDIO HAS THE POWER TO MOVE THE HEARTS OF MANY PEOPLE.
ウィー VWEEEEEE
DON'T CREEP ME OUT. THAT'S A LOAD OF CRAP.
YOU'RE GOING TO MAKE WORKS OF ART WHICH WILL DELIVER STRONG MESSAGES TO SOCIETY.
SO IS THAT MARKETING? OR LITERARY ANALYSIS? WHICH IS IT?
THOSE TWO THINGS ARE THE SAME THING.
THE AUDIENCE WILL ALWAYS MISUNDERSTAND THE CONTENT.
THAT'S WHY I DON'T CARE IF THERE'S NO MESSAGE.
DAIKON RADISHES GROWING BY THE SIDE OF THE ROAD DON'T MEAN ANYTHING, BUT SOME PEOPLE MAY BE MOVED BY THE SIGHT...
RRLL
RRLL
RRLL
... AND TAKING VIEWING FEES FROM THEM IS A CALLOUS BUSINESS.
TSHHOOO

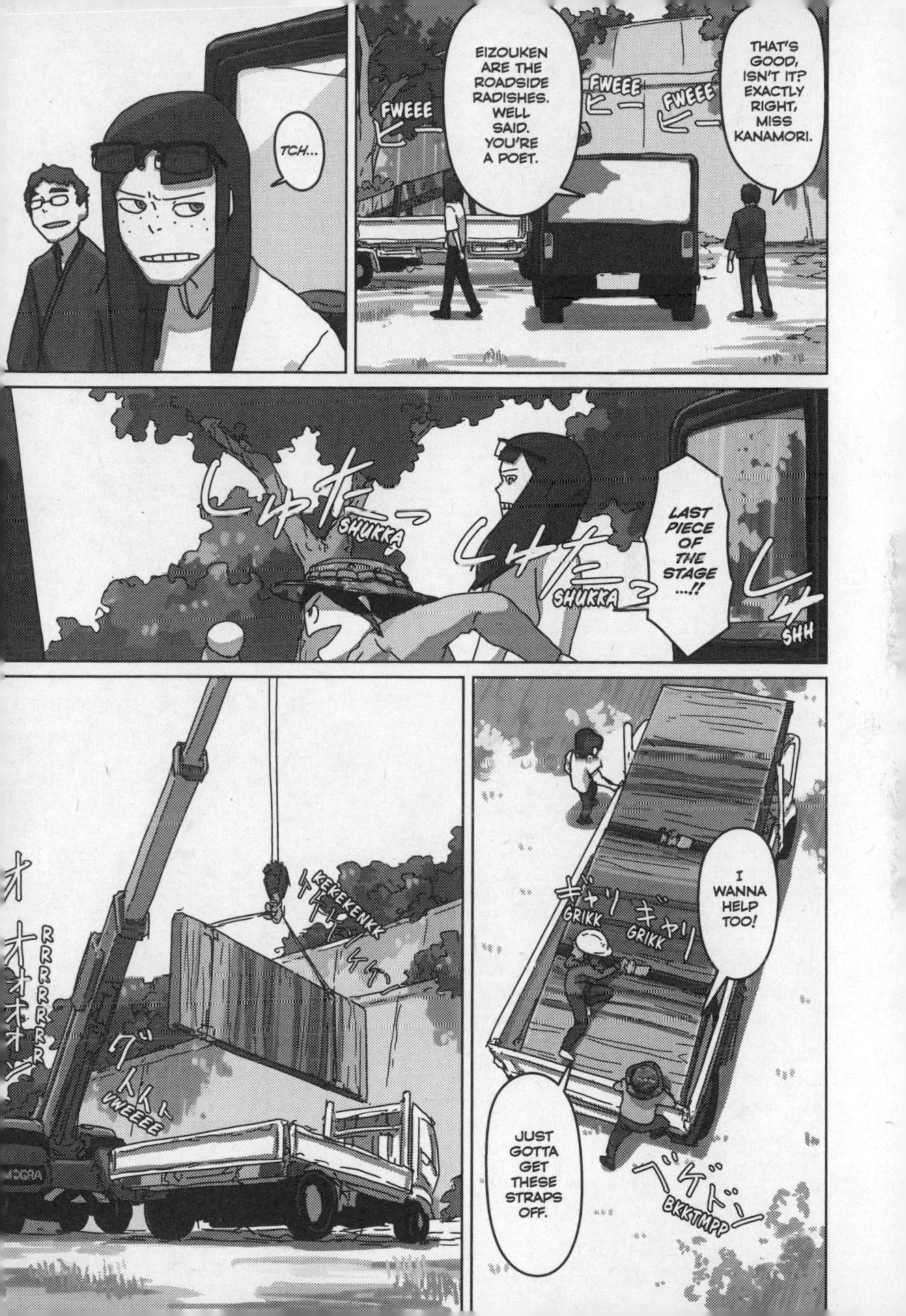
THAT'S GOOD, ISN'T IT? EXACTLY RIGHT, MISS KANAMORI.
FWEEE
FWEEE
EIZOUKEN ARE THE ROADSIDE RADISHES. WELL SAID. YOU'RE A POET.
FWEEE
TCH...
SHH
LAST PIECE OF THE STAGE ...!!
SHUKKA
SHUKKA
I WANNA HELP TOO!
GRIKK
GRIKK
JUST GOTTA GET THESE STRAPS OFF.
BKKTMPP
KEKEKENKK
VWEEEE
RRRRRRR

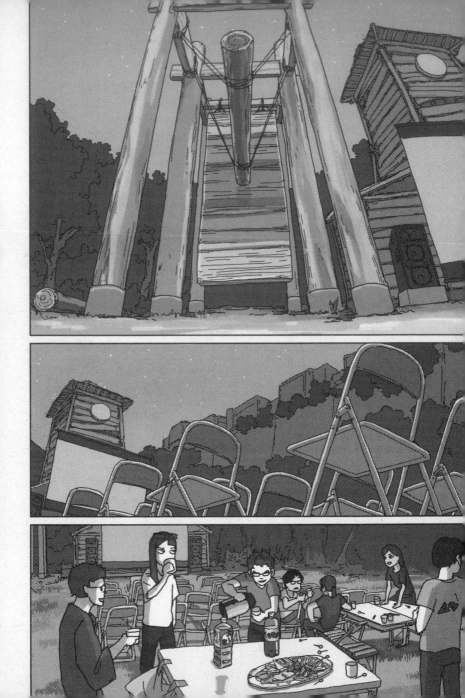

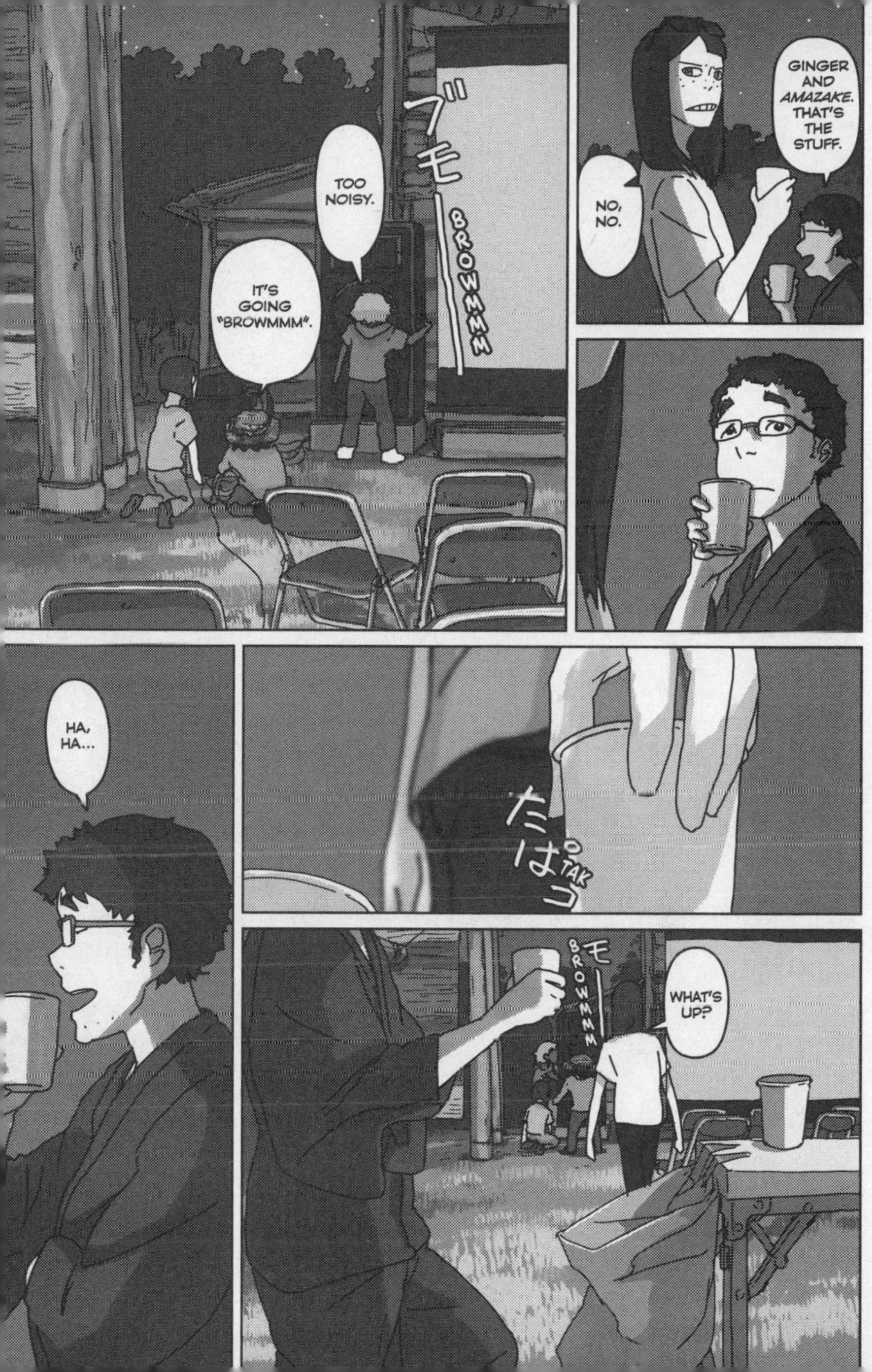
GINGER AND AMAZAKE. THAT'S THE STUFF.
NO, NO.
ブモー
BROWMMM
TOO NOISY.
IT'S GOING "BROWMMM".
たぱっ
TAK
モー
BROWMMM
WHAT'S UP?
HA, HA...

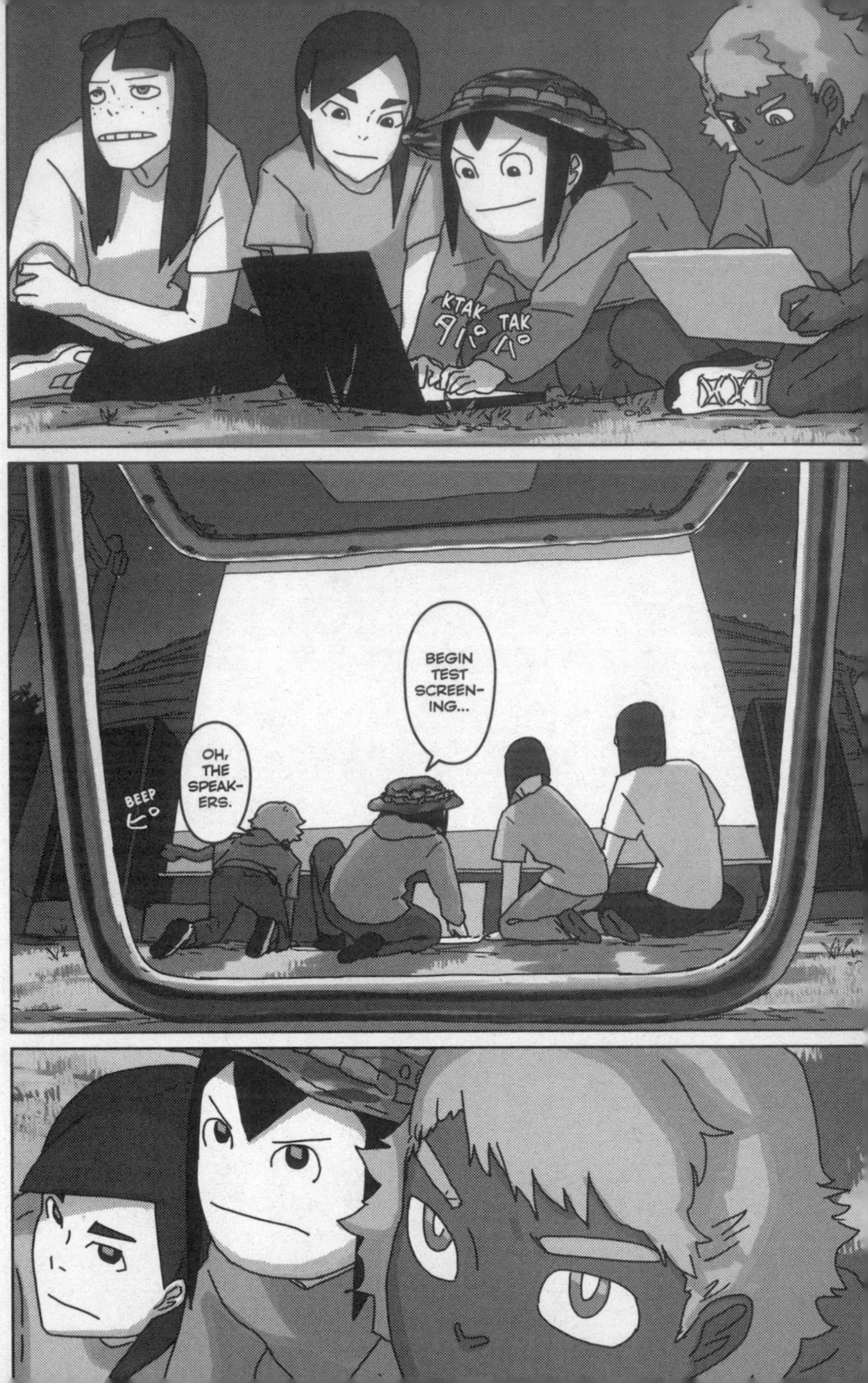
KTAK
TAK
BEGIN TEST SCREEN-ING...
OH, THE SPEAK-ERS.
BEEP

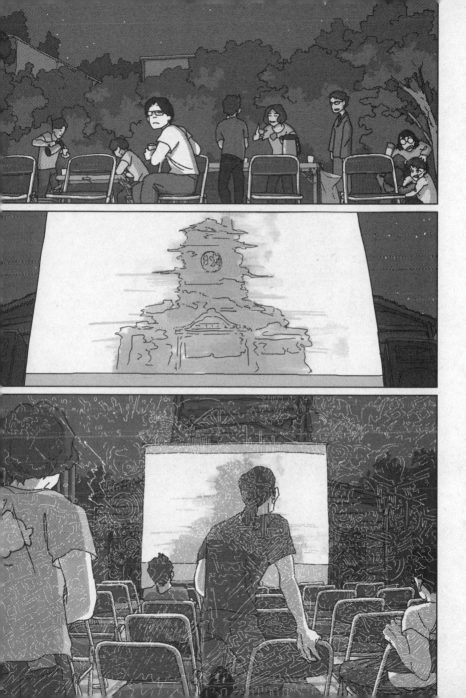

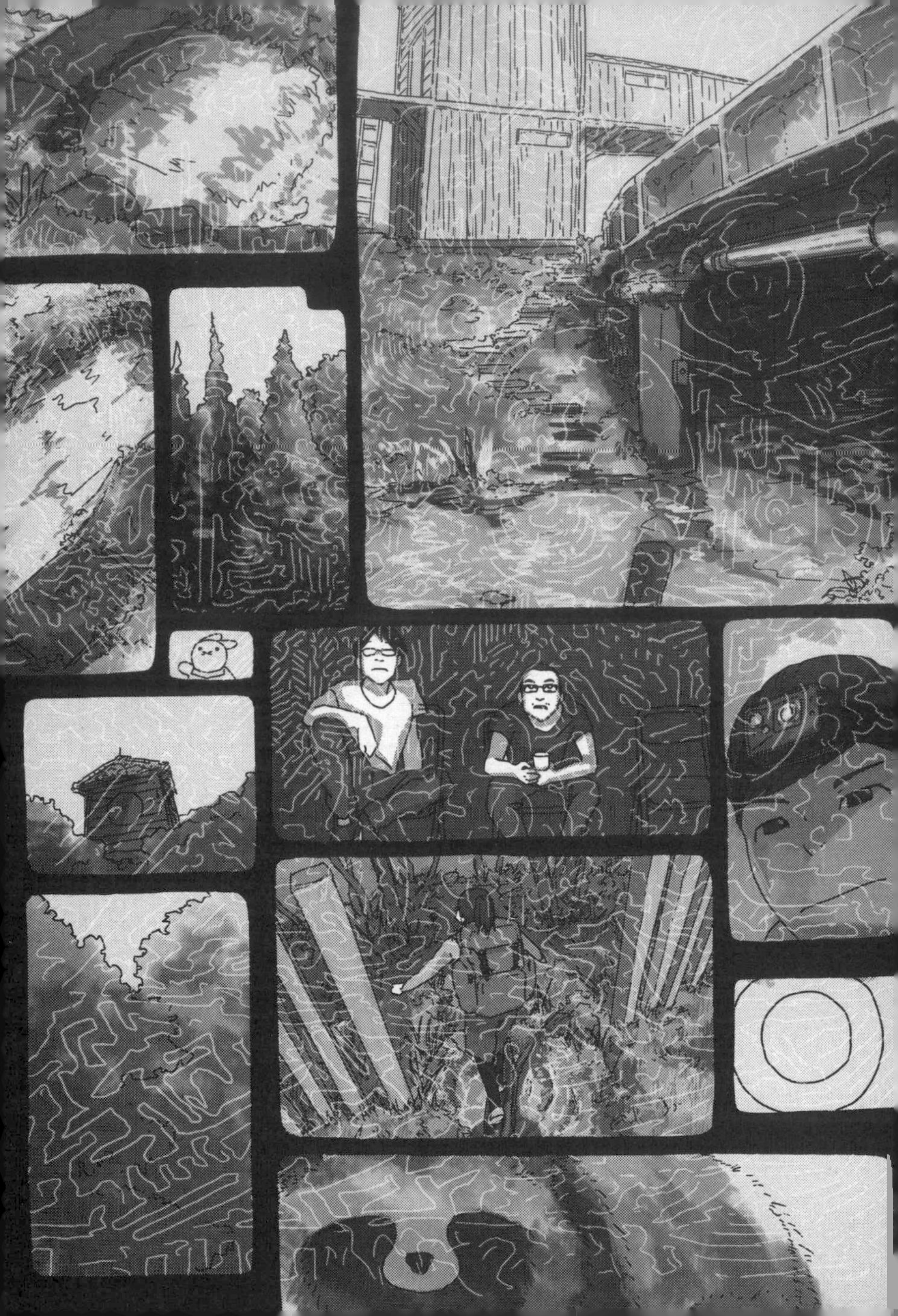

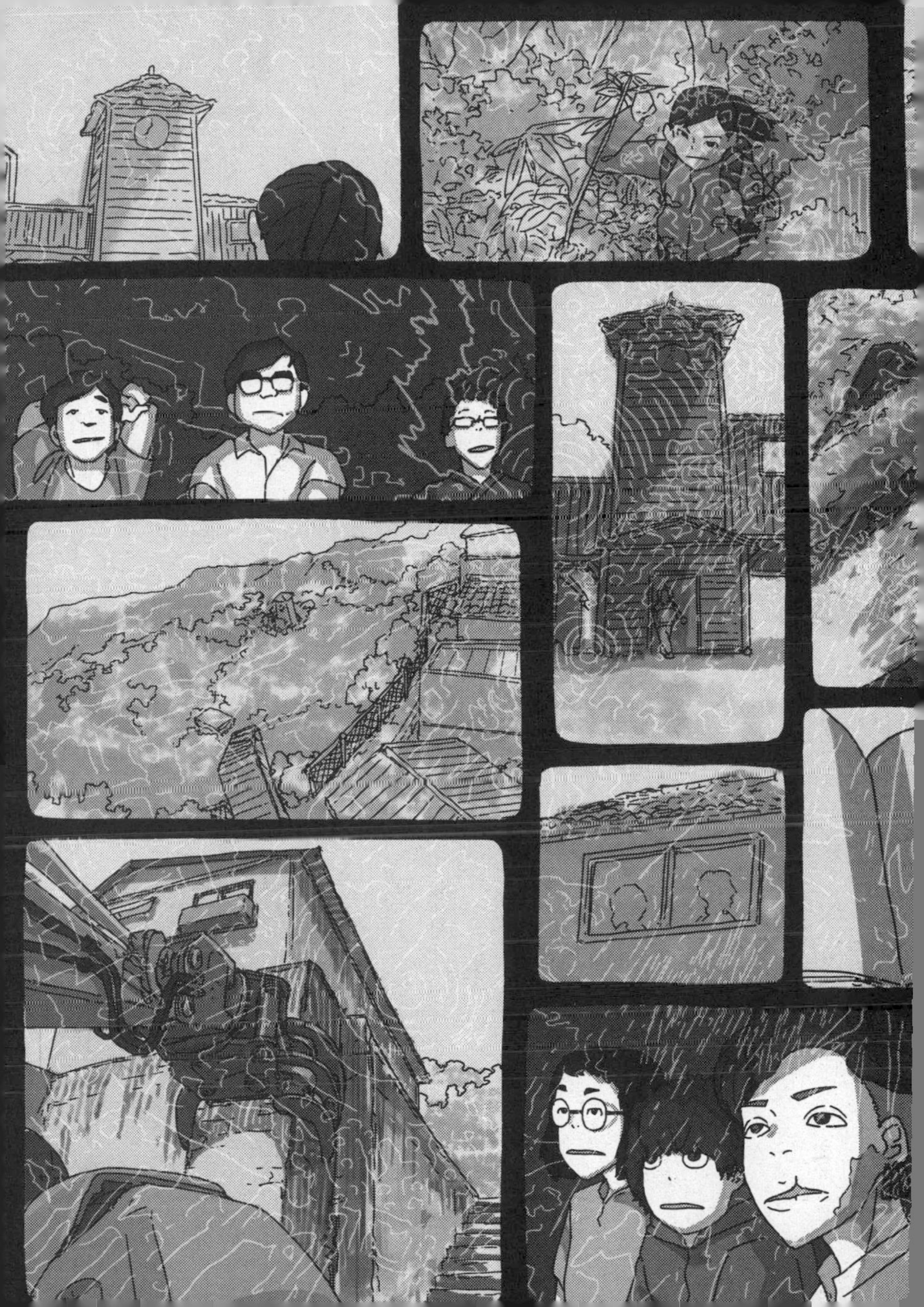

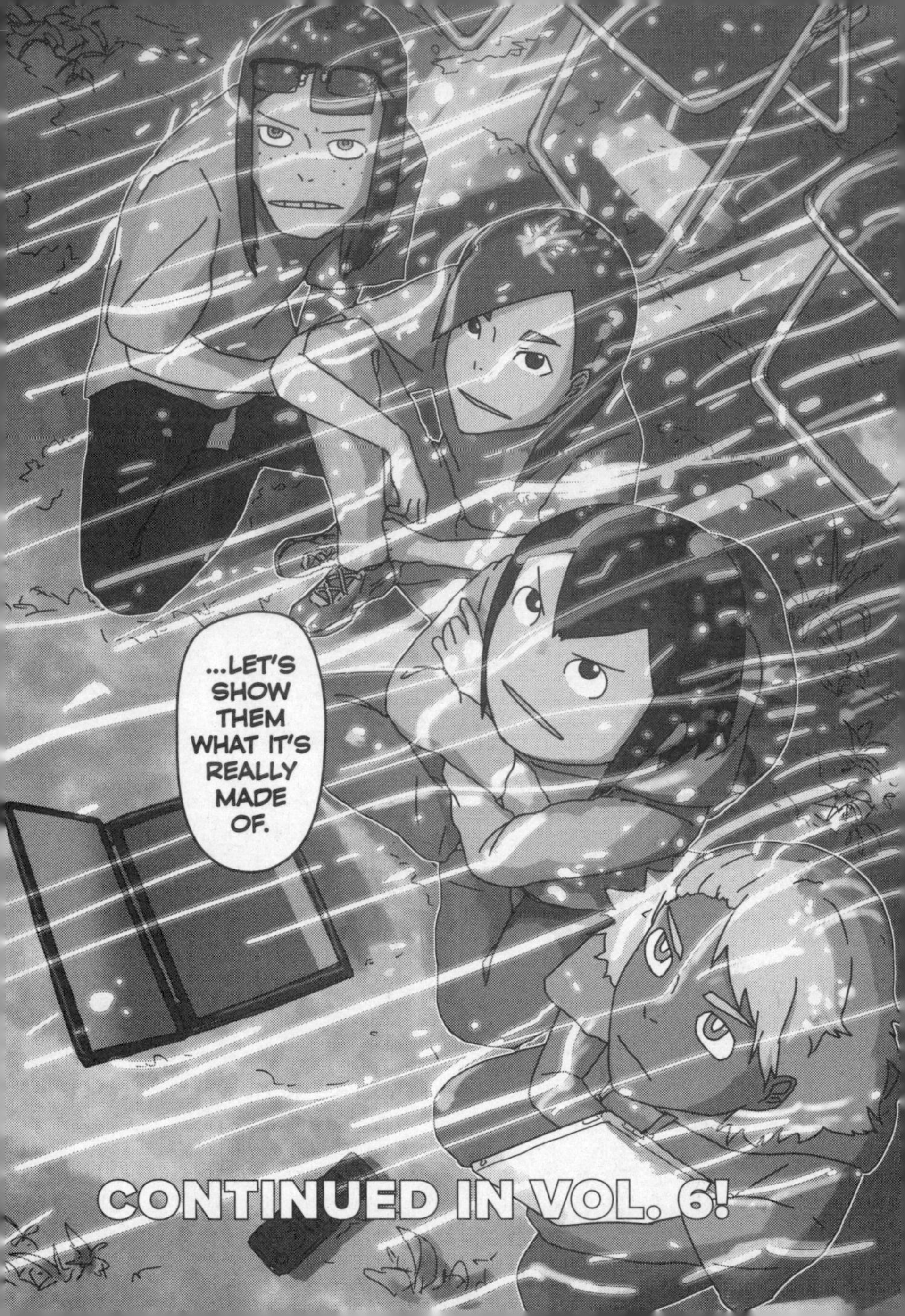
...LET'S SHOW THEM WHAT IT'S REALLY MADE OF.
CONTINUED IN VOL. 6!

President and Publisher
MIKE RICHARDSON

Editor
CARL GUSTAV HORN

Designer
SKYLER WEISSENFLUH

Digital Art Technician
CHRIS HORN

English-language version produced by Dark Horse Comics

Published by
Dark Horse Manga
A division of Dark Horse Comics LLC
10956 SE Main Street
Milwaukie, OR 97222

DarkHorse.com

To find a comics shop in your area, visit comicshoplocator.com.

First edition: May 2023
ISBN 978-1-50673-150-6

1 3 5 7 9 10 8 6 4 2

Printed in the United States of America

NOTES ON VOL. 5 BY THE TRANSLATOR AND EDITOR

Welcome back! First of all, some more good news—in the notes for volume 4, I mentioned that we planned to release an English version of *Eizouken* volume 6 . . . now we can say we're adding volume 7 to the schedule as well! That's actually as far as the *tankobon* (collected manga volumes) have gotten in Japan to date, although of course new chapters of *Eizouken* continue to be serialized in its home magazine, *Monthly Comic Spirits*, published by Shogakukan. So hopefully it won't be too long until there's a volume 8 in Japan as well . . .

As always, Oowara-sensei has given us a lot to take note of :). On the very first page of the story, we get introduced to the trash-talking Fishing Club (you might say they like to bait each other—sorry). As you might guess, the "Revros" referred to in panel 3 of page 4 is a model of fishing reel, made by the Japanese firm Daiwa. Note how in the panel just before (panel 2) there's also evidently a couple taking a selfie. If so, it's the first instance of a relationship between students we've seen so far in the manga; while there are lots of school manga with relationships and romance, the story we see in *Eizouken* (fanfics, as always, may take a different approach ^_^) is about partnership (in the work sense) and problem solving.

I've seen *Eizouken* described as being in the "slice of life" genre, but perhaps that term gets a bit overused . . . ? I personally think of "slice of life" manga and anime as being about characters' reactions (often funny or charming) to various day-to-day occurrences . . . i.e., slices of life. By contrast, Eizouken (as in the anime studio who are the protagonists of this story) are basically active, rather than reactive characters—rather than sit around and eat slices, they're baking a cake. *Eizouken* also isn't the kind of anime or manga where characters are caught up in a much larger conflict and have to make the best choices they can under the circumstances (as in, for example, a war story). That's not to say Shibahama High School doesn't have mysteries and secrets, and of course, we've seen their more mundane issues with the faculty and administration. But Eizouken themselves are writing the plot and driving the drama. Is there a term for stories like this, where the narrative is about characters who plan out an objective for themselves and work towards a goal, facing and (hopefully) overcoming challenges along the way? "Goal driven" stories...? There's the term used for some anime, *iyashikei* 「癒し系」 which is sometimes expressed in English as "healing," although I think "soothing" is better (and if you stop to think about it, there's an important difference between something that heals and something that soothes), but these kind of stories are also often described as having a calming effect. There's nothing wrong with that, but again, I see *Eizouken* as a story of motivation, effort, struggle, debate, and conflict—its fundamental positivity is grounded in the fact the core of the conflict is between its artistic sparring partners: Asakusa, Kanamori, Mizusaki, and Doumeki thus far; people who are not trying to tear each other down or backstab each other, but learn from each other and learn to work together. And because they're artists (have you noticed that Kanamori, too, has been expressing her opinions?) this is not just a clash of different personalities, as it might be in some stories, but an ongoing clash of ideas as well.

In the same panel, there's also another group of students in the lower left engaged in some unknown activity, and then, to the right of the couple, a student sitting alone at their desk. So Oowara has portrayed four separate groupings of students in a single panel, all of whom seem to be doing things independent of each other—and also independent of our protagonists, Eizouken, whom we see on the next page are in a different part of the room. It may seem to contradict what I said earlier about this being a manga where the main characters are the ones writing the plot, but I think it's good world building to have things going on in the background that aren't necessarily related to the plot—just as the real world is full of people and things with no particular connection to us, or interest in our goals and aspirations, no matter how motivated and driven we are (Gainax's first work, *Royal Space Force*, portrays this kind of worldbuilding well). In other words, even though we can and should write the plot for our lives, in the real world, turn the camera away from us a little, and suddenly we look like supporting characters; turn the camera away some more, and now we're in the background; turn the camera still further, and then we're no longer in the shot at all.

On pages 8 and 9, many readers will have caught that the student from the Security Club is re-enacting the scene from the opening of *Blade Runner* where Holden administers the Voight-Kampff test to Leon (despite Leon supposedly not being one of the smarter replicants, it's worth pointing out neither Holden nor Deckard get the better of him), and may be wondering about the dialogue here. In fact, even though the *Eizouken* manga is referencing the movie scene visually, in the original Japanese the Security Club dude doesn't ask Doumeki any of the questions from the Voight-Kampff, but instead that odd thing about the bread crusts and milk. Well, it's 2023 instead of 2019, so maybe they added some new questions in the past few years :) Amusingly, in the original Japanese version of the diagram on page 16, Asakusa initially wrote the name of her own club, Eizouken, wrong, as well as the word for "farm," by drawing what looked like the correct words, but on closer inspection were not real kanji. Don't be discouraged if you make mistakes in writing Japanese; plenty of Japanese people do, just as people who can read and write English still may misspell words all the time.

In case you were wondering, although Asakusa is often compared to a tanuki, in panel 5 of page 21, Kanamori compares her to an *araiguma*, which is the Japanese word for raccoon. Raccoons are not native to Japan, but are now an invasive species there. Ironically enough for Eizouken, the problem is blamed on an anime—the 1977 TV show *Rascal the Raccoon*, which inspired many fans to import raccoons as pets, some of which eventually got into the wild. On page 24, you'll notice Oowara-sensei introducing something new between chapters: examples of his *neemu* 「ネーム」, "names" used in the making of the *Eizouken* manga. This is a technical term within the manga industry to refer to a rough draft version of a page, showing the basic layout of panels, position of characters, and dialogue. As you can see from the examples in vol. 5, the "name" can be very minimal, leaving out most of what will be in the finished page. A manga creator draws up such "names" to show their editor so they can discuss and/or critique a particular chapter before the actual version gets drawn (of course, this is also a practice in American comics, where the rough versions might be called "layouts" or "thumbnails" [the expression "thumbnail" for a small image long predates digital media]). It is thought that manga uses the English word "name" for these rough layouts in the sense of the verb "to name", having the implication of "designate"—in other words, to designate where things will go on the manga page. Continuing with the Fishing Club's comments on each other's hairstyles, the owner of the two-block haircut "retaliates" on their shaggy comrade in panel three of page 34 by dubbing them "Valais Blacknose," after the Swiss sheep of the same name. If you look closely at the final panel in this chapter, there's also a suggestion that the six-meter Shibahamassie may exist after all. On page 50, we see a visual gag grounded in anime (and so worthy of Eizouken). Look at the jagged, broken-up effect as Doumeki runs in panels 2, 5, and 6. Because anime traditionally used fewer drawings per second than Western animation, this trick was used as a kind of shortcut to convey rapid motion. Of course, it wasn't meant to be seen as a still image, but as part of a rapid sequence of drawings to fool the eye; Oowara-sensei uses it as a joke here, since manga panels are all still images.

Many people's early impression of Kanamori was that she was simply hungry for money, but as she explained to Sakaki in vol. 3, "What I love is not money itself . . . but activity that generates returns." It's become clear for a while now that, even if she's not thought of as one of the "creatives" (what a bone-dry term that is) of Eizouken, she thinks about art and philosophy just as her partners do. In panel 2 of page 65, Kanamori quotes one of the most famous phrases in Japanese Buddhism, *shogyōmujō*「諸行無常」. Also translated as "the impermanence of all things," the phrase is in the opening lines of *The Tale of the Heike* referenced in the notes for *Eizouken* vol. 3. And just in case you were wondering if Doumeki's reference to Michael Bay on page 74 was in the original Japanese version of the manga, yes, it was. Not only was it in the original, but Bay's 2001 film *Pearl Harbor* was considered a box office hit in Japan, and according to *Variety*, "critics [there] were far more positive than in the U.S. and most other countries," despite, naturally, the Japanese being the bad guys in the movie.

In the original manga, Doumeki's "buzz box" on page 76, panel 2, read *Bōzu*「坊主」, a term which refers to a Buddhist priest, but also to close-cropped hair (as might be worn by a Buddhist priest) and by extension can mean "sonny boy" due to young Japanese boys being traditionally given such a haircut. I liked the fact that "buzz" in English refers to both a short haircut and a sound effect, and for a bonus it even sounds like *bōzu*, so that's why it's "buzz box" in the Dark Horse version ^_^ By the way, Kanamori also referenced the same term on page 80 of vol. 1 when she quoted the old Japanese saying "A priest's earnings are pure profit," in the original language「坊主丸儲け」*bōzu marumōke*.

If you think about it, Doumeki is a challenging character for a manga, since her artistic field is sound design, and manga are a silent medium. Page 104, panel 2 contains 19 different sound effects, including some that are seemingly accompanied by echoes (appearing first as white kana with black outline, and then again as thin black lines). Recently I gave a presentation on Dark Horse's manga at Purdue University together with our senior director of licensed publications, Michael Gombos, and used this particular panel in a segment on *Eizouken* as an exemplar among contemporary manga. One issue discussed was the endeavor of simply trying to make sure all the sound FX in this panel were identified; for example, on the illustration hanging on the wall behind the woman, there appears (when you view the original raw 1200 dpi file) to be writing and possible kana-like marks. I determined as editor that they weren't actually sound FX, but it's perhaps a tribute to Oowara-sensei's intricacy that I'm only 95% sure of that, not 100%. ^_^

On pages 108-9, we finally get to meet the "other" anime club on campus, evidently the one whose screening Eizouken disrupted in vol. 1 (well, it wasn't their fault, and also they weren't even Eizouken yet). They seem determined in their club room to preserve the classic aesthetic of a cigarette smoke-filled anime studio, but as they're on a high school campus, if you look closely, the "cigarette smoke" is from a mosquito coil, and they fill their ashtrays with rolled crepe cookies. Another gag is that all the members of the club look like youthful versions of real anime directors. Page 108 has the most famous faces in the first two panels, modelled on Hayao Miyazaki and Mamoru Oshii, but *Eizouken* fan Midori Ogiwara has identified those on page 109 as (top row, right to left): Isao Takahata,

Yoshiyuki Tomino, Satoshi Kon, (middle row, right to left): Shinichiro Watanabe, Hideaki Anno, Makoto Shinkai, (bottom row, right to left): Masaaki Yuasa, Naoko Yamada, and Mamoru Hosoda. Masaaki Yuasa, of course, directed the anime adaptation of *Keep Your Hands off Eizouken!*

The exception may be Suzuki, on page 110, who is seemingly modelled on a young Toshio Suzuki, the former president of Studio Ghibli, who early in his career became an editor on the great Japanese-language anime magazine *Animage*, where he first promoted Miyazaki and Takahata's work—well before either director was known to the general public (or even necessarily known to many anime fans). *Animage* was famous in the 1970s and 80s for its wide-ranging discussion of anime both past and present (at that time, a "classic" anime might mean one from the 1940s!) and Eiji Otsuka, author of the manga *The Kurosagi Corpse Delivery Service*—also available from Dark Horse ^_^—goes as far as to credit *Animage* with creating the media voice of what we now know as otaku culture (in the first part of Gainax's *Otaku no Video*, set in the early 1980s, the protagonist Kubo is visibly upset to suddenly realize the new *Animage* is on the stands and he hasn't read it yet). *Animage* was a major influence on Viz's former magazine *Animerica*, veterans of which would later start the magazine *Otaku USA*, which itself recently celebrated its 15th anniversary—so the legacy of *Animage* can be seen at work even today in the English-language fan scene (and the original *Animage* is still running in Japan).

The Anime Culture Studies Club shows the eclecticism of the *Animage* tradition in their

Second Wave newsletter; besides the works of Eizouken, they're discussing the 1967 anime TV series *The King Kong Show*. This program was a very early example of a joint production between a Japanese and an American animation studio, in this case, Toei Doga and Videocraft. Videocraft later changed its name to Rankin/Bass and perhaps remains best known for its classic stop-motion children's TV specials that are still shown around Christmastime in the US (more on that below). *Flying Phantom Ship*, which has just recently been released on Blu-ray from Discotek, is a 1969 Toei film. Containing key animation by a young Hayao Miyazaki and his wife Akemi Ota, Dave Merrill (known for his always-packed "Anime Hell" events at cons)—who does a commentary track on the Blu-ray together with Anime News Network columnist Mike Toole—has described *Flying Phantom Ship* as "ignored for years by anime fandom," but once seen, a reminder of why we "got into this stuff in the first place; that sense of outlandish did-I-just-see-that nonsense . . . " Even though it didn't come out nearly as long ago, the 1996 film *Chocchan Monogatari* is somewhat obscure even in Japan, perhaps because, reportedly, the video version is not sold or rented; it is only authorized to be viewed in libraries. It's based on an autobiographical essay by the late Cho Kuroyanagi, mother of the famous television personality, author, and goodwill ambassador Tetsuko Kuroyanagi. *Gundress* was a 1999 anime feature film known principally for two things: having characters whose look and personalities were designed by the creator of *Ghost in the Shell*, Shirow Masamune (he also allowed his Landmate mecha designs to be used in the anime), and for being released to theaters largely unfinished to meet a release deadline; audiences going to see it were handed flyers with an apology and a form that could be filled out to receive a copy of *Gundress* on video once it was finished! *Angie Girl vs. Conan* is evidently the title not of an anime, but of two different detective anime series counterprogrammed against each other: *Detective Conan* (known as *Case Closed* in the US) against the 1977 anime TV series *Jōheika no Petit Ange* (*Her Majesty's Little Ange*), about a 19th century British girl who, after recovering a ring belonging to Queen Victoria, is granted a medal by the Queen and authorized to work as a detective for Scotland Yard. The series was perhaps best-known outside Japan under the title used for its Italian dub, *Angie Girl*, although evidently some episodes were released on video in the English-speaking world during the 1980s with the lead character re-named "Charlotte Holmes," (the supposed niece of Sherlock Holmes) under the title *Sherlock & Me* in the United Kingdom and *The Casebook of Charlotte Holmes* in the US—the anime portions are bookended by live-action sequences with actors portraying Holmes and Watson.

Did you know that *Animage* considered Rankin/Bass's *Rudolph the Red-Nosed Reindeer* to be an anime? In fact, all of its stop-motion work was done in Japan, under the supervision of Tadahito Mochinaga, an animator experienced in both cel and stop-motion techniques; Jonathan Clements writes on his career in some detail in the highly recommended book *Anime: A History* (grounded in extensive translation of Japanese-language sources, it's a book of special interest to *Eizouken* fans, as its emphasis is not on the history of anime as a medium, but as an industry in Japan—technical progress, organization of labor, financing, distribution, marketing—all the things Kanamori thinks about). It's true that we don't usually think of stop-motion animation as being part of "anime," but we should consider that techniques we take for granted in anime today, such as computer animation and digital ink and paint, were absent from many classic anime shows of the past (such as the 1978 series that inspired Asakusa to become a filmmaker, *Future Boy Conan*). You could make the counter-argument that even if it now uses digital techniques, anime is defined by its aesthetic—that is, it still preserves its 2D look, so stop-motion, which is a 3D technique, cannot have the "anime look." But we should also consider ^_^ how Mizusaki said in vol. 2 that she wants to make animation, not anime. The late animation director Yasuo Otsuka (who partnered for years with Miyazaki) has remarked further on the influence of puppet theater on anime production in the 1960s—you'll remember in Isao Takahata's 1991 film *Only Yesterday*, Taeko's favorite TV series as a child was the puppet show *Hyokkori Hyotanjima*—and of course, the film uses anime to depict the visual style of a puppet show! Glenn Kenny made the cogent remark in his review of *Only Yesterday* that Takahata showed "interest in expanding and changing up the aesthetic of anime"—you can certainly see this also in his *My Neighbors the Yamadas* and *The Tale of the Princess Kaguya*. Come to think of it, doesn't Masaaki Yuasa show his own independent style in the anime for *Eizouken*?

On page 116, I couldn't help but note that even though this is a high school manga, this is also the first time we've seen anyone actually attending class (as opposed to hanging out in a classroom). Kanamori doesn't seem to agree with her teacher, and we already know she disagrees with the school administration. I guess her "problem" is that while she is thoughtful, motivated, and organized, she is already building a career of her own (in her case, as an anime producer). Put bluntly, Kanamori might wonder what relevance this class has to her future, when she is already building a future together with her partners. On the other hand, at this point Eizouken still seems far from being able to make anime for a living, and as Sakaki alluded to in volume 4, it wouldn't be fair to say Shibahama H.S. has nothing to do with Eizouken's success, as the school provides them with studio space, budget support, and a built-in potential audience. What sets Eizouken apart, of course, is what they do with those resources they were given. You'll have noticed that a recurring motif at Shibahama is of student clubs that are full of history, but that don't really accomplish much, or that lost their ambitions long ago. Eizouken, full of speed and energy, is shaking things up, and their energy is putting new motivations into some clubs, and disrupting others.

When I was reading manga in high school (in the 1980s ^_^) it actually did make me ask myself, "Am I having enough fun in school?" Sometimes we see the struggles of everyday life reflected in the manga we read, but they can also remind us of the positive possibilities, including using student clubs to make cool and/or strange things happen, although *Keep Your Hands Off Eizouken!* also shows that this too can be a struggle, both for the club itself and sometimes with the school rules and administration. I remember in 1986 there weren't any student anime clubs yet, so instead we got our high school's "Philosophy Club" to sponsor a one-day anime convention. We held it in the biggest classroom on campus, which was a lecture hall—you know, the kind with a slanted floor, where the seats in the back are higher up than the seats in the front, so everyone can get a better view—because it was also the only place on campus that had a video projector. I think at the time the projector was mainly used by the football team to study their play after a game. By the way, at least one person on the team was watching anime, even back then. There was an English-dubbed anime series called *Robotech* that came on TV after school. It was controversial among many fans because of the considerable changes it made from the original Japanese (*Robotech* was made by taking three separate anime series, *Macross*, *Southern Cross*, and *Mospeada*, and rewriting them in English as if they were three generations in the same storyline) but nevertheless it exposed many people here to contemporary anime, and it was certainly far more sophisticated than any domestic animated series at the time on North American television. Ironically, maybe the very fact there wasn't an anime club yet at my school meant *Robotech* could transcend social cliques (he wasn't the only jock that was into it ^_^).

I have to thank the Anime Culture Studies Club for pointing out in their newsletter on page 121, panel 3 that the people from the planet on which *Tanuki El Dorado* takes place have six fingers. I went back and looked at vol. 4, and they do have six fingers! I'm the editor of the manga, and I hadn't noticed that! Page 129, panel 1, seems to be another playful use of sound effects—several of them seem almost like a find-a-word puzzle in the original Japanese, in that they are (or resemble) the titles of various manga by Fujiko Fujio—the big 「ド」do, with the 「ラえもん」 *raemon* to its lower left (*Doraemon*), 「パーマン」 *paaman*, (*Perman*), and 「オバQ」 *obaQ*, (which could be short for 「オバケのQ太郎」 *Obake no Q-taro*. I'm sure there might be some I'm missing, too.

On the phone screen in panel 5 of page 143, Doumeki dubs herself "Houichi the Moneyless," a play on "Houichi the Moneyless," a folktale about the eponymous minstrel (who in fact was famed for performing *The Tale of the Heike*, mentioned above). On pages 146-47, does Asakusa ever notice that Mizusaki has made an origami bunny out of her towel and placed it on Asakusa's head? I don't think so ^_^ The elastic band around Mizusaki's wrist, by the way, is lent out at some *sento* (public bathhouses) as a place to store your locker key. Kanamori, you'll notice, is keeping her glasses stowed in her hair bun (she didn't do this when Eizouken went to the bathhouse in vol. 2). I'm likely reading too much into her remarks, but to the extent Eizouken reminds me of Daicon Film, Kanamori's comments about the daikon radishes on page 150 are interesting. Anyway, thank you for reading this volume, and we'll look forward to seeing you again in vol. 6 of *Keep Your Hands Off Eizouken!*

—CGH